They Live on the Land
Life in an Open-Country Southern Community

Paul W. Terry
and
Verner M. Sims

with an Introduction by Clarence L. Mohr

The University of Alabama Press
Tuscaloosa & London

The Library of Alabama Classics edition is a facsimile of
the 1940 edition published by the Bureau of Educational
Research at The University of Alabama.

The paper on which this book is printed meets the minimum
requirements of American Standard for Information
Science-Permanence of Paper for Printed Library Materials,
ANSI Z39.48-1984.

Library of Congress Cataloging-in-Publication Data

Terry, Paul W. (Paul Washington)
    They live on the land : life in an open-country southern community
/ Paul W. Terry and Verner M. Sims : with an introduction by
Clarence L. Mohr.
        p.   cm.—(Library of Alabama classics)
    Originally published : University, Ala. : Bureau of Educational
Research, University of Alabama, 1940.
    Includes bibliographical references (p.   ).
    ISBN 0-8173-0587-4 (alk. paper)
        1. Southern States—Rural conditions.   2. Sociology, Rural.
3. Country life—Southern States.   4. Social surveys—Southern
States.   I. Sims, Verner M. (Verner Martin)   II. Title.
III. Series.
HN79.S85T47   1993
307.72—dc20   92-31416
                                                                    CIP

British Library Cataloguing-in-Publication Data available

To

*Those people in Upland Bend who were
striving to make their community a better
place in which to live.*

Contents

Introduction*

Clarence L. Mohr

In 1934, with the South's chronic pattern of rural poverty thrown into sharp relief by global economic crisis, Paul Washington Terry and Verner Martin Sims began work on the book that follows this essay. Funded initially as part of a larger information-gathering effort by New Deal agencies, the survey of a tiny rural locale in Tuscaloosa County, Alabama, quickly outgrew its bureaucratic purpose. When finally published in 1940 the book carried a title—*They Live on the Land*—that was almost an anachronism. What Terry and Sims had produced was more nearly an eleventh-hour snapshot of a way of life doomed to rapid extinction in the wake of World War II. Viewing their subject through a lens untinted by sentimentalism, the authors collected and analyzed a staggering amount of evidence obtained from interviews, questionnaires, standardized tests, and firsthand observation during visits to 196 of the 209 families residing within the twenty-one-square-mile area identified by the fictional name "Upland Bend." In seeking to reveal "who the people were, what they thought, and what they did," the authors began with local history and went on to explore the entire spectrum of social, economic, political, psychological, and demographic information available during the mid-1930s. Organized around such themes as religion, education, leisure, civic life, and economic activity, the book's eleven topical chapters left few subjects untouched, including potentially explosive matters like race relations and injustice stemming from class stratification. Even gender, a category alien to most scholars of the authors' generation, received thoughtful consideration in a separate section of the chapter on local leadership. Only a few community studies, before or since, have attempted so much in a single volume.

Emerging as it does from the catastrophe of the Great Depression, *They Live on the Land* might seem at first glance to be little more than a period piece—an example of that vague and sprawling thirties genre that bears

*Preparation of this essay was facilitated by generous grants from the National Endowment for the Humanities, the Rockefeller Archive Center, and the Tulane University Senate Committee on Research. Each organization has the author's sincere thanks.

the label "documentary expression."[1] Further scrutiny reveals, however, that the book has little in common with the work of contemporary photojournalists, and for good reason. Terry and Sims were social scientists rather than social documentarians. Trained in the quantitative methods of psychology, they showed a concern for precision, objectivity, and analytic rigor that stood in marked contrast to the elevation of emotion over intellect and uniqueness over typicality that pervaded the documentary field.

The differences become clear upon making even a casual comparison between *They Live on the Land* and the more widely known Alabama study *Let Us Now Praise Famous Men,* often cited as the finest example of 1930s documentary presentation.[2] Researched and written at roughly the same time and published in 1940 and 1941 respectively, the two books examine daily life among impoverished rural families in contiguous counties of west and central Alabama. The authors of each study developed an intimate firsthand knowledge of the people they wrote about and combined prose with photography to depict the mundane reality of their subjects' daily lives. In the published versions of both investigations, moreover, the privacy of individual informants was carefully preserved by altering personal names and geographical references. Beyond these superficial resemblances, however, the two works share relatively little in the way of purpose or method. *Let Us Now Praise Famous Men* is the achievement of two creative artists, Walker Evans the photographer and James Agee the Harvard-trained poet, novelist, reporter, screenwriter, and film critic. In Agee's hands the white sharecroppers of Hale County compel recognition as fellow human beings precisely because the author's response to them is viscerally human in its intensity. Yet when all is said and done the book's emotive power is also

---

1. William Stott, *Documentary Expression and Thirties America* (New York, 1973) has defined the genre and given currency to the phrase. Stott's effort to place depression-era social science beneath the "documentary" umbrella creates a certain degree of conceptual confusion.

2. James Agee and Walker Evans, *Three Tenant Families*[:] *Let Us Now Praise Famous Men* (New York, 1941); Stott, *Documentary Expression,* 261–314; Richard H. Pells, *Radical Visions and American Dreams: Cultural and Social Thought in the Depression Years* (New York, 1973), 246–51. On the 1960s revival of interest in Agee's work and its continuing influence, see John Hersey's introduction to Houghton Mifflin's 1988 edition of *Let Us Now Praise Famous Men.* See also Dale Maharidge and Michael Williamson's sequel volume *And Their Children After Them: The Legacy of Let Us Now Praise Famous Men, James Agee, Walker Evans, and the Rise and Fall of the Cotton South* (New York, 1989).

its chief source of analytic weakness. Despite its intermittent outrage and its occasional chapters of expository prose, *Let Us Now Praise Famous Men* is less a work of social analysis than a subtly nuanced portrait of the artist as a young man.

In stark contrast to the Evans and Agee volume, *They Live on the Land* is permeated by the technique and temperament of quantitative social science. Written in what charitably might be called straightforward prose, the work is animated by a spirit of rigorous objectivity and disdain for artistic contrivance. Whatever similarity it shares with the work of depression era photojournalists is dramatically overshadowed by a much clearer and more direct connection with the vast body of statistical surveys conducted by economists, educators, and sociologists in the years following World War I. Although not patterned directly on any previous study, the "Upland Bend" project employed methods and posed questions that would have been familiar to readers conversant with longstanding scholarly debates over the basis of rural community formation, the measurement of human intelligence, and the relation of schools and schooling to America's class structure.[3] For all of these reasons the social upheavals of the 1930s provide little more than a convenient point of departure for assessing either the underlying aims or the specific content of *They Live on the Land*.[4] By examining the Alabama activities of the Civil Works Administration and the newly created Tennessee Valley Authority, one may discover the immediate stimulus for the research that Terry and Sims conducted. Here, amid the efforts of New Deal bureaucrats to gather "data" for social planning, lies the book's proximate cause. Its intellectual origins, one need hardly say, must be sought elsewhere: in the history of rural sociology, in the intellectual terrain of American psychology during the 1920s and, to a certain extent, in the personal and professional lives of the two authors.

If published today *They Live on the Land* probably would be charac-

---

3. The nearest analog to *They Live on the Land* in terms of methodology, topical organization, and geographical focus is Charles S. Johnson's *In the Shadow of the Plantation*. Published in 1934, the year that Terry and Sims began their research, Johnson's book is a detailed survey of religious, educational, economic, and family life among some 612 black tenant families in the lower third of Macon County, Alabama.

4. For additional treatment of 1930s artistic and intellectual activity, see Pells, *Radical Visions* and David P. Peeler, *Hope Among Us Yet: Social Criticism and Social Solace in Depression America* (Athens, Ga., 1978). Neither work concerns itself with academic writing or scholarship in the social sciences.

terized as a work of interdisciplinary scholarship. The principal foundation for such a claim has less to do with the academic training of the authors than with the topic of their investigation. The social sciences, as Louis Wirth has noted, are distinguished from each other "not so much by subject matter as by the different questions that are raised about the subject matter."[5] The field of community studies offers a case in point. During the first third of the twentieth century the study of community became an endeavor that linked the social sciences together in subject matter even as it helped to set them apart as separate disciplines. In the case of sociology, for example, community scholarship must be viewed ultimately as part of the larger process through which the young academic field cast off its intellectual dependence upon natural science and psychology by defining sociological inquiry as the study of groups per se, rather than the behavior of sentient individuals.[6] But viewed from a slightly different angle, explorations of community were equally important as an area of convergence for what otherwise would have been separate lines of investigation in the fields of education, sociology, psychology, and cultural anthropology. There are many explanations for the proliferation of community studies in the social sciences but perhaps none is more important than the sheer inclusiveness of the term "community." In the vague and general sense that the word is usually employed it encompasses questions of human ecology, social organization, and collective behavior—all major subfields of sociology—while shading over into social psychology on the one side and into field ethnography on the other.[7] At the more practical level the study of communities, as variously defined, reflected an impulse toward microcosmic research that was rooted in the reigning "positivist" or "objectivist" credo of scholars seeking to legitimize the academic study of education, society, and human behavior. For specialists in each of these fledgling endeavors the ability to secure reliable data in a form and on a scale that would facilitate quantitative analysis became a litmus test of disciplinary claims to scientific stature.[8] In

---

5. Louis Wirth, "The Social Sciences," in *Community Life and Social Policy: Selected Papers by Louis Wirth*, ed. Elizabeth Wirth Marvick and Albert J. Reiss, Jr. (Chicago, 1956), 55.

6. Hamilton Cravens, *The Triumph of Evolution: American Scientists and the Heredity-Environment Controversy 1900–1941* (Philadelphia, 1978), 138–53, incisively delineates sociology's intellectual transformation in the decades after 1909.

7. Louis Wirth, "The Scope and Problems of the Community," in *Community Life and Social Policy*, 9–20.

8. Robert C. Bannister, *Sociology and Scientism: The American Quest for Objectivity, 1880–1940* (Chapel Hill, 1987), argues for the existence of "nominalist" and

education the chief vehicle for data gathering was the ubiquitous school district survey, while in psychology the group intelligence test was most frequently administered to specific school populations. Sociologists cast a somewhat wider net in studying patterns of association in both urban and rural settings but inevitably resorted to survey methods and units of analysis that linked sociology to the field work of its sister disciplines. Schools, for example, came to represent one of many different "community making factors" that both shaped and reflected the development of group identity as sociologists understood it.[9]

Any full discussion of cross disciplinary influences in community studies literature falls beyond the scope of this essay. For present purposes it is sufficient to point out the virtual impossibility of studying rural life in the depression era without violating at least some of the academic world's imaginary boundaries. For Terry and Sims the act of intellectual trespass began (but did not end) with the phrasing of the book's subtitle. By describing the locale of their study as an "Open-Country Southern Community" the authors acknowledged their implicit debt to a tradition of rural sociological analysis initiated a generation earlier by reformist scholars like Charles J. Galpin, Warren H. Wilson, Kenyon L. Butterfield, and others. Inspired by the country life movement of Theodore Roosevelt's day and driven by Progressive Era anxiety over the impact of modernization on traditional values and mores, early students of the "rural problem" hoped to rehabilitate American agriculture and stem the rising tide of farm-to-city migration. In seeking remedies for rural poverty, isolation, poor health, inadequate schooling, religious stagnation, and a host of related ills, reformers developed a variety of survey and mapping techniques to inventory community resources and examine patterns of group life that long had been taken for

---

"realist" variants of objectivism linked by the "fashionable enthusiasm for quantification."

9. On the proliferation and aims of school surveys, see Robert M. W. Travers, *How Research Has Changed American Schools* (Kalamazoo, 1983), 130–32; Wayne E. Fuller, *The Old Country School* (Chicago, 1982), 239–40, 290; and Thomas Pogue Weinland, "A History of the I.Q. in America, 1890–1941" (Ph.D. diss., Columbia University, 1970), 89–90, 153–54. On intelligence and achievement testing in schools after 1900, see Paul Davis Chapman, *Schools as Sorters: Lewis M. Terman, Applied Psychology and the Intelligence Testing Movement, 1890–1930* (New York, 1988), chapters 2 and 4. On sociological methods and the school, see Wirth, "The Social Sciences," 76–77, and Newell Leroy Sims, ed., *The Rural Community, Ancient and Modern* (New York, 1920), 146.

granted.[10] Fundamental to such inquiries was an operational definition of "community" elastic enough to encompass not only the nucleated farming villages of New England but also the dispersed agricultural settlement patterns of the Midwest and South. Building upon initial studies that equated rural communities with the trading and service zones of small towns, advocates of "central place" theory went on to describe an increasingly intricate system of more restricted rural "neighborhoods" defined by the existence of some external institution or group beyond the family to which local residents attached conscious importance.[11]

The questions that Charles Galpin posed in his celebrated 1915 study of a single Wisconsin county remained at the heart of rural community scholarship for the next generation.[12] From the beginning, however, Galpin and other central place theorists ran the risk of giving undue emphasis to relationships based upon labor specialization and technologically generated patterns of economic interdependence. The communities thus described tended to represent only one side of the conceptual dichotomy established by Ferdinand Tönnies's categories of *Gemeinschaft* and *Gesellschaft* or Émile Durkheim's distinction between mechanical and organic forms of social solidarity.[13] By the decade following World War I it

---

10. William L. Bowers, *The Country Life Movement in America, 1900–1920* (Port Washington, N.Y., 1974), 62–88; James H. Madison, "Reformers and the Rural Church, 1900–1950," *Journal of American History* 73 (December 1986): 645–68. Cf. David Danbom, *The Resisted Revolution: Urban America and the Industrialization of Agriculture* (Ames, Iowa, 1979).

11. Lowry Nelson, *Rural Sociology: Its Origin and Growth in the United States* (Minneapolis, 1969), 34–42.

12. Galpin's seminal study "The Social Anatomy of an Agricultural Community," *University of Wisconsin Agricultural Experiment Station Research Bulletin,* 34 (May 1915) was reprinted in Galpin's 1923 volume *Rural Life.* Among the many questions that Galpin raised were the following: "Is there such a thing as a rural community? If so, what are its characteristics? Can the farm population as a class be considered a community? Or can you cut out of the open country any piece, large or small, square, triangular, or irregular in shape, and treat the farm families in this section as a community, and plan institutions for them? Would the Norwegian settlement, bound together by one church organization, form a community? Has each farm a community of its own, differing from that of every other? What is the social nature of the ordinary country school district? What sort of social unit is the agricultural township?"

13. Ferdinand Tönnies, *Gemeinschaft und Gesellschaft* (Community and Society), trans. Charles P. Loomis (New York, 1957); Louis Wirth, "The Sociology of Ferdinand Tönnies," *American Journal of Sociology* 32 (November 1926): 412–22; Émile Durkheim, *The Division of Labor in Society* (Glencoe, Ill., 1933).

was evident that neither a strict geographic nor a narrowly behavioral definition of community would suffice to depict the full complexity of rural social organization. Alternative approaches often drew upon the work of sociologist Charles H. Cooley, who added a new element to the scholarly equation in arguing that both individual and collective identity emerged from a single interactive process involving membership in "primary groups" like the household, the childhood play group, and the "neighborhood or community group of elders." As expressed by John Dewey in 1916, what allowed any group of people to form a community was the existence of common "beliefs, aspirations, knowledge—a common understanding—likemindedness, as the sociologists say."[14] In the South, scholars like Carle E. Zimmerman and Carl C. Taylor quickly discovered that such intangible factors as "race, class status, social practices, and standards of conduct" could create many overlapping neighborhoods in the same physical space.[15] Schools, churches, farmer organizations, lodges, and other visible agencies of community formation necessarily rested upon a foundation of shared culture and thus embodied what often was described as "community sentiment." Whether viewed as a precondition or as a consequence of group association, morals, folkways, customs, traditions, and collective ideals assumed an important role in establishing the existence of rural communities based upon factors other than physical propinquity.

In 1920, after reviewing the scholarly literature on rural social organization, University of Florida sociologist Newell L. Sims returned to the central question "What makes a community in the open country?" His answer was noteworthy in that it anticipated the increasingly broad and sophisticated range of analytic strategies that students from several social science disciplines would bring to rural field studies in the years ahead. "Those . . . who have anything in common, by virtue of their having it, live in a community," Sims announced. Community in the open country could therefore be defined as "a number of families dwelling on farms lying adjacent to one another and having something in common." Although the pattern of reasoning was obviously circular it reflected Sims's belief that only a "unitary" approach would bring stability to rural life. Sims anticipated a temporary period of continued decline in the countryside to be followed by transitional changes that would move farm families into the mainstream of national life.[16] During the remainder of the 1920s, however, the South's

14. Charles Horton Cooley, *Social Organization: A Study of the Larger Mind* (New York, 1909), 24; John Dewey, *Democracy and Education* (New York, 1916), 5.

15. Nelson, *Rural Sociology*, 42.

16. Sims, *The Rural Community*, 141, 150–52; Nelson, *Rural Sociology*, 112.

slumping cotton economy gave little evidence of an approaching millennium. In fact, the Southern version of America's larger rural crisis assumed a particularly acute form in which endemic problems of lagging institutional development were compounded by deepening indebtedness and economic stagnation. After 1930 the virtual collapse of the sharecropping system added new and compelling urgency to the task of rural modernization, endowing depression era studies like *They Live on the Land* with practical significance and tangible policy implications that generally had been absent from earlier investigations.

II

If Paul Terry and Verner Sims had done no more than produce an exceptionally thorough case study addressing the central preoccupations of rural sociologists during the 1920s and 1930s, their work would merit serious attention from present-day historians of Southern community life and folk culture. In reality, the book's intellectual agenda was somewhat different and in certain respects more ambitious than that which shaped rural scholarship in sociology or any other single discipline. What ultimately sets *They Live on the Land* apart from the bulk of contemporary field studies is the distinctive conceptual and methodological framework the authors brought to the project from their background in education and quantitative psychology. In order to comprehend the scope and design of the published monograph one must look first at Terry's and Sims's larger research interests and inquire at least briefly into the nature of educational psychology between the two world wars.

Born a dozen years apart in Nashville, Tennessee, and Mount Olivet, Kentucky, Paul Terry (1887–1959) and Verner Sims (1900–1960) took undergraduate degrees at Vanderbilt and Transylvania universities respectively before embarking upon teaching careers that eventually would include service at the high school, college, and university level. Each man received his psychological training within a school or department of education at a time when the two fields had become professionally interdependent in both a practical and an intellectual sense. Long regarded as a subdivision of philosophy, American psychology established a separate disciplinary identity around the turn of the twentieth century by asserting its claim to recognition as an experimental science, grounded in Wilhelm Wundt's laboratory study of stimulus and sensation at the University of Leipzig. Although Wundt provided psychologists with a model of rigorous and mathematically precise experimental design borrowed largely from physiology, his emphasis on disciplined "introspection" as a technique for examining the elements of consciousness had little appeal in the United States. American psychologists, including most of Wundt's returning students, quickly abandoned German structuralism with its emphasis on abstract or "pure" research. In its place they substituted the "functionalism" of William James and John Dewey, which defined its subject matter as the study of mental processes viewed as adjustments to environment. By broadening the scope of their discipline to include behavior, functionalists anticipated the more radical formulations of John B. Watson and opened the door to a variety of practical applications for both the methods and results of experimental research.[17]

Education provided the earliest and largest arena for the development of applied psychology. From the beginning, educators and psychologists made common cause on the basis of professional self-interest. A dramatic expansion of public-school enrollments and tax revenues in the decades after 1900 went hand in hand with the efforts of American educators to clothe their activities in the garb of pedagogical science. Psychologists possessed both the laboratory training and the quantitative expertise so necessary to legitimate education's claim to scientific stature. With other psychological research positions in short supply, new Ph.D.'s gravitated toward state and university education departments or the numerous normal schools and teachers colleges that strained to meet the burgeoning demand for duly certified classroom instructors. Experimental collaboration between educators and psychologists occurred initially within the framework of the child study movement, a massively empirical but somewhat amateurish endeavor rooted in the developmental "genetic psychology" of G. Stanley Hall. In the years before World War I, however, emphasis shifted to the more esoteric and rigorously quantitative field of "connectionist" learning theory based upon Edward Lee Thorndike's model of stimulus-response reinforcement.[18]

At the practical level, most educational psychologists devised, administered, and interpreted a wide array of standardized tests and scales

---

17. Generalizations in the preceding paragraph draw heavily upon John M. O'Donnell's excellent study *The Origins of Behaviorism: American Psychology, 1870–1920* (New York, 1985). For a more detailed discussion of various psychological schools, see Edna Heidbreder, *Seven Psychologies* (New York, 1933).

18. O'Donnell, *Origins of Behaviorism*, 152–58, 164–65, 229; Lawrence A. Cremin, *The Transformation of the School: Progressivism in American Education, 1876–1957* (New York, 1961), 110–14.

designed to measure ability or achievement in particular school subjects. In itself, the Progressive Era vogue for testing and measurement was pedagogically neutral. Depending upon a psychologist's prior assumptions, differences in individual performance could be interpreted as stemming primarily from environmental or hereditary sources. Educators, in turn, could employ test results to justify either individualized instruction within a common curriculum or the hierarchical grouping of students into academic and vocational courses according to presumed differences in innate mental capacity. Conservative hereditarian conceptions of intelligence gained wide national publicity as a result of the written and pictorial mental tests administered to almost two million U.S. Army recruits (plus selected prostitutes) during the First World War. As interpreted by Lewis M. Terman and other prominent psychologists, the tests ostensibly proved that the average "mental age" of Americans was less than fourteen years, a figure low enough to invalidate the entire concept of mass education beyond, or even through, high school. For educators the potential implications of the army tests were staggering and throughout the next decade controversy over the accuracy and meaning of IQ socres would shape debates over schooling, immigration, and social welfare policies.[19]

It was more or less at this juncture, with American psychologists caught up in what one contemporary would later describe as an "orgy of tabulation," that Paul Terry and Verner Sims began their doctoral studies.[20] Although Terry had participated in the wartime testing program as a lieutenant in the Psychological Service of the Army Medical Department's Sanitary Corps, there is little indication that he shared the socially conservative hereditarian bias of leading IQ testers. On the contrary, his decision in 1919 to study with Charles H. Judd at the University of Chicago suggests a decidedly liberal orientation. Among pre-1930 educational psychologists Judd is something of a paradoxical figure. A student of Wundt and an able statistician, he nonetheless rejected both structuralism and the behavioristic assumptions of

19. Chapman, *Schools as Sorters,* 173–77 passim; Robert M. Yerkes, ed., *Psychological Examining in the United States Army* [Memoirs of the National Academy of Sciences, Vol. 15] (Washington, D.C., 1921), 807–8; Franz Samelson, "World War I Intelligence Testing and the Development of Psychology," *Journal of the History of the Behavioral Sciences* 13 (July 1977): 271–82; Nicholas Pastore, "The Army Intelligence Tests and Walter Lippmann," ibid. 14 (October 1978): 316–27; Richard T. Van Mayrhauser, "Making Intelligence Functional: Walter Dill Scott and Applied Psychological Testing in World War I" ibid. 25 (January 1989): 60–72.

20. Harold Rugg, quoted in Cremin, *Transformation of the School,* 187.

Thorndike and other testing and measurement experts. Convinced that psychologists should study mental processes in their social context, Judd insisted that graduate students explore topics of practical significance to classroom teachers seeking guidance on how to do a better job with conventional school subjects.[21] For Paul Terry this meant a Ph.D. dissertation on how numerals are read in both sentences and arithmetic problems. Conceived as the introduction to a broader study of the way children acquired number reading skills over time, the work employed introspective observations by graduate students in conjunction with detailed photographic records of eye movements.[22] After completing the project in 1920 Terry taught for three years at the University of Washington where he demonstrated a thoroughly Judd-like interest in the relationship between public schooling and informed citizenship. Disturbed by America's postwar retreat into isolationism, he surveyed several hundred west coast high school seniors to determine their level of knowledge about Japanese Americans and the history of diplomatic relations between Japan and the United States. The results were less than encouraging. School curricula contained virtually no information on either subject, and teachers considered the "Japanese problem" too controversial for classroom discussion. Pervasive ignorance compounded by "virulent race prejudice" suggested that fear and propaganda would carry the day politically as the nation rushed headlong toward more restrictive immigration quotas.[23]

In 1924 Terry left Washington to begin a three-year stint as professor of education at the University of North Carolina, a school already well on the

---

21. Biographical information on Paul Terry comes primarily from the following sources: Guy A. Matlock, ed., *Who's Who in Alabama, 1939–1940* (Birmingham, 1940), 243–44; *Who Was Who in America,* vol. 4: 1961–1968 (Chicago, 1969), 933; and "Professional Career of Paul W. Terry," unpublished typescript, University of Alabama Library. On Judd and Chicago see Travers, *How Research Has Changed American Schools,* 319–40; Alanson A. Van Fleet, "Charles Judd's Psychology of Schooling," *Elementary School Journal* 76 (May 1976): 455–63.

22. Paul W. Terry, *How Numerals are Read: An Experimental Study of the Reading of Isolated Numerals and Numerals in Arithmetic Problems* (Chicago, 1922). See also Paul W. Terry, "The Reading Problem in Arithmetic," *Journal of Educational Psychology* 12 (October 1921): 365–77. Terry's graduate director, Charles Judd, had written a Ph.D. dissertation under Wundt on space perception and binocular and monocular vision.

23. Paul W. Terry, "Is the High School Developing a Citizenship Intelligently Informed of Japanese-American Relations[?]" *School and Society,* 18 (October 1923): 475–80.

way toward establishing its reputation as the "Wisconsin of the South." Although his affiliation with Chapel Hill was brief, it brought the young psychologist into an intellectual environment energized by the presence of sociologist Howard W. Odum and the newly created Institute for Research in the Social Sciences.[24] What influence, if any, the embryonic "regionalist" movement may have exerted on Terry is unclear, although he could hardly have remained oblivious to the ambitious program of rural field research that Odum was sponsoring. All that can be said with certainty is that the focus of Terry's own research shifted in North Carolina to the study of junior and senior high school extracurricular activities, a matter educators had begun to regard as crucial for shaping acceptable patterns of student socialization. Describing the modern school as a "community similar in nature to the community at large," Terry stressed the civic value of training in the "practical arts of social experience." Specifically, he defended organized group activities as a prerequisite for educating "socially useful" adults who would cooperate effectively in religion, politics, and government as well as in philanthropic and recreational activities.[25]

By the time Terry reached North Carolina his future colleague Verner Sims had exchanged a high school principalship in Kentucky for a position as mathematics instructor at Hillhouse High School in New Haven, Connecticut, where he taught from 1923 through 1926 while pursuing graduate

---

24. George B. Tindall, "The Significance of Howard W. Odum to Southern History: A Preliminary Estimate," *Journal of Southern History* 24 (August 1958): 285–307; Dewey W. Grantham, *The Regional Imagination: The South and Recent American History* (Nashville, 1979), 165–69; Louis R. Wilson, *The University of North Carolina, 1900–1930* (Chapel Hill, 1957), 450–53. Shortly before Terry's arrival, the University of North Carolina had established a Bureau of Educational Research. An organization of identical name and similar purpose at the University of Alabama would later publish *They Live on the Land*.

25. Terry's major writings on extracurricular activities include: "The Social Experience of Junior High School Pupils," *School Review* 35 (March 1927): 194–207 and ibid. (April 1927): 272–80; "Administration of Extra-Curriculum Activities in the High School," ibid. 33 (December 1925): 734–43 and ibid. 34 (January 1926): 15–25; *Extra-Curricular Activities in the Junior High School* (Baltimore, 1926); and *Supervising Extra-Curricular Activities in the American Secondary School* (New York, 1930). The passages quoted here are from "The Social Experience of Junior High School Pupils," 194. For an assessment of the claims made on behalf of extracurricular activities in the 1920s, see George S. Counts, "Procedures in Evaluating Extra-Curriculum Activities," *School Review* 34 (June 1926): 412–21.

work in educational psychology at Yale University.[26] From an institutional standpoint the timing of Sims's enrollment at Yale was excellent. In 1920, after decades of disciplinary infighting, education had achieved departmental autonomy under the chairmanship of Frank Ellsworth Spaulding, a Leipzig Ph.D. and veteran big-city school administrator who came to the university from a post on the General Education Board. By 1923 Spaulding had revived education's faltering graduate program and recruited able new faculty members like George S. Counts and J. Crosby Chapman.[27] Although Counts would gain prominence during the next decade as an outspoken leftist critic of the nation's educational establishment, he was already well known for his trenchant analysis of class inequities in public secondary education.[28] Chapman, a British radiation physicist turned educational psychologist, specialized in educational measurement and had helped formulate the vocational tests used for military classification of recruits during the First World War. Yet despite his Columbia Ph.D. and his earlier collaboration with Edward L. Thorndike, Chapman was no educational determinist. Openly scornful of those who drew social-Darwinist conclusions from the results of "so-called intelligence tests," he cautioned

---

26. Unless otherwise indicated, biographical information on Sims was obtained from the following sources: J. McKeen Cattell, ed., *Leaders in Education,* 1st ed. (New York, 1932), 852; ibid., 2d ed. (New York, 1941), 925; draft typescript of Sims's obituary, University of Alabama Library; published obituary, *Birmingham News,* May 19, 1960; and telephone interview with Ms. Carolyn Palmgreen, Transylvania University Library, April 4, 1989. A seventy-five-year time seal precluded access to Sims's academic records at Yale University.

27. The following reports by Frank E. Spaulding afford a detailed picture of the development of Yale's Department of Education during the 1920s: "Outline of a Plan for Organizing and Maintaining Courses for Connecticut Public School Teachers . . . December 7, 1921"; "Notes on the Study of Education as a Profession at Yale [January 1925]"; "Department of Education, Report for the Year 1928–29"; "Memorandum Submitted at the Request of the Provost, March 8, 1929," all in Miscellaneous Manuscripts no. 17, Sterling Memorial Library, Yale University. For a useful overview of the program's rise and fall, see John S. Brubacher et al., *The Department of Education at Yale University, 1891–1958* (New Haven, 1960).

28. Two works by Gerald L. Gutek explore Counts's ideas in some detail: *The Educational Theory of George S. Counts* (Columbus, Ohio, 1970) and *George S. Counts and American Civilization: The Educator as Social Theorist* (Macon, Ga., 1984).

educators against "putting too much faith in the instruments which a short while back were the objects of their distrust."[29]

Chapman's warning was prompted in part by the postwar boom in group testing that followed public disclosure of the details of the army's massive program of psychological examinations. With hundreds of thousands, and perhaps millions, of school children being tested by the early 1920s, IQ measurement and its broader social implications became a subject of intense professional and public debate. National interest peaked during 1922–23 when the liberal journalist Walter Lippman subjected the testers' methods and a priori hereditarian assumptions to scathing criticism in the pages of the *New Republic*. The army experts, he charged, had failed to define intelligence or distinguish its environmental component. By refusing to acknowledge the limitations of their measuring instruments, they invited educational abuses that could usher in an "intellectual caste system." Professional silence, Lippman argued, made psychologists accomplices to a larger reactionary deception and left them vulnerable to the charge of furnishing "doped evidence to the exponents of the New Snobbery."[30]

The intellectual shock waves from Lippman's assault were still reverberating through the scholarly world as Verner Sims entered graduate school. Under the circumstances it was hardly surprising that the young mathematics teacher gravitated toward educational measurement and elected to study with Chapman, whose skepticism about IQ testing's exaggerated claims went hand in hand with a commitment to rigorous experimental design and open-minded scientific inquiry. Like most psychologists of his day Chapman regarded intelligence as the product of both nature and

---

29. *National Cyclopaedia of American Biography* Vol. 20 (New York, 1929), 341; J. Crosby Chapman and Verner M. Sims, "The Quantitative Measurement of Certain Aspects of Socio-Economic Status," *Journal of Educational Psychology* 16 (September 1925): 380–90 (first quote on p. 380); J. Crosby Chapman, "The Unreliability of the Difference Between Intelligence and Educational Ratings" ibid. 14 (February 1923): 103–8 (second quote on p. 103).

30. *New Republic,* November 29, 1922, 10. See also the sources listed in note 19 above. Recent overviews of the controversy surrounding intelligence measurement include Raymond E. Fancher, *The Intelligence Men: Makers of the I.Q. Controversy* (New York, 1985) and a more critical assessment by Stephen Jay Gould, *The Mismeasure of Man* (New York, 1981). In terms of intellectual breadth and contextual richness, no work surpasses Carl N. Degler's brilliant synthesis *In Search of Human Nature: The Decline and Revival of Darwinism in American Social Thought* (New York, 1991). See especially chapter 7.

nurture. But in contrast to many colleagues he was not content to let the matter rest there. Although quick to warn future teachers against basing educational theory upon a naive trust in the "omnipotence of environmental forces," he reserved his harshest criticism for the doctrinaire hereditarianism of American test architects whom he accused of "loading the dice" by subsuming biological and environmental influences within the same measurement categories.[31] In a series of penetrating articles published between 1921 and 1923, Chapman argued that existing IQ tests failed to allow for differences in vocabulary and basic skill development between older and younger children, thereby resulting in "great injustice to individuals whose environmental opportunities are not essentially normal." One solution to the problem lay in restricting statistical comparisons to children of the same age and developing test items that were "freed from nonessential experience factors." A second approach, and the one eventually taken by Sims, was to attempt quantitative measurement of environmental influences as such.[32]

Working in the New Haven school system under Chapman's guidance and with financial support from the Columbia-based Character Education Inquiry, Sims developed a preliminary questionnaire to gather data on the social, economic, and cultural background of nearly seven hundred sixth-through eighth-grade students whose neighborhood schools represented the entire range of urban living conditions. Subsequent refinement and

---

31. J. Crosby Chapman and George S. Counts, *Principles of Education* (Boston, 1924), 181 (first quote); J. Crosby Chapman, "An Additional Criterion for the Selection of the Elements of Mental Tests," *Journal of Educational Psychology,* 12 (April 1921): 232–35 (second quote on p. 232).

32. J. Crosby Chapman and A. Barbara Dale, "A Further Criterion for the Selection of Mental Test Elements," *Journal of Educational Psychology* 13 (May 1922): 267–76 (quotes on p. 268). The series of articles referred to includes the publications cited here and in notes 29 and 31 above. For additional evidence of Chapman's interest in the relation of environment to intelligence and school performance, see J. Crosby Chapman and H. L. Eby, "A Comparative Study, by Educational Measurements, of One-Room Rural-School Children and City-School Children," *Journal of Educational Research* 2 (October 1920): 636–46; J. Crosby Chapman, "The Relation of Family Size to Intelligence of Offspring and Socio-Economic Status of Family," *Pedagogical Seminary* 32 (September 1925): 414–21. As one careful student of the subject has noted, Chapman was virtually alone among psychologists of the early 1920s in attacking the validity of Raymond Franzen's "accomplishment quotient," an alleged measure of teaching efficiency derived from comparing achievement test scores to IQ scores. Weinland, "History of the I.Q. in America," 151–53.

simplification resulted in a twenty-three item "score card" covering such topics as parental education and occupation, possession of books and magazines, participation in social and cultural activities, and access to luxuries and creature comforts. All answers had specific, weighted point values that were averaged to obtain a final score between zero and thirty-six. This number, carried to one decimal place, formed the basis for a comparative ranking of students according to class background or what Sims preferred to call "socio-economic status."[33] Keenly aware of the "fallacy of labeling" in quantitative social science, Sims nonetheless believed that his scorecard measured something real—a hierarchy of qualitatively different domestic experiences that would either facilitate or impede a child's ability to function within a larger external environment dominated by upper-middle-class norms and expectations. This at least would appear to constitute the unstated assumption behind his willingness to designate home backgrounds "favorable" or "unfavorable" as measured by the "Sims score."

Although Sims made no attempt to pinpoint either the dimensions of personality or the processes of cognitive development that were influenced by home environment, he clearly saw his scale as a device that would promote critical reassessment of prevailing assumptions that all children enjoyed "equal exposure" to the intellectual and cultural content of IQ tests. In discussing the possible uses of his score card Sims found it "rather amusing" that the test designers gave lopsided emphasis to material that students from "superior homes have obviously had more opportunity of coming in contact with, and then registered surprise when children from a superior environment, such as the children of professional men, show a higher average score."[34] Objective measurement of socioeconomic status, Sims believed, would help clarify distinctions between formal and incidental learning and thus facilitate the study of intelligence in situations where environmental factors were minimized or held constant. In the school itself a

---

33. Verner Martin Sims, *The Measurement of Socio-Economic Status* (Bloomington, 1928), 1–11, 23. On the Character Education Inquiry, see Earle Wayne Kenyon, "The Character Education Inquiry, 1924–1928: A Historical Examination of its Use in Educational Research" (Ph.D. diss., University of Texas, 1979); Stephen M. Yulish, *The Search for a Civic Religion: A History of the Character Education Movement in America, 1890–1935* (Washington, D.C., 1980), 75–77, 181–82, 203–5, 233–36.

34. Sims, *Measurement of Socio-Economic Status*, 1; Verner Martin Sims, "The Need for Objective Measurement of the Socio-Economic Status of the Child," *Phi Delta Kappan* 15 (June 1930): 10–13, 14.

thorough knowledge of student social levels might give focus and direction to efforts at educational reform. Instead of working at loggerheads with family and community influences, public schools should "take the [student's] home background as the logical starting point, and work upward" from there. In practice, "working upward" could involve policies as diverse and potentially contradictory as publicly financed preschool training, vocational courses in high schools, "moral education" for students who failed to assimilate appropriate values within the family, and even the use of Sims scores to ensure that homogeneous ability grouping did not result in systematic segregation of students according to social status.[35]

By linking the IQ controversy to a larger concern over the relationship of schooling, class, and individual opportunity in America, Sims followed in the footsteps of Yale's outspoken education professor George Counts, whose 1922 monograph *The Selective Character of American Secondary Education* established a clear connection between parental occupations and the attendance patterns, dropout rates, and curricular choices of high school students. Convinced that public high schools were serving the "upper social strata," Counts urged future scholars to move beyond occupational analysis and relate school patterns to the "cultural level and standard of living" in student homes. Illuminating the latter issue would require specific information about the "number and character of books, magazines, and newspapers" in households, the presence or absence of telephones, the "character of conversation," levels of exposure to music, art, and a number of similiar matters.[36]

Having included most of these categories in his home background questionnaire, Sims was ready to pursue Counts's central theme of socioeconomic "selection" within student populations. An opportunity to explore the subject arose during 1926–27 when Sims joined the faculty of Louisiana Polytechnic Institute, a former industrial school in the rural cotton region of the state's northern hill country. Making the most of his position as a quantitative expert in the education department of a local teacher-training institution, Sims proceeded to gather data on the socioeconomic status and intelligence scores of more than one thousand elementary and high school students in rural Lincoln Parish and the town of Ruston where the college was located. Subsequent analysis of the mass of statistical evidence revealed tendencies sharply at odds with public education's pro-

---

35. Ibid., 15.

36. George S. Counts, *The Selective Character of American Secondary Education* (Chicago, 1922; rpt. New York, 1969), 87–88.

fessedly egalitarian aims. Among the parish's white schoolchildren a process of class-based academic winnowing began very early as pupils from the poorest and least educated families dropped out. A profound change in the social composition of the student body seemed to take place at the end of the fifth grade rather than at the beginning of high school as many educators had supposed. With the state's compulsory attendance law largely unenforced, each successive grade from the sixth onward became less representative of the general population in terms of measured IQ and socioeconomic status. Had data been available for black students and the most culturally disadvantaged whites in one- and two-room schools, the contrasts would have been still more pronounced.[37]

Aware that some psychologists would attribute high dropout rates to a supposed lack of innate ability among lower-class families, Sims rejected the hereditarian argument and called for additional study of the social and economic forces governing school attendance. In addition he urged administrators to consider the role of "curricular content, aim, or method" in determining which students remained in school and for how long. Since good teaching would be crucial to any effort at reaching and retaining working-class children, Sims made a detailed assessment of the sixty-seven freshmen women enrolled in Louisiana Tech's two-year normal course and compared them with the ninety-two women beginning various four-year degree programs at the same institution. Once again, the results were less than encouraging. By virtually every available measure, including intelligence, vocabularly, English ability, and socioeconomic status, the two-year students seemed inferior to their four-year counterparts. Indeed, in their general grasp of elementary school subjects the "normal freshmen" actually ranked lower than pupils in the college's demonstration high school and only slightly above ninth-grade achievement norms. These sobering revelations, in conjunction with what must have been frustrating personal experiences in the classroom, were sufficient to jolt Sims momentarily out of his usual posture of controlled scientific detachment. The inadequacy of Louisiana's normal school students was "striking enough to cause concern," he announced in a prominent national education magazine. "Working with such raw material," professors engaged in teacher preparation would "do well to give the students a fair mastery of elementary subject matter plus a few 'rule-of-thumb' methods," hardly the caliber of training necessary to

---

37. Verner Martin Sims, "The Selected Nature of a Particular School Population," *School Review* 36 (April 1928): 296–301.

produce graduates "capable of handling our education at this most critical period." The solution, if there was to be one, would necessarily involve upgrading the status of the teaching profession in order to attract the South's more able and qualified students into education programs.[38]

Sims's impatience with the lacklustre quality of prospective elementary school teachers reflected more than the exasperation of a talented Yale Ph.D. marooned in the Louisiana hills. Behind the young psychologist's unflattering conclusions lay a deeper concern with the acquired aspects of intelligence and a growing conviction that local schools were inadvertently squandering potential talent and denying opportunity to lower-class youth. Given the role of hereditarian dogma in reinforcing political and economic roadblocks to educational reform, Sims's analysis of the Lincoln Parish test results could scarcely have been expected to ignore the theoretical implications of socioeconomic selection among grade school students. In an article that became the intellectual centerpiece of his Louisiana research Sims attacked the nature-nurture issue directly and, in the process, committed himself irrevocably to the liberal environmentalist wing of his profession.

Sims's 1931 study of the influence of blood relationship and common environment on measured intelligence represented a fresh and highly original adaptation of a familiar experimental concept.[39] By the late 1920s, comparing sibling IQ scores had become an accepted technique for distinguishing between native and acquired mental ability. Leading critics of hereditarianism like the University of Chicago's Frank N. Freeman arrived at rough estimates of environmental influence by studying brothers and sisters who were separated early and reared in different homes.[40] Armed with his socioeconomic scorecard data, Sims took precisely the opposite approach. That is, he sought to compare the intelligence of siblings reared in the same home with that of unrelated children reared in different homes at the same socioeconomic level. Following a line of reasoning similar to the one set forth in J. Crosby Chapman's earlier critiques of IQ and achievement tests,

---

38. Ibid., 301; Verner Martin Sims, "A Comparison of Normal-School Students with Certain Other Groups," *School and Society* 30 (July 13, 1929): 70.

39. Verner M. Sims, "The Influence of Blood Relationship and Common Environment on Measured Intelligence," *Journal of Educational Psychology* 22 (January 1931): 56–63.

40. Weinland, "History of the I.Q. in America," 233–37; Frank N. Freeman et al., "The Influence of Environment on the Intelligence, School Achievement and Conduct with Foster Children," in *Nature and Nurture: Twenty-Seventh Yearbook of the National Society for the Study of Education* (Bloomington, 1928), 104ff.

Sims employed an ingenious method of statistical grouping calculated to isolate genetic and environmental components of IQ while controlling for such external factors as age and school attendance. The intricacies of Sims quantitative procedures need not concern us here. Described by one modern authority as a "sophisticated and elegant" study based on "impressive" data and guided by "impeccable logic," Sims's investigation must have raised a cheer from the environmentalist ranks.[41] When full allowance had been made for margins of error and all extraneous factors, the IQ correlation for 203 pairs of "unrelated individuals reared apart" in similar home environments was .29, a figure not significantly lower that the .40 correlation observed among 203 pairs of true siblings. Since the siblings shared a virtually identical environment while the unrelated pairs were grouped according to a far less precise environmental standard, even the small observed differences in correlation probably were overstated. With characteristic scholarly restraint Sims concluded that his findings might be interpreted as either a "condemnation of present day 'intelligence' tests" or as evidence that IQ represented the "interplay of environmental forces on hereditary characteristics." Whichever the case, there could be little doubt that intelligence, "so far as we are today able to measure it," was "greatly influenced by environment."[42] Coming at a time when environmentalist forces were steadily gaining ground in psychology and the other social sciences, Sims's essay, for all its scientific caution, was clearly a step in the direction of more explicit challenges to the existing social order. Although he did not personally address the rapidly brewing controversy over alleged racial differences in IQ, Sims certainly knew that his finding lent indirect support to scholars like Thomas Russell Garth, Otto Klineberg, and Franz Boaz who were advancing cultural explanations of intelligence that threatened to undermine the entire philosophical defense of racial and class hierarchy.[43] The culmination of these developments was, of course, still far in the future. During the next three decades the realities of Sims's position as a college professor in the Deep South would force him to tread lightly in matters of race. Eventually, however, history would come full circle and allow him to witness at close quarters the assault on segregated education that environmentalist scholarship had helped set in motion.

---

41. Leon J. Kamin, *The Science and Politics of I.Q.* (Potomac, Md., 1974), 80.

42. Sims, "Influence of Blood Relationship and Common Environment," 62–63.

43. Thomas F. Gossett, *Race: The History of an Idea in America* (New York, 1965), chapter 16; Degler, *In Search of Human Nature*, chapters 3, 4, 7, and 8.

III

In 1928, just as the first of his Lincoln Parish studies was making its way into print, Sims joined the education faculty of the University of Alabama in Tuscaloosa. Only two years earlier Paul Terry had moved to the same institution at the behest of Dean James J. Doster, an able administrator who aspired to make Alabama's College of Education "one of the leading schools in the South."[44] Doster's stated policy was to seek out faculty members who possessed "more than a sectional view of education." In practice, this meant recruiting Ph.D.s trained outside the South since "the best universities are in the North and the West."[45] With his Chicago doctorate and his experience in Washington state, Terry filled the bill splendidly, and in 1926 he was appointed to chair the College of Education's new Department of Psychology. Initially he was the lone professor in his discipline, a department head "in name only," as he would recall later.[46] That situation changed in 1928 when, after close consultation with Doster, Terry doubled his department's size by hiring Verner Sims. Quite possibly Sims's candidacy benefited from the good offices of Chicago's Frank N. Freeman who previously had recommended Terry for the Alabama chairmanship and certainly would have been familiar with Sims's home background scale.[47] In any case both Terry and Sims cast their lot with the University of Alabama at what appeared to be an auspicious moment. After decades of frustrating struggle against deeply entrenched political conservatives, the state's school forces had united in 1926 behind progressive gubernatorial candidate Bibb Graves. Elected through a bizarre alliance of educators, organized labor, World War I veterans, and Ku Klux Klansmen, Graves proceeded to push measures through the legislature authorizing some $25 million for educational purposes during the next four years, including some $3 million for higher education. An early cooperative agreement between the state's college and university presidents facilitated efficient use of the money and permitted needed expansion of various

---

44. Paul W. Terry to James J. Doster, March 26, 1937, College of Education, Dean's Office Papers, box 1, University of Alabama Library.

45. James J. Doster to Earl Hudelson, November 13, 1941, in ibid., box 17.

46. Paul W. Terry to James J. Doster, March 26, 1937 in ibid., box 1. This is a different letter from the one cited in note 44 above, though the date and recipient are identical.

47. James J. Doster to Frank N. Freeman, November 3, 1927, in ibid., box 9. See also Frank N. Freeman to James J. Doster, March 26, 1928, in ibid., box 9.

professional programs including those within the College of Education.[48] Amid the optimism and relative affluence of the Graves administration, school reformers could find grounds to hope that the corner on educational modernization at last had been turned. Only the most naive enthusiast, however, would have been tempted to believe that victory was at hand. By almost any standards Alabama in the late 1920s presented a picture of stark cultural contrasts and unresolved social contradictions. The instability of Graves's "progressive" electoral base became evident as early as 1927 when the same legislature that enacted generous educational appropriations defeated bills to unmask the Klan and thus check the sudden outburst of floggings that was causing the state national embarrassment.[49] On the educational front, policies designed to reconcile progress with tradition yielded mixed results. Civic boosters could point with pride to the thoroughly modern white schools and their inferior but improving black counterparts in the metropolis of Birmingham, while no less a figure than John Dewey turned the spotlight of national publicity on Marietta Pierce Johnson's experiment in "organic education" at Fairhope, Alabama.[50] In the countryside, moreover, the administrative panacea known as consolidation continued to generate reassuring statistics, as more and more rural children traveled farther to study longer in bigger, sturdier buildings with more and presumably better teachers.[51] On those rare occasions when white reformers turned their attention to black schooling, it was possible to ignore or rationalize the virtual theft of state appropriations by white authorities at the county level, as long as outside philanthropies like the General Educa-

---

48. Albert B. Moore, *History of Alabama* (University, Ala., 1934), 769–72, 775–76; William E. Gilbert, "Bibb Graves as a Progressive," *Alabama Review* 10 (January 1957): 15–30; Henry Clifton Pannell, *The Preparation and Work of Alabama High School Teachers* (New York, 1933), 10–12.

49. Moore, *History of Alabama,* 774–75.

50. Carl V. Harris, "Stability and Change in Discrimination against Black Public Schools: Birmingham, Alabama, 1871–1931," *Journal of Southern History* 51 (August 1985): 375–416; *An Educational Survey of Alabama* [Department of the Interior, Bureau of Education, Bulletin No. 41] (Washington, D.C., 1919); Cremin, *Transformation of the School,* 147–53; Marietta Johnson, *Thirty Years with an Idea* (University, Ala., 1974), 131–39 passim; Paul M. Gaston, *Women of Fair Hope* (Athens, Ga., 1984), 77–117.

51. *Educational Survey of Alabama,* 119–23; cf. Alabama Educational Survey Commission, *Public Education in Alabama* (Washington, D.C., 1945), 25–27.

tion Board and the Julius Rosenwald Fund provided enough money to create visible signs of improvement in a few places.[52]

For both races, if the truth were told, the actual pace of educational change in Alabama was highly uneven. As late as 1929 an official report of the state Superintendent of Education described the typical Alabama white teacher as a single, twenty-three-year-old woman with less than two years of formal education beyond high school. Responsible for sixteen recitations per day in seven different subjects, she walked nearly six miles over sand-clay roads to and from school for an average monthly salary of $85.50.[53]

Judged by the most common statistical measures, such as literacy rates and years of schooling completed by percentiles of state population, Alabama ranked near the bottom, surpassing only South Carolina and Louisiana.[54] In Tuscaloosa County the quality of classroom instruction was probably enhanced by the university's practice teaching program, but school conditions were far from ideal. During the early 1930s the county still contained 31 one-teacher white schools enrolling a higher-than-normal percentage of overage pupils in the lower grades. White illiteracy rates were above the state average and expenditures per pupil for both whites and blacks fell substantially below the statewide norm. A slightly higher than average rate of black literacy apparently bore testimony to the work of small private tuition schools like St. Mary Magdalene, St. Paul's Lutheran, and Stillman

52. Horace Mann Bond, *Negro Education in Alabama: A Study in Cotton and Steel* (Washington, D.C., 1939); Glen N. Sisk, "The Educational Awakening in Alabama and Its Effect upon the Black Belt, 1900–1917," *Journal of Negro Education* 25 (spring 1956): 191–96; Irving Gershenberg, "The Negro and the Development of White Public Education in the South: Alabama, 1880–1930," ibid. 39 (winter 1970): 50–59.

53. Report of Alabama State Superintendent of Education, 1929, as quoted in George Howard, *Teacher Supply and Demand in Alabama, 1948–49* (University, Ala., Bureau of Educational Research, 1950), 20.

54. Sanford Winston, *Illiteracy in the United States* (Chapel Hill, 1930), 16–17; Charles S. Johnson, *Statistical Atlas of Southern Counties* (Chapel Hill, 1941), 53. In 1930 Tuscaloosa County had a white illiteracy rate of 5.2 percent and a black rate of 23.6 percent. As late as the 1940s Alabama ranked twelfth among the fourteen southern states in the percentage of adults with no formal schooling (see Alabama Educational Survey Commission, *Public Education in Alabama*, 122–23).

Institute, which together assumed at least some of the educational responsibilities that society as a whole had abdicated.[55]

For scholars like Terry and Sims, with their southern roots, northern training, and national frame of reference, Alabama's educational scene presented challenges that looked formidable, but not insurmountable, given the right combination of money, political will, and professional expertise. A long road unquestionably lay ahead for school reformers, but change had begun in the state and its momentum showed signs of increasing. Or so it seemed until 1929 when events on Wall Street punctured the bubble of New Era capitalism.

The onset of the Great Depression in Alabama and its deepening local impact defy any effort at brief description. University faculty members saw salaries drop by 20 percent as state revenues plummeted, although the employed professor's position remained vastly superior to that of white and blue collar workers who forfeited both jobs and personal dignity as the economy ground to a virtual standstill.[56] Among rural folk who had never really participated in the prosperity of the twenties, conditions went steadily from bad to worse. Mortgage foreclosure threatened many in the landed class, while the sharecropper's already grim struggle for survival took on a desperate edge. For black farmers, of course, the economic crisis was compounded immeasurably by the crushing weight of the racial caste system. Ignored or exploited by more affluent whites, black tenants facing the specter of starvation took help where they found it. In several plantation counties the part humanitarian, part political program of the Communist-led Sharecroppers Union attracted sufficient grass-roots interest to provoke fierce repression by local authorities.[57] Radical organizers also worked to

---

55. [Arthur F. Raper, et. al.], *The Plight of Tuscaloosa: A Case Study of Conditions in Tuscaloosa County, Alabama, 1933* (Atlanta, 1933), 38–39; Earl M. Meadows, "Some Factors Associated with Slow Progress in the First Grade of the White Schools of Tuscaloosa County, Alabama" (Master of Arts thesis, University of Alabama, College of Education, 1932), 22–26.

56. Suzanne Rau Wolfe, *The University of Alabama: A Pictorial History* (University, Ala., 1983), 58, 159. For an excellent account of the depression's impact upon the state's white workers, see Wayne Flynt, *Poor But Proud: Alabama's Poor Whites* (Tuscaloosa, 1989), chapter 11.

57. Robin D. G. Kelley, *Hammer and Hoe: Alabama Communists During the Great Depression* (Chapel Hill, 1990), chapters 2 and 9. For the vivid recollections of a black participant, see Theodore Rosengarten, ed., *All God's Dangers; The Life of Nate Shaw* (New York, 1974).

mobilize unemployed miners, steel workers, and assorted urban wage laborers in and around Birmingham, the state's chief industrial center. Amid growing public hysteria over left-wing threats to white supremacy and capitalism, however, all forms of labor militance faced stiff resistance in the form of legal harassment and covertly sanctioned acts of terrorism.[58]

No one who challenged the status quo was exempt from the bludgeoning force of intolerance that journalist Wilbur J. Cash would later describe as the "savage ideal." Intellectuals like University of Alabama physics professor Joseph Gelders discovered that defending the civil liberties of arrested Communists was tantamount to forfeiting his own access to legal protection. Unfortunately, Gelders's 1936 kidnapping and savage beating at the hands of known but unindicted assailants was only one in a long list of object lessons on the dangers of academic activism.[59] If meddlesome eggheads failed to get the message conveyed by the infamous Scottsboro trials in northern Alabama, a more immediate demonstration of the limits of socially permissible dissent was provided in the city of Tuscaloosa itself following the arrest of three black men on rape and homicide charges during the summer of 1933. Under the best of circumstances black defendants stood little chance of obtaining justice in Alabama courts, but in mid-1933 Tuscaloosa County was in the grip of an unprecedented crime wave. Lax law enforcement, the shutdown of nearby coal mines, and the desperate plight of cotton tenants helped explain why more than seventy killings had occurred since the spring of 1931, giving the county a murder rate proportionately higher than that of Chicago.[60] Another dimension of the problem could be read in the county's burgeoning relief rolls, which by the autumn of 1933 contained nearly 8,000 names.[61]

With unemployed miners, sharecroppers, and transients loitering aimlessly in Tuscaloosa's streets, the arrest of three black suspects helped

---

58. Kelley, *Hammer and Hoe,* chapters 3 and 7; Flynt, *Poor But Proud,* 321–32.

59. On the details of the Gelders episode and its larger context, see Thomas A. Krueger, *And Promises to Keep: The Southern Conference for Human Welfare, 1938–1948* (Nashville, 1967), 3–11; Jerold S. Auerback, *Labor and Liberty: The La Follette Committee and the New Deal* (Indianapolis, 1966), 94–96; Hollinger F. Barnard, ed., *Outside the Magic Circle: The Autobiography of Virginia Foster Durr* (University, Ala., 1985), 112–15.

60. Dan T. Carter, *Scottsboro: A Tragedy of the American South,* 2d ed. (Baton Rouge, 1984); [Raper et al.], *Plight of Tuscaloosa,* 36.

61. [Thad Holt], *Two Years of Federal Relief in Alabama* (Wetumpka, Ala., 1935), 46.

transform individual resentments into support for collective violence. Temporary removal of the prisoners forestalled an initial mob in June, but when the trial opened in July the presence of lawyers retained by the International Labor Defense, a Communist organization, precipitated a crisis of local authority. Only the intervention of National Guard troops armed with fixed bayonets and tear gas grenades allowed the ILD attorneys to escape Tuscaloosa unharmed. In the wake of the incident a Klan-style vigilante group known as the Citizens Protective League took virtual control of the community with an elaborate campaign of masked parades, spying, secret reporting, and night-riding violence. Before the reign of terror began to subside county sheriff's deputies had delivered the black defendants to a group of masked gunmen who killed two of the men and seriously wounded the third. Another black prisoner, arrested on unrelated charges, was lynched a few weeks later. Meanwhile, a special grand jury protected by barbed wire entanglements and some 120 soldiers failed to return indictments in the initial mob murders. Moderate forces eventually reasserted themselves in the city, but not before local vigilantes effectively had made their point.[62]

The apparent timidity of local police and grand jurors stood in marked contrast to the zeal of the field investigators sent into town by the Southern Commission on the Study of Lynching. In what was probably the most thorough assessment of Tuscaloosa's flirtation with anarchy, SCSL researchers directed by University of North Carolina sociologist Arthur F. Raper sought to establish the basic facts concerning the lynchings and to place the mob violence in economic and cultural context. Refusing to absolve educators from a share of responsibility for existing conditions, the Commission concluded that, for all practical purposes, the University of Alabama had "merely acquiesced" in the prevailing attitude of "inaction and apology" for bigotry and lawlessness. Instead of taking the lead in social change, the university had allegedly "lived quite within itself," exerting little influence over the surrounding community.[63]

Whether or not such criticisms were entirely fair, Paul Terry and Verner Sims undoubtedly would have agreed that university faculty members had a legitimate role to play in improving local life. As early as 1930 they had

---

62. [Raper et al.], *Plight of Tuscaloosa,* 10–19 passim; Kelley, *Hammer and Hoe,* 88–89; Clarence Cason, *90 ° in the Shade* (Chapel Hill, 1935; rpt. University, Ala., 1983), 113–20, contains a firsthand account of the 1933 Tuscaloosa disorders.

63. [Raper et al.], *Plight of Tuscaloosa,* 38.

organized an extension class of Tuscaloosa County teachers who became the "main working corps" for the testing program conducted as part of the school survey of 1930–31.[64] Terry gave lectures and extension classes at various points throughout the state from 1928 onward and was also active in the Tuscaloosa Kiwanis Club, which joined with other civic groups in sponsoring a ten-point campaign to increase respect for law and order during the autumn of 1933.[65] Significantly, one of the program's stated goals was increased emphasis on "law observance . . . good citizenship and character development" in the curriculum of the public schools.[66] Within his own institution Terry helped found the local chapter of the American Association of University Professors whose members, including Sims, worked to expand the faculty's role in university governance.[67] Although Sims's activities leaned somewhat more heavily toward scholarship, his sociological approach to educational psychology gave little evidence of a sheltered "ivory tower" perspective. During the year following the lynchings of 1933, for example, he collaborated in a comparative study of personality differences between black and white college students in the North and South, using test data secured in part at the University of Alabama and Tuskegee Institute.[68] Nor did the prevailing climate of bigotry and intolerance deter him from supervising a 1934 master's thesis that explored the relationship between IQ scores and home background among one hundred pairs of black and white Tuscaloosa County sixth graders from comparable socioeconomic backgrounds.[69]

Activities like those just described, when placed alongside Terry's ac-

---

64. Paul W. Terry to N. F. Greenhill, October 5, 1930, College of Education, Dean's Office Papers, University of Alabama Library.

65. [Raper et al.], *Plight of Tuscaloosa,* 32–33; "Training, Experience, and Professional and Civic Activities of Professor Paul W. Terry . . . July 1957," typescript in University of Alabama Library.

66. [Raper et al.], *Plight of Tuscaloosa,* 33.

67. "Paul Washington Terry, 1887–1959," resolution adopted by the University of Alabama chapter of the American Association of University Professors, February 1960. Typescript in University of Alabama Library.

68. James R. Patrick and Verner M. Sims, "Personality Differences Between Negro and White College Students, North and South," *Journal of Abnormal and Social Psychology* 29 (July–September 1934): 181–201.

69. Irene De Moville Elliott, "The Difference in the Intelligence of Negro and White Children of the Same Socio-Economic Status" (Master of Arts thesis, College of Education, University of Alabama, 1934).

knowledged reputation for a "sincere belief in the theory and practice of democracy," suggest the outlines of a basic reform mentality that found expression in the research and writing of *The Live on the Land*.[70] As progressive educators, Terry and Sims were drawn almost automatically to the idea that social improvement required a fusion of popular will and professional expertise. Amid the domestic turbulence of the early 1930s both men looked upon public schools as stabilizing mechanisms that would mitigate class differences, promote cultural bonding, and foster long-term stability by linking the world of higher learning with the realities of day-to-day existence for most Alabamians. Presumably a more literate citizenry would also be more rational, more civic minded, and less prone to dispel frustration through violence. The path to enlightened politics and constructive action for social reform began at the schoolhouse and led, if still rather circuitously, to the university campus. Although less emotionally exhilarating than the manifesto of "social reconstructionism" proclaimed from the ramparts of Columbia University's Teachers College, the incremental approach to social uplift was closer to American education's philosophical mainstream.[71] More important, it was thoroughly compatible with southern liberal orthodoxy and thus was also in harmony with the spirit and substance of the New Deal.

In the end it would be one of the so-called alphabet agencies created during Franklin D. Roosevelt's first hundred days that provided a framework within which southern academicians could safely address regional problems and influence public policy. At its best the New Deal's eclectic bureaucracy helped encourage moderate intellectual dissent by enlisting the cooperation of social scientists on something resembling their own terms.

---

70. "Paul Washington Terry," 1.

71. Cremin, *Transformation of the School*, 227–33. Terry and Sims, like many of their academic counterparts across the South, shared elements of the ambiguous reform outlook associated with Howard W. Odum, Rupert P. Vance, and their fellow "regionalists" at the University of North Carolina. While ignoring race and eschewing direct political action, Odum and his colleagues pursued social reform through a program of modernization involving scholarly research and analysis, central planning, and improved education. For Terry and Sims no less than for Odum and Vance it would appear that "education took the place of politics," as one recent student of regionalism has argued. See Richard H. King, *A Southern Renaissance: The Cultural Awakening of the American South* (New York, 1980), 48. For a less sympathetic treatment of regionalism's purported deficiencies, see Daniel Joseph Singal, *The War Within: From Victorian to Modernist Thought in the South, 1919–1945* (Chapel Hill, 1982), chapter 5.

For educators in Alabama and several neighboring states, the door to federal sponsorship opened almost effortlessly during the winter of 1933–34 when Tennessee Valley Authority officials invited scholars at southern land grant universities to help collect fundamental social and economic information about virtually any aspect of life in their respective locales.[72] Funded as part of the Civil Works Administration's effort to generate emergency white-collar employment, the TVA's "Compilation of Basic Data" program encompassed the entire range of social science disciplines and supplied personnel to some twenty-three Alabama research projects, including nine directed by University of Alabama faculty members. Paul Terry and Verner Sims received a total of $2,800 during the program's second phase (February 15–April 26, 1934) for "A Comprehensive Survey of the Behavior Patterns of the People of a Single Rural Community and of the Social, Cultural, Intellectual and Economic Forces That Influence Them."[73]

From the beginning Terry and Sims envisioned their project as both a contribution to rural scholarship and a tool for social action. The place selected for study was Gorgas, Alabama, a predominantly white farming settlement located near a tributary of the Black Warrior River in northern Tuscaloosa County. Although situated outside TVA's territorial jurisdiction, Gorgas struck the authors as a "more or less typical rural community" of landowners and tenants occupying an isolated river valley in the north Alabama foothills. Together with much of the upland South, it represented a vast "neglected sector" of America that had received little in the way of scholarly attention or tangible assistance from outside experts. This, of course, was precisely the situation that Terry and Sims wanted to help alter.

---

72. William C. Cole, "Personality and Cultural Research in the Tennessee Valley," *Social Forces* 13 (May 1935): 521–27.

73. Ibid., 521. As explained in Bonnie Fox Schwartz's definitive study *The Civil Works Administration, 1933–34* (Princeton, 1984), "the CWA served as the technical authority for other government agencies to undertake white collar and professional work relief" (134). See also Floyd W. Reves and T. Levron Howard, "Compilation of Basic Data Projects, TVA-CWA: A Report of Projects Conducted . . . December 15th, 1933 to February 15th, 1934 and February 15th, 1934 to April 26th, 1934, Classified by States and Social Science Field. Also a Table Showing Number of Projects Personnel, Amount of Payroll by States and Duration," unpaginated typescript in folder 97Z7, box 20, Tennessee Valley Authority, Office of Economic and Community Development, Department of Regional Planning Studies, Social and Economic Research Division, Record Group 142, National Archives, Atlanta Branch. For official purposes the Terry and Sims project was designated "B-107," the B indicating authorization for the second funding period.

After compiling a detailed and objective record of local conditions, the two psychologists planned to compare Gorgas residents with their counterparts in other rural communities and point out "directions in which betterment in the lives of such people" could be attempted. "Suggestions of this kind," they believed, would "prove useful to any social agency . . . interested in assisting a community in adjusting . . . to such changes in social conditions as may confront it."[74]

Whether or not Gorgas actually typified farming neighborhoods "throughout the Southern Appalachian range and the Tennessee Valley" as initially claimed, the exhaustive nature of the proposed study all but guaranteed that its findings would have wider significance. Once federal funding was assured, Terry and Sims moved quickly to set their ambitious research effort in motion. Since the project was partly a work-relief measure, all staff members were hired from the CWA registration rolls of unemployed persons in Tuscaloosa County.[75] As a practical matter, however, the Parent-Teacher Association of the Gorgas Consolidated School seems to have been the initial point of contact with at least some of the local residents who were employed to gather data on virtually every aspect of community life. Nearly all of the area's 209 families would eventually be contacted by field workers who visited homes to conduct interviews, distribute survey forms, and make notes on house size, domestic conveniences, proximity to neighbors, roads, mail service, school bus routes, and a host of related matters. Firsthand reports of funerals, church services, community singings, and political rallies helped breathe life into the dry statistics generated by survey forms, although few subjects except community history proved immune to quantitative analysis. Working more than a decade before historians like Frank L. Owsley would revolutionize local history through the use of statistical evidence derived from the manuscript U.S. census, Terry and Sims sought to reconstruct the broad outlines of Gorgas's past from oral interviews and written accounts of pioneer life, religious and school development provided by Harvey Kuykendall, O. N. Andrews, and J. Edward

---

74. Between March 27 and May 11, 1934, Terry and Sims submitted a total of nine bound typescript volumes of material to T. Levron Howard, Executive Secretary of the TVA's Compilation of Basic Data Project. The volumes were designated part I through part IX of the B-107 Project. All quotations in this paragraph are from the "General Description" in part VIII, TVA Social Studies, 901.02, B-107, box 23, National Archives, Atlanta Branch.

75. Ibid. (all quotations); James J. Doster to W. L. Walker, January 4, 1934, College of Education, Dean's Office Papers, box 11, University of Alabama.

Rice—who also served as the project's documentary photographer. Local schoolteachers became the project's major source of unpaid labor when they devoted what must have been days of class time to administering a formidable array of survey questionnaires and standardized tests to Gorgas's unsuspecting youth. Terry and Sims supervised all of the project's data-gathering efforts and participated directly in some of them. Records indicate, for example, that on April 18, 1934, Paul Terry accompanied two stenographers and a local CWA worker to a political rally at Ralph School, where verbatim accounts of most speeches were secured.[76]

The short duration of the TVA grant placed a premium on obtaining as much information as possible while support was available. On March 27, 1934, when Terry and Sims submitted a twelve-page summary of the project's findings, there had been time for only "rough examination of [lengthy field] reports" and "preliminary tabulations of outstanding gross facts readily accessible to statistical treatment."[77] Work on the project would continue for two more years under the auspices of the Federal Emergency Relief Administration and the Works Progress Administration, followed by three additional years of writing and revision before the manuscript was ready for the printer in December 1939. Still, despite the painstaking analysis and correlation of statistical evidence that preceded publication, the basic outlines of the Gorgas study were apparent from the outset. In essence, Terry and Sims produced a microcosmic survey of rural socioeconomic stratification and its far-reaching cultural and behavioral consequences. From the standpoint of both methodology and topical emphasis, the book represented an extension of each author's prior research on such matters as adolescent socialization, civic education, racial and ethnic prejudice, and the intricate relationship between social class and intellectual achievement or access to economic opportunity. These questions and a welter of subordinate issues were examined with quantitative evidence that was often filtered through several layers of strong personal commitment to public schooling as an engine of democracy and egalitarian consensus.

On the face of it Gorgas seemed to represent a textbook illustration of how the school per se could serve as an institutional focus for rural group

---

76. All of the individuals mentioned are specifically identified in part VI of the B-107 Project, "Representative Samples of Reports by Field Workers."

77. Paul Terry to T. Levron Howard, March 27, 1934, accompanying ibid., part IX, "Preliminary Summaries of Data." All quotations are from the foreword of the latter document.

identity. Throughout most of its 115-year existence the community had been known simply as "camp ground" in recognition of the loose social cohesion provided by Bethel Camp Ground Methodist Church, the area's oldest religious body. It was only after World War I with the creation of a new consolidated high school named for General William Crawford Gorgas, a native Alabamian famed for his medical triumph over yellow fever in Cuba, that local residents came to equate their community with the boundaries of the school district. The result was a new name: "Gorgas" (or "Upland Bend" in the altered nomenclature of the published volume).

The story of school consolidation, as Terry and Sims told it, resonated with the passionate optimism of educational history's heroic age. The scenario was a familiar one that, with slight variations, might have been found in almost any pre–World War I textbook or state superintendent's report. After decades of fruitless bickering between partisans of rival neighborhood schools, Gorgas parents ostensibly placed their children's welfare ahead of petty differences and proceeded to vote for the tax levies necessary to make consolidation a reality. The entire episode proved civically regenerative and helped "train the people in the method and spirit of cooperation." The students, it seemed, were soon "learning cooperation" by "growing up together in a single institution," while the chief local advocate of consolidation had emerged from the struggle as one of Gorgas's "outstanding leaders." Education thus had become the "most poweful of the social forces" that held local residents together, and the new consolidated high school stood out as both the source and symbol of popular unity.[78] By describing school consolidation in a narrative that fell somewhere between history and allegory, the authors betrayed an understandable need to believe in the ultimate social efficacy of their chosen profession. As Sims had long since demonstrated, and as the book repeatedly showed, public schooling often gave the least help to those who needed the most. But for either author to have embraced the view that education merely replicated existing patterns of social inequity would have been tantamount to stepping off an intellectual precipice. For academic liberals in the depression South, education simply had to work because change was essential and the constraints imposed on direct political activism were hopelessly—at times brutally—narrow. Terry and Sims surely

---

78. *They Live on the Land*, 12–14. Presumably the published account drew upon Harvey B. Kuykendall, "Comments Concerning How the Consolidation Idea Was Started in the Gorgas Community," one of the field worker reports submitted in part VI of the TVA project.

needed no reminder of the darker possibilities inherent in the social turbulence of the 1930s. Like other Americans who had peered into the abyss, however, they came away doubly determined to find secure footing on the terrain with which they were most familiar.

And, on balance, there was little in their study of Gorgas that could be described as romanticism or wishful thinking. From the earliest draft report onward the two psychologists were guided by a hard-nosed scientism that penetrated the surface of local life and viewed all institutions, including schools, with a mixture of sympathy and critical detachment. Both authors, moreover, possessed the analytic skill and sense of professional mission necessary to tackle the problems most germane to the crisis of the early thirties. Terry's longstanding concern with ethnic prejudice and inadequate civic education took on sharp local significance in the wake of Tuscaloosa's lynching spree. Civic instruction in Gorgas, the authors discovered, ignored virtually all the major social problems of the day, leaving students to absorb prevailing folk attitudes on issues ranging from taxation and public ownership of electrical power facilities to rural poverty and race relations. Neglect of the latter theme was especially sobering in a society where roughly one-third of the white adults placed blacks "on the same social basis as . . . a mule" and agreed that "no Negro has the slightest right to resent or even question the illegal killing of one of his race."[79]

In a formal sense the authors shared equal responsibility for the entire Gorgas study, but at the conceptual level it was clearly Verner Sims's overarching concern with class structure that gave the project definition and shape. Evidence of Sims's guiding influence abounds throughout the published work, becoming most explicit in the extended discussions of school and home life. Much of the material in chapters six and nine, particularly the detailed information on household routine and "cultural equipment" among landowners and tenants, can be read as a more or less direct effort to refine and flesh out the original descriptive categories of Sims's socioeconomic score card. Similarly, the treatment of such themes as school curriculum, age-grade retardation and dropout rates among different social classes bears a striking resemblance to Sims's analysis of Louisiana school problems a few years earlier. Finally, the book's exceptionally precise classification of rural households into a scheme that distinguished not only the full legal complexity of tenure systems (e.g., sharecroppers, furnishing tenants, cash renters, "free" renters, etc.), but also took account of the crucial

---

79. *They Live on the Land,* 270–71, 284–88.

importance of kinship ties across all legal categories, certainly must have owed something to Sims's ongoing efforts at creating an occupational taxonomy that would illuminate levels of culture. At the same time, however, it is important to recall that Eugene C. Branson, one of the few contemporary scholars to look carefully at the mitigating influence of family relationships among tenants, had been a colleague of Paul Terry at Chapel Hill during the mid-1920s.[80]

Although concerned with subjects as diverse as rural health services and the content of adolescent daydreams, the central, recurrent theme of *They Live on the Land* was class inequity. When reduced to its essentials, the book told the story of a community in which the maldistribution of what little wealth existed led to injustices as glaring as any to be found in more affluent towns or cities. In a review that praised the "provocative" study for its "candid portrayal of rural society," sociologist Chester McArthur Destler provided what may rank as the most lucid and concise summary of the book's key arguments:

> With agriculture as the predominant occupation, social status of the people is determined by land ownership and tenure. Barely forty per cent of the farmers are owners. Their children monopolize the high school, marry later, and have fewer offspring than the tenants. Most of the things that constitute the so-called American standard of living, from insurance policies to automobiles and hospital treatment, are enjoyed almost exclusively by the owning class. Led by eleven large holders they deliver the vote, govern the churches, and dominate the PTA. The tenants, irrespective of race in this predominantly white community, are virtually disfranchised. They exist on marginal incomes and can give their children no more than an elementary education. But one generation away from farm ownership, they are developing into a permanent class whose substandard houses and shifting residence undermine the churches, the school, and civic ethics. Into this class small owners are sinking as they fail to lift the burden of debt, and land ownership continues to become concentrated.[81]

Additional reviews of the book appeared mainly in education and sociology journals and were overwhelmingly favorable. Rural sociologist Edmund de S. Brunner of Columbia University described *They Live on the*

---

80. E. C. Branson, "Farm Tenancy in the South: The Social Estate of White Farm Tenants," *Journal of Social Forces* 1 (November 1922–September 1923): 450–57. During the 1950s, Sims's concern with occupational hierarchy led to the publication of an occupational rating scale that was aimed at eliciting information about class consciousness.

81. *Social Education* 5 (November 1941): 554.

Land as "far more than an ordinary community survey." It was, he believed, the "most intensive case study ever made in the South" and, as such, its publication represented "an event of real importance" for scholars in the field. Brunner was especially impressed by the use of standardized attitude scales to determine popular opinion on numerous subjects. He even went so far as to pronounce the discussion of "what the people thought" (chapter nine) as "superior" to the comparable portion of Robert and Helen Lynd's famous *Middletown in Transition*.[82] Both Terry and Sims were keenly interested in exposing patterns of thought or assumption at different social levels and both knew how to approach the task with quantitative precision. Still, one is struck by the fact that Sims personally prepared the standardized tests on folk superstitions and attitudes toward the New Deal and also may have been responsible for the use of four additional tests published by the Character Education Inquiry, which had earlier helped underwrite his dissertation research.[83]

Perhaps the most thoughtful and searching assessment of the book came from the pen of an education specialist, the University of Chicago's Herman G. Richey. Focusing on the chapter-length treatment of local schools, Richey praised the authors' honest depiction of "conditions arising from poverty . . . and the failure of America to think of education in terms of the national interest." "Upland Bend" offered convincing proof that it was "not the failure of education but rather the failure to educate" that expressed itself through statistics on "curtailed school terms, small enrollments, high tuition fees in public schools, excessive absences, meager facilities, selection of both elementary and high school pupils on the basis of the economic status of their parents," and the consequent patterns of low academic achievement. Richey agreed with the authors' contention that school curricula should make more use of community resources, but he went on to sound a cautionary note. The strategy of linking school activities to the "realities of the immediate environment" could prove self-defeating if it led to neglect of "essential and basic" social insights that did not arise from community experiences or the study of local problems alone. In a passage that anticipated the kinds of criticism eventually leveled at post–World War II "life adjustment" education, Richey tried to point out that by criticizing existing

---

82. *Rural Sociology* 6 (June 1941): 180.

83. Part II, "Standardized Tests Used," TVA Social Studies, 901.03, B-107, box 23, National Archives, Atlanta Branch. Of eleven attitude scales used in the Gorgas study, four were from the Character Education Inquiry Series and two—one on superstitions and one concerning attitudes toward TVA—were devised by Sims.

curricula for an excessively academic emphasis, egalitarians like Terry and Sims inadvertently might be taking schools down the path toward a new process of class-based social sorting. "For better or worse," Richey argued, "the people of America's Upland Bends must, during the coming years, participate in making decisions which will require vision not circumscribed by the boundaries of the local community." It would be a "serious mistake," he warned, if advocates of "social quietism" seized upon *They Live on the Land* as an "argument for a program of education aiming at the adjustment of underprivileged persons to an inferior culture."[84]

By linking Terry and Sims's work to the larger philosophical issues facing policymakers in the depression South, Richey effectively underscored the book's dual significance as both a source of immediate factual data and a chapter in the intellectual history of rural modernization. Taken on its own terms *They Live on the Land* remains a valuable case study, a precise and finely detailed portrait of a specific Alabama community at a particular historical moment. But with the passage of half a century the book has also become a primary source that illuminates the struggle of southern educators to bridge the gap between a dying world of cotton and poverty and a new economic order that had only begun to take shape. Although influenced by the previous decade's IQ debates, Terry and Sims's treatment of schooling and social class inevitably reflected the 1930s vogue for "progressive" pedagogy aimed at transforming schools into centers of community revitalization. Indeed, at one level, the entire Gorgas study can be seen as part of a larger professional metamorphosis that began in response to the collapse of rural culture and continued under the stimulus of financial support from the federal government and private philanthropy. For Terry and Sims the reordering of scholarly priorities triggered by the TVA in 1933 soon came to resemble a permanent way of life. The driving force behind Alabama education's new spirit of creativity and social activism was a Rockefeller-financed study of thirty-three representative southern high schools conducted by the Commission on Curricular Problems and Research of the Southern Association of Colleges and Secondary Schools. Conceived as a regional counterpart to the Progressive Education Association's highly publicized "Eight Year Study," the southern project looked toward radical modifications of pedagogy and curricula within the framework of what were often described as "community schools."[85] Sims joined

---

84. *Elementary School Journal* 41 (April 1941): 627.

85. Cremin, *Transformation of the School,* 251–56; Edward A. Krug, *The Shaping of the American High School, 1930–1940* (Madison, Wis., 1972), chapter 10 and

the "Southern Study" as a paid consultant in 1938 and spent considerable time during the next five years visiting participating schools, conducting summer workshops for teachers, and attending numerous conferences arranged for project staff members.[86] Although the work in local high schools constituted a natural extension of the community outreach philosophy Sims had espoused during and even prior to the Gorgas project, the ground rules were considerably different. Sims now encountered local teachers as peers and colleagues rather than as students or subordinates to be evaluated. The new relationship changed his educational perspective and imbued him with a spirit of egalitarian enthusiasm. At a 1939 Southern Association meeting in Memphis, Tennessee, Sims spoke for some ten minutes about "what the study had done to him."

He said in [a] semi-humorous vein that it had ruined a perfectly good college teacher. As a test measurement expert he had virtually finished . . . organizing his courses and had looked forward to a relatively easy future in which he might repeat year after year his well arranged material. The study upset this. He learned that teachers did not think so well of his courses as he himself did. He found he was missing the real problems; that he as a college instructor needed

---

especially p. 266; *General Education Board Annual Report, 1936–37* (New York, 1937), 20–21; ibid., *1937–38* (New York, 1938), 36. Two printed reports from the Southern Association's Commission on Curricular Problems and Research (*Southern Association Quarterly* 2 [May 1938]: 269–74 and 4 [May 1940]: 186–202) provide a detailed account of the origins, aims, and evolution of the "Study in Colleges and Secondary Schools." The concept of "community schools" emerged from the study's fifth formal goal or "characteristic": "More satisfying teacher-pupil-parent relationships." In pursuit of this aim many schools, by 1940, were "developing programs which are becoming an integral part of community life." Illustrations of the activities included cooperative attempts to develop local recreational facilities, "the increased use of school facilities by adult groups, and in general cooperative attempts to improve life in the community." Ibid. 4 (May 1940): 188.

86. Leo M. Favrot Diary, September 12, 1938, General Education Board Records, Series 12, Rockefeller Archive Center, Pocantico Hills, North Tarrytown, New York. See also Verner M. Sims, "Evaluation in the Southern Association Study," *School and Society* 57 (January 16, 1943): 76–79; Verner M. Sims, "Problems Relating to Effective Study for Workshop Participants," *Southern Association Quarterly* 7 (August 1943): 418–43; V. M. Sims, E. A. Waters, and W. A. Robinson, "Experimental Programs in the Southern Associations," in *Secondary Education in the South*, edited by W. Carson Ryan et al. (Chapel Hill, 1946), 140–66.

these visits with high school teachers. He has come to realize that evaluation of instruction is not a thing apart, but an integral part of the teaching process.[87]

Much of Sims's consulting work during the late 1930s and early '40s involved the Holtville High School in Elmore County, Alabama. Under Sims's guidance the institution eventually abandoned the conventional pattern of subject matter organization in favor of a more or less unstructured approach that emphasized independent learning through individual or group projects. Cooperation, democratic decision making, and community service became mainstays of the school's program, which increasingly centered around the personal preferences and occupational interests of individual students.[88] Concurrently, at the University of Alabama, both Sims and Terry helped formulate proposals for an experimental program of teacher training based upon the same progressive concepts that prevailed at Holtville.[89]

If one were to take the rhetoric of depression-era school reform at face value it would be easy to conclude that Terry, Sims, and other leading state educators had succumbed unabashedly to the radicalizing influence of John Dewey. The reality, of course, was considerably more complicated. Behind the reformers' undeniably sincere efforts to make schooling more relevant to local conditions stood a shaky intellectual substructure riddled with contradiction, ambiguity, and ultimate confusion of purpose. Pedagogical innovations at schools like Holtville might be novel and even daring, but the educational consequences often were more accommodationist than revolutionary. By focusing relentlessly on the present and its problems, reformist educators fostered an unnecessarily static conception of rural society and became parties to a disturbingly utilitarian instructional agenda. At Holtville, for example, the number of graduates attending college dropped sharply during the study years even as the student population substantially increased.[90] Like most other regional educators and social scientists, Terry and Sims were slow to grasp the implications of structural

---

87. Leo M. Favrot Diary, March 28, 1939; see also *Southern Association Quarterly* 3 (May 1939): 318.

88. Whilden Wallace, James Chrietzberg, and Verner M. Sims, *The Story of Holtville* (n.p., 1944), especially 62–66, 164.

89. "A Tentative Proposal for an Experiment in Teacher Training at the University of Alabama," undated (ca. 1939); Richard C. Foster to Fred McQuiston, June 13, 1941; Foster to Frank C. Jenkins, June 13, 1941, all in College of Education, Dean's Office Papers, box 17, University of Alabama Library.

90. Wallace, Chriezberg, and Sims, *Story of Holtville,* 141.

economic changes set in motion by the Agricultural Adjustment Act and later accelerated by the advent of farm mechanization. In *They Live on the Land* the authors had sharply criticized Gorgas High School's academic, college-preparatory curriculum for ignoring the needs of children from sharecropper families. Their call for increased emphasis on vocational agriculture had a certain plausibility in 1933 when New Deal farm policy included an anachronistic "subsistence homestead" program that left the economic future of the old Cotton Belt somewhat in doubt. Within a few years, however, circumstances had changed dramatically as displaced tenant farmers fled the countryside en masse in search of nonagricultural employment. Among the first scholars to confront the migration's long-range significance was University of North Carolina sociologist Rupert P. Vance, who predicted in 1936 that the six southeastern cotton states were destined to experience a rural exodus equal to 86 percent of the actual farm population. A demographic shift of such magnitude, Vance argued, would necessitate "certain changes in education whereby rural people would receive training to fit them for the transition to [an] urban and industrial environment."[91] Although Terry and Sims probably would have agreed, in principle, with Vance's contention that education should equip students with "flexible skills" and "adaptable personality traits," their skepticism about the value of traditional academic training was out of step with the approaching requirements of post–World War II modernization and economic development. As late as 1942 Sims would renew the call for community schools where learning could occur through a "direct attack on the problems of the immediate environment."[92] Such institutions made sense in a society composed of poor and isolated communities like Gorgas where rhythms of continuity rather than visions of change framed the social expectations of local residents. In Gorgas and hundreds of comparable Alabama communities the long-standing problems of maldistributed wealth and truncated educational opportunity were painfully real. Their solution, however, would depend more upon the advent of mechanical cotton pickers, junior colleges, and suburban housing tracts than upon the success or failure of short-term measures for embellishing a moribund pattern of rural life.

---

91. Rupert P. Vance, "The Old Cotton Belt (1936)," in *Regionalism in the South: Selected Papers of Rupert Vance,* ed. John Shelton Reed and Daniel Joseph Singal (Chapel Hill, 1982), 124.

92. Verner M. Sims, "Education Through Community Improvement," *Progressive Education* 19 (October 1942): 332–35. The passage quoted appears on p. 334.

From the preceding pages one may derive a context of sorts for evaluating the questions raised and the answers provided in *They Live on the Land*. To go further in establishing what the book represented for each author would require a far more detailed knowledge of the personal lives of both men than is possible at this distance. There is a certain irony in the fact that two individuals who spent decades studying the socialization, personality, and behavior of others should remain largely immune to personal scrutiny by later historians. Other than the limited kind of intellectual biography that emerges from each man's scholarly publications, what can one know—or deduce—about Terry and Sims as flesh-and-blood human beings? Unfortunately, very little.

Both men were husbands and fathers. In 1921 Paul Terry married Jessie Louise Owens of Milton, Wisconsin. The couple had one child, a son Paul Beauchamp Terry, who occasionally accompanied his father on visits to Gorgas during the 1930s, a period when the elder Terry was also active in the Black Warrior Boy Scouts Council. Verner Sims had two sons, John and Edward, and by the 1950s he could count five grandchildren. Even in the relatively traditional social atmosphere of pre–World War II Alabama, rearing children was undoubtedly a humbling experience, and one suspects that the two professors must have perused the survey data on generational conflicts between parents and youth in the Gorgas community with more than an academic interest.

Surviving evidence affords only fleeting glimpses of either man's personality and temperament. Sims seems to have been a modest and unassuming figure who pursued original research with the single-mindedness of a true intellectual. He clearly had little taste for academic pretensions, and, if one may judge from his extemporaneous remarks on the 1939 Southern Association study, he could display considerable finesse in disguising implied criticism behind a cloak of self-deprecation. Sims's most revealing comments about himself and how he perceived his own professional situation came in a 1951 response to a Yale University poll indicating that psychologists considered education courses largely irrelevant to the training of educational psychologists. Rankled by the arrogance of his colleagues, Sims responded with a statement that affirmed his convictions concerning the scholar's obligation to society at large. "After 25 years of trying to be an educational psychologist," Sims wrote "I freely admit that his lot is not a very happy one."

> He is closely associated with two disciplines neither of whose followers have any great respect for him. His psychological brethen generally consider him of an

inferior breed; while his fellow educators look upon him as an impractical theorist (seldom as well paid as they) whose courses are usually required by state certification laws, and must therefore be taken, but who really has little to contribute to the training of effective teachers. Educational psychologists seemingly have decided to reduce the tensions thus created in them by striving diligently to look more and more like "real" psychologists, while they withdraw from their colleagues in teacher education.

Sims deplored the trend toward separatism and argued that educational psychology could succeed only as a cooperative undertaking. In order to do his job well the educational psychologist "must himself be a teacher skilled enough to 'practice what he preaches.' . . . Furthermore, he must have sympathy with his fellow educators and some respect for their fields of concentration. And added to all these, he must understand what makes administrators click; must be able to translate the language of the philosopher into symbols which have meaning to him; must have sympathy for the half-caste 'special methods' people; and must often come to the defense of the poor benighted classroom teacher."[93]

No comparable statement of principle from the pen of Paul Terry has come to light. But in a memorial resolution adopted in February 1960 the members of the University of Alabama chapter of the American Association of University Professors spoke eloquently of the personal qualities that had distinguished Terry's tenure as a department head, chapter president, colleague, and faculty elder statesman. What endured beyond any formal record of service and professional accomplishment was the memory of "Paul Terry the Man." Colleagues remembered his "gentleness, his softspokenness, his tolerance, his unbelievable understanding of people resulting from a grasp of psychology that cannot be learned from books." Possessed of a "subtle sense of humor that was always catching one off guard," Terry had learned to lead without seeming to do so. His personal style was altogether disarming and people often "followed him without realizing that they had been persuaded by a master."[94] If the richness of information contained in *They Live on the Land* is any indication, both Terry and Sims were skilled practitioners of the art of human relations as well as trained analysts of psychological data.

---

93. Verner M. Sims, "More 'Education' for Educational Psychologists," *American Psychologist* 6 (August 1951): 459–60.

94. James Holiday, Verner M. Sims, Frederick L. Wectover, and I. Willis Russell, "Paul W. Terry, 1887–1959," February 1960 resolution of the University of Alabama chapter of the American Association of University Professors, University of Alabama Library.

Explanatory Note

The photographs that follow are reproduced from photographs submitted to the Tennessee Valley Authority on April 26, 1934 as part IV of the formal report on Project B-107 in the Compilation of Basic Data program. The captions are those originally given the pictures by Terry and Sims. As far as can be determined, all photographs appear to have been taken by J. Edward Rice, who was listed as the project's photographer.

View of First Grade in Classroom This interior view of the first grade illustrates the type of farm children who attend schools in the Gorgas community. Overalls are worn universally, by sons of parents well-to-do, and otherwise.

An Aged Farmer This aged farmer is a descendant of one of the pioneer families of the community; too old to plow now, but with that restless spirit characteristic of his forefathers, he sits in his fields watching his son and grandsons carry on with the crops.

Rolling Plateau Land This view is typical of the rolling plateau land, which comprises most of the topography of the Gorgas region. Once covered with timber, most of the land in the community is now cleared.

A Timber Covered Hillside This hill, whose size is apparent from the clothes-line, figures, and barn in the left middle-distance, lies near the north boundary of Gorgas. Behind it is a region of jagged hills which form the last of the Appalachians in this section of Alabama.

A Brush-Arbor Typical of the brush-arbors which were so characteristic of the camp-meeting era of the past century is this arbor of the Original Church of God in the Gorgas community. Gathered under the arbor is the church congregation.

(top) **Hewn Log House with Stone Chimney** This hewn log house has withstood the elements for more than a century successfully enough to be used today as a tenant residence. Built by a pioneer resident of the Gorgas community who came from Buncombe County, N.C., the old cut stone chimney is reminiscent of many old houses in North Carolina.

(bottom) **Hewn Log House Used for a Barn** This old log house, once a dwelling but now used for a barn, is indicative of the age of this agrarian hill community. This house was the original homestead of one of the pioneer families, of which there are many descendants living in the community today.

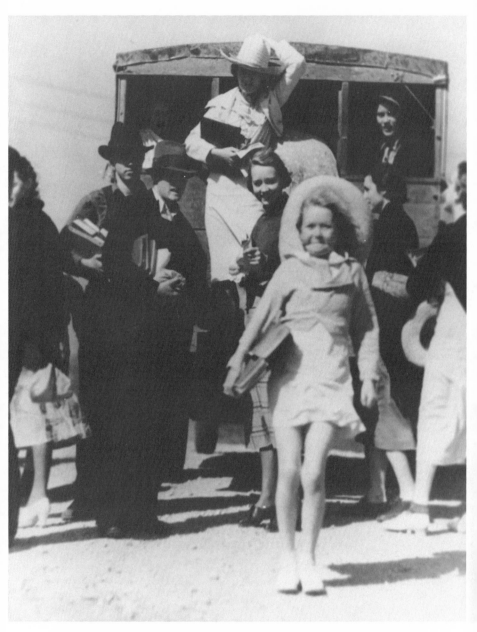

Pupils Entering School Bus Overalls are also often worn by many high school boys, but girls at this stage of school life are more addicted to town clothes.

Elementary School Building and Boys Playground The Elementary School shown in this view, like the High School is located on the crest of a hill included in the rolling plateau area, which comprises most of the land in this community.

Plowing a Hillside Terrace These plowmen rest for a moment on a hillside terrace; and as the field they plow is quite steep, the workers appear to be on a hill top.

They Live on the Land

CONTENTS

CHAPTER I   ORIGINS OF THE COMMUNITY

CHAPTER II   THE PEOPLE

CHAPTER III ECONOMIC LIFE OF THE COMMUNITY

CHAPTER IV CIVIC LIFE

CHAPTER IX HOW THE PEOPLE SPENT THEIR TIME

CHAPTER X WHAT THE PEOPLE THOUGHT

CHAPTER XI LEADERSHIP OF THE COMMUNITY

LIST OF TABLES AND ILLUSTRATIONS

TABLES

ILLUSTRATIONS

PREFACE

The study of social conditions has made great progress in recent decades throughout the country. The development of practicable techniques and the availability of financial support have contributed to this end as has an increasing recognition, on the part of thoughtful citizens, of the necessity of understanding how people live before promising steps can be taken in the direction of improvement. In the South especially much has been done in the nature of broad surveys and in the study of special problems of limited scope.

Few of the investigations, however, have been concerned entirely with single open-country communities and few of these have been comprehensive in nature. For this reason it appeared desirable in the present instance to concentrate on one typical group of rural folk whose environment both physical and social could be examined in an intensive way with the hope of presenting a detailed picture of who the people were, what they thought, and what they did. Such a picture, it was believed, would be useful to social scientists, educators, and intelligent laymen in general who are interested in current conditions and who consider careful analysis the best approach to understanding.

Several methods of collecting data were employed in this investigation. Most of the quantitative material was gathered with the aid of formal interviews with families, individuals, and representatives of institutions. Questionnaires, standardized tests, and ratings were also used for this purpose. Informal interviews, and observations by members of the staff were employed to obtain descriptions of persons, events, and things. As the facts are presented the technical reader who is interested in such matters will be able to tell which methods were used in any given case.

The names of persons and places have been changed to prevent identification but this has been done in such a way as to preserve the nomenclature of the region in which the community is located. Interpretations have been offered here and there and rather consistently topics have been concluded with brief observations on the part of the authors. Yet in the main the facts have been allowed to speak for themselves and the reader is invited to draw his own conclusions as to their significance. Elements of local color that illuminate the data have not been neglected, but the intention has been to rely chiefly on an impersonal, objective account of findings. The collection of data was begun early in the year 1934 and finished in the latter part of 1936.

The work of organizing and conducting the survey and the burden of preparing the report for publication were shared equally by the authors. For such interpretations as are offered and for numerous short-comings the writers are solely responsible. For aid in several forms, however, the writers are under obligation to a number of agencies and to many individuals which it is a pleasure to acknowledge. The investigation was initiated under the auspices of the University of Alabama with Civil Works Administration funds alloted to it by the Tennessee Valley Authority. Later clerical help was supplied by the Emergency Relief Administration and by the Works Progress Administration. Writing the report was made possible by a reduction in the authors' teaching loads which was arranged by the Bureau of Educational Research of the University of Alabama. Publication was effected through the Bureau of Educational Research with the aid of financial support contributed by the University of Alabama Chapter of Phi Delta Kappa. Services of far greater value than those imposed by contractual obligation, were contributed by the Birmingham Printing Company. Helpful assistance, likewise, was received from the Alabama Engraving Company. To these several organizations and to the capable men and women who worked with untiring zeal and devotion to collect the data under their direction, the authors are very grateful. And likewise they owe a great debt to colleagues and friends who lent encouragement and especially to the people of Upland Bend who patiently answered innumerable questions.

UNIVERSITY, ALABAMA   V.M.S.

DECEMBER 15, 1939   P.W.T.

CHAPTER I

ORIGINS OF THE COMMUNITY

In the first decade of the Nineteenth Century the area that is now Alabama was a great unpeopled wilderness. There were a few scattered settlements around the struggling village of St. Stephens on the lower Tombigbee River and a small but rapidly growing community of planters around Huntsville in the Tennessee Valley. Both communities cultivated cotton which was soon to become the chief marketable product of the entire region. Between these clearings lay hundreds of miles of territory, much of it rough and broken, that was inhabited by Indians and by straggling white traders and squatters. Irregular and precarious communication between these outposts of civilization was maintained over the rivers and forest trails that traversed the region. The government of Mississippi Territory which officially controlled the country was far away in New Orleans.

Not many years before this time events took place in other parts of the nation that exercised a far-reaching influence over the area with which we are concerned. Power machinery was applied to the spinning and weaving of cotton cloth and the invention of the cotton gin had made commercially profitable the cultivation of short-staple cotton. The good prices thereafter available for this fibre induced the piedmont farmers of Georgia and the Carolinas to abandon tobacco and plant their fields in cotton. But transportation to the coastal markets from these areas was difficult, the lands were wearing out, and the population was increasing rapidly. A great army of landhungry people began to look with covetous eyes across the old frontiers to the new lands of the Southwest that seemed to be just what was needed. The pressure grew and it was but a matter of time before the swarm would break loose in a mad rush for new homes.

Events in Alabama and elsewhere moved fast to open the new country for settlement. When the War of 1812 ended the demand for cotton was tremendously increased and the price rose rapidly. Mobile, which was the natural export market for the entire region because it lay at the mouth of a great system of navigable rivers, was taken from the Spaniards in 1813. Jackson's victory over the Indians at Horseshoe Bend in 1814 broke the power of the savages and cleared the country of the Indian title. New land offices were set up and millions of acres were offered for sale. Alabama was soon established as a territory and shortly thereafter as a state. While these events were taking place small numbers of immigrants had trickled in but by 1817 the stream of new-comers turned into a great flood as thousands upon thousands laboriously worked their way over the hard trails to the virgin acres that lured them on.

THE FIRST SETTLERS

One of the chief routes over which the pioneers traveled in Alabama was the Huntsville Road which started from Madison County in the Tennessee Valley and ran south until it struck the headwaters of the rivers that flowed through the southern half of the State toward Mobile. The first bands of settlers pushed down the streams until they came to the broad bottom lands of the main rivers and their tributaries. Later comers left the road higher up and worked into the interior searching for fertile lands along the smaller streams that flowed through the region of broken hills in the central and northern parts of the State. Thus it was that in the year 1818 a family named Brum left the little town of Shallow Ford on the Huntsville Road and pushed south along an Indian trail for about twenty-five miles until they came to a bend in East River that is now known as Upland Bend.

The Upland Bend section looked good to the pioneers. The river, a clear upland stream that was rarely more than twenty yards across, was plentifully supplied with fish. A half dozen little creeks made their way over the bottoms and several strong springs furnished a never failing supply of wholesome water. The sandy loam soil of the lowlands was very fertile. Higher up a wide expanse of rolling ridge land reached to the eastern hills at the foot of which ran the road that came from Shallow Ford. The soil on the plateau was not the best in the world but it was much like that of the piedmont sections and the settlers knew how to cultivate it. Stands of virgin short-leaf pine and smaller growths of cedar here and there provided an abundance of wood. In the open places there were fine patches of the wild pea vine which attracted large herds of deer and other wild game that was valuable for food. The only undesirable feature of the situation was the distance to a navigable stream and the difficult nature of the road that led that way. This was a serious handicap to the wealthy planter who owned a large number of slaves and who had to ship considerable quantities of cotton to Mobile. But most of the immigrants were small farmers who grew only the few bales that their own families could raise. Having little money to pay for land they were forced to confine their choices to the less accessible places. Upland sections were preferred by many who considered them more healthful than lower locations. The immigrants liked to settle, moreover, in a country such as that from which they came. Thus it was that sections like Upland Bend were just what large numbers of the pioneers were hunting for.

So the Brum family was soon followed by others. Several of these, like the Brums, came from Elbert County in Georgia but most of the newcomers were from Anson and Buncombe Counties in North Carolina or from the piedmont sections of Virginia and South Carolina. A few Tennesseans arrived at this time and there was one family of Dutch extraction from Pennsylvania. Some of the early families settled in the bottom lands but others took to the ridge. As fast as they could they erected modest log cabins, girdled the trees on small patches of ground, and planted crops. Corn was raised for the family and for the animals but cotton was cultivated for money. Pigs and cattle were turned loose to forage for themselves in the woods. Whenever the family wanted a change of diet one of the men bagged some game in the forest nearby or caught a mess of fish in the river. After the cotton was picked the farmer laboriously carted it to Shallow Ford and sold it to one of the merchants there.

The farmers from Upland Bend probably sold most of their cotton to John Brum who was the brother of their neighbor of the same name. John Brum was the first merchant to bring goods up the river from Mobile to Shallow Ford. Poling or warping a keel boat that distance up stream required from a month to six weeks though a flatboat could float down in about two weeks time. The boats headed for Mobile carried cotton mainly, fifty to a hundred bales a trip. Those coming up brought sugar, coffee, flour, and whiskey for the most part. In 1820 when the steamboats came to Shallow Ford transportation was more regular and rapid. But this improvement did not mean very much to the pioneers in Upland Bend because the road to Shallow Ford was too hard to travel often and most of them lacked money with which to buy what the boats brought. Thus isolated the settlers learned early how to live on a self-sustaining basis. But at that life in Upland Bend must not have been unpleasant for later comers continued to trickle in until by the end of the 1820's most of the original families had arrived.

CORLEY'S TURNPIKE ROAD

Fortunately for the scattered settlers in Upland Bend the wood path over which they came from Shallow Ford led to other and more populous settlements to the south. There was thus created a strong demand to make the path into a turnpike. In 1819 the State Assembly honored a petition to that effect and authorized a Mr. George Corley to construct the road. Scarcity of funds delayed completion until 1830. But for twenty years thereafter the builder had the right to collect tolls that ranged from 75 cents for a four-wheel carriage to ½ cent a head for a drove of hogs.

Some of the most colorful happenings in the early history of Upland Bend centered around this old road. Of these incidents one of the most memorable was the passage through Upland Bend of the Choctaw Indians who were on the way to their new lands across the Mississippi. One band of several hundred, some on foot and some on horseback, reached this section late in the afternoon and camped for the night. From all about the settlers came to inspect the quarters of these unusual visitors. With her father, who was one of the leading farmers, was a beautiful dark haired girl nineteen years of age. Her attractions struck the eyes of a burley warrior who tried to purchase the girl as a slave. When the father refused the Indian raised his price several times until at last he was given to understand that the girl was not for sale at any price. During the night one of the Indian babies died and before the band left in the morning the baby was buried in the hollow trunk of a large oak tree that stood beside the road.

Animals with which to stock the new farms were needed soon after the settlers arrived. These were supplied by drovers who brought horses, cows, hogs, and turkeys from the older settlements in Tennessee and drove them south to Shallow Ford, Upland Bend, and points beyond. When they learned that a herd was moving down Corley's Road the farmers who wanted animals repaired thereto and waited. A number of the oldest residents remembered purchases made by their fathers in this market. One recalled a flock of several hundred turkeys that was driven by a group of men on horseback. The turkey drovers, he said, never could tell when or where the birds would stop for the night. Late in the afternoon, when they got ready, the whole flock suddenly took wing with a thunderous roar and flew up into the nearest trees where they roosted until morning. And there was nothing their masters could do but stop and make themselves as comfortable as they could. Before the railroads came stage coaches drawn by four to six powerful horses passed up and down this road. These often met farmers going to town in large covered wagons drawn by one or two yokes of oxen. During the Civil War Confederate soldiers, then Union soldiers, and later carpetbaggers traveled by Upland Bend on Corley's Road. There were reports of camels that went by. One family that owned a beast of this description stopped in Upland Bend but they did not stay long. In later years when the westward movement began anew some of the Upland Bend families with all their worldly goods piled onto a wagon or two left the community by this same road. The last of the passing incidents was that of the herds of wild western ponies which horse-traders drove down Corley's Road. These animals were cheap and many of the Upland Bend farmers bought them. But the ponies were so hard to break and so poor to work that they were soon discarded for the small mule that for many years has been the farmer's favorite work animal.

Reminiscences of the Civil War

Upland Bend like other parts of the State suffered from the Civil War. Only two or three families owned slaves and only a few slaves at that. For this reason and the isolated situation of Upland

Bend it is difficult to believe that sentiment in the community was overwhelmingly in favor of the war in the beginning. But the conscription law had its effect here as elsewhere and before the end practically all of the eligible men had enlisted in the Confederate cause. In the southern part of the community near Corley's Road, there was a drill field to which recruits from this section of the county reported for preliminary training before they were sent to larger military centers.

In the final year of the War when Union troops marched into Shallow Ford and later when a peacetime garrison was stationed there small parties of marauders disturbed the peace of Upland Bend over a considerable period of time. Incidents connected with these raids were still fresh in the minds of a few of the oldest inhabitants who witnessed them as children. One old man described his encounter with a squad of five or six Yankee soldiers on an April morning in 1865. He was barely old enough to ride the mule that was carrying him and a sack of meal home from the mill. Coming upon the soldiers unexpectedly he had just brought the mule to a halt when one of them called, "Say, boy, is that flour you've got there?" "Naw, it's only corn meal", the boy retorted as he started to move on. "Wait a minute, let's see", returned the soldier as he reached his hand into the sack. Having verified the lad's statement the soldier said, "You can keep that stuff, boy, we're looking for flour." Then he added, "Where is your daddy, son?" "He's off fighting in the War", was the immediate response. At this the soldiers laughed good humoredly and took off down the road. Parenthetically the old man added "Them damn Yankees didn't know corn meal was fit to eat."

An old lady who was born in 1850 recalled the war period as one of great hardship. Corn pone, the only bread that was available, was so scarce that each person in her family was rationed daily a single piece no larger than a man's hand. There was practically no meat, so vegetables were cooked with milk. Corncob ashes were substituted for soda and parched meal for coffee. Salt was very scarce. Some families boiled the earth crust of the smokehouse floor for this commodity while others evaporated water from a weak salt lick near the river. Federal soldiers visited her father's house several times. One group demanded money or jewelry under threat of dire punishment if these were not produced immediately. When convinced that no valuables were obtainable the raiders shot a turkey and three chickens two of which were left dead in the yard. On another occasion a squad of soldiers was accompanied by three negroes. The soldiers directed the negroes to take three good saddle horses from the barn and leave in their place a broken down old mare with a sore back. The horses were needed for an important mission, they said, but suspicion was aroused in her father's mind by the fact that the animals were ridden away by the negroes. When the party reached Corley's Road the soldiers turned north toward Shallow Ford but the negroes went south. Quickly collecting a number of friends the father went in pursuit of his horses. By nightfall the animals were back in the stalls of their owner but the recipients of the soldiers' bounty were buried in a small lake not far from where they were found.

Another old resident told of two raids on his home. On the first occasion the soldiers threatened to burn them out if money was not forthcoming immediately. His mother assured her callers repeatedly that nothing of that nature was in the house. Unwilling to believe her the raiders proceeded to build a fire on the floor with the aid of such papers and clothes as they could find. The mother continued her denial and as the fire died down the soldiers departed leaving a large charred spot in the middle of the room. On the second visit money was again the object. Receiving none the soldiers began wandering about the place poking their heads in here and there to see what they could find. Presently one entered the smoke house and began throwing hams and shoulders into the yard. When the leader saw this he commanded the man to "leave the lady's meat alone." Returning to the front yard the leader saw a pile of cotton at the edge of an adjoining field and he told the boy's mother that he would burn the cotton if she did not give him some money immediately. This he would have to do, she firmly replied, because there was none to give. So the men attempted to fire the cotton but it was too damp. Disgusted with this failure they all got on their horses and left cursing cotton and the country in general.

The First Two Churches

After the Revolution conditions in the young nation were ripe for a fresh sowing of the seeds of religion. The people had drifted away from their old creeds when Whitefield and the Wesleys began to preach a new faith that meant strength to those who were bent on conquering the wilderness. The Methodist and Baptist societies were peculiarly well fitted to cope with conditions on the frontier. Little in the way of education was asked of the clergy by the church or by the people with whom they labored. All that was needed was a fiery zeal for the Cross, courage to endure the hardships of an unsettled life, and willingness to work for small compensation in a material way. In those days men were inclined to be open and definite in the expression of their views; if they were for religion, they were for it. Thus they were ready to be moved by the strong emotional appeals with which the intrepid old circuit riders preached the Gospel.

The original settlers of Upland Bend had not long to wait before the church made its appearance among them. The first institution to be formally organized was the Shady Grove Missionary Baptist Church which was founded in 1824—only six years after the arrival of the first family. A few years later the second and last of the early institutions, the Tabernacle Methodist Church, was established. These two churches were among the first to be set up in Chehaw County and both were soon taking a prominent part in the religious activities of the denominations to which they belonged. In the beginning the people of Upland Bend were Baptists or Methodists as they have remained to this day.

The first of the two institutions to achieve outstanding recognition in the surrounding country was the Shady Grove Baptists. Soon after the founding of this church the denomination to which it belonged was attacked with a terrific schism on the subject of Arminianism and open communion. A long and bitter debate between the factions ensued, sharp lines were drawn, and many members felt compelled to leave their old congregations and to shift their letters to others with more congenial views. Shady Grove became a stronghold of the more liberal faction and among those who moved to it was a famous preacher who had already made an outstanding reputation in Shallow Ford. The original building at Shady Grove was a cabin of peeled log walls twenty-two feet wide and twenty-six feet long lighted by a single window. On the loose plank floor sat rows of backless splitlog benches supported on pegs. In these primitive surroundings under the leadership of the distinguished evangelist that had recently joined were conducted a series of revivals which lasted throughout the years 1832 and 1833. To hear this powerful preacher large numbers came to Shady Grove from miles around and soon all the Baptists in the country were afire with a new religious fervor. The membership of Shady Grove grew by leaps and bounds nearly 200 people having been added at this time.

The Tabernacle Methodist Church did not win a place of unusual prominence in the life of its denomination until after the middle of the last Century when the camp meeting came into vogue. The Tabernacle was the first institution in Chehaw County to subscribe to meetings of this kind. Its log building was situated on a knoll that overlooked a small creek and the whole site was shaded by a beautiful grove of large oak and poplar trees. An abundant supply of pure cold water was available from a spring nearby. The location, in short, was ideal for camp meetings which always were held in the summer. To accommodate the crowds that overflowed the church a large arbor forty feet wide and sixty feet long was erected. Unlike the hastily built brush covered structures that were used in other places this arbor was of a permanent nature. Strong upright logs around eighteen inches in diameter supported a roof of homemade split pine shingles. The dirt floor was covered with straw and sometimes as many as 100 men and boys slept there at night. In a semi-circle back of the arbor a number of prosperous families built small log cabins. Others brought tents for their accommodation. In the early evening the grounds were illuminated by large pine-knot fires. The leaders were serious and dignified but the people, especially those who were young expected to have a good time as well as to worship. Three of the charter families of the Tabernacle that had negroes on their places brought most of them along to care for the stock, cook meals, keep hot coffee ready for all, and to prepare the barbecues with which the whole company now and then was fed. The meetings lasted from ten days to two weeks and during this time the atmosphere was much like that of a wholesome open-air summer resort.

There was no bell in the arbor but one of the charter members always brought along a large hunting horn which was used to awaken the people in the morning, to call them to preaching, and to send them to bed at night. Two sermons ordinarily were delivered in the forenoon after which a recess was allowed for dinner. An abundance of food which the campers brought with them was available for all. Visitors from the surrounding country brought picnic lunches and stayed for the day. In the afternoon there was a third sermon at the end of which sinners were called to repentance. As the ministers worked and prayed with those who had gone to the altar the crowd sang songs and went into an ecstacy of religious excitement. Several of the exhorters who preached at the Tabernacle in those days were evangelists whose names are honored in the history of Southern Methodism. The doctrines which they preached had much of hellfire and brimstone. One of the aged residents of the community, who lived within sight of the Tabernacle, had this to say of the services which he attended there as a boy. "Those were the days of real religion. Folks would go off into the woods to pray late in the afternoons, the men going off to one side and the women to the other. Along about dusk after they had got religion they'd come out of the trees shouting so loud the woods would ring. You couldn't hear your ears."

In the dark days of Reconstruction that followed the Civil War the religious life of Upland Bend declined. The quality of the records of the Tabernacle, which had been kept for nearly a hundred years by a succession of church clerks, deteriorated to a marked extent. Whether the later clerks were less impressed with the sacredness of their office or whether they were simply men of less training it is difficult to tell. From what the old residents said one would judge that the years of Reconstruction tore down the morals of the community to a considerable extent. Theft, adultery, and murder were committed with an openness that was new. Some of the perpetrators of evil deeds were strangers who drifted into Upland Bend in the wake of troop movements but others were natives who had backslid. As early as 1854, however, the State Legislature in passing an act for the establishment of a system of public schools had sown the seeds of a new institution which would enable the community eventually to regain the moral and intellectual fibre which seemed to have been lost.

EDUCATIONAL BEGINNINGS

The pioneers in Upland Bend did not set up formal facilities for the education of their children until they had been in the community for several years. An act of Congress had set aside the sixteenth section of land in every township for schools but in Upland Bend this land was so poor that it was practically worthless as an aid to education. The facilities of the churches were available, however, and the first school was organized about 1840 in the log cabin of the Shady Grove Church. A few years later a second school was established on the site of the Tabernacle Church. Only the 3 R's were taught at first. The method of financing was the so-called scholar-payment plan. Each pupil was expected to pay a fee of $1.00 a term although some who lacked money but who wanted to come were permitted to enroll without charge. A term usually lasted about three months between the planting of the cotton and the beginning of the picking season.

One of the old residents of the community recalled an unusually large school which he attended at the Tabernacle in 1862. Nearly a hundred pupils were enrolled that year. Quite a number of the scholars were young soldiers home on furlough whose grey uniforms were regarded with envy by the other boys some of whom were no more than five years of age. Most of the scholars wore garments of coarse homemade cloth. Paper was too scarce to use for writing so slates taken from the river bed were made to serve this purpose. The session lasted that year for the extraordinarily long period of five months. Instruction in the 3 R's was provided by a single teacher who was assisted by four or five of the older scholars.

The early educational life of Upland Bend was profoundly influenced by an academy some distance away from the community that was conducted by a famous teacher of boys during the years 1849 to 1885. Quite a number of lads from Upland Bend sat at the feet of this distinguished instructor. The guiding principle of his method was "Learn how to learn" and he always insisted that the regular course in Latin, Greek, and mathematics was the best approach to the mastery of this principle. For youngsters who were not able to drink deeply from the true springs of learning he offered natural science, bookkeeping, and practical arithmetic. Some of the Upland Bend boys whom he trained became preachers, others taught in the local schools, and still others became the community's leading supporters of education.

The first of two schools from which later a consolidated institution was to be developed was founded in 1884. It was called the Chism School after a leading citizen of that name who had studied at the academy and who was chiefly responsible for organizing the new school. The teacher was one of the first graduates of the State University to serve Upland Bend in that capacity. In addition to the 3 R's this man was able to offer instruction in such subjects as algebra and geometry. The building, which was blown down in 1897, was replaced the following year but from that time on the institution was known as the Knoll School. The second of the two institutions that were later absorbed in the consolidation was Killian's Chapel School which was founded at the other end of Upland Bend about the same time. Killian's Chapel, like the Knoll was the successor of several smaller institutions that had been taught by different teachers in different places over varying periods of time.

These two schools, unlike most of their predecessors continued in existence for about nineteen years. Killian's Chapel recruited its pupils from the families in the northern part of the community while the Knoll drew from the southern part. Each school had grown until it offered nine grades that were taught by three teachers. But the term lasted only four and a half months and the salaries of the teachers averaged only $50.00 a month. In years when the price of cotton was good supplementary popular subscriptions extended the terms by a few weeks. There was a good deal of rivalry between the two schools and the patrons who supported them tended to divide the citizens of Upland Bend into two opposing camps.

Neither group was satisfied, however, with the school it had. Greatly improved facilities could be provided by consolidation. Sooner or later something of this kind would have to be done but each group wanted the new school to be built at its own end of the community. The contention between the sections became bitter and the county board of education did not know how to proceed

in the matter. In the meantime the patrons of the Knoll School
had divided over the election of a principal—the question being
whether a local man or an outsider should get the job—and a
furious factional fight developed. Seeing opportunity in the confusion of their rivals the Killian leaders got together with the
leaders of the stronger Knoll faction and asked the county superintendent to call a meeting of the patrons of both districts who
were interested in consolidation. Not many came but those who
did decided to press ahead and a committee of six including three
from each district was appointed to proceed with the matter. The
center of the community seemed to be the best location and a
prominent landowner agreed to donate a site of ten acres where
two of the chief roads crossed. Subscriptions for the erection of
a building were quickly procured. The recalcitrant Knoll faction
swore they would never send their children but the committee
went ahead and won the consent of the county board of education.
At an election held in 1918 a majority of the voters of both districts approved consolidation together with the necessary levy of
taxes and within a few months a $6,000.00 two-story building was
erected on the chosen site. The new school was a great improvement over its predecessors. Equipment was purchased to the
extent of $1500.00, seven teachers with better training were em-
ployed, there were fewer recitations per teacher, salaries were
increased, two grades were added, the enrollment stepped up, and
the regular term was lengthened to six and a half months. In the
course of time the resentment of the Knoll dissenters was softened
by the tactful assignment of some of the much coveted bus-driving
jobs to sons of the right men. The transportation routes for the
high school were extended and soon pupils were coming not only
from all over Upland Bend but from several adjoining districts
as well.

When the old differences subsided the minds of the people were
turned toward appreciation of the superior advantages which their
children now enjoyed. Many good things yet remained to be done.
So they turned their faces to the future and set to work in ways
that will be explained in later chapters to improve upon the great
gains that had already been made. These additional efforts tended
further to submerge antagonisms and to train the people in the
methods and spirit of cooperation. The man who had taken the

leading part emerged from the movement for consolidation as one
of the outstanding leaders of the community. The other outstanding leader controlled the road work in the Upland Bend end of
the county. As will be shown later these two men seemed to have
reached an understanding that divided the leadership of the community between them. As long as they held their grip and worked
in harmony the forces of integration would prevail. The children,
who were growing up together in one school, were learning cooperation. In these several ways the consolidated school was
binding all elements of the population together. It was the only
local institution that served them all and for which all were willing
to do whatever they could. In so being it was the cause as well
as the symbol of their unity. Thus the people of Upland Bend
strengthened themselves as a community and the school that
worked to that end was the most powerful of the social forces that
held them together.

GEOGRAPHICAL FEATURES

The description of how Upland Bend looked when the pioneers
arrived needs to be supplemented by a brief sketch of the geographical features that greeted the eye of the observer when the
survey was made and the general effect of these on the people who
lived there. The wide bend of the river in which Upland Bend lay
formed the boundary of the community on the south and east
sides. On the west side the boundary was Corley's Turnpike Road.
Toward the north it blended with the Mount Moriah Community
being separated therefrom by the school district line. Within
these limits there was an area of approximately twenty-one square
miles which centered about the Upland Bend Consolidated Rural
School from which the community got its name. It was fairly
well supplied with roads there being a total of approximately
thirty-three miles within the area. The roads were comparatively
narrow but they were graded and surfaced with sand clay or top
soil. They were more or less passable except after prolonged rains
when the hills, on account of the lack of gravel, became so slippery
that they were impassable except for horses and wagons. Being
treacherous after rains and always rough and bumpy the roads were
more likely to be traveled for business than for pleasure. Good
gravel highways led out of the community both north and south

but only country roads led east and west and there was very little travel in these directions.

The nearest town of any size was Shallow Ford but Corley's Road also connected Upland Bend with De Soto, a town of a few thousand people that was located approximately eighteen miles to the southwest. One of the country roads that ran through the community led to Chocco, a village that was about ten miles from the center of Upland Bend. Chocco supplied the nearest connection with a railroad, the nearest telephone and telegraph service, the nearest power lines, and the nearest post office. The railroad at Chocco which was a branch line that was built originally to transport timber, offered no passenger service and very inadequate shipping facilities. Other than these the nearest marketing facilities and the nearest passenger service as well were at Shallow Ford twenty-five miles away.

The situation thus described was one of substantial isolation. And so it had been throughout the life of the community. The people who lived in Upland Bend were descendants for the most part of the original settlers. Generation after generation they had intermarried to an extent that made nearly every one kin to everyone else. From the beginning they had churches, schools, and stores that were adequate for their needs. These facts plus that of isolation have caused the people to develop a community life that was rather highly integrated, to leave the world outside alone, and to depend mostly on themselves. To such an extent was this true that a description of their life is apt to give an impression of "historical lag" but this effect would be produced by a penetrating account of the lives of almost any rural group in the foothills of the Southern region.

The area in which Upland Bend lay was within the foothills of the Appalachian Mountains, a part of the Cumberland Plateau. The territory surrounding it to the south and west especially was rugged hill land covered with second growth pine and valued chiefly for mineral rights. The farms in this territory were rough and poor as compared with those within Upland Bend where the land was gently rolling and relatively fertile. Geologically two formations were represented—"light and varicolored irregularly bedded sand, clay, and gravel with some lignite" which shaded off into "shale and sandstone with thin coal beds" as the river was approached. It was all cut-over timber land. To make it profitable for farming careful handling was needed which it had not always had.

When the pioneers came into Upland Bend they brought with them the methods of tilling land that prevailed in the sections from which they came. These were primitive and wasteful and it is worthwhile to trace the steps that led to improvement. This was done by piecing together the accounts of several old men who had witnessed the changes that took place. The sandy loam soil that covered the rolling hills was loose and susceptible to washing by the torrential rains that fell at certain seasons of the year. The loss of topsoil did not greatly worry the farmers in the early days, however, because as late as fifty years ago only 10 per cent of the land was cleared and when one field washed away they simply went to new ground and opened another. Each man plowed his rows in any way he saw fit. Some even argued that it was best to run the rows straight up and down a slope in order that each row might take care of its own water.

The more farsighted men realized, however, that such a rapid waste of land could not continue indefinitely if they were to have farms at all. Yet it was not until about 1896 that one of the leading farmers learned from a man he met in Shallow Ford of the value of hillside ditches. The hillside ditch was simply an open cut on the surface that fell away more gently than the natural slope of the land, the number of ditches constructed depending on the steepness of the slope. This system of drainage represented improvement and its use was gradually extended.

The loss of soil, though not as rapid as before continued nevertheless, the ditches tended to become gullies, and a better system of conservation was needed. In those days agricultural experts seldom appeared in Upland Bend but in 1907 one who was visiting in the county convinced a leading farmer of the value of the narrow base terrace that followed the contour of the land. Once made the terrace remained unplowed and was allowed to grow up in grass and weeds. This system reduced washing to a great extent and in the course of about ten years it displaced the hillside ditch throughout the community. Certain disadvantages, on the other hand, kept it from being entirely satisfactory. The terrace itself was out of cultivation and a row on either side was "busted" by the grass and weeds that flourished on it. Thus the yield was reduced and the fields assumed a very ragged appearance.

The situation then was ripe for the introduction of a more modern system of protecting the land. This was the broad-base terrace several rows wide which could be plowed and sowed with the rest of the ground. When properly constructed it permitted little washing and the entire field was available for cultivation. This plan was introduced to Upland Bend by a new county agent in 1924. Three years later a vocational agricultural department was added to the school under the leadership of an energetic, well-trained teacher. This man recognized immediately the necessity of encouraging the use of the broad terrace and within a few years he succeeded in interesting practically all of the landowners and their sons. Some still doggedly adhered to "old fogey" methods, and some constructed poor systems, but in general the land in Upland Bend was much better terraced than that of adjoining communities.

Upland Bend as a Part of the American Scene

Having completed this brief survey of the origins of Upland Bend it is desirable to emphasize the salient features to which the reader's attention has been called. The inhabitants of Upland Bend have in their veins the blood of the pioneers who were a part of the great westward movement of the people of the United States in the early decades of the Nineteenth Century. The lands on which they settled, if not the best, were nevertheless good in many ways. Soon after the settlers arrived they built churches for themselves and later schools for their children. Like other communities in the South they were engulfed in the disasters of the Civil War. But when the storm had passed they reconstructed their institutions, began to emphasize education, and made progress in the husbandry of their lands. They were a part of larger human and physical wholes yet the geographical features of the environment which surrounded them produced a state of isolation and the cultural patterns that flow from that condition.

A new day dawned for Upland Bend when, after the sharp conflict of interest that usually precedes such an event, they pulled themselves together and built a consolidated school. Rallying about the new institution they moved forward to better their lives in many ways to achieve an integration superior to anything they nad known in the past. When the survey came to Upland Bend the community was more than a hundred years old. What manner of life the people have come to lead after all these years it is the intention of the writers to tell as best they can in the chapters that follow. The attention of the reader will be directed first to the people themselves. After this the fundamental factors of economic and civic life will be discussed and, following these, health and the medical services that were available. We shall examine then the people's homes, their churches, and their school, the ways in which they spent their time and what they thought about various matters. Finally an effort will be made to describe the leaders of the community and the contributions they have made to its development.

In the long history that lies behind them the people of Upland Bend have coped manfully with the many substantial difficulties that confronted them. What the future holds belongs to the precarious realm of prophecy but this much seems fairly certain that problems in the years to come will be more subtle and more complicated than in the past. What the community will be able to make of its life will be determined in large part by what it was at the time of the survey. This, succeeding chapters will show in some detail. The study is a mass of facts objectively presented and there are dark sides in the picture as well as bright. If the reader is disturbed as shadows flit across the pages here and there let him remember that human life is all mixed up with good and bad. And he who would understand it must look at both without dismay. Life in Upland Bend at the time of the survey was like that of thousands of other communities. Taken together these constitute a very important part of the life of the American people. The facts about Upland Bend, including such as seem to be faults as well as those that seem to be virtues, are thus undeniably warp and woof of the American Scene. After years of study the writers have arrived at some measure of understanding of Upland Bend, and with it of that sector of our society which Upland Bend represents. And with understanding respect has come—respect for a people who, as a community in the case of education but otherwise as individuals for the most part, have done well with an environment, physical and social, the structure of which was not always of the best.

CHAPTER II

THE PEOPLE

In this chapter a body of material concerning vital factors of the population has been assembled. Such matters as birth-rate, death-rate, marital status, and size of family are considered because they determine the present and future vitality of the community. But other conditions, such as the amount of education, the occupational pursuits, and the mobility of the people, their ancestors and their children will also engage attention. These factors, though perhaps less significant as regards the actual perpetuation of life, are nonetheless fundamental to an understanding of the qualitative aspects of living. When maintenance of life over and above mere existence is of concern they become in a very real sense vital factors. Throughout the discussion it is well to keep in mind the mutual interaction between all such factors and the economic, social, and cultural levels of the community. The fertility of the population, the amount of schooling, and the occupations followed are to some extent certainly determiners of the economic compentency and the cultural attainments of the people. At the same time this competency, these attainments, retroactively influence the vital factors.

THE POPULATION

Within the twenty-one square miles which make up the community we have called Upland Bend there lived 209 families, 196 of which were interviewed. The facts concerning the people of the community which are reported in this study were obtained from these 196 households. With the remaining families, for one reason or another, the interviewers were not able to make contact. These few families have been ignored throughout the study.

The estimated total population of the community was approximately 1150 persons. In the 196 homes visited the population, men, women, and children, was 1064, or something over five persons to the family. This, of course, does not include members who were living away from home, a group that will be considered later. It does, however, include a total of 91 adults other than householders and housewives. Most of these adults were relatives of the families with which they were living. Usually they were parents, maiden sisters or bachelor brothers of the householder or his wife.

Distributed over the twenty-one square miles, the density of the total population was approximately 50 persons, or ten families, to the square mile. The density of the population varied for different parts of the community. Expressed in terms of the number of families to the section of land (one square mile), the range was from three to seventeen families. The most populous sections ran north and south through the community, following one of the main highways. The greatest density was found around the school. In the four sections surrounding it, less than one-fifth of the total area, almost two-fifths of the entire number of families, lived.

In most Southern hill communities negroes make up but a small part of the total population. In Upland Bend the ratio of whites to negroes was more than five to one. Of the families interviewed, 166 were white and 30 were negro. There were 882 whites and 182 negroes living in the homes visited. But since racial differences are always of interest in Southern groups the negroes have been consistently considered not only as a part of the total, but separately also.

OCCUPATIONAL CLASSIFICATION

Practically every one in Upland Bend lived off the land. Of the householders interviewed, 189 were farmers, two were professional men, one was a widow without land, and four were unemployed and without land. This does not imply that the population was a homogeneous one. The survey had not progressed far before it was discovered that occupational differences were so pronounced that if the life of the people was to be successfully portrayed it would be necessary to consider the occupational classes separately. The classification finally evolved is presented here in some detail and a thorough understanding of it, on the part of the reader, will greatly simplify the perusal of the report.

As in any American rural community, some of the farmers were owners, others were tenants. But significant differences appeared within these two groups as well as between them, consequently both were further subdivided. Slightly less than 40 per cent of the householders, all but four of them white, were owners. These were divided into two main groups, *landowners without tenants*, or small owners who worked their own land, and *landowners with tenants*, or larger owners who although they usually raised a crop of their own had enough land to be able to rent some of it. In this latter group were eleven men with large farms, 300 acres or more, that supported from four to nine tenants. This small group was economically so favored and politically and socially so influential that they have been treated separately as the eleven *large owners*.

The other householders, 60 per cent of the total, were tenants. In studying these we found two factors having important bearing on their status and consequently have classified them in two ways. The first division was on the basis of the financial arrangement with the landlord, the second on the basis of kinship to the landlord.

On the basis of the financial arrangement there were two main classes, the *sharecroppers* and the *renters*. At the foot of the economic ladder were the sharecroppers. They had no resources of their own, no tools, no animals, and no finances. Consequently they made an arrangement with the landlord whereby he, the landlord, furnished the necessities for farming, and often supported the tenant's family until the crop was sold. With such an arrangement the landlord got one-half and the tenant the other half of all crops raised. Hence the title sharecropper. All of the negro, and approximately two-thirds of all tenants belonged to this class. The more fortunate ones, those who owned a mule and the necessary equipment for farming and had enough resources to finance the family for a year were able to make a more satisfactory arrangement with the landlord. On condition that they furnish the tools and animals for farming and support for their families these men receive two-thirds of the cotton and three-fourths of other crops raised. This group was known locally as *furnishing tenants*. Most of the group of tenants called renters belonged to this class, but there were others who had enough money to pay cash rental for land and thus get everything produced. This last group, the *cash renters,* was small. There were only six in the community. In addition to these two groups of renters there were seven house-holders who lived on a relative's farm for which they paid no rent at all. These have been called *free renters.* These two small groups have been combined with the furnishing tenants to make up the group of renters. Throughout the study, on the basis of the arrangement with the landlord, the two main groups referred to are the sharecroppers and the renters.

The above classification of tenants appears to be the most satis-factory one on all matters economic. Consistent differences have been found between the groups. But oftentimes a more significant distinction could be made on the basis of kinship to the landlord. Approximately 40 per cent of the white tenants were close relatives of their landlords; usually a son or son-in-law, occasionally a brother or brother-in-law, a nephew or cousin.

In many respects, especially in the realm of the social rather than the economic, these *related* tenants were more comparable to the owning classes. In other respects they very definitely represented "poor relations." So significant were certain differences between the related and *unrelated* tenants that we have rather consistently broken the white tenants into these two groups as well as into sharecroppers and renters. The two classifications are of course not mutually exclusive. Rather all of the white tenants were classified under both headings. Although the negro tenants have been treated simply as negro sharecroppers, they belonged to the unrelated group. Most of them had white owners for landlords. The four negro owners had a total of four tenants, all negro but none related.

Only twelve families could not be classified in the above groups This *miscellaneous* group was made up of the seven householders who were mentioned in the beginning of this section as not being farmers and five hired men who worked on a monthly wage basis. The group was so small and so heterogeneous that scant attention has been paid to it.

The topic may seem to have been rather labored but the various terms are used throughout the study and consequently want under-standing. By way of summary and for purposes of convenient reference the occupational classification outlined above with the number and per cent of householders falling in each class is reproduced in Table I.

TABLE I

DISTRIBUTION OF HOUSEHOLDERS BY OCCUPATIONAL CLASSES

Occupational Classification	Number of Householders		Per Cent of Total	
White Owners				
Large landowners		11		6%
Landowners with tenants		32		16
Landowners without tenants		26		13
Total		69		35%
White Tenants				
Renters				
Related	18		10%	
Unrelated	26		13	
Total		44		23%
Sharecroppers				
Related	18		9%	
Unrelated	23		12	
Total		41		21%
Total related	36		19%	
Total unrelated	49		25	
Total white tenants		85		44%
Negroes				
Owners	4		2%	
Sharecroppers	26		13	
Total		30		15%
Miscellaneous		12		6%
Grand Total		196		100%

AGE, MARRIAGE, AND SIZE OF FAMILY

Having arrived at a working classification of the population next in line for consideration is an analysis of vital statistics. The age, marital condition, and size of family found in a population are matters of interest within themselves, but they also reflect the fertility of the population and thus have wider implications. Many married, at early ages, with large families constitute social problems which are quite different from those had in a society where many do not marry and those who do marry late and have small families. All signs point toward the fact that Upland Bend had an extremely fertile population.

The population was made up of a preponderance of young people. The median age of the approximately 1000 persons in the community was 18.5 years. A figure, incidentally, more comparable with the United States of 1820, when the median age was 16.7, than with 1934, when it was approximately 26.4. The *fertility rate,* that is the number of children under five years of age per 1000 women aged twenty to forty-four, was found to be 780. This was practically the same as the rural ratio of the United States of 1910, much higher than the ratio of 653 reported for 1930. The death-rate, to the extent that it is indicated by the proportion of old people, likewise, was relatively high. The 1930 census figures report 5.8 per cent of the population in rural communities as sixty-five years or over, but in Upland Bend this percentage was only 4.6.

The percentage of young people, as a result of those conditions, was abnormally large. Of the entire population 52 per cent were under 20 years of age. People at this age are not prepared to assume the full responsibilities of making a living. The chief dependence of a community for the production of material goods rests on that part of the population that falls in the age range of 20 to 44 years. This part of the population in Upland Bend constituted only 31.5 per cent of the whole. In 1930 the comparable percentage for the entire Southern region was 36.4 per cent. This fact undoubtedly set definite limits to the economic productivity of the community.

The median age for some 200 heads of families interviewed was 43 years. Slightly less than 10 per cent of these men were under

25 years and the same percentage were 65 or over. They had married women who were several years younger. The median age for the housewives was 37 years. Thirteen per cent of them were 25; 5 per cent under 20, and less than 5 per cent were as much as 65.

The ages of the householders and their wives varied decidedly with the occupational classes. The landowners were the oldest. Their median age was 49 years. Next in order came the negroes, with a median age of 47; then unrelated tenants with a median of 42; and the youngest, the related tenant group, of which the median was 31 years. The upper class tenants, the renters, were older than the sharecroppers, 41 years as compared with 34.

Approximately four of every ten persons in the community were married. Eight per cent of those married had been married for more than 40 years. Fourteen per cent had been married less than 5 years and 8 couples had married within the year. Certainly, as compared with urban groups, they had married at an early age. The median age at which men had married was 23, that for the women was 18. Four women and no men were married at an earlier age than 15, but almost 60 per cent of the women and 20 per cent of the men were married before they were 20.

In marital status, too, there were some interesting differences among the occupational classes. The negro men were the oldest at marriage, but their wives had married at the same age as had white women. Among the whites, the tenants, being younger, had of necessity been married a shorter time, but they married at an earlier age than did the owners. The median age at marriage of the landowners was 24 years, that for tenants was 21 years. The same difference existed between the tenants of higher and lower rank. The sharecroppers were married at 20, the renters at 22. The age of the wives at marriage varied in a similar manner. The typical owner married a woman who was twenty, while the tenant married a girl of sixteen or seventeen years, 16.6 years old to be exact. The nature of this relation between ages of marriage and the economic level attained was not definitely determined. It may be that owning classes delay marriage in order to get more schooling, or to more carefully select a mate, or because they require a more elaborate material background for marriage. On the other hand, it may be that early marriages, with the accompanying "hostages to fortune", doom the participants to a low economic class.

Families are typically large in rural communities, and Upland Bend was no exception in this respect. The average family had 4.4 children. The number of children varied greatly among the families. Ten per cent had no children, but most of these couples had been married less than two years, and only two of them had been married as much as ten years. Seven per cent of the families had ten or more children. The largest had fourteen. The unrelated tenants had the largest families, in spite of the fact that they were younger and had been married less time than had the owners. The negroes had fewer children than any white group comparable in age and length of time married. The related tenants had fewer children but they had been married less than half the time that any other group had. The differences in family size were not pronounced, however. The two groups most comparable in length of time they had been married were the unrelated furnishing tenants and the group known as owners with tenants (omitting the eleven very large owners who were older than any other group in the community). These groups had been married 25 years and had 5.1 and 4.5 children per family, respectively. The total unrelated white tenant group had been married approximately the same time that negroes had and their average family size was 5.0 while the negroes had 4.3 children per family.

The children were evenly divided between the sexes, but male children were more plentiful among the owners, females among the tenants and negroes. The ratio of males to females among the owners was 1.1; for the tenants it was .9.

Among the older families, there was no evidence of a decreasing birth-rate. If it can be assumed that families in which the wife is 45 years or older, are complete, only one-fourth of Upland Bend's families had reached their final size. For these completed families the average number of children was 6.5. This figure is practically the same as that describing family size in the immediately preceding generation. The average householder was one of a family of 6.7 children and his wife one of 6.8. Not enough of the families were completed in the different occupational groups to justify breaking the figures down, but a hint of the differences in the ultimate size of family for these several groups is furnished by the fact that the white tenants and their wives consistently came from larger families than did the owners and their wives.

If we can judge from relatively small numbers there is some evidence that for certain of the occupational groups the birth-rate was on the decline. So long as the birth-rate is increasing young children predominate, consequently the number of children under five years of age is greater than that found in any other five year age group. This was true for the community as a whole. Among the owners it was not true but they were older and consequently had a larger number of completed families than any other group. However, the related tenant group, largely sons and daughters of these owners, although they were the youngest group in the population had fewer children under five than they had between the ages of five and nine. These figures are suggestive but the numbers involved were so small that one would hesitate to interpret them as indicating a definite descending trend of the population.

EDUCATION

Perhaps no other single item so adequately reflects the qualitative aspects of life as does the amount of education received by the members of a social group. In America, particularly, there has been a tendency to use amount of schooling as a crude index of the cultural level of a community. Later inquiry will be made into the educational facilities of Upland Bend. Here our concern is with the extent to which the opportunities available had resulted in an educated populace.

The typical male adult in the community had attended school into the fifth year, had not entered the sixth grade. His wife went into but did not finish the sixth grade. Every third householder and housewife entered and every tenth one graduated from high school. Every twentieth one entered college, but aside from the teachers in the local school and the two professional men in the community there were only two persons, one man and one woman, who had received a degree from college. On the other hand, 12 per cent of the men and 5 per cent of the women did not attend school at all. The related tenants received the most education, eighth grade for the average. This was probably to be expected since not only their economic connections but their age was in their favor. The unrelated tenants had spent the shortest time in school of any white group, an average of five years, but the average negro did not reach the third year, and 40 per cent of them had never attended school.

Education was very definitely on the increase. Information on the education of the present householders, their parents, and on those of the children of the householders that had left school makes available figures on the education of three generations of men. The same figures are had for the women. The average years attended school by those of the men for whom the information was available were:

For the fathers of present householders............ 3.5 years
For the householders themselves....................... 5.8 years
For those sons who had left school................. 7.4 years
For the women the average were:
For the mothers of present housewives............ 3.7 years
For the housewives themselves......................... 6.5 years
For those daughters who had left school........... 7.5 years

The years attended roughly represent grades reached. They are reported in years because the older people attended ungraded schools and were not able to report their education by grades. We find, then, an increase of approximately two years of education each generation with insignificant differences between the sexes.

The same facts are more strikingly shown through consideration of the number with no schooling. More than one-third of the fathers of the householders had no schooling; one-eighth of the householders had none, but only one thirty-third of their sons had not attended school. The women, likewise, exhibited the same trend. One-fourth of the mothers of housewives did not attend school while only one-twentieth of the wives and one thirty-third of their daughters did not.

While this increase had taken place for all classes of people, it had been more pronounced among the owning groups. There is some reason for believing that for the sharecroppers the increase had ceased. The fathers of the sharecroppers attended school but slightly more than two terms, they themselves reached the fifth grade which was the grade at which the school careers of their sons had ended. The only educational advantage the sons seemed to have over their parents was that they had all attended school for a time at least.

A most striking picture of the educational inequalities among the occupational groups came from an analysis of the graduates of the local high school. During the twenty years of its existence, there were 75 children from the community who had graduated from the high school. Of this number 66 were from the land-owning classes and only 4 were children of sharecroppers. A part of this difference came from the fact that more of the owners had lived in the community during the time their children might have been in school. Moreover, being older they had more children who were of an age that would have permitted them to have graduated during the life of the school. But these are not the only factors. The fact is that more than one-half of the owners' children and less than one-tenth of the tenants' children who might have graduated did graduate from the high school. Without raising the issue of the responsibilities involved, it must be pointed out that rather than having universal education Upland Bend reserved a large part of its educational offerings for the owning families.

MOBILITY OF THE POPULATION

In addition to facts concerning the age, marital condition, size of family and schooling, information on movements within the population, both geographically and occupationally, are essential for adequate understanding of the people. Movements from place to place, for succeeding generations and within a generation, are to a certain extent inevitable. Change of occupation, too, is bound to result as the social structure changes. The extent of such change, that is the fluidity of the population, influences such matters as receptiveness to new ideas, ability at large scale cooperative endeavor, and adaptation to social change. It may actually determine the ultimate future of the people.

So far as geographical movement was concerned, the population of Upland Bend was undoubtedly an extremely stable one. Information on the places of birth and residences of the householders and the housewives, their ancestors, their brothers and sisters, and their children all support such an assumption. The householders and their wives were indigenous to the immediate locality. Four of every ten householders were born within the limited area of the community. Among the owners and related tenants this number was more than five in ten; among the tenants it dropped to three, and among the negroes but two in ten were born locally. The proportion of locally born wives was slightly less, three in ten, for the total population. Among the owning classes there were as many native women as men.

Those who were not born locally came from nearby communities. It will be remembered that the community was on the border between two counties. From these two counties, Chehaw and DeSoto, came more than 80 per cent of both householders and housewives. Those who were not from these counties came from other parts of northern and central Alabama. Seven couples of which only one was negro came from out of the state. Four of these came from the adjoining state of Mississippi, the others from Tennessee, Arkansas, and Louisiana. Two of the seven were not outsiders as their parents were only temporarily living out of the state at the time of their births.

Most of the people who were born in the community had resided there all their lives. The one in ten that had lived elsewhere, had lived in a nearby community usually. A few had moved out of the state for short periods. Two whites and three negroes had lived for a time in northern states. Those persons who were not born in the community had lived there for varying lengths of time, but in general they were not very mobile. The owners who had come into the community after birth had lived there for an average of 29 years, the tenants for 15 years. Only 4 families came in during the year prior to the survey and slightly less than 13 per cent of the total number of families had moved in during the previous five years. The white sharecroppers were the most mobile group. Every fourth one of them had come in during the previous five years. Next to the owners, the negroes were the most stable. Those who were not born in the community had been there for an average of 25 years. Of the four families that had moved into the community within the year of the study two had lived there previously. One of these was a native. Of the newcomers, one came in after having married into a local small owner's family, the other was a cronic "mover", having had five different landlords in the previous seven years. The problem of tenant transiency was largely confined to moving about within the community. This changing of landlords was quite common, usually because of friction between the owner and tenant, because of a chance to get better land or "just to be moving." A complaint occasionally heard among the renters was that when they worked hard to improve the soil and increase its productivity the landlord then raised the rent and thus compelled them to move.

Many of the parents of the householders were born in the community or nearby. Those who were not born locally, usually the parents of the older people came from the states to the east. Approximately 70 per cent of the fathers of the householders and of the housewives came from the two counties Chehaw and DeSoto; 20 per cent from other parts of Alabama, and 10 per cent came from other Southern states. Most of the people were not too sure concerning the nativity of their grandparents, but enough evidence was accumulated to identify their forbears as having taken part in the great westward movement of the early and middle part of the last century. The grandparents of the younger householders were born in Alabama; those of the older ones in Virginia, the Carolinas, Georgia and Tennessee. Only one person reported an ancestor from the North. This was a case in which the grandfather of one of the small owners came down from West Virginia during the Civil War, and after the war returned with his young wife and settled in the County. The ancestry of Upland Bend would need to be traced back further than the people were able to trace it to reach the "old country." Only one person reported an ancestor within the second generation back who came from a foreign country. This was an old sharecropper who remembered hearing his mother, whose maiden name was Campbell, say her father came as a boy from Ireland. If this report is true, it should be possible to trace this ancestry further back into Scotland.

The many brothers and sisters of the householders and housewives were also located nearby. Seventy per cent of the brothers and sisters of the white householders lived in Upland Bend, in Chehaw, or in DeSoto County. Most of the others (20 per cent) lived in other parts of Alabama. The small percentage remaining lived in other Southern states. Unlike their parents, those brothers and sisters who had left the state had moved westward. At the time of the survey they were residing in Mississippi, Arkansas, and Texas. Of some 800 brothers and sisters whose addresses were known only six had gone into the North to settle. For the white housewives the story is the same. Three of every four of their brothers and sisters lived in Upland Bend or in communities nearby. Those who had left the state had moved westward. Only three were known to be in the North. Among the negroes, most brothers and sisters were nearby, but those who had left went northward in much greater numbers. One-tenth of the brothers and sisters of the negro householders and wives resided above the Mason and Dixon line. The fact is more of them were in the North than were in other parts of Alabama, and a negligible number lived in other Southern states.

The stability of the general population and its ancestors is very well shown in the family tree of one of the families in the community. In 1826 a young farmer and his newly-wed wife came from Buncombe County, North Carolina and settled in the community. In five generations, that have come down from this mating, the residences of 343 descendants were located. Of this number:

138 lived and died or were living in Upland Bend.
128 lived and died or were living in Chehaw or DeSoto counties.
58 lived and died or were living in other parts of Alabama.
10 lived and died or were living in other Southern states.
9 lived and died or were living in the North or West

Even more convincing evidence of stability is found in a study of the interrelations among the families. These were closely intermingled in Upland Bend both by blood and by marriage. This fact is very well reflected in the family names. There were precisely 100 different surnames among the 196 families of which we had record. In other words, there were two families for each family name. But this does not tell the whole story. The twelve most common of these 100 names accounted for more than four of every ten white families and for 37 per cent of the total population of the community. That this similarity of names indicated common blood is supported by the fact that eight of these twelve names were borne by original settlers in the community.

The kinship of families was no less marked among the negroes. Three family names accounted for approximately one-half of the total negro population. The most common name among the negroes was one of the twelve most frequently found among the whites. The negroes of this name were very proud of their ancestry. They all stemmed from a common ancestor, a slave owned by the original white settler of the same name. Upon being freed this negro took his former master's name.

But even more direct evidence of family interrelations is available. For one-third of all families either the householder or his wife, was a child of some other householder then living in the community. In 25 homes (more than 12 per cent of the total) the father of both man and wife was then living as a householder in Upland Bend. The matter did not stop there. Five of the large landowners, for example, had a total of seventy-five grandchildren living in the community at the time of the survey. Relations beyond this were not ascertained but there is no doubt that a very large part of the community, both tenants and owners, have some of the same blood coursing in their veins.

Common blood was found more often among the owning classes. The daughters of landowners were more apt to acquire husbands locally and the sons of owners married locally more often than did other classes. In general these marriages were within their own occupational group. Only four of the daughters of owners who had married locally had married unrelated tenants. Of all the owners who had married locally two married daughters of unrelated tenants and these were furnishing tenants rather than sharecroppers.

Family names also followed economic lines. Seven of the twelve most common names, mentioned above, accounted for 45 per cent of the total landowning class, and six of these seven did not appear among the unrelated tenant population. There were six families of one name who were all small owners, without tenants. Four names appeared very frequently among tenants, the most frequent being Jones. Eight different families bore it, and like Joneses everywhere, it is probably not safe to assume that it indicated close blood relationship.

In occupation, too, the population was a relatively stable one. Not only were the people farmers but most of them had never engaged in any other occupation. They almost invariably came from farming families. Their brothers and sisters lived on farms, and many of their sons and daughters, even those who had left the community, were engaged in farming.

Three of every four householders in Upland Bend had never tried any occupation other than farming. Every fourth man had tried something else, but almost half of those who had were land-owners, and the owners who left farming temporarily did not give up their land, consequently their jobs would best be treated as part-time ones. Those who definitely gave up farming for varying periods of time, tenants usually, commonly engaged in some closely allied occupation like mining or saw milling. Three men, however, had "worked on the railroad"; two had served as truck drivers; and one had worked in a machine shop. One sharecropper preached for a time, but said he "couldn't make a living at it." One negro worked in a packing house in Chicago for several years, and another old one reported being a slave as a former full-time job which he had engaged in. Among the owners, two had done some trucking, two some preaching, one had served as deputy sheriff, and one had been a traveling salesman. A few of the men had tried two different jobs, only three had tried as many as three. One versatile man had varied his farming with storekeeping, preaching, and bricklaying. He was never too sure of himself in these wanderings because he continued to hold a farm in the community, to which he returned early in the depression.

Well over 90 per cent of the fathers of the householders had been or were farmers and the same proportion of their grandparents, both paternal and maternal, had engaged in farming. For the women the figures were comparable. In the few exceptions found the parents were commonly engaged in some work closely allied to farming such as saw-milling, stock trading, or storekeeping (country merchants). One householder and two wives were children of coal miners; one woman was the daughter of a minister; and the father of one sharecropper's wife had been a shoemaker in a nearby small town.

Brothers and sisters, too, were typically farmers or farm wives. Numbers of them had drifted into the towns where they typically engaged in unskilled, semi-skilled, or skilled labor. But, at that, six of every ten brothers and sisters of the householders and more than this proportion of those of the housewives were living, or had lived during their lifetimes, on farms.

Occupationally, the people were extremely stable. Certain facts, on the other hand, indicate that stability of the same high order did not characterize the various economic groups found within the farming population. In fact, the evidence suggests that during the past few years there had been considerable movement among the whites from the owning class into tenancy. Large numbers of the tenants were but one generation away from ownership. Most of the tenants as well as the owners reported that their parents were landowners. Two of every three householders had fathers who owned land, and slightly more of the housewives had. The proportion of landowning parents was higher for the owning classes. The percentages varied from 100 per cent for the free related tenants to 54 per cent for the unrelated sharecroppers. However, 63 per cent of all unrelated white tenants and 65 per cent of their wives had parents who owned their own farms. This finding was not true for the negroes. The negro ancestors probably never owned land. Only two reported fathers who were landowners, and if one goes back another generation most of them were slaves.

The permanency of this stratification can only be inferred. Facts just presented in addition to one reported earlier to the effect that the tenants were a relatively young group would seem to extend hope that with the passage of time some of them might move into the owning class. This will surely happen in the related tenant group. Many of them will inherit land if they come by it in no other way. But for many others, for most of those who were classed as *related sharecroppers,* the small holdings of their relatives, the heavy indebtedness on the land, and the large families which their parents had greatly reduce the chances of the inheritance of any land.

For the unrelated tenant groups the hope is even less. Several facts seem to preclude the possibility of any very large natural shift from tenancy to ownership. It will be remembered that the

unrelated tenants were already well into middle life, forty-two
years being their median age. An even more important fact is
that most of the owners were never tenants, and those who were,
acquired their land at a much earlier age. The average owner
reported that he had owned some land since he was 26 years old.
Although quite a number of the owners had come into their present holdings in relatively recent years, within the five years previous to the survey only three householders moved from the unrelated tenant into the landowning class. And, finally, there is little
doubt but that during the past few decades the movement has
been toward an increased concentration of the land rather than
otherwise. The eleven large owners, who made up less than 6
per cent of the total population, 15 per cent of the owners, owned
55 per cent of the total acreage of the community. They had
gradually bought up these holdings during their own lifetimes,
however, and, if we can judge from the inheritance, their fathers
did not own such large farms. Less than one-half of the owners
had inherited any land and these not very much. The average for
those who did inherit was 54 acres and only one person in the
community inherited as much as 200 acres. All of which would
suggest that the tenant group will probably increase rather than
decrease in the future.

Perhaps because of a relatively high degree of occupational stability the problem of absentee landlordism was not a pressing one
in Upland Bend. The typical landlord lived on his land, supervised any tenants he had, and raised a crop. There were only
sixteen tracts of land, all of them relatively small, owned by absentee landlords. Four of these were parts of unsettled estates,
three were the holdings of widows who had moved out, and only
five were owned by men who had left farming and moved into
nearby towns. The four remaining tracts were owned by outsiders.
Two of these were acquired by individuals through mortgage
foreclosures and two were owned by corporations, one by a land
company and the other by the Gulf States Steel Corporation. This
Corporation held mineral rights which were acquired some 20
years earlier on most of the land in the community, and to the
East had large land holdings; but this tract of some 200 acres
represented their entire ownings in this community.

Drainage of the Population

Although the population was a stable one, nevertheless, it was true that the community annually lost a goodly portion of its inhabitants through the leaving of sons and daughters. Of the 343 older children, children out of school, had by approximately 200 families, exactly one-half of the sons and three-fifths of the daughters had left the community. A fairly detailed study of these children was made, not only to ascertain what became of them, but also to determine the extent to which they represented a selected group intellectually. A rather common comment seen with reference to rural communities is to the effect that the best blood is being drained off. It was desirable to discover the extent to which this was true in Upland Bend.

The children who had left home had not gone far. Most of them were in neighboring communities or towns. Eighty per cent of both the sons and daughters were in the two counties Chehaw and DeSoto; 12 per cent of the daughters and 9 per cent of the sons had left the state, and only 12 of the children, eight of them negroes, had gone North. There were no differences among the occupational classes as to the proportion of sons that left the community, but tenant daughters, probably because of greater difficulty in finding husbands locally, left much more often than did the daughters of owners. Only one-third of the tenants' older daughters lived in the community while more than one-half of the owners' daughters did. The negroes had gone farthest away. The white tenants' children were mostly all nearby. This was particularly true of the daughters, who seemed to have married farmers in neighboring communities. However, almost one-half of all of the children who had left had gone into towns and cities. Sons left farming more often than daughters did, and the children of landowners more often than tenant children. Birmingham, the only large city in the state, had drawn more than 8 per cent of the children who had left home. This fact, incidentally, is of current interest. At the time of writing there was criticism in certain quarters of a state policy which was designed to equalize educational opportunity throughout the state by distributing funds on the basis of need. Under this plan Upland Bend received a larger proportion of the funds than did Birmingham, but to a certain extent at least it was being used to educate future citizens of Birmingham.

To the extent that the amount of education received is an indication of intellectual ability, Upland Bend was losing its extremes and keeping the great middle group. Those with little education as well as those with comparatively much tended to leave. Approximately one-half of all the children had left the community, but two-thirds of those with less than fourth grade education had left, and nine-tenths of those who went to college had never come back. Those of the latter who did return were daughters who came back to teach in the local school. The most striking fact was that of nineteen children who had graduated from college, only one, a woman teacher, had returned to the community.

In general the uneducated children who left were the sons of tenants and small owners, and they went to farms in nearby communities. (It will be recalled that the surrounding communities were in general inferior to Upland Bend). The daughters who married farmers in nearby communities had just as much educa- tion as those who stayed in Upland Bend, but belonged to lower economic groups. The median son who went into urban centers had reached the tenth grade, the median daughter the ninth grade. Not all of those who went into the cities and towns were well edu- cated, however. Birmingham, for example, drew more than twice as many persons with less than sixth grade education as it drew high school graduates, which, again, should intensify Birming- ham's-concern over Upland Bend's educational program.

The occupations which were entered by the children who left farming were quite diverse. Unskilled or semi-skilled labor ab- sorbed the greatest number. Six of these who were graduates of the local high school were working in a paper mill. Mercantile work came second, teaching third. In general the amount of education received determined the nature of the work in which they engaged. Aside from teaching the professions were poorly represented. The success that they had with these various occu- pations was difficult to determine. However, Upland Bend did seem to have contributed its share of eminence. One of her sons was general counsel for a large southern railroad, one was a Doc- tor of Philosophy from Yale, another a superintendent of schools in a small city, and a fourth was a successful physician in a nearby town.

In this chapter has been presented a body of more or less related factual material. The many facts have in common one thing, they throw light on the vitality of the community. No attempt will be made to summarize them in detail. Rather, the intention is to point out what appear to be some of the high points of the material.

The population of Upland Bend has been seen to be a homogeneous one with reference to occupation engaged in. When considered in terms of success in coping with this occupation, however, there were great differences among the people. Not only between owners and tenants, but within both groups, there existed very definite stratifications. As the reader proceeds with the chapters he will find that life at these various strata was very different.

A preponderance of young people, such as were found, sets definite limitations on economic productivity, particularly where dependence on manpower is great, as it is in any rural community. At the same time, it places an abnormally heavy educational responsibility on the community. Local maintenance of an adequate educational program would tax to the limit the financial resources of the community. But there is scant social justification for the burden being borne by the small, local community alone. When every other son and daughter leaves the community to live elsewhere it seems reasonable to expect that the burden be shared.

Although education had been on the increase for three generations at least, the level reached by the average person was still low. The most discouraging part of the educational picture was the gross inequalities in opportunity for the differing economic groups. High-school training, in particular, was found to be almost entirely limited to the owning classes.

A similarity of ancestry and limited mobility, both geographically and occupationally, characterized the population. These suggest a great sameness in customs, traditions, and outlook, but they also lead one to expect a high degree of provincialism, a limited understanding of and appreciation for the problems facing other peoples in other times and other places.

Finally there is in Upland Bend a constant drainage of the population. To the extent that the losses are unselected this is not necessarily undesirable. A high birth-rate, limited fertility of the soil, and absence of opportunities other than agricultural, would preclude the possibility of the community's maintaining the total population that it produced. But those who left the community did not represent an unselected group. Although they were not drawn entirely from the upper economic levels, the indications did point to a constant loss of some of the community's best intelligences.

The welfare of a community is, of course, measured in terms of the well-being of the individuals who make it up. To the extent that the welfare of one's children is a social good, the movement away from the community should perhaps be evaluated in terms of the relative prosperity of those who had left. But there is another side to the matter. In terms of the immediate future, the community needed the leadership which potentially these bright young men and women possessed. In terms of longer periods, this failure to hold the most intelligent offspring can but mean a gradual deterioration in the intellectual quality of the population. The Upland Bend of the present is paying a high price that its urban neighbors may profit; but the irony of the situation is that the community will gradually get even by sending out a product of less and less quality.

CHAPTER III

ECONOMIC LIFE OF THE COMMUNITY

Modes of making a living and the kind of livelihood the economic order will maintain are matters which have important bearing on many aspects of the life of a people. Most of the energies of a community go into the making of a living. The degree of success which is achieved in this undertaking determines more than most other factors the quality of the recreational, cultural, and institutional life which can be developed and sustained. Realizing the fundamental character of the economic life, efforts were made in the survey to secure rather detailed information on the income, the wealth, and the material goods which the people had and the sources from which these possessions came. At the same time, the uses to which available funds were put were not neglected. The buying, trading, and economic self-sufficiency of the families were also given attention.

WEALTH AND INCOME

Arriving at a precise figure for the wealth of the average householder of Upland Bend was rather difficult. The value of the land they had is a useful index for the owning classes, at least. This is not true of the tenants for, with them, the amount of land rented tended to vary with the number of members of the family who were old enough to work, and did not give much indication of economic resources. As farms in the South go, those of Upland Bend were not large. The average farm consisted of 142 acres. Eleven farmers owned large tracts ranging in size from 300 to 800 acres. The 62 other owners had much smaller farms, from 10 to 200 acres, averaging only 72 acres. Fifteen per cent of these were so small that the owner needed to rent other land to raise the size of crop he desired.

So little land had been bought and sold in the community in recent years that it was practically impossible to estimate its worth. Prices paid for the land owned ranged from $2 to $75 per acre and in one case a small tract was bought at $100 per acre. Prices asked ranged from $15 to $150 per acre. The more productive and better located land was priced highest. The most valuable location at the time of the survey was in the neighborhood of the school. The opinion of one of the larger owners in the community was that a fair average valuation for land at present market prices would be $35 per acre, but this figure was much too high according to a leading real-estate agent in the neighboring county-seat.

The attempt to arrive at the wealth of landowners on the basis of the value of the land was rendered more difficult by the fact that many farms were mortgaged. The land holdings of more than six of every ten farm owners in the community were mortgaged. Fifty-four per cent of the owners with tenants and 65 per cent of the smaller owners had mortgages on their land. This indebtedness ranged from $150 to $9000. The median debt was roughly $900; for the larger owners, those who had tenants, it was $1200 and for the small farmers $500. The principal value of many of the mortgages amounted to far more than the land would have brought on the market. According to the real-estate agent quoted above, at least one half of them were mortgaged for more than they could be sold for. Most of the mortgages were held by banks in neighboring towns and by private individuals. Only seven farmers had taken advantage of the Federal Government's assistance to obtain Federal Land Bank Loans. There was very little foreclosure activity, however. During the year of the study only one farmer had lost his land because of a mortgage foreclosure.

The resources outside of land may be taken as another indication of wealth. Analysis of these resources threw interesting light on the economic level of the various occupational classes as well as on that of the community as a whole. The estimated wealth, aside from land but including household goods, cash and other personal property, was reported by practically all householders. For the eleven large landowners this average wealth was $2350, but one of them reported $18,000 in bank deposits while a second reported only $100 of assets. The average for all owners was $915.

For the related tenants the average was $275, for unrelated tenants it was $190, for white sharecroppers $125, and for negroes $55. Thirty-five householders in the community, or about 17 per cent of them, estimated that if they sold out everything they owned the cash raised would be less than $50.

A better estimate of the economic status of the people can be made in terms of their cash income; although one cannot, of course, compare the income of farmers with that of urban groups, because the farm contributes far more to economic support than is indicated by such income. The year in which the study was made was a "depression" year, but because of the contributions which were made by the Federal Government in the form of cash advances on cotton and through other agencies it may be considered fairly typical. The total income of the community during the year with which we are concerned amounted to approximately $75,000. Of all the householders, 186 reported their incomes and the total for them was $74,028, an average income per family of $367. The range from householder to householder was great. The eleven large owners averaged $1691; the average owner with tenants made $850; the small owner without tenants, $293; the furnishing tenant, $290; and the sharecropper, $148. The related tenants probably because of greater dependence on their landlords made less money than the unrelated tenants did. There was but little difference between the income of white and negro sharecroppers, $153 as compared with $144. Forty householders made less than $100. The most made by any man was $2400. Only one sharecropper made as much as $450. The 3 per cent of the families with the highest incomes received more than 20 per cent of the total income, and the 20 per cent with the lowest incomes received slightly less than 3 per cent of the total.

The amount of insurance carried, the number of bank accounts, the amount of taxes paid, and the automobiles and livestock owned reflect the limited incomes. Life insurance is very widely used in the United States to safeguard the income of the family in case of the death of the chief earner. But it is costly, and probably because of this was not very often found in Upland Bend. There were a total of 29 policies owned by members of the community. Twenty of these were for $1000 or less and only two were for as much as $5000. Eighteen of the policies were held by owners and eight of them by young related tenants. Only two of the unrelated tenants and none of the negroes had life insurance. Six of the holders of life insurance had a disability clause. Burial insurance, which is usually thought to be common among negroes, was owned by only one in Upland Bend. Among the whites only a single sharecropper had such a policy. Fire insurance, too, was a form of protection that was rare. In the tenant classes there was none. Even among the owners only eight had policies. The families were thus exposed in general to being wiped out by fire and in such cases were thrown on their neighbors. It was not uncommon for a collection of clothing, food, and money to be taken up for such occasions.

Checking accounts call for the possession of considerable amounts of cash and the current use of the same in the daily routine of living. Twenty-six householders, about 13 per cent of those in Upland Bend, had checking accounts in a nearby bank. All but four of these accounts were had by owners. One of these was a negro, and he was the only negro in the community who had contact with a bank. The four other accounts were held by related tenants. Savings accounts represent what a family is able to lay aside against a rainy day and are thus measures of the power of accumulation. In this community they were entirely limited to the landowning class and only ten owners had such accounts.

The amount of taxes paid not only gives a measure of governmental support, but to the extent that taxes are equitably assessed they throw light on the economic competency of the people. The average landowner in the community paid $35 in direct taxes, the average tenant about $2.50. Sixty whites and 24 negroes, almost one-half of the community, paid no direct taxes. This did not include poll tax which was $1.50 for all registered voters, but only one-half of the householders and one-fifth of their wives were registered for voting.

There were 41 automobiles in the community, approximately one to every fifth family. Aside from one Dodge, one Oldsmobile, and a ten year old Chandler owned by the one negro who had a machine, the cars were either Fords, Chevrolets, or Plymouths. Fifty-three per cent of those owned were bought second-hand. Only two new cars were bought during the year previous to the study. The ownership of cars was confined to the landowners and related tenants. Only two unrelated tenants owned cars. All of the large landowners and 43 per cent of all owners had them. The one negro who possessed a machine was the largest negro landowner.

The typical work animal was a mule. In fact, it was common to estimate the size of the farm not by the number of acres but by the number of mules necessary to cultivate it. In these terms the largest farmer had an eleven-mule and the typical owner a two-mule farm. In all there were 216 mules for 192 families reporting. They were, however, not very equitably distributed. All owners had at least one, most of them had more, and the renters typically had one, almost one-half of them had two. But only six sharecroppers, two white and four negro, owned a mule. The few automobiles owned, in addition to an even greater scarcity of horses, there being only nine in the community, meant that large numbers of families had to depend on the mule for transportation. The limited number available to the sharecroppers undoubtedly influenced the amount of travel that they were able to do.

The cows per family ran even higher than did mules, there being an average of more than two cows per household. Although many of these were concentrated on the farms of the community's three dairymen, 80 per cent of all families had a cow. The 20 per cent without were largely from the sharecroppers. One of every three of the negro sharecroppers had no milk supply. For these families, most of them with large numbers of young children, there was no dependable supply of milk and butter. And so it went with chickens and pigs. The average householder had 25 chickens and two hogs. Thirty-five per cent of the sharecroppers had no chickens and 45 per cent had no hogs. Hogs were rather obviously raised for home consumption only, the largest number owned by any farmer being 15, and but three farmers had as many as eight. On the other hand, one-fourth of the families sold or bartered eggs and chickens at certain seasons of the year.

The animals which were owned were probably not of a very high quality. Few farmers reported any purebred stock. Ten had at least one purebred cow, one had eight. Four others had some purebred chickens and three had purebred hogs. There was only one purebred bull in the community, although practically all cows were bred locally. The purebred chickens owned by one man were "game chickens", used for fighting purposes, and three other men had purebred dogs. One had fox hounds, the others bird dogs. Incidentally, dogs other than purebred were very plentiful among the landowners and the negroes, but the white tenants reported very few. All of the purebred stock except two Jersey cows was concentrated in the hands of owners and related tenants.

Farming was dependent chiefly on mule- and man-power rather than on machinery. There were three tractors, ten trucks, used for hauling rather than farming, and two stationary engines in the community. Other farming equipment was equally scarce. Three farmers had manure spreaders; three had planters, six had cultivators; seven had harrows; and six had hay rakes. As would be expected, these tools were owned by the large farmers, people who had some resources beyond those necessary to feed and clothe the family.

SOURCES OF INCOME

The gains which proceed from the labor of farmers cannot be measured entirely in terms of cash income, but in spite of this the income probably most adequately reflects the current and potential economic sufficiency of life in a rural community just as it does in urban centers. Second only in importance to the size of the incomes are facts concerning the sources from which they are obtained. Through such information one may obtain valuable insights into how the people spend their time and what they must think about many matters.

Mentioned earlier was the fact that practically everyone in Upland Bend was tied to the land in one way or another. Coming to the point more specifically it was found that more than 190 of some 200 householders were farmers. Some owned land, some rented, and some hired out for wages but all had their roots in the soil. Most of what they earned, therefore, came from the land. By far the largest part of their cash income came from the sale of cotton raised on this land. This was true for both landowners and tenants. Less than one-half of the landowners made any money from the farm except from that source. One-third of them sold some corn and 10 per cent took in small supplements from other crops such as peanuts, syrup, and strawberries; but only six farmers in the community had revenues of any size from another crop. Three of these men depended on dairying for their chief income and three made sizable supplements through raising chickens. The income of the tenants was even more from cotton. The typical tenant raised some corn but a large part of this was ground into meal to make cornbread which was a staple in his diet. Those tenants who had stock used corn to feed their animals. The sharecropper usually sold or bartered a small amount of corn. But for no farmer in the community did the sale of this grain account for as much as 10 per cent of the total earnings.

Although the farm crops contributed the largest part of the income there were several rather important regular supplements had by numbers of families. A rather common one came from the work of the housewives. One-half of the wives in the community had through one method or another earned some cash during the year previous to the study. They did it by selling produce, eggs and butter, chiefly. Other sources mentioned were part-time or full-time work at boarding teachers, sewing, teaching, cooking, hiring out as a farm hand, and washing. A leading store in the community was operated by a woman and two housewives taught regularly in the local school. Although quilting was one of the most popular leisure-time activities in feminine circles, there were two women in the community who did such beautiful work that they were kept busy quilting for their neighbors. Sometimes they worked "on the halves" sometimes for cash. For fancy quilts (The "Double Wedding Ring" and the "China Plate" were very popular models) they received $1.75 if the materials were furnished, from $3.50 to $5.00 per quilt when they were not furnished, by the purchaser. Each of them estimated that she sold about ten quilts per year. A few negro women had full-time jobs as servants in the homes of larger owners. Several others did part-time work at cooking and washing. Aside from these negro women, the women who earned this extra money were drawn largely from the landowning classes. Sixty per cent of the wives of owners as compared with 27 per cent of sharecroppers' wives reported such earnings. The amounts received were usually small, but they represented definite contributions to the livelihood of the family.

The most substantial supplements to the family income, however, came through regular, part-time or full-time jobs, which were pursued regularly by several householders. Fifteen per cent of all householders reported such work in addition to their farming. The jobs consisted of trucking, hauling, carpentering, painting, store-keeping, milling, ginning, black-smithing, furniture making, hair cutting, veterinary work, preaching, and one man reported whiskey making. Having one of these jobs meant in general that the individual had developed special skill along some line of work needed in the community or possessed the specialized tools needed, but there were indications that being well-connected was often quite an important factor. It is impossible to determine with certainty the cause and effect relations involved, but the fact is that the jobs were almost entirely confined to the owning classes and their relatives. Only two unrelated tenants, both renters rather than sharecroppers, and no negroes reported regular employment other than farming while 20 per cent of the owners reported such work.

The industrial life of the community, aside from home industry, was in the hands of the part-time workers. There were within the community two cotton gins, two small stationary sawmills, and a grist mill. The gins were owned and operated by two of the larger owners. One of these men also owned the grist mill and one of the sawmills. The second sawmill had been bought and operated for a short time by a small landowner but being unable to make it pay he had abandoned it. The gins were operated through the cotton picking season, that is between two and three months in the fall. During this time one of the gins employed two and the other, three men in addition to the owner. The jobs which these men performed represented skilled labor. One served as engineer, (one gin was operated by a steam engine burning wood, the other by a jacked-up tractor), a second man operated the press and the third weighed and operated the suction unloader. The gins charged a flat rate per bale for ginning and the seeds as well as the cotton fibre were returned to the farmer. At the time of ginning the farmer received an official sample from the ginner to which a number identifying the bale was attached. This sample was passed around among the buyers in nearby towns until a satisfactory sale was made.

This combined cotton gin and sawmill, operated by a "jacked-up" tractor, was only an adjunct to the main occupation of farming. Such a plant represented too heavy an outlay to be financed locally. It was owned by "outside money."

The sawmill and the grist mill were operated by the owner or by one of his farm hands from the same steam engine which ran one of the gins. During the ginning season, when a "head of steam" was available, they were operated on demand. At other seasons of the year corn was ground on certain days of the week only and lumber was sawed up when a sufficiently large order had accumulated. The grist mill ground corn "on shares", one-eighth for grinding; the sawmill cut logs at a cash rate per thousand board feet.

The incomes obtained from these industries were sufficient to place the two owners among the six persons in the community having a total income of more than $2,000. The investment was, however, too heavy for them to manage alone. Both owners were backed by large furnishing merchants in nearby towns. These two merchant backers were not and never had been residents of the community. One of them had married into the family of a local large owner who was a relative of the ginner. The other merchant was one of the community's few absentee landlords.

The community had a blacksmith, a furniture maker, and a third man who was both a blacksmith and a furniture maker. None of these men worked at his trade full time. The blacksmith and the furniture maker were both furnishing tenants; the third man owned a farm of 40 acres. Two of these three men raised a crop; the third was in poor health and had not worked his land for several years. The three of them, aged 77, 59, and 60 years respectively, had developed their skill under the tutelage of their fathers. Although they had a total of eight sons, all mature, no son had been interested in his father's trade sufficiently to gain a competent skill in it.

The shops which the above mentioned artisans operated were scantily furnished, but their apparatus included many ingenious homemade substitutes for standard equipment. The blacksmith's work consisted in shoeing mules, sharpening plow points, and repairing farm implements. The furniture maker specialized in making chairs, baby cribs, and dining room tables. But the highest development of skill was found in the third man. Depending entirely upon homemade equipment except for a draw knife, he made elaborate furniture, the designs for which were taken from his Sears-Roebuck catalogue. In his blacksmith shop he would attempt any need that one might have in the metal field. Some of his apparatus was extremely complex, but it did the work he required. He had made tables, beds, ironing boards, stoves, locks, for doors, a unique posthole digger (one of his favorites), and at the time of our interview was working on a reproduction of a $21.90 Sears-Roebuck bed which he thought was "nice but too expensive." He had begun this bed at the instance of one of the women of the community who had torn the picture from her catalogue, brought it to him, and ordered one like it. He made any kind of chairs to order. Rocking chairs were sold for $3.00; dining room tables for $4.00; and straight chairs, $1.25. If the purchaser wanted it he would make a ladder-back chair with split-bottom seat, the whole beautifully proportioned, for a charge of $1.00. The back posts of these chairs were bent in graceful curves. This effect he produced by means of a process which he claimed

A chairmaker displays his wares. Ladderback chairs, ax handles, and such were carried in stock. More elaborate furniture was made to order, Such skill was fast disappearing from Upland Bend. This elderly worker had no successor in the community.

was all his own. As a first step in the process the post was shaped on the lathe. It was then boiled for 3 or 4 hours in water. After its removal it was twisted slightly, set in a block, which he had designed, to give it the proper bend and allowed to dry. When fairly dry, holes were bored and the rungs, which had previously been kiln dried and processed, were inserted. These chairs were old fashioned but very substantial, he thought.

The earnings of these men from their skills, like those of other part-time workers, were not very large. During the previous year the especially skilled furniture maker took in $97 from his shop. The other cabinet maker had earned approximately $50 and the blacksmith had taken $25 in trade. Their sales were confined entirely to people living in the community.

Hair cutting was another of the part-time activities which members of the community engaged in. Five men had either developed the skill or had acquired the necessary tools for hair cutting. Although only two of them received pay for this work, their services were in great demand. One of the amateurs, who was a young man, took a three weeks barbering course in Birmingham. For a year he ran a small shop which his father bought for him near Birmingham. He had expected to be a town barber but after some experience he concluded he did not like the work so he had moved back to the home of his father. His motive for cutting hair, as he reported it himself was to "to help the poor people out who can't pay for hair cuts." Another of the unpaid barbers went into the business because several men in the community, who liked his work, agreed to buy him the necessary equipment—a barber cloth, two pairs of shears, one barber comb, and a straight razor, if he would cut their hair. He reported service to men and women at the rate of five a week. The two men who received some pay for their work charged 15 cents per haircut, but it was "all right if you didn't have the money." They estimated earnings of $7.50 and $12.50 for the previous year.

The above described activities constituted the most important regular supplements to the farm incomes that were had by the people of the community. During the year of the survey, however, there were two other very important supplements shared by a rather large part of the community. These, though temporary, were of such size that attention must be given to them. They were the work of the Federal government, done through the Civil Works Administration and the Chehaw County Emergency Relief Committee.

During the winter prior to the survey the CWA engaged 43 per cent of the householders, or members of their families, for parts of approximately six weeks. Most of these persons were engaged in building and repairing roads and bridges in the community. For this work they received a total of $3524.35, an average of almost $42 per worker. Those employed were scattered throughout the occupational classes. One-fourth of them were landowners, one-fourth were related tenants, 40 per cent were unrelated tenants and the others were from the miscellaneous group. In general the work was distributed in such a way that it augmented the incomes of the lower economic classes. The average worker from the tenant classes received approximately $48 while the average owner who worked earned only $32. The largest earnings were received by the sharecroppers, an average of $57 for those employed. Expressed in terms of amount earned *per member of the occupational class,* the average owner received $12, the average tenant $22. But when the earnings are expressed in such terms facts are brought to light which suggest that in some cases factors other than need may have influenced the distribution. The average large landowner with tenants received more aid than did the small owner, roughly $12 per householder as compared with $9. Among the white tenants, those related to their landlords received more than did the tenants who were not related, the respective sums being $35 and $27. The group receiving least aid, however, was that of the negro. Only three negroes in the community were employed at all, and they for an average of less than two weeks. The average negro sharecropper received 88 cents from the CWA during the year.

The second source of aid came through the County Emergency Relief Committee, the CERC. This organization was set up for the purpose of giving relief to needy people. During the four months prior to the survey, the period for which figures were available, a total of $1660.91 in cash or goods was given to various families in Upland Bend. Approximately one-half of this was distributed as home relief in the form of food, clothing, seed, household necessities or medical care, the other half came as pay for work done. In either case the help was presumably given only to needy persons. Twenty-nine per cent of all the families in the community received some assistance. The aid given to the various occupational classes varied. Less than 15 per cent of the land-owners, 34 per cent of the renters, and 43 per cent of the share-croppers received help. The average received per family receiving aid was $29. The average per family for all families in the community was $8.50.

Indications are that this aid was distributed more directly on the basis of need than were the CWA funds. The average landowner received only $3, the average related tenant $10, the average un-related white tenant $13.50, and the average negro $9.50. Aid through this agency was granted only on application, and an analy-sis of the percentage of those applying who were granted aid lends support to the assumption of equitable distribution. Of all fami-lies applying, 70 per cent were granted some aid. Three of every five applications from related tenants, three of every four from un-related tenants, and five of every six applications from negroes were accepted. The negroes seemed to hesitate about applying but a larger percentage of their applications were granted than were those of any other occupational group.

The differences between the distributions of the CWA and the CERC are probably accounted for in terms of two factors. First, there was some difference in the objectives of the two organiza-tions. The chief objective of the CWA, it will be recalled, was to stimulate spending through an extensive distribution of funds among those with limited incomes, while the CERC was designed more directly to relieve distress among the underprivileged. A second factor which may help to explain the differences was the nature of the personnel of the two agencies. The CERC was rather carefully staffed with people who had some profes-sional training. The CWA staff was of necessity hastily drawn together and matters other than professional fitness probably had a part in determining the selection of the personnel.

From such varied sources as those we have described came the income of the people. Depending chiefly on the sale of cotton, nevertheless, large numbers of families had additional funds from the sale of other crops, from the endeavors of the housewives and from work, on the part of the householders, at occupations other than farming. Temporarily, these were further supplemented with Federal aid through two of its agencies. In terms of dollars earned the returns from these sources were, with few exceptions, never great. It was obvious, however, that having such supplements placed the recipients among the favored few. The best evidence of the need for additional cash was found in the struggles that ensued when the possibility of part-time work presented itself. A chance to board the teacher or drive the school bus or work on the road was the occasion for bringing to bear all available pressure. A political following would be developed if necessary and possible for the sole purpose of keeping a daughter on the teaching staff of the local school. And the men responsible for such matters as distributing work relief were almost sure to incur the lasting enmity of persons who felt that the distribution was unjust because it failed to include them.

BUYING

For people with limited incomes, such as were found in Upland Bend, the story of what their money went for is quickly told. The demands of those who had some resources did not seem to be great, and for the masses of the people buying was of necessity reduced to a minimum. For large numbers even the small amount of buying done was made possible only through a credit arrangement. In order to finance a living through the long months of producing a crop they were compelled to borrow against this crop. Consequently, most of them had spent their income before it was secured.

The stock of country stores is commonly limited, consequently the extent to which the needs of a people are satisfied by such stores is an item of considerable significance. In Upland Bend the buying was most all done locally. There were a few exceptions such as more expensive items of clothing, farm equipment, and incidental purchases made on a trip to town. All of the householders interviewed listed some one or more of the local stores as their most common buying place, and every tenth one of them, every third sharecropper, reported he never bought anything elsewhere. Three-fourths of the families bought all food, other than that produced on the farm, and one-third bought all clothing except that which was made at home from the local merchants. The small amount of goods that were not purchased locally were obtained from nearby towns. Usually such purchases were made irregularly or whenever they were in town. It was found, however, that sales advertised by stores from the nearby towns were often the occasion for a trip to town. Only three families in the community mentioned mailorder houses as among the three most common buying places and less than one-half of the families in the community had ever "ordered anything from the catalogue." The mail received in the community, which will be given more complete analysis in a later chapter, supports the conclusion that the large number of mailorder catalogues which the people had served actually to entertain their possessors more than to guide them in buying goods. The ten-cent stores and cheap chain stores located in a nearby larger town were most often patronized on out-of-the-community buying trips. These emporiums also served as loafing places as well as satisfiers of more material needs.

In number at least the community was fairly well supplied with stores. There were four within its boundaries and five others within three miles of the homes of certain of the householders. The average home was within three-fourths of a mile of a store and only four homes in the entire community were as much as three miles away. Two of the local stores, one operated by a local landowner and the other by a daughter of one of the owners, received the largest part of the trade of the community. The stores were all of the type that is very familiar in the country, namely, the general store. The stock which they offered their customers, would be best described as 'staple' rather than 'fancy', and very little choice was offered in any department. The significance of this point can be understood by examining the list below of the entire stock of groceries and of dry goods and clothing that was found in the largest and most popular store in the community:

GROCERIES

Apples—dried	Jello	Rice
Baking powder	Lard—packages	Spices—mixed
Beans—dried	Lye	Salt meat
Bon Ami cleanser	Matches	Sardines—canned
Catsup	Mackerel—canned	Sugar
Corn—dried	Meal	Syrup
Coffee	Oranges	Turnips
Dill pickles (barrel)	Pepper—black	Vanilla extract
Flour	Peas—dried	Vinegar—barrel
	Washing powder	

Clothing, Dry Goods, Notions

Buttons	Shirts—work	Hats—straw
Caps—boys aviation	Socks—cotton	Needles
Cloth (in bolt)	Stockings—cotton	Overalls
Organdie	Underwear	Pins
Cretonne	men's one-piece	straight
Duck	Dress binding	safety
Gingham	(2 kinds)	Thread
Outing	Elastic	
Shirting	Gloves—cotton	

The items having the most rapid turnover according to the merchants' reports were: flour, lard, gasoline, coffee, snuff, smoking and chewing tobacco, turpentine, and castor oil. An analysis of the actual annual purchases for a number of families, most of which were tenants, indicated the items most often bought. These in order of frequency were: flour, snuff, lard, sugar, coffee, cloth, overalls, tobacco, salt, shoes, and oats (for animal feed). The demand for snuff was so great, it is interesting to note, that one merchant claimed he had once made a single purchase of $1000 worth.

That these stores did serve the needs of great numbers is shown through an analysis of the purchases made by selected families. Typically the sharecroppers and many of the smaller owners who were "short on cash" bought everything from or through one of the local merchants. If the merchant did not have in stock the article desired—or a substitute—an order from him to some other merchant was given. In this way, all purchases made by persons having such arrangements were reported in the one account. Availability of the books of a merchant in the community made possible a detailed study of the purchases made over rather long periods of time by several families. As the reader examines these accounts he should recall the amount of money which these people made and he will see that the accounts are in keeping with the purchases made possible by such incomes.

A tenant, who had resources enough to pay cash rental for his land during nine months spent $131.62. His account for the month of June, which appeared to be typical, included the following list of items:

June 2 Oats ($2.50), flour (.80), sugar (.50), coffee (.30),
           oil, kerosene, (.20), socks (.10)........................ 4.40
    " 6 Vinegar, lard, snuff ($2.55), cash ($1.00)............... 3.55

June 10 Sugar, shoes.. 2.35
  "   13 Flour (.80), 1 sack oats, ($2.55), sweep plow
          (.35) 3.70
  "   23 Flour, coffee, snuff ($1.35), soap, lye (.15)......... 1.50
  "   29 Cash ($1.00), flour, matches, soap, soda, lids and
          rings for jars, ($1.90)....................................... 2.90

        Total purchases for month..$18.40

A furnishing tenant whose year's expenses amounted to $196.48
made purchases during the months of March and April as follows:

March 4 Flour, sugar, coffee, soda................................. 2.15
  "   6 Two curry combs, potatoes (.40),
          rat poison (.35),... .75
  "   9 Snuff and insect powder................................... .55
  "   14 Bolts and nuts.. .20
  "   17 Flour and 2 plow points................................. 1.50
  "   21 Overalls, shirts, rat poison............................. 4.40
  "   24 Potatoes and bolts.. .40
  "   28 Plow, three shovels.. .65
  "   30 Two sacks flour... 1.20
  "   31 General (.34) mule collar and snuff ($1.25).......... 1.59

        Total purchases for month $13.39

April 4 Cloth, 19½ yards.. 1.95
  "   4 Sugar .... .50
  "   8 Cash ($5.00), plow points, crickets, (.40).......... 5.40
  "   10 Two sacks flour ($1.30)................................. 1.30
  "   12 Two yds. oil cloth (.75), overalls (.55).............. 1.30
  "   15 Tobacco .... .15
  "   18 Planter 4.80
  "   19 Thread, lye, snuff.. .70
  "   22 Flour and sugar... 1.90

        Total purchases for month $18.00

A small owner with 25 acres and one mule spent $103.46 in a
year. During August when his garden was probably supplying
most of the needs of his family, the following list of commodities
were bought:

August 2 Syrup... .30
  "   4 Flour .... .90
  "   5 Five lbs. lard.. .40
  "   15 Flour, tobacco, snuff....................................... .65
  "   18 Twelve lbs. flour, snuff, tobacco..................... .65
  "   22 Flour .... .55
  "   23 File and tobacco (.30), flour, lard ($1.55)......... 1.85
  "   26 Salt .... .10
  "   30 Matches, soap, snuff....................................... .15

        Total purchases for month.................................$ 5.55

A negro sharecropper during a year made total purchases of $112.36. His account for December included the following:

Dec.	3	Flour	.95
"	9	Sugar	.25
"	10	Two pr. shoes (bought in town but charged to acct.)	3.50
"	16	Flour	.95
"	30	Flour, 100 lbs. salt, overalls	3.30
		Total purchases for month	$ 8.95

None of the people bought everything with cash, but one-third of the householders, most of them tenants, reported that they never paid cash for their purchases. The sharecroppers almost invariably bought on credit, paying up when the cotton was sold. Ninety per cent of them had credit at one of the local stores arranged through either the landlord or the merchant. Merchants who handled such accounts were known as "furnishing merchants." The two larger stores in the community furnished a large number of tenants and several small owners. The accounts were secured ordinarily by a mortgage on the crop and on any personal property which the borrowers owned. The interest rate was reported as 8 per cent annually. Examination of the details, however, showed that the rate of interest was actually much higher than this. Eight per cent was charged for the total amount bought for the total period of time during which purchases were made. If we assume that purchases were made at regular intervals this actually represents an annual interest rate of approximately 14 per cent. A fee of $1.35 for filing the mortgage at the courthouse also had to be paid by the borrower. In the case of some tenants the landlords handled the account, at the same rate of interest. When the landlord furnished the tenant no mortgage was required since the law gives the owner a lien on all crops produced on his land. In either case the tenant settled—if he could—annually. If he was lucky he came through the year even; if unlucky, he owed more at the end than at the beginning.

The following summaries of the accounts of four men substantiate this last point. It will be seen that the first man having a good year managed to wipe out his old debt and finish the year with a balance of $3.32. The second man made but slight reduction in his debt, the third man started even and cleared $3.67, but the fourth man was $10 further in debt at the end of his year's labors. These accounts were summarized at random from the merchant's files and he said they were in no sense unusual.

A White Sharecropper

Jan. 1, balance due		$104.31
Purchases for 9 months and 18 days	186.74	
Oct. 18, Balance due		291.05
Paid (upon delivery of his cotton)		294.37
Credit (left with merchant for starting a new year)		3.32

A Furnishing Tenant

Mar. 25, Balance due		$123.17
Purchases for year	127.62	
Apr. 1, Balance due		250.79
Paid (upon sale of his cotton)		159.94
Balance due		90.85

A Small Owner

Apr. 15, Opened account		
Oct. 15, Balance due		96.64
Paid (upon delivery of his cotton)		100.31
Credit		3.67

A Negro Sharecropper

Mar. 1, Balance due		$105.79
Purchases for year	157.11	
Feb. 22, Balance due		262.90
Paid (turned over 4½ bales cotton to the merchant)		147.50
Balance due		115.40

Not all of the trade of the community was carried on through the medium of cash or credit. A considerable part of it was done by means of barter. This was especially true among the land-owners and renters. The renters, the highest group of tenants, did more bartering than any other group of people in the community. The unrelated tenants did more than the related groups, probably, again, due to the tendency of the related tenants to depend on their relatives, the landlords. Only 30 per cent of the white sharecroppers and 23 per cent of the negroes reported they ever had anything to barter, while roughly 70 per cent of the others did. Eggs, chickens, butter, corn, potatoes, cotton seed, syrup and peanuts, in that order, were the most common items exchanged. The extent to which trading of this sort was prevalent may be understood when we report that 10,000 dozen eggs were taken in on this basis each year by the leading merchant. Not only did he take them in trade, but often he in turn traded them to traveling salesmen for new stock. One of our interviewers was present on an occasion of this sort and overheard a "drummer" agree to accept seven dozen eggs in exchange for twelve boxes of Chipso. Barter was usually on the basis of latest market quotations, although when the trade could not be made on such a basis neither party to the transaction was averse to bargaining.

ECONOMIC SELF-SUFFICIENCY

The average farm home has far more economic self-sufficiency, particularly in food and clothing, than does an urban home. In this respect the homes of Upland Bend were typical ones. A summer garden, which they claimed supplied all of the vegetables for the family during the long summer months, with some left over for canning and drying, was reported by all of the families in the community except four. In addition, one-half of the families cultivated winter gardens. In this way a year-round supply of fresh vegetables was available. Winter gardens were found on as many as 74 per cent of the places of the owning families. Among the tenants, especially the sharecroppers, they were not so common. Only every sixth white sharecropper and every fourth negro reported this type of food supply. Tomatoes, beans, cabbage, potatoes, sweet potatoes, peas, and corn were the summer vegetables most often grown, while the winter gardens were largely confined to collards, turnips, and cabbage. There were no regular orchards in the community, but a few fruit trees were often found about the places. Three-fourths of the owners and one-half of the tenants had a number of fruit trees, mostly peaches and pears, in their yards. These sources of fruit supply could be supplemented materially, however, with blackberries, wild grapes, scuppernongs, and muscadines which were very commonly found in the fields.

Much of the produce from the gardens and fruits and berries from the fields were canned, dried or preserved for the use of the family during seasons when fresh supplies were not to be had. The curing of meat, too, was very common. Pork was the universal meat. Those who did not raise their own hogs bought salt pork from the local merchants. But numbers of people supplemented their pork supply with an occasional beef, the surplus of

This paling fence, being built at odd times by the owner, was intended to enclose a vegetable garden.   Such fences were frequently seen in Upland Bend, probably because wire was expensive.

which was canned.   Even young chickens were canned so that "fried chicken and hot biscuits" could be enjoyed during the winter months.

The amount of foodstuffs "put by" in the homes gives a picture of the independence which they enjoyed in this realm and, partially at least, explains the limited stock of groceries which we have seen the local merchants carried.   A group of housewives reported that during the year prior to the survey they had canned an average of approximately 600 quarts and had dried on the average almost 30 bushels of foods.   This represented more than 100 quarts of canned goods and five bushels of dried food per member of the family.   Vegetables, relishes, pickles, fruit, meats, even soups were canned.   Potatoes, apples, pears, peaches, beans, and peas were dried.   In addition, the typical family had killed and cured two hogs and rendered 15 gallons of lard.   The owners had a much larger supply than the tenants.   This was particularly true of dried foods and meats.   In canned goods they had on the average one-third more, but had twice the amount of dried foods and cured meats that the tenants had.

Below is reported the materials canned, dried, preserved, and cured by two families during the summer and fall prior to the survey. One was the winter supply for a large landowner's family of six. The other supplied a sharecropper's family of five.

CANNED	A Large Land-owner Had:		A Sharecrop-per Had:	
Apples	---		6	quarts
Beans	---		16	"
Beef	65	quarts	---	
Beets	18	"	6	"
Blackberries	50	"	16	"
Chili Sauce	30	"	---	
Chowchow	12	"	12	"
Cucumbers	20	"	8	"
Jellies	50	"	---	
Krout	50	"	25	"
Muscadines	---		10	"
Peaches	200	"	60	"
Pears	15	"	10	"
Sausage	30	"	19	"
Soup mixture	30	"	15	"
Tomatoes	200	"	15	"
Total	770	quarts	218	quarts

DRIED, STORED, AND CURED:

Apples	2	bushels	1	peck
Beans	1	bushel	½	"
Peaches	---		1	bushel
Peas			½	peck
Potatoes (Irish)	20	bushels	---	
Potatoes (Sweet)	40	"	---	
Cured Meat				
Hams	8		2	
Shoulders	8		2	
Middlings	8		2	
Lard	25	gallons	7	gallons

Clothing did not appear to be as plentiful, comparatively, as the store of foods. Like the food supply, however, a large part of the clothing, particularly that of the women and children, was made at home. The average man had a "Sunday suit", a pair of "Sunday shoes" and a good shirt. For everyday wear he had two pairs of overalls, two work shirts, a pair of work shoes, and two suits of long underwear. Among the men, work shirts and often underwear were made at home. The "good" clothes were usually worn for several years. The average age of suits owned by 17 selected men was 4 years, and one householder was pleased to

report that he was still wearing the suit in which he had been
married 11 years before. There was some difference between
the occupational groups, but not much. The larger owners usually
had an overcoat or raincoat, two Sunday shirts instead of one,
and perhaps a tie. Seven large owners, of whom inquiry was
made, reported in fact an average of 14 different garments while
the average number was 11 for a like number of small owners and
tenants.

The complete wardrobe of a large owner and of a tenant consisted of the following garments.

Garments	An Owner Had:		A Tenant Had:	
	No.	Age	No.	Age
Sunday suit	1	5 yrs.	1	4 yrs.
Sunday shirt	2	2 "	2	2 and 3 yrs.
Sunday shoes	1	1 yr.	1	Unknown
Socks	6	Unknown	2 prs.	New
Overalls	3	"	3	1 and 2 yrs.
Work shirts	6	"	1	New
Work shoes	1	"	1	1 yr.
Underwear	2	"	2	2 yrs.
Raincoat	1	2 yrs.	None	
Tie	1	2 "	None	
Odd trousers	1	1 yr.	None	

The women had but few more items of wearing apparel than the
men. In fact, the families investigated reported for the average
wife only one more garment than for the husband. The garments
of the women were in general less expensive than those of men
and many more of them were made at home. More than two-thirds
of all garments reported by 17 housewives were made at home.

The clothing of the young children was entirely homemade except for shoes and stockings and an occasional coat or sweater.
With the older children the same sex differences were found as
between husband and wife. The boys and girls had about the same
number of garments, but most of the items for boys were ready-
made, those for girls were homemade. Class distinctions, again,
were not pronounced. On the average, tenant wives had three
less garments than did landowners' wives, and the children of
tenants had correspondingly less. Too, more of the male children
of tenants wore homemade clothes.

Typical for a small owner's family were these items:

Garment	Age	Where Made
The housewife had:		
1 cotton print dress	New	At home
4 work dresses	2 yrs.	" "
2 suits underwear	3 "	" "
1 coat	9 "	Ready made
1 pair light shoes	2 "	" "
1 pair work shoes	1 "	" "
2 pairs cotton stockings	New	" "
1 pair silk stockings	2 yrs.	" "

Her daughter (16 years old) had:		
1 cotton print dress	New	At home
2 cotton print school dresses	"	" "
2 cotton print dresses	2 yrs.	" "
2 blouses	1 "	" "
2 suits of underwear	2 "	" "
1 wool skirt	2 "	Ready made (made over)
1 coat	5 "	" "
1 pair oxfords	1 "	" "
2 pairs of stockings	1 "	" "

And the baby (1 year old) had:		At home
1 pair white rompers		" "
3 gingham aprons		" "
3 cotton socks (pairs)		" "
3 flannel petticoats		" "
3 shirts		" "
13 diapers		" "
1 pair shoes		Ready made
3 pairs stockings		" "

A tenant's family had the garments listed below:

Garment	Age	Where Made
The housewife had:		
2 print dresses	1 yr.	At home
3 work dresses	1 "	" "
2 suits underclothes	2 yrs.	" "
2 nice print dresses	New	Ready made
1 pair work shoes	1 yr.	" "
1 pair Sunday shoes	1 "	" "

A son (15 years old) had:		
1 Sunday suit	1 yr.	Ready made
2 pair overalls	1 "	" "
1 pair work shoes	1 "	" "
1 pair Sunday shoes	1 "	" "
2 work shirts	1 "	At home

A daughter (10 years old) had:		
5 cotton dresses	1 yr.	At home
3 work dresses	2 yrs.	" "
1 Sunday dress	New	" "
4 suits underwear	1 yr.	" "
1 pair shoes	1 "	Ready made
1 coat	1 "	" "
1 sweater	2 yrs.	" "

And the baby son (3 years old) had:

8 suits unionalls	1 yr.	At home	
2 Sunday suits	1 "	" "	
3 suits underwear	1 "	" "	
1 Sunday suit	1 "	Ready made	
1 pair Sunday shoes	1 "	" "	
1 sweater	1 "	" "	

When tools are scarce and money is scarcer, ingenuity is at a premium. This homemade lathe was typical of many clever aids to work developed by the more skilled workers in Upland Bend.

Other evidences of self-sufficiency were found in the homes themselves. Quilting was the favorite leisure time activity of the older women and was popular with many of the younger married women. Three-fourths of the women reported they made towels and wash cloths from cotton bags. The average farmer was a fair blacksmith, a shop being a rather common outbuilding among the owning classes. Automobile owners or their sons fixed punctures, pumped up their own tires, and did simple repair work. Most householders had a shoe-repairing outfit. And hair-cutting, though developed as a semi-skilled activity by a limited number of local persons, was done by some member of the family in many homes. The typical home was furnished with some homemade furniture, a favorite being a long bench or two which served to seat the family at the dining table. The dining room of one of the largest landowners, the man reporting the highest income for the year of the study, had two such benches. Other pieces of home-

This homemade lye hopper, although still in use, was considered old-fashioned in Upland Bend. Lye was still used extensively but was more commonly bought at the store

made furniture included chairs, tables, dressing tables, and occasionally a bed or a mattress.

On the farm itself economic self-sufficiency was not so much
in evidence as in the home. Enough feed for their stock was
normally raised by only two-thirds of the farmers. This percentage was lower for the small owners, and but slightly more
than one-third of the sharecroppers raised feed sufficient for the
few animals they had. This in spite of the fact that the owner
usually permitted the tenant to raise such feed. Commonly all
feed except cotton seed was bought. The farmers usually kept
the cotton seed from their crops to feed their stock, but, at that
some of them had to buy from the surplus supply of other local
farmers. Corn was reported as sold by only 22 owners, less than
one-third of the total number. Cribs for storing corn, in fact,
were altogether lacking on two-thirds of the farms. The animals
which the farmers used were in most instances imported from outside. None of the farmers bred mules although large numbers of
them were used. Cattle and hogs were bred locally but not to an
extent that would supply the community needs. Though the implements used for farming were usually simple in construction,
they came largely from out of the community. The local black-
smiths made very little of what the farmers used in the way of
tools. The local merchants carried nothing in stock except small
items such as plow lines, horse collars, and mule shoes. They were
not averse to serving as the middleman, however, making such
purchases for the farmer at a commission. Approximately 40 per
cent of those tenants who furnished their own tools and 23 per
cent of the owners bought their equipment through the local merchants.

For maintaining the fertility of their farms, too, the community
had recourse to outside aid. Cover crops and manures from the
animals were far from furnishing the degree of productivity which
cotton demanded of the soil. The use of commercial fertilizers
was practically universal. A poor cotton year was commonly expressed as a year in which "the crop didn't pay for the fertilizer."
The cost of fertilizer was shared by the owner and the tenant. If
the landowner could pay the bill and deduct the tenant's part at
eight per cent interest before the final settlement, the price was
cheaper; but, if this cash was not available, the furnishing mer-

chant would supply the needs at the credit price, which ran from 12 to 20 per cent higher, and add it to the purchaser's account. The total cost for enough fertilizer for one man's crop was typically about $50.00, but it was not unusual for it to amount to as much as $100.00. For the larger owners, on whose land several crops were being raised, the cost was, of course, much greater.

Life in Upland Bend was built on an economy of scarcity. Limited incomes with an accompanying lack of material possessions were the rule. The crying need for cash was so evident in many directions. But there are other facets to the picture that perhaps will bear reformulation for purposes of emphasis.

Economic inequalities among the occupational groups, while perhaps not so great as would be found in modern urban communities, did nevertheless exist. The people in general had little, but for large numbers of them, for most of the sharecroppers and for many of the other tenants and the smaller owners, only the barest necessities were available. The standard of living made possible for a family with an annual income of $2500 may not be too high even in the country, but an income of $150 must be well below a "subsistance level."

Distinctions between negroes and whites in the economic realm appeared to be occupational rather than racial in nature. Most of the negroes were sharecroppers, but there were no consistent economic differences between them and white people of the same occupational grouping. The only serious exception to this, the distribution of CWA work in the community, probably resulted from the fact that the *mores* of the people were such that the allotment of government work was as much a political as an economic matter.

The one-crop farming which they engaged in, aside from its effects on the land itself and aside from the element of risk involved in depending on one crop alone, caused most of the people to live without cash for a large part of the year, and necessitated their operating on credit—at a high rate of interest. The farmers seemed to realize this and were willing to do anything about it except change their methods of farming. Part-time jobs were in great demand, but diversified farming was practically non-existent.

The tenants were not situated so they could initiate such a program and the owners with few exceptions had not found it possible to move in that direction.

The homes, through necessity or choice, were self-sustaining to a rather high degree. It was among the homes of the well-to-do, the economically superior where this self-sufficiency was most evident. And, finally, on the farms themselves there was no such independence of outside aid. Farm animals were imported, even a large part of their feed came from the outside, and the fertility of the soil was maintained chiefly through the use of commercial fertilizers.

Chapter IV

CIVIC LIFE

Contacts with government constitute an inevitable part of the experience of the people of a community. In rural sections where the population is scattered and the volume of business is comparatively small the citizen is not made aware of the presence of government as frequently as is the case in urban areas. The tendency of government to exercise an increasing influence over the activities of the people is now being felt in the country as well as in the city. The people of Upland Bend met agencies of government when they recorded deeds, registered mortgages, built roads, followed health regulations, entered into agreements concerning the animals and crops they raised, received emergency relief funds, and when they sent their children to school. These events and their effect on life in Upland Bend have been treated elsewhere. In the present chapter it is our purpose to describe the official representatives of the county who resided in the local community, its services in the nation's wars, and its relations with the courts of law. After this attention will be given to the subject of voting and to the activities that were connected with it. For reasons that will be explained later the treatment of this subject will be comparatively elaborate.

County Officers, Veterans, and the Courts

The government of Chehaw County was represented in Upland Bend by a number of local persons who held official positions. The people of the community met these officers as friends and neighbors for the most part but, as occasion demanded, business of an official nature was transacted with them. In Beat 36, in which most of Upland Bend was located, there was one justice of the peace. He was an elderly man, not otherwise employed, but in former years he had been a prominent landowner and merchant. As compensation for official services he received 75 cents for issuing warrants and $1.00 for conducting trials of petty misdemeanors. The constable and deputy sheriff was a tenant farmer who was a distant kinsman of a prominent landowner. Landowners themselves ordinarily did not hold positions of this sort. This officer received 25 cents for serving court summons, 75 cents for summons and complaints, and $3.00 for making arrests. The local Registrar of Vital Statistics of Health, a large landowner, was paid 25 cents for each registration of birth or death. Five Upland Bend men, all large landowners, acted as managers, clerks, or returning officer for the voting box in Beat 36 during the May and June primaries. For this work each received $2.00 for each of the two days he served. Three large landowners served as trustees of the local school. One of these was also a member of the county board of education, for which service the maximum compensation was $50.00 a year. Thus all told twelve Upland Bend men served the county and the local community during the year in which the survey was in progress. With a single exception they were or had been landowners. The official capacities in which they worked were of a minor nature, for the most part. Only small sums of money were received by way of compensation but these were welcome on account of the generally low level of income.

The men of Upland Bend had not failed to serve their country in its wars. Complete records of services rendered were available in the cases of sixteen men only. Fifteen of these were white men; one was a negro. One veteran had served in the Spanish-American War; the others, in the World War. Three were in the navy; the rest, in the army. None of those of whom we have record had risen to commissioned rank in either service. Several World War veterans had asked for pensions but only one request had been granted. The beneficiary in this case was a negro who received $37.50 per month.

A few of the citizens of Upland Bend, like those of other communities, had fallen into the hands of the law. During the two years prior to the survey two white men and one negro had come before the inferior court. The charges were trespassing after warning, escaping jail, abusive language, and forfeiture of another's bond. Only one man, he against whom the two charges last named had been made, was taken to jail. He was found guilty, fined $20.00, and sentenced to a total of 150 days hard labor. The second case was nol-prossed; the third, that of the negro, was set aside. Two of the three, including the negro, were small landowners; the remaining one was an unrelated tenant.

Six men, all white, had come to the attention of the circuit court. Two of these had been charged with grand larceny and concealing stolen property and both had been jailed. The case against one, a small landowner, had been nol-prossed; but the other, the son of a small owner, had been sentenced to four years in the penitentiary and was out on a $3000.00 bond pending the outcome of an appeal. This man was the one against whom two charges had been made in the inferior court. The four remaining men, all of whom were related tenants, were charged with violation of the prohibition law in one case and with distilling in the others. The first of the four plead guilty and had been sentenced to 110 days hard labor for costs and punishment. The other three also had been found guilty and each had received a sentence of one year. The evils of liquor troubled the ministers of Upland Bend to a considerable extent. The cases above recited provided some of the incidents, no doubt, that moved the ministers to the decided views they held on this subject.

Taking as examples the seven white men who had been brought before the courts we can describe the typical man to be arrested in the following terms. He was about twenty-eight years of age, a husband, and the father of children. He had been born in the community and was a tenant. The small farm he occupied was not worked very hard if at all. From this and from some supplementary work, such as that on the roads, he obtained a cash income of $75.00 per year which probably did not include returns from violation of the liquor laws. The possessions he owned were reported as worth about $75.00. In general he was not as well-to-do a man as his neighbors. The smallness of the number of court cases over a period of two years in a population that numbered more than 1000 souls is impressive. The people tended to be tolerant, doubtless, of minor illegalities on the part of friends, neighbors, and relatives but it seems reasonable to conclude that the great majority of the population kept well within the law as far as serious violation was concerned.

VOTING AND THE VOTERS

Voting is one of the most important of the civic responsibilities that demand attention in a democratic society. By this means the citizens express their will on questions of policy and choose the men who are to manage the public business. In so doing they determine the course of political development over the next succeeding period of years and exercise the sovereign right of control over the government that belongs to them. Voting takes place in rural sections usually in only one year of every two. But the preliminary events which the candidates stage last over a period of several months during which time the attention of the voters is continually solicited. The exciting nature of an election campaign causes it to stand out as one of the most conspicuous features of life in a rural community. On this ground alone a considerable amount of attention should be given to the subject of voting in a study of country life.

The fact that a campaign leading to the Democratic Primary election of May the first was under way at the time facilitated the effort of the survey to obtain reliable and detailed information. It was desirable to learn who the voters were, to examine the nature of the task the voters faced, and to look into the situation of the candidates. Especially interesting were the campaign techniques which the candidates employed to persuade the voters. What the people of Upland Bend saw and did under these circumstances and how well prepared they were to cope with the problem are matters of great concern to those who desire to understand social conditions. What went on in Upland Bend was not wholly detached from the political situation that existed in the county and in the state at large. To this wider background reference will be made whenever it is necessary to promote understanding. For these several reasons it was decided to study voting and the activities connected with it in considerable detail and the remainder of the chapter will be devoted to the subject.

The number of citizens who fail to exercise the sovereign right of suffrage in American communities is astonishingly large. Upland Bend was no exception to the rule. Of the 195 householders whom the surveyors interviewed only 85 or 44 per cent reported that they were qualified to vote. All of the 85 were white men— 47 being landowners, 21 related tenants, 13 unrelated tenants, and 4 of the miscellaneous group. Of the total number of landowners in the community 68 per cent were qualified; of the related and unrelated tenants 58 and 27 per cent were qualified. As for the housewives only 35 had registered. These included 24 landowning women, 5 related tenants, 3 unrelated tenants, and 3 of the miscellaneous group. In general, the situation was as follows. The negroes did not vote. Of the 330 eligible white householders and housewives only 37 per cent were qualified. The great majority of these (81 per cent) were landowners or their related tenants. Voting was pretty largely a prerogative of the men.

Why did so many of the people fail to vote? The preponderance of the landowning classes in the registration lists suggests that economic considerations had much to do with it. Registration for voting cost $1.50 a year in the form of a poll tax. In a community in which cash was as scarce as it was in Upland Bend, $1.50 was a lot of money. If a householder and his wife both wanted to vote the cost would be $3.00 a year, or a considerable percentage of the average annual cash income of many families. If they failed to pay the tax one or more years they could not register again except by paying the entire accumulation of back taxes. Only veterans were legally exempt from these demands. The vicissitudes of fortune in Upland Bend, where so many of the families lived very near to the margin of existence, had piled up heavy accumulations of back taxes against the names of a very large proportion of the people who, otherwise, were eligible to register. To pay $30.00, $15.00 or even $5.00 in back poll taxes was simply beyond their capacity unless they valued voting more than they did shoes, flour, or plow shares. The right to vote thus depended on a substantial money qualification that to many people in Upland Bend was practically prohibitive: it was the right of a privileged minority.

It is possible that the men and women of Upland Bend who did not go to the polls needed some other important things more than they needed the right to vote. But people who cannot vote are not in the best position to press directly for the consideration of such of their needs as can be met by agencies of government. Their interests, economic and social, can be neglected more or less with impunity by more favored classes of the population, if these were disposed to do so. Lack of effective access to the suffrage may thus operate to increase the difficulties that attend the efforts of submerged elements to rise above the conditions which oppress them. The dangers to a democratic society that inhere in this situation have not escaped the attention of public-minded citizens and statesmen. In the State Legislature, that assembled in Montgomery after the election with which we are here concerned, a constitutional amendment was proposed to change the law in such a way as to restore to the voting rolls persons who were delinquent in their poll taxes. A vigorous debate ensued in the Legislature and the question was widely discussed in the newspapers; but the bill failed of passage. The situation in Upland Bend, therefore, continued as it was and the problems remains to challenge the best efforts of thoughtful citizens to find a sound solution.

The Voters' Task

The citizens of Upland Bend who were qualified were confronted with a task of considerable magnitude when they attempted to exercise the right of suffrage. Of the factors that made voting difficult one of the most obvious was the multiplicity of offices and of candidates. For the office of district Representative in Congress there were 3 candidates. For 16 state executive and judicial offices 30 men were running. Seven candidates had offered for 3 state legislative posts. There were 22 aspirants for 9 county offices and 8 candidates for places on the State Democratic Executive Committee. The total number of offices to be filled was 30 and 71 candidates aspired to fill them. The ballot on which the names of the offices and candidates were printed, was more than two feet long.

The nature of the duties of some of the many offices must have been very obscure to some of the electors of Upland Bend as indeed it was to their fellow citizens in numerous other communities. A considerable number of the candidates, especially those who were running for state offices, did not appear in the community in person. As far as these applicants were concerned the voters were forced to make up their minds on the basis of indirect evidence that had been shuffled and reshuffled considerably before it reached them. More than thirty of the candidates, however, did visit Upland Bend. Choosing between these alone was enough to tax the abilities of any group of conscientious electors. The long ballot is said to be very democratic by those who favor or who profit from it. The points above mentioned suggest that the words, *confusing* and *baffling,* describe it more precisely. Much of the voting with a ballot of this kind in Upland Bend, as elsewhere, must have been like a blind stab in the dark.

Further increasing the difficulties connected with voting was the fact that the ballot was not certain to be secret. It was indeed supposed to be secret in Upland Bend as elsewhere but the mechanics of the voting made it possible for unscrupulous politicians to ascertain the choices of any of the electorate whom they wished to investigate. It was a common saying in the county that a citizen who had forgotten how he voted could tell well enough by noticing the looks the candidates gave him the next morning. The significance of experiences of this kind had not escaped the understanding of the people of the community. These conditions, they well knew, placed penalties on independent action and made it easier for selfish men to control them.

The difficulties of voting did not end here. During the several months of active campaigning that preceded the election the voters were subjected to all of the forms of appeal and propaganda which the seventy-one candidates and their workers could devise. The nature of the campaign techniques, as they impinged on the electorate in Upland Bend, will be described in some detail in a later section of this chapter. In the midst of the storm and stress of the battle the voters had to try to make up their minds on the innumerable issues which the candidates called to their attention. Many of the issues such as improved systems of taxation, uniform methods of county accounting, and the reorganization of city and county governments were highly technical in nature. Others such as a minimum school term of seven months, reduction of the ad valorem tax on homesteads, and the establishment of a state department of labor involved economic, social, and political implications of the gravest nature. On major problems of this kind even the experts disagreed: yet the average voter was asked to make quick decisions concerning them. At the same time he had to try to determine what a candidate actually could or would do about them if he were elected.

Confronted with difficulties as above described the voters might well be expected to be very grateful for anything of an amusing nature that cropped out in the campaign. All the more welcome would such fun be if it came at the expense of the candidates who appeared to be so intimately connected with the troubles the voters were experiencing. Immediate benefits of a more tangible nature might not be unwelcome to many. Of these matters more will be said later. For our purposes here it is sufficient to add that the magnitude of the difficulties connected with voting may have bewildered many citizens to the extent that they were unwilling to undertake the responsibility. Thus a cultural equipment that was not equal to the demands made upon it may have cooperated with inadequate economic resources to reduce the number of voters.

THE CANDIDATE'S SITUATION

The candidates who sought the approval of the voters of Upland Bend were an interesting lot of men. In respect to schooling, breadth of experience, and economic resources the seekers-for-office were obviously superior to the general run of the electorate. Some had entered politics for the first time; others were veterans at the game. Some were liberally supplied with funds; others were comparatively poor. Some were young; others were well along in years. Most were men of good reputation; a few had records of questionable behavior in the past. But all, apparently, had been "bitten by the bee of politics."

Politics, it has been said, is the greatest game on earth. It is concerned with every kind of issue and the lives of all men are on the board. The competition is fierce but it is loaded with human interest. The players organize as fighting gangs but none knows what the next moment will bring. They must be prepared to cope with every trick of ingenuity their opponents can devise.

The men who threw their hats into the ring as candidates needed to be moved by powerful allures to be able to stand the gaff. They could count on a patient and courteous reception at the hands of the people if the situation was relieved with a reasonable amount of fun. They had to expect to be gouged for money in all sorts of ways—as presently shall be seen. Fear of the arguments or tactics which their rivals used against them was much on the candidates' minds. Some of their grounds for fear were frankly disclosed in newspapers and hand-bill literature. Examination of a few excerpts from materials that were distributed by aspirants for county offices will yield interesting insights into the situation that the candidates faced in Upland Bend as elsewhere in the county:

Fear of Younger Opponents

"In the evening of his life with his faculties unimpaired, and his heart more tender than ever, let us give him the greatest majority of votes ever given any citizen of this County. Thus endorsing his life's record of faithful service."

Should the Doors of Opportunity Be Barred Against the Younger Generation?

"Some day your boy or your girl may ask for a public office and surely today you are making sacrifices and efforts that your sons and daughters may become capable of filling some position. Change is inevitable and changes have the effect of promoting efficiency in government."

Gold Should Never Determine the Outcome of Any Election

"The amount of money I can and will be able to spend in my campaign will necessarily be limited. I have only a small income and have not been able to accumulate much of this world's goods, neither do I have any relatives who are able to finance any expensive campaign for me. What chance has a poor man if gold is to determine the outcome of an election; I earnestly seek your vote with the plea that the doors of opportunity not be barred against a poor man."

To the Legal and Illegal Voters Who Vote

"If you sell your franchise are you a man? If you let yourself be voted and do not exercise the right of freedom in this land of liberty for which our forefathers fought and died how can you expect to bring relief to the masses? You are, my friends, a traitor to your wife and babies when you sell your vote. Your vote is more precious than gold—certainly a drink of whiskey or the likelihood of a job should offer no inducement. Frankly I think Chehaw County needs just one election where whiskey and money do not do all of the talking."

Fear of Questionable Record in the Past

"To the moral Church element in the county which felt it was their sacred duty to defeat me I cherish nothing but good feeling. I know they did their duty as they saw it and chastised me with their votes as they would a child who had misbehaved. I hope they feel they have squared any punishment debt they owed me and that they will love me as I do all people and will give me an opportunity to show them I can take defeat in the right spirit and permit me to go ahead and accomplish something in life."

PRINTED MATERIAL AND LETTERS

Having considered the voters' task and the candidates' situation the reader is prepared to examine the methods by which candidates attempted to win the voters' approval. The customs attached to election campaigns are of many years standing. Rather well defined techniques have been developed which are described below under the headings—*Printed material and letters, political rallies, a single candidate's appearance,* and *"expense money."* How these were employed in Upland Bend and some of the values and abuses that adhere to each will be set forth in the following pages.

Printed material and letters constituted a substantial part of the total effort of the candidates to reach the voters of Upland Bend. Most of this material appeared in the form of "paid political advertisements" in the Daily News which was read regularly by a majority of the citizens who were qualified to vote. The ads varied greatly in size and the ads of some candidates appeared with greater frequency than those of others. A direct approach under his own name was the usual method but not infrequently the ad was signed by "friends" of the candidate. The content was concerned in some instances with arguments over issues. This was the case most notably with gubernatorial and legislative aspirants. Examination of these arguments would be interesting but the issues were too numerous and the discussion too complicated to be presented here. In most instances, however, the content of the ads, and especially of those dealing with county offices, was comparatively simple and quite personal.

Excerpts from a few ads of this nature are given elsewhere in this chapter. Supplementing these there is presented below a detailed list of ideas or points (other than argument on issues) that were taken from a large number of ads. This list of ideas may be thought of as a word-book of voters' interests, campaign stereotypes, and political shibboleths. The language in which they were couched tended to be general in nature if not quite vague. As to the motives involved and the value of such appeals in determining the selection of men to public office the reader may use his own imagination.

The candidate's past experience was referred to in most ads. It was described as wide, seasoned, successful, or qualifying for the office concerned. The candidate had a good education, long residence in the county, business or farming background or he was politically experienced. There were details of previous public service, he had worked for the church, for the people's welfare, he had helped the poor and needy, was poor himself or had worked his way through school.

Much was made of the candidate's personal traits. He was described as competent, efficient, progressive, ambitious, a "silver tongued" orator, fair, impartial, sympathetic, appreciative, optimistic, sober, courteous, courageous, honest, unselfish, unprejudiced, unbiased, trustworthy, conscientious or sincere. He was a veteran, a plain man, or a Christian gentleman of unquestioned character. He knew people, loved them, they loved him, he was young and vigorous or he believed in democracy. No man, no selfish interest, no political ring ever had or would hang its collar on his neck.

Promises were made. The seeker for office would secure men of good reputation to assist him, support all progressive and constructive tendencies, work for prosperity, give everybody a square deal or put new blood into the office. His administration would be business-like. Those who helped him bake the pie would help him eat it. There were no private axes which he wanted to grind for himself or anybody else.

The last group of ideas that appeared in the ads were miscellaneous in nature. Confidence of winning was expressed. The candidate had never sought office before or his previous administration had been approved by higher authorities and it was not wise "to swap horses in the middle of the stream." Friends too numerous to resist had urged him to run. No "hampering promises" had been made and all who were interested were invited to advise him or to investigate his record. The present encumbent had had the office long enough. Finally, he said, he had slung no mud but entertained only generous sentiments toward his rivals and other opponents.

A day or so afterwards, when the results of the election were known, all of the candidates or at least those who hoped to run again, inserted ads thanking the people who supported them. The winners promised faithful performance and expressed generous attitudes toward those who had not voted for them. The losers congratulated their successful rivals and promised to abide by the verdict. The heat of the battle was forgotten and foundations of good will were laid for the next campaign.

Handbills were used in Upland Bend to a considerable extent, especially by the candidates for governor. Some handbills merely gave the time and place where a speaking was to be held. Others amounted to as much as four pages of newspaper space. In these there was elaborate discussion of the stand of the candidate or of his opponents on numerous issues as well as much of the wordbook material that has been presented above. Handbills were gotten out occasionally by county candidates. Of these the following is an interesting example.

To the Voters of Chehaw County

"Even were I without physical handicap it would be impossible to see each of you personally before the Election on May 1st. So, I take this crude method of letting you know that I want your vote and valued friendship to help make me your Circuit Clerk. I am just a poor man in politics. I am crippled and have no money. For the past several years fate has dealt harshly with me, decreeing, that I deal largely in hospital bills and the endurance of much physical pain. However, I have made a living and I am now physically capable of handling the affairs of this office and I am qualified for it by experience, ability, and temperament. Whoever may come to see me as Circuit Clerk, whether on business or a social call, can count on receiving not only courteous treatment but the sympathetic attention of a friend. I am running this race on little more than Faith, Hope, and Love. As one of my many friends, may I count on your support and your vote on May 1."

The third type of printed material to be distributed consisted of small cards. These were usually one and one half by three or four inches in size. Ordinarily they contained the candidate's name, mention of the office for which he was running, a word or two of appeal, and the statement that he was subject to the action of the Democratic Primary. Occasionally a small photograph of the candidate appeared on the card. These, unlike the handbills which tended to be broadcast, were given personally to the voters by the candidate or his supporters as they "shook hands" with the people.

A few days before the election date some of the candidates sent personal letters to the voters of the community. Usually the letters were very short containing simply the following message, "In view of the fact that it will be impossible for me to see each of you in person I am taking the liberty of writing to you and asking for your vote for the office of _____ on May 1st." Sometimes the letters were longer. In these cases any of the appeals above mentioned might be included.

POLITICAL RALLIES

In the rural sections of Alabama the political rally is one of the most interesting of the customary campaign activities. The sponsor of the occasion is usually a school or a church. It may be held at either of these places, at a well-known store or at the home of a leading landowner. Ordinarily the sponsors plan the rally for the purpose of making money. The voters want to see the candidates. The latter are fortified with considerable sums of loose change. Cash is scarce in church and school alike and the planners of the rally intend to get as much of this as they can. But everybody has a good time.

The attractions they offer for this purpose besides the candidates who are afraid not to come include plate, box, pie or chicken suppers or fiddlers' conventions. These are supplemented by various features of entertainment provided by the local people such as songs, instrumental numbers, exhibition dances, and recitations. In addition to these there are auctions and guessing contests. The master of ceremonies is usually a man from the county seat who has the reputation of being a forceful and amusing presiding officer.

During the campaign for the May primary four rallies were held at Upland Bend. Two of these, the CWA Rally and the Plate Supper and Political Rally given by the P.-T. A. are described as social gatherings in Chapter IX, *How the People Spent Their Time*. The third rally was also called at the school. A chicken supper at 35 cents per plate was served to sixty-five persons. When the speaking began about 100 people were present. Nearly a third of these were candidates and their backers or visitors from town. The local company appeared to be very largely of the owning groups.

One of the candidates, who was a little boisterous, entertained the audience on this occasion very effectively. Every now and then he would shout, "I'm a statesman" or "They don't dare say a word against this old countryman because everytime they do they lose a country vote." When time was called on him toward the end of his talk he brought the house down with the remark, "You allowed Jim Keene (an opponent) to stay in Congress four years and here you call me down in four minutes." Seizing the advantage this hit brought he went on for four minutes more without interruption from the chairman. This candidate had the reputation of being eccentric, to put it mildly, and none of the political wiseacres thought he had a chance. But he was having a great time, the people enjoyed him, and anything he said was received with tolerant amusement.

The fourth rally was held on the place of a large owner at 7:30 P.M. one very chilly but beautifully clear, moonlight night in April. About 100 people appeared. Supper at 35 cents a plate was served by the ladies on long plank tables. Soft drinks, coffee, sandwiches, and ice cream were also sold. The money thus earned went to the singing organization of one of the churches. A leading county singer had been asked to serve as chairman. The audience was seated on rough hewn two-by-twelve timbers that rested on pine logs. Dim and wavering electric lights from a Delco system provided illumination over the chairman's platform which was very close to the stable and barnyard.

The proceedings were opened with a guessing contest. Holding up a half-pint jar filled with shelled peanuts the chairman invited estimates of the number in the jar at 5 cents a guess. The candidates and their friends guessed freely. There were 415½ and the man who estimated 420 got the prize which was a small bag of nuts. The chairman then offered a large four-layer cake with white frosting. After spirited bidding this went for $1.00 to a Bill Beasley supporter who returned it for a second auction. This time it brought 75 cents. Then, at 5 cents each, the candidates were asked to guess what was in the cake. It was a marble which no one had guessed. A small box of 2-for-5 cigars, which was said to be for the ugliest candidate, was then offered for bidding. By this time, however, the candidates were wary. Even the pretty young ladies who had been going from one to another to encourage bidding were unable to stir much enthusiasm. Finally the cigars went to a man who had bid little if any more than they cost.

After these preliminaries the chairman invited the twenty candidates to be seated on a long bench facing the audience. Each man put a card with his name in the hat from which various people in the audience were asked to draw to determine the order of speaking. Five minutes was the time allowed candidates for major offices. Three minutes went to county aspirants. One of the candidates was appointed to act as time keeper. When the alloted period was up he pounded a plank with a rock until the speaker sat down. This the speaker did by slowly stepping backward toward the bench continuing to speak and stumbling as he went which was very amusing to the audience.

During the speaking some of the many dogs that were hunting for scraps from the supper were continually going up to the candidates and sniffing at their legs and feet. The woods were full of the mournful call of the whippoorwill. At the wire fence just back of the candidates a group of cows, hogs, and mules had collected to watch these strange proceedings. Most of the time the animals listened as respectfully as human beings do when what is going on is beyond them. But of the latter one could not be too sure because, now and then, they punctuated a candidate's remarks with a chorus of bellows, grunts, and heehaws in a most timely manner. This was almost too much for some of the speakers but the audience found it vastly entertaining.

The chief feature of the political rally is the series of talks that are made by the candidates or their representatives. To hear what the candidates have to say, to size them up, and to learn how to vote are the motives, presumably, that draw the crowd. The doings and sayings of the candidates are determined by their desire to win the goodwill of the voters. In working out their remarks they are guided not only by their own judgment but by that of numerous friends and supporters, including some in the local community. The candidates and their advisers are the most skillful judges we have as to what is effective in political persuasion.

When one examines candidates' remarks he is studying material which offers significant insights into the nature of the mental processes of candidates and voters alike. The degree of intelligence, level of emotion, and quality of attitude are all available for inspection. In respect to the extent that they possess these values individual candidates differ widely. The voters differ likewise. What one has, therefore, is a situation in which all kinds of candidates attempt to reach all kinds of voters with all kinds of speeches.

Some of the speakers were well educated; others had had few advantages of this nature. Some talked briefly; others took all the time they had. A few were impersonal in their remarks. Some defended themselves; others attacked their opponents. Some were shy and bashful; others, bold and fluent. Attempts at humor were frequent. Simplicity and sincerity were contrasted with insinuation and guile. Some knew what they wanted to say; others were badly confused. Promises of a very broad nature were made by some. Gubernatorial and legislative aspirants, generally speaking, were more concerned with issues than the others. Appeals to many types of common prejudice were readily apparent. Again and again the charges were rung against big business, the Negro, the "ring politicians", and the "ins." The speakers were "for" the poor man, the farmer, the laboring man, and the veteran. Several attempted to ride the President's coat tails. Allusions of a pietistic nature appeared now and then. There was much, in short, of being all things to all men.

It is customary in sophisticated circles to dismiss the remarks of candidates with an attitude of cynical amusement. Much of what candidates say is indeed amusing to persons of broad cultural background. But this attitude fails to take into account the fact that such talks figure significantly in the civic training of the masses of the people, especially those in rural sections. As such they constituted an important part of the political life of Upland Bend. Realizing their value, pains were taken to make verbatim stenographic records of the talks of candidates and their representatives on several occasions. These records are worth careful study on the part of social scientists, educators, and intelligent citizens generally.

For these reasons and because they are filled with human interest quite a number of talks are presented below. For the convenience of the reader they have been grouped according to the office to which the speakers aspired. This arrangement has the additional advantage of facilitating discrimination of the different types of appeals that were employed by different candidates for the same post. To save space the customary opening address to the audience, "Mr. Chairman, Ladies, and Gentlemen," and the customary conclusion, "I thank you", have been omitted.

Representatives of Gubernatorial Candidates

"I want to tell you that I am just a plain country citizen. I am one of the citizens of Chehaw County and a loyal supporter of Major Dixon. I am not going to condemn Mr. Graves' policy in the paying of school teachers. However, he can't spend as much money as he has done in the past. He was entirely too extravagant. We have got to try something new. Mr. Roosevelt tried something new. Governor Byrd of Virginia tried something new and really organized the state of Virginia. The very same thing happened in Indiana; $100,000,000 was saved in two years. Major Dixon wants to really organize the state of Alabama. He can save five million dollars. We are being attacked about the short ballot. We have Mr. Graves and Judge McCord, who represent the old-time politicians as our opponents. According to statistics from the state government, we have an indebtedness in this state of over $210,000,000. That is the result of the old-time politician. We young men want something new. We believe that Major Dixon's, Roosevelt's, and Byrd's plan will bring us out of the mire. If you believe like we do, you are going to vote for Major Dixon."

"I am glad to be with you here tonight to have the privilege and honor of representing Judge McCord who is running for governor of the state. We have three men who are in the race for governor of the State of Alabama. At this time the burden rests upon my shoulders and your shoulders to seriously consider those men to whom we shall turn over our chief office of trust. I represent tonight a man who is known not only in the state of Alabama but throughout the United States. He is a scholar, a gentleman, and a jurist. He is one of the truest Democrats of this whole country of ours. I have not time to talk of the platform of Dixon but he tells you of the short ballot. I am opposed to that. I believe in the Democratic principles. I say to you men and women of this state that you can think and have the right to march to the polls on election day and vote for every man you think is best and vote for those principles. Major Dixon's first act will be to so change our laws as to have votes only for a few men and I say to you with all seriousness and I firmly believe that he is distinctly opposed to the principles set forth by Thomas Jefferson. We have had Colonel Graves for four years. You know of his extravagance. McCord promises you that you will have at least a seven months school and that if any other employees of the state be paid, the school teachers will be. I earnestly beg you to carefully think of the men who are candidates and cast your vote for the best one."

————————

"I am indeed happy to be here to speak in behalf of my friend and your friend the ex-governor and the next governor of Alabama. Not any of the people who supported Bibb Graves in his last race, or those who did not, have ever been able to accuse him of misappropriating funds. He left schools and highways. He gave you something for your money. He told you at the time you elected him that your boy and girl would have the advantages of those in the city. He is asking you again to let him do the great things that he did for you eight years ago when he was governor. He doesn't ask of you any additional taxes. Ad valorem taxes he will reduce. He will reduce the automobile license tag more than 50 per cent. He will pay the teachers and run the schools full term and pay off. When Bibb Graves was governor eight years ago he paid off every time. If you go to the polls on May 1st, Ladies and Gentlemen, and cast your vote for Bibb Graves you will vote for your boy and girl. He was a great man in the history of Alabama."

"I am only a stranger to you. You all know The Star and also know that The Star is back of Frank Dixon, with all its power. The state is in a serious condition just as the nation was before F. D. Roosevelt. Frank Dixon will do for the State of Alabama just what Roosevelt is doing for the nation. If you call Dixon a radical, then you call Roosevelt a radical too. We all know what Roosevelt did for the State of New York. Dixon will do for Alabama the same thing Roosevelt did for the State of New York and what he is trying to do for our country. When we ask you to reorganize the government, we do ask you to put a man in Montgomery to take out the dead wood. You will be the ones to decide whether you want it or not. He is an honest man. Frank Dixon is the only man who tells you to stand up for him and put him in Montgomery and if he doesn't do the right thing, just to blow him out of office. Frank Dixon, ladies and gentlemen, is an honest man and worthy of your consideration and vote."

"We are approaching the Democratic Primary on May 1. There are three men running for governor. When you go to mark your ballot for the highest office of the Democratic Primary, I want you to remember the extravagance of Bibb Graves, the inexperience and radicalism of Dixon, the levelheadedness and experience of Leon McCord. It is a serious thing, my friends, when we go to elect a governor. In 1931 the State of Alabama had a deficit of $16,000,000. I say it in all seriousness, that deficit is largely the work of Bibb Graves. We cannot stand four years more of such a regime as he gave us. The radical change offered by Dixon is the short ballot plan by which I judge he will take from the people the democratic right to make their own decisions in selecting their candidates. It might be said that McCord is backed by capitalists. This is not true. One of the biggest lawyers representing large capitalistic organizations like railroads, the power company, telephone company, etc. in Birmingham, is working might and main for Bibb Graves. Any lawyer will tell you that the most unjust law ever written on labor and capital was written for Major Dixon. I want you to vote for Leon McCord."

"I am glad tonight to be here with you folks, and I am also glad that I have the privilege of speaking in behalf of our next Governor, Bibb Graves. When I noticed in the paper about there going to be a meeting at Upland Bend, I immediately thought about if it rained, how would we get here? Then I remembered that we could come on a Bibb Graves' road right to the door. You can speak of progress, of keeping schools open, of spending money, roads, etc., but it is all worth while. We all know that as well as we know who is going to be elected governor.

"All nations are today looking for leadership. The biggest trouble in the world is on account of not having leadership. Some of the countries feel that they have found a leader. We *know* that we have found our leader in Franklin D. Roosevelt. Next, the states are looking for leadership, not only states, but counties and municipalities, looking for leadership. The people realize from past experience and observation, that they have found the leader they want in Alabama, and on May 1, will meet and elect Bibb Graves for governor."

State and National Legislative Posts

"Folks I have had a difficult time trying to make a speech for Bill Beasley to satisfy the Keene forces, cause they just can't be satisfied. I want no quarrel. If you admire anything about Jim Keene it is your privilege.

"Bill Beasley is a man that was trained in the experience of a humble fellow. He is up for the poor folks. If Jim Keene is all that he is expected to be Bill wouldn't be running against him. If he had been, Beasley's campaign wouldn't have reached what it has.

"Jim Keene is a professed wet. Bill Beasley has the only platform that can pretend to be dry. He will go to Congress and represent you to the best of his ability. What is Jim's platform? It is true that he brought the Army Post to Shallow Ford but he took the money part of it, the Quartermaster Department, to Washington, his home town. I am glad to give him credit for what he has done, but what has he done? Let me call your attention to one thing. He is a mighty rich man in Congress and has been for many years. Just a short time ago when cotton was 5 cents a pound all the farmers were bending low and deciding on charity or suicide, what did your rich man do about it? Did he introduce a bill? No he didn't. He can't say it can't be done either 'cause John Bankhead went up there and did it. Jim was up there and could have saved you before John got there but he didn't. Now laugh that one off. I would be glad to discuss it with you. All we need is a representative and Bill Beasley is a boy wonder and will represent you. He is surrounded by opposition and it takes a man of courage. Beasley is a fine young Christian man trained to go to Congress to represent the poor folks."

"You know Mr. Keene's record stands for itself. I am not going into the record of his opponents. I am going to talk for Mr. Keene and not against his opponents. Mr. Keene supports the great man who is now in the White House, Mr. Roosevelt. He is and has been a credit to his congressional district. Mr. Keene is not only a great man in the State of Alabama, but throughout the entire United States. We will certainly do a great thing by ourselves if we support a man who is trying to lead us out of this great depression. Mr. Keene is a citizen of Chehaw County. He has brought a number of things to this county. It would be foolish for me to try to enumerate them here tonight. He is rated as one of the most capable leaders of the Democratic Party. It is certainly a privilege to have been able to speak here tonight in favor of a man who has done so much for his state and for the South as Mr. Keene."

"I want to thank the Chairman for the manner in which he introduced me tonight. Most of the time I am introduced as the "little bitty" man. I was walking down the street from a football game which Alabama had won and I felt like I was about as big as anybody. About that time I passed a small boy and his mother. The little boy looked at me and said to his mother, 'Mother, look what a little man.'

"I am here tonight to represent a real big man. A man who has the courage, ability, and leadership to represent our people. How often have you heard the expression that we need a business man for this office. Now we have the opportunity to vote for such a man as that. I would appreciate your vote for Mr. Arthur Caldwell on May the first."

"The Chairman told us that I had only three minutes to speak, but if I had more time I would not be able to make a good speech.

"I am a candidate for State Senate. We could probably have no more serious a problem in the State than the school situation. Then there are finances, and inmates of eleomosynary institutions. But the heads of those institutions, superintendents, professors, and teachers are in a bad fix and taking proper care of them is a serious matter. Hence, it is a business proposition for all. I believe the people of Alabama will do the proper service to our State to send a business man to the government. Its debt, its inability to pay school expenses this year is a business proposition. The state is only paying 63 per cent and this situation cannot continue. This question of license tags, gas tax, the whole problem is a business problem. Our duty is to find who is the best one and then stand for him and vote for him. Send men that you can trust as business men having some abilities and men you have confidence in. Your duty is to send a man to Montgomery who can do a good job and who can handle a business job."

———

"I am a candidate for the office of state senate from this county. It is an important office and means much to the people of this county and the State of Alabama. I cannot come before you purposely as a man of large affairs. I come to you as a plain citizen. I come to you in person. I appeal to you to vote for me and I sincerely believe you are going to. You have sincerely stood by me in the past and I count on you now

"Big business!' We live in a democracy and we don't need rich men to run our affairs. Big business! When the Master of Men was here on earth in the midst of His career, He drove the big business men out of the temple. I will try to represent the most humble citizen. I want to do my best to be fair and square to all kinds of business. I cannot take the time to tell you of my entire platform, but I will give you a few of my principles. I have had experience for some time. I have the ability or I would not have the audacity to stand before this intelligent audience and ask for your support. I stand for human happiness, to lift the load, if possible, off the burdened people. I stand for everything that is good and against that which is bad. I stand for white supremacy, especially at this time.

"I want your vote and I think that I am going to get it and when I get there, I will not be a man of so large affairs that you cannot get to me. I want your advice and counsel."

"I seek Post Number One to represent you in our county in the next Legislature. The major plank in my platform is lower interest rates in the State of Alabama. It would mean additional purchasing power, money that will be kept in the boundaries of this state. Today the money is being controlled on Wall Street. Ninety-five per cent of the wealth today is controlled by five per cent of the people. If we give the little business men a chance with the big business men, we would have a square deal. We must use careful consideration to vote for a good man. With your help we will get at the bottom of this trouble. We are looking from the bottom up and not from the top down. My next plank is old age insurance to take the place of the poorhouse system, which is a disgrace to any state in the Union. We should eliminate the poorhouse system entirely. I say that if you use your vote wisely, the government can begin to remedy this situation. It is up to you to see that our poor old people in the State of Alabama are taken care of. I hope you will help me to put this over. I think that it is time that we balance the little business man with the big business man. Think of the enormous salary of Mr. Aldrich of the Chase National Bank and Mr. Harriman of the Harriman National Bank of New York. Where is Mr. Insull today, floating around in disgrace.

"Now, friends, if you want to vote for a man who will fight for you, vote for me and you will have the right man."

"I am pleased to have the honor of having a few words to say in behalf of my candidacy for Post Number One in the Legislature from Chehaw County. Ladies and Gentlemen, most all of you know me. I have resided in this county for twenty-five years. I do not feel like I am much of a stranger in this community and I am asking the citizens of Chehaw County to support me for the Legislature. In doing this, I deem it necessary to lay out before the people, which I have done in print, what I stand for as my platform. I first stand for free schools and free schoolbooks and I stand for a free home taxation, to reduce the ad valorem. I stand for no more raise of taxes whatever. I oppose any sales tax and I stand for a compensation act to be enacted in the State of Alabama for our workmen. We are facing some great problems in this next administration and I think that I should and every voter in Alabama should get their senses together before they cast their ballot and cast it for the man who has the courage and ability to fight for the County and for its rights, to save our schools and pay our teachers above all things. There are many things we are facing that the next Legislature has got to contend with in our state government. I am in favor of reducing all useless offices in the state as we have many of them prowling about the country at the hands of the poor class of people and the people are already burdened to death with taxes. I will do all I can to serve you as a state official. Ladies and Gentlemen, I wish to say that I wear no collar of no organization or any group of men. I represent the people at large."

"It was my pleasure to appear before you a few weeks ago, and I will save the time and just announce that I am still a candidate for the Legislature, Post Number One. I have a great many things to discuss, among them being taxes, my desire to serve the people fairly, squarely, and honestly, and support the governor that you elect, and do what I think the people of this County want their representative to do, namely: to talk with them and find out what they want in order that he may know how they feel about the various issues."

A Candidate for Attorney General

"While in Shallow Ford tonight, I heard of this political rally and I am glad to be here and to meet you people of Chehaw County. I am a candidate for the office of Attorney General of the State of Alabama. You are very much interested, of course, in the county races and this is only natural, but please do not forget these state offices because they are almost as important to you as the county offices.

"I was born and raised in southern Alabama and practiced law successfully for about seventeen years. I served in the State Senate of 1923, served as prosecuting officer of my county and the long and short of it is that I am a successful country practicioner asking for you people to elect me to the office of Attorney General. If I am elected, I will do my best."

Circuit Solicitor and Circuit Clerk

"I have enjoyed the hospitality of this community. Both my feet and hands are cold, but my heart is still warm. I will tell you something of the importance of the office of solicitor. Naturally I am interested in the other races too, but I want to say that the sheriff's and solicitor's offices are two of the most important offices in this county. Law enforcement in this county depends on these offices. On the solicitor depends the law enforcement in this county for the next four years. Get a man with experience and ability.

"My brother, Joe R. Moore, is now in the western part of the county and I am here tonight to represent him. I am naturally interested in his race and would like to see him succeed. He is now in his forties. I believe that if he is given an opportunity, he will make this county a splendid solicitor. I will appreciate your vote and influence in his behalf."

"This is a sad occasion for me. I stand beside the daughter of a man whom I loved and her eyes are not yet dry of the tears for her beloved father. He meant more to me than almost any man I know. I was unable to attend his funeral but my heart was with the people of this community that day.

"Tonight, I am representing a man who was his friend. George West loved him and he loved George West. Everybody loves him and George West. George West loves Upland Bend as they love him. George West loves me and I love him as a brother. He was born and raised in Chehaw County, he was educated here, and knows the people of this county. The people of this county love him and he loves them and wants to serve them as solicitor. If you will vote for him in May you will put in that office a man who knows you and loves you as I know him and love him."

"I don't know how you feel but I am about to freeze to death. I have cold hands and head but I haven't cold feet yet. I am very glad to be here. I will not detain you long. I am a candidate for the office of solicitor of our county. I offer you ambition. I worked my way through high school and the university. I offer training with the advantage that I am supposed to have from twenty-two years in the experience and practice of law. I offer you the twenty-two years experience with several years in the school room, which is a good background for this kind of work. I offer you human sympathy in abundance. Sympathy with a man who violates the law but is not a criminal. I want to try to bring citizenship instead of sentencing those to our penitentiary who should not be there. I offer you character. I believe the people of this county know my life. I do not believe anyone in this county has yet had to question my character. I believe that I can conduct this office to save expenses and I believe it can be done. And I will try to save expenses to the tax payers of this county. If I am elected your solicitor I will be open to consult any citizen and I shall give you the best I am able. I am conducting this campaign by myself except with the good citizens that believe in me. I will appreciate it if you will vote for me for your solicitor."

———————

"I have certainly enjoyed the wonderful feed down here to-night. I am glad to see so many here tonight. Ladies and Gentlemen, I hope I have all of your votes.

"I have spent $153.45 for pies and box lunches, made 81 speeches and am still living. There are five of us in this race. It is true I am the first boy candidate. Mr. Carter is a good man but is getting pretty old and all I can say for that is you can't learn an old dog new tricks. Judge West has been in office 12 years. He is now asking for a decreased office you might say. His office pays $300. A solicitor's office pays $250. If you will elect me to this office of solicitor I will increase, at any rate I will not decrease. Mr. Rogers will hand you a card about himself. But it is your duty to vote for the man you think can fill the office the best. Anybody can make a talk but it takes a man or woman to think right. Mr. Rogers eight years ago was asking you to experiment and you did experiment and now it is time for you to experiment again. I say to you that I am the most logical candidate in this race. I am a boy candidate and it is time to put a young man in this place. I don't think I could work fifteen years sweeping, milking cows, nursing babies trying to get my education and let it go to the chaff. I have my career ahead of me and I can't fail and throw it away. If I do fail where will I be? I have everything in my future. I have obtained all I have by the sweat of my brow. Not one penny has been given to me.

"Ladies and Gentlemen, I am asking you to give me an opportunity, to give me a chance, and if I don't make good I will get down and out. Remember me on May 1st. I am here tonight to ask you to give me your vote and I am sure to make you a servant worth while. Vote for me and I will certainly appreciate it."

"I believe this is the third time I have been in this community in the last few months. It seems to me I came when you were having a fiddlers' convention. I spoke a few minutes, but I think everybody looked as if they wanted to get back to their fiddles. I think in a few months I came back and enjoyed a supper like I have enjoyed tonight. I again say that not only have I enjoyed the wonderful food that we have had, but I have enjoyed your hospitality, good fellowship, and mingling with you. The office of solicitor is an important one. It should be filled by a lawyer of ability and experience; should be filled by a lawyer who is able to cope with the finest talent in Alabama. Whether I be the best man or not, I ask you to go before the polls and vote for the man that you think will be the best solicitor.

"I promise, if you elect me, I will be a good solicitor, say that the laws will be enforced to the best of my ability, that I will be reasonable, that I will try to render justice, to handle it in such a manner that when you come in the court room, whether you be lawyer, witness, or visitor, you have that feeling of confidence, and that the State of Alabama is well represented. No man could appreciate your vote on May 1 more than I will. From the expression that I have received from this community, I am confident that the large part of the people are going to help me retain my office. If you make it a point to do so, I am going to see that you will never regret your vote."

" 'You can always tell a barber by the way he parts his hair
You can always tell a dentist when you get in his chair
You can always tell a musician by his air
You can always tell a candidate but you cannot tell him much.'

"There are many people in Shallow Ford that can tell you a great deal. The things Mr. Evans would like to tell you people here tonight, if he were able to come, is how much he wants your vote. Do you think, voters, that it is fair to a man who has served you as faithfully as Mr. Evans has not to give him a chance to serve you a second time. Mr. Evans has been in this work and he knows it. Most of us would be mighty particular about our own personal things.' You would want a man with experience to handle your own things. Surely we want to be just as careful of the public affairs as we would of our own affairs. We are not here to tell you how to vote. The freedom of choice is everyone's privilege. We are here to ask you to consider and choose the person you think is best fitted, the more efficient, and consider his moral character. Then elect the one you see fit.

"If you elect Mr. Evans he will promise to serve you in the same efficient manner as in the past."

County Officers

"I am not going to stand here and speak very long. I am a candidate for Tax Collector, and I shall appreciate your vote on May 1. I will not make you a promise and say that I will make you the best tax collector, but I will do my best."

"I am a candidate for the office of tax collector. It has been said that my old daddy is going to give me the office. He can't give it to me. If he could I would not be running. When I get in I am not going to turn out my old daddy into the cold who has been in this office for thirty years. I will keep him right with me. If you put me in the office I promise you it will be run with the old-time Field's efficiency."

"I am glad to be out here tonight to represent my husband. He is very sorry that he could not be here tonight and he asked me to tell you so. He promises you that if he is elected that he will stay on the job and make you one of the best tax collectors you ever had."

―――――

"It gives me great pleasure to represent to you tonight my boss, your friend, my friend Jesse Ray. I would like to take just a moment to pay tribute to a man whom I consider was one of the best citizens of Chehaw County and who was one of the best tax collectors Chehaw County ever had, Mr. John Cleveland, the father of the man who just spoke.

"Ladies and Gentlemen, about the time the present man was appointed to this office of Tax Assessor Jesse Ray offered his services to the United States Army as a soldier, upholding the principles of Jeffersonian Democracy. He is now asking for a rotation in public office. If we believe in those persons who served us we must give them a chance. We should not do any other way. Why did we send Jesse and those others that did not come back to fight? If we believe in public offices, Ladies and Gentlemen, why don't we support those who were unwilling to submit to the iron heel. Ladies and Gentlemen, I appeal to you for your vote for a man who is in your favor. I guarantee you as good service as you have ever had. I realize I am making a broad statement, but I know a fine man when I see one.

"I will appreciate your vote for Jesse Ray."

―――――

"Most of you, no doubt are familiar with Mr. Freeman and his record in the past administrations. He has served you honestly, sincerely, and courteously. It is of vital importance to you, as land and home owners, to have a man in the Tax Assessor's office who is thoroughly familiar with the work because a survey of the state shows that numerous suits have resulted from incorrect entries of land in this office. As to the reason of my speaking in his behalf I wish to say that on different occasions he has helped me to continue my education at the University of Alabama. For this reason and the fact that he will continue to serve you to the best of his ability, I shall sincerely appreciate your vote and influence in the coming primary."

―――――

"The sheriff's office is a very important office and ought to be filled by somebody that has had experience, a man with some detective knowledge, knows human nature, and other qualifications. I have had experience. No longer ago than Christmas I caught a negro in Birmingham who had held up several merchants in the town at the point of a gun. Not only men but white ladies. The last robbery he pulled, the lady has never got over the effect. That negro is serving 124 years in the penitentiary. He ought to have gotten the death penalty which he deserved. He had two cases against him. He got ninety-six years in one case and twenty-five in the other. Anybody can be an officer who can serve a paper or make an arrest but it takes a qualified man to do it properly."

"I am very glad to be here and glad to see so many friends here. I will indeed be grateful to you for your support in this campaign. Out of 68 crimes which we have had only two remain unsolved. Only last Sunday I had a case. A negro boy had been stealing automobile tires, and in less than one hour I had the boy in jail with the automobile tires and all. We try to solve crimes just as soon as possible. In this county today, I am glad to say crime is on the decrease. This office is being conducted and shall continue to be conducted, as this office should be, above reproach."

"I am glad to be here indeed. I am glad I am alive today. I thoroughly enjoyed the banquet tonight.

"All of you know what I stand for. There is no use in making a long speech. Only 5 per cent of the people need me; only one per cent of the people are really bad. If the 95 per cent of the people will join hands with me and conduct the office in such a manner, we will crowd the others out and work together.

"I am proud of the profound confidence you have already expressed in me."

"I have not been in this community before and spoken to you, but I have ridden over 200 miles today to get here and be with you. I am not going to make a speech, however. I am glad to be here and talk about my candidacy for Probate Judge. In the space of three minutes it is hard to give you the things you should know, the ideas I have about the duties of this office. I will try to do it briefly.

"When I announced for this office, I stated that I would limit my salary to $6000. The law that now governs this office is that on and after October 1, the $6000 limitation shall not apply and the income shall be put back on a fee basis. I think the candidate should express himself on this and I have done so. I know you all know that it is reported that my opponent was in Montgomery lobbying against having his salary cut. His income has averaged a gross of $17,000 for the last three years. Out of this he pays his own clerks. I don't know what this costs, but I think it would net at least $11,000.00. You are taxpayers and I think you ought to have the candidate's expression on that thing. I am going to limit my salary and it can be done if you will demand of the legislature a constitutional amendment. When you consider that the Probate Judge gets 2½ per cent of the licenses for automobile tags, why shouldn't the Circuit Clerk get it, why shouldn't the Sheriff get it, why shouldn't the Tax Assessor or Tax Collector get it? There is no reason why the Probate Judge should have been getting that. He gets 50 cents for issuing the tag and 2½ per cent of the cost of the tag. I have said and I *now* say that a new law should be adopted by this county. I think my opponent is not out here to ask you for your vote. I am here asking you personally."

Not every one in Upland Bend was convinced that the political rally was the best possible means of considering the merits of candidates or of deciding on the issues that developed in an election campaign. A few thoughtful citizens were of the opinion that it was not quite fair to take too much advantage of the susceptabilities of candidates and that the costs involved might keep poor men from running for office. The candidates themselves felt that the system was something like a "holdup", and that few, if any votes were changed by this means. Some of the officers of the county P.-T.A. were of the opinion that no community should hold more than one rally during a campaign and that every one should be invited to attend without cost of any kind. The whole time should be given without distraction to political discussion. The latter should be organized in the nature of a public forum, they thought.

What the people in general felt about these suggestions is not known. But the fact is that the schools and churches alike wanted the money the rallies brought and it did not appear likely that a custom so well entrenched in the traditions of the community would be discarded soon.

A Single Candidate's Visit

It was not possible, of course, for all of the candidates to make special individual visits to as small a community as Upland Bend. This was done, however, by several aspirants for county and congressional offices. In such cases the appearance of the man was announced in advance and all citizens were invited to attend. The main effort of the candidate himself was a speech, but he shook hands with everybody and his supporters "worked on the voters." Having learned that Mr. Bill Beasley, who desired to represent the district in Congress, was to speak at Prude's store at 3:00 o'clock one afternoon in the middle of April a member of the staff arranged to be present. The following report of his observations will describe the nature of the work that was done on such occasions.

"A handful of people were already at the store when I arrived. Every few minutes a car drove up and parked nearby. The fact that the people came in automobiles indicated interest on the part of landowners. Some of the men sat on the edge of the porch, reclined on sacks of cotton seed or leaned against the posts. Inside a number were sitting on the counters or standing around watching a game of pool. Others sat in the cars outside or rested on a clay bank nearby. By 3:00 o'clock 150 men, 25 boys, 6 women, and 8 girls had assembled. They talked quietly and made themselves as comfortable as possible.

"About 3:30 the candidate and his party of ten men, including some local supporters, drove up in two automobiles. Although most of the men present had expressed themselves as being "friendly" none rushed up to greet him. One of the candidate's county advisers asked Mr. Kellum, a large owner, to introduce him. This Mr. Kellum did by taking the candidate from one small group to another. Every one shook hands cordially, and passed the usual pleasantries of greeting. Otherwise they remained where they were and the pool game kept on.

"About this time a school truck drove up to discharge about twenty high-school boys. Mr. Kellum took the candidate to the boys and asked one to introduce him to the others. The boys talked freely. One said, 'Mr. Beasley, I wish you would help our school get some better busses. Look how dusty I got riding that thing today; and I took a bath last night, too.' Another remarked to the candidate, 'I reckon as near as I will ever get to the White House is by talking to fellows like you.' A third responded to his introduction by saying, 'I can't vote, but I can wish for you.'

"It was about 4:00 o'clock when all had been introduced. Three or four farmers then spoke up, 'Mr. Beasley, everybody is ready now when you are ready.' A large barrel was quickly rolled to the center of the porch and a pitcher of water and a glass were placed on the top. The crowd gathered slowly around. Mr. Kellum presented the candidate briefly and the speaking began. During the hour it lasted the people listened attentively. There were no outbursts of applause but quite a number of individuals from time to time indicated approval of the speaker's remarks by nodding their heads in a decided manner or by saying in audible whispers, 'That's right, that's right', 'We know that to be a fact', 'Yes Sir, yes, sir', 'You're right about that', 'He's telling the truth, ain't he?', etc.

"When the speaker concluded his remarks several men shook hands and complimented the talk he had made. In the meantime members of the candidate's party began to take aside and talk seriously in low tones to certain of the leading local men whom they knew. After conversing in this manner for a few moments the local leaders in turn spoke in a confidential way with certain of their friends. This was continued for about a half hour when the people began going home. At about 5:30 the candidate and his party climbed into their cars, hot and tired but well satisfied with their work apparently, and left for the county seat."

"EXPENSE MONEY"

An election campaign costs the candidates a good deal of money. Each of the techniques above described calls for the expenditure of considerable sums for materials, services, and travel. Money is used to influence the electorate, however, in more direct and less open ways than these. The politicians know how it is done and they know the people in every community who are subject to such persuasion. Laymen who keep their eyes open do not lack information, for there is no great secret about the matter. Under these circumstances it was not difficult for members of the staff to inquire concerning what was done along these lines in Upland Bend in the Democratic Primary campaign. That which follows is offerd as what the writers have reason to believe is substantially true. It all came from men who unquestionably were in position to know and who, like the writers, believed that good might come from the telling.

Beat 36 in which most of the voters of Upland Bend lived, was known as an expensive section to carry. All during the campaign some money was used there and a lot more was "put in" by frightened candidates two or three days before the election. This inflow of cash, some of the local people said, meant something like as much to them as the distributions of the CWA. In former years one or two men were able "to deliver" the vote of Upland Bend but this power at the time of the survey was more widely distributed. Beat 36 was also known as "slippery" which means that a candidate was not always certain to get what he bargained for. A large proportion of the voters were approachable in this way. Voters in the rural areas, it was said, were more subject to simple and direct suggestions of this nature than those in the towns. The latter were also moved by material influences but these were of a larger or more subtle nature.

Some of the candidates had no money or would not use it in this way. When all of the candidates for a post were thus situated the voters were forced to choose more on the basis of merit. But when one candidate was better "heeled" the others were placed at a serious disadvantage. If a candidate who was known to have money was too close, his case was weakened. Some voters accepted encouragement only from the candidate for whom they expected to vote. Others received from all and voted as they pleased. But this attitude eventually was discovered and help in the future would be denied men of that reputation.

All of the candidates were approached many times. One or two Upland Bend groups sent representatives to the candidates to collect for the group. Some of the men who thus came to collect had very little influence in the community. Informed candidates knew who did and who did not, and acted accordingly. The visitors usually approached a candidate indirectly. They sat talking in the office, hinting that they liked him well enough but that it would take money to "put him over" in the community. It was difficult for them to believe that some of the candidates would not use money in this way. Other callers simply refrained from expressing their intentions concerning the seeker-for-office until he had given them proper recognition. Some approachable men would not come in but waited to be sought out. When found they expressed interest but, like the others, they thought that considerable sums would be required "to get the candidate across." Numerous individuals approached candidates with a plea for $2.00 with which to fill a prescription for a sick baby. One candidate cleverly met this approach by sympathetically writing an order on a drug store to fill the prescription. But his orders were almost never presented. To avoid overtures of this kind some candidates practically stayed away from their offices during the later stages of the campaign. If an opponent had already reached a leader the candidate made overtures to the leader's following. He inquired if the leader had given them their share. When the leader had not, the opponent's case was seriously prejudiced especially if the candidate who discovered it was himself generous. A few candidates, who were well supplied with funds, got candidates for other offices to work for them. These workers were faithful in some instances but in others they spent the money thus obtained on their own campaigns.

The men in Upland Bend with whom the candidates dealt in such matters were leaders who were interested in politics. Most of them were landowners. Some were large owners. One or two prominent men, who once responded to inducements of this nature, were no longer approachable in such a manner. It was difficult to learn the total amount of money that went into the community in this way but it was certain that many hundreds of dollars changed hands. One candidate alone was reported as having put $600.00 into the region in which Upland Bend was included. Of this a single leader received $400.00. Other candidates put in $5.00 to $50.00. The leaders distributed $1.00, $2.00, or even $5.00 sometimes to their followers. Some of the leaders were accustomed to see to it that the poll taxes of their followers were paid in order that the latters' votes might be available when needed.

The leaders and other voters in Upland Bend who handled "expense money" were not inclined to be talkative on the subject to strangers. But with friends they were no more reticent on this than on other matters pertaining to their personal business. They had not learned the use of "expense money" from the school or at church but they did not think of it as being very wrong. These institutions were preoccupied with higher things so much that they tended to neglect the more tangible details of ordinary life. Thus the people were left free to meet practical problems in what appeared to be the most practical ways. Nor was there anything to fear, for nothing was likely to be done about a custom in which so many office-holders and prominent citizens were implicated. It was, in short, a matter that everybody seemed to understand. So much was this true that it was considered a huge joke by the crowd when a speaker at one of the political rallies referred to the Upland Bend beat as the "mystery beat that would not declare its political allegiance until the candidates had spoken to it *in the right way.*"

It was not difficult to explain how this point of view developed. As far as the Upland Bend people could see it made little difference to them who held the offices at the court house as long as the officials were courteous. The jobs were "soft as dirt" and paid an awful lot of money for "just sitting around in town." Very different was this situation from that of the men of Upland Bend. They worked hard and long with their hands in the fields under the heat and cold of the weather and they got "mighty little money" for it. When an election rolled around it was their chance to get something back from the big, fat politicians who lived off them. There was plenty of money floating around at such times. Somebody would get it. Why shouldn't they get their share? When they left off plowing to hear a candidate speak wasn't it fair for him to pay them for the time he used? So they contended for what appeared rightfully due and voted for the candidates who were generous with them.

If there was adequate cause for the behavior we have described, there was likewise history behind it. Some of this it was possible to discover. Candidates have always been accustomed to reimburse some of their chief workers at least for expenses legitimately incurred for printing, postage, travel, etc. If anything was left over the candidate was glad to give it to his helpers as a gesture of gratitude. If he had plenty of money he gave enough in the first place to make certain that something would remain. The chief workers, in turn, asked friends to assist them on the same basis. Until the roads were improved in comparatively recent years Upland Bend was isolated from other sections of the county and the people developed ideas and customs more or less distinctly their own. Like other isolated rural communities they were united against the more prosperous people of the county seat who had held slaves before the Civil War and who appeared to be having things their own way now. When these seemingly big men came asking favors at election time it was a great chance to make them pay. Without realizing why, perhaps, this was precisely what many of the men of Upland Bend proceeded to do to the best of their ability.

Before concluding this section of the chapter it may be desirable to add a few words for the purpose of bringing the picture that has been drawn into true perspective. The reader who has not taken pains to investigate the practical details of political manipulation may be surprised by a description of civic behavior that is not in strict accord with the highest theoretical principles of public ethics. In the disturbed frame of mind thus engendered he may rush to the conclusion that the community with which this report is concerned was strikingly different, and that in an unfavorable way, from communities of like nature in other respects. That this conclusion is illfounded will be realized immediately by those who are in close touch with the actualities of political activity. The report has spoken continually of Upland Bend because Upland Bend is the subject of this study. What is said of Upland Bend holds with inevitable local variations, however, for numerous other communities similarly situated. The fact that its characteristic activities are general in nature is what makes the study of Upland Bend significant.

It will be interesting to know finally how the voters of Upland Bend responded to the many types of persuasion that were brought to bear upon them. In the May Primary, the count of ballots cast in Beat 36 showed that in general the electors of Upland Bend voted for the candidates who won. The influences which predominated in the minds of voters elsewhere in both state and county predominated here. Notable exceptions, however, were the races for governor, attorney general, circuit solicitor, tax assessor, and inferior judge. In these cases the vote was widely scattered or concentrated on one of the unsuccessful candidates. The average number of votes cast for an office in Beat 36 which included Upland Bend and some adjacent territory was 191. A few more votes were cast for congressman, governor, lieutenant-governor, and the county offices. Most of the candidates for these offices or influential representatives had appeared in the community in person. The smallest number of votes cast for any office was that for one of the public service commission posts on which only 160 persons in Beat 36 voted. These offices and some of the other state administrative posts may have been less well understood and neither the candidates nor their representatives appeared in the community.

A Concluding Note

When the attempt is made to see the several elements of civic experience, which have been examined above, as parts of a greater whole certain features of the situation stand out in sharp relief. The people of Upland Bend received customary and emergency benefits from government. In turn they contributed manpower to the national defense and served as official representatives of local government in their own community. Only a few had disturbed the public peace and these usually with offenses of a minor nature. Circumstances over which they had little control prevented a majority of those who were eligible from participating in the periodic selection of officials and determination of public policy. Those who could not register for voting on account of poll tax qualifications were effectually denied the right of citizens in a democratic society to decide the conditions under which they lived. They were in the economically and socially dangerous situation of being forced to accept decisions concerning their welfare which were made by others who were free to think first of their own needs, if they so desired.

Those who did exercise the right of suffrage found themselves in an exceedingly complicated position. They were exposed to the shrewdest scheming of veteran politicians who coveted intensely the rich political plums which the electors awarded to the aspirants who won their favor. The circumstances under which the struggle took place were not conducive in some respects to the wisest decision. If the candidates who played the great game of politics asked much for themselves the cost was dear, many things were to be feared, and more than one in two would fail. The voters were confronted with a bewildering multiplicity of choices to make in a confusing welter of emotional appeal. If they demanded a good deal in the way of entertainment and picked up what they could of the loose funds that dangled temptingly before their eyes one need not be surprised.

In the activities of the election campaign it was difficult for the observer to discover any rich fruition of the many years of instruction concerning the exercise of civic responsibility which the public school and the church have intended to give. It is not profitable to expect great changes in human behavior to be produced quickly. But the wise use of the right of suffrage in a democratic state promises too much for the welfare of society to permit the tolerance of small hopes of achievement. It seems reasonable, therefore, to suggest that the school and the church may well make a fresh examination of the civic activities of Upland Bend and of other communities and seek anew to put their powerful resources to work in the direction which their ideals prescribe.

CHAPTER V

HEALTH AND MEDICAL SERVICES

The health of a people is an important factor in determining the kind of life which they have. Its attainment is generally recognized as one of the immediate ends of living. As such it was a matter to which attention needed to be given. The assistance of medical experts was not available in studying this phase of life in Upland Bend, consequently the materials presented represent a layman's picture of the health and of the means for promoting health which the community had.

HEALTH OF THE PEOPLE

The evidence on health came from questions asked at the time of the family interviews and from certain data concerning the school children furnished by the County Health Office. The first concern will be with the information obtained from the families. The questions asked at the time of the home visitations had to do with the amount and kinds of serious illness which members of the families had. The facts obtained from this source are to be interpreted for what they are, reports on family-recognized illnesses rather than information obtained from expert examinations. As such they probably represent minimum statements of the amount of illness and not too reliable accounts of the nature of the ailments.

The amount of sickness as indicated by the reports seemed large. Almost 40 per cent of the homes visited had one or more persons sick or seriously crippled at the time of the visits. Only the related tenant group was relatively free of illness. Forty per cent of the landowners and of the unrelated tenants and 50 per cent of the negro homes had some one or more members incapacitated. Most of the cases were classified by the family as sick persons.

Of the sick, slightly less than one-half were chronic or permanent cases, that is, "sick all the time"; the others were acutely but temporarily ill. In addition, a number of homes reported no one sick, but some one so seriously crippled as to be unable to carry on normal activities.

Many of the homes had persons "sick all the time." One-fifth of them had at least one person chronically ill. The percentages varied but slightly with the occupational groups. Age, rather than economic status, appeared to be the most important determining factor. The related tenants, the youngest age group, reported no one permanently sick and the large landowners, the oldest group in the community, reported the greatest number. Next to the large landowners in percentage of sickness were the negroes. The sharecroppers as a group had no more illness of this sort than did those classed as renters or owners.

The types of ailments from which the people suffered were usually mentioned. These reports should not be accepted in all cases as though they had been clinically diagnosed. They were often given in non-technical terms, and, occasionally, symptoms, rather than the diseases themselves, were named. But since most of the ailments were easily recognized and others had been diagnosed by the family doctor, they can probably be taken as representing fairly true reports. The most common disease causing permanent illness was tuberculosis. This malady, which was usually called "lung trouble", accounted for one-third of all cases reported. Cancer, chronic malaria, pellagra, rheumatism, heart trouble, and high blood pressure were the only other ailments that appeared except as isolated cases. Four known cases of cancer were reported, four of malaria, and three persons had rheumatism so bad as to be completely disabled. Only two homes named cases of pellagra. Single homes had some one suffering from paralysis, blindness, "stomach trouble", "abscessed side", "broken down from childbirth", "diseased eye", and from a broken hip. One other family reported a case of "nerves" and another simply an "invalid."

In addition to these more or less permanent illnesses, 15 per cent of the homes had some one or more members of the family temporarily but acutely ill at the time of the visits. Differences among the occupational classes were entirely negligible in these illnesses and there were no differences between whites and negroes. A measles epidemic from which the community had suffered during the winter prior to the survey had not completely run its course with the result that three families reported measles. In one of these families there were eight cases. Four homes had influenza, in two others some one was in bed with a "bad cold." One child had chicken-pox and another had tonsilitis. The other ailments, so far as it was possible to ascertain, were non-contagious. Two persons with kidney trouble, two with "stomach trouble", which in the country might be any ailment involving the abdomen, one with piles, and one with "headaches" were mentioned. Two women were suffering from "change of life", another was recovering from childbirth. Two children had broken bones, and one man, a negro, was ill from gunshot wounds.

Persons crippled, rather than sick, were reported from an additional 10 per cent of the homes. The records on these crippled people were not as conclusive as those on the above cases. The people of the community seemed to feel that to classify a person as "crippled" was adequate, and because the interviewers failed to press the subject the cause and nature of the crippled condition was not usually given. Most of the known cases were old people crippled from rheumatism or partial paralysis. Accidents seemed to be involved in very few cases.

The above analysis was made in terms of the number of families having some one or more of their members ailing. Perhaps a clearer picture of the health of the community is obtained when the same facts are reported as the percentage of the population that was sick. Expressed in such terms, almost 10 per cent of the people, men, women and children, were seriously ill. Five per cent were either sick all the time or so crippled as to be unable to get about, and more than 4 per cent were acutely ill at the time of the visitations. Since the interviews were all made during the spring, a time when country people tend to be "rundown" after a winter on limited diet, this latter figure may be higher than the year-round average. On the other hand, one must remember that the reports dealt only with very serious illnesses. It cannot be assumed that all others were physically fit; rather it seems safe to believe that there were many other persons who, though not completely incapacitated, were in a state of ill-health serious enough to interfere with normal efficiency. In fact the known nature of the distribution of human traits suggests that this "borderline" group was actually larger than the number of extreme cases, the only ones which the survey identified.

Other evidence on the health of the community came from records of physical examinations of the school children that were made by the county health nurse while the survey was in progress. These included measurements of height and weight and examinations for common physical defects. The facts reported here are for white children only as no physical examinations were made of negro children. Height-weight records, when there is only one measurement available, are not too dependable as indices of general health, but the results are suggestive at least. Using the records provided by the nurse, and comparing them with the normal height-weight relationships, the percentage of children who were as much as 10 per cent overweight or underweight was calculated. One-fourth of the school population, 30 per cent of the boys and 20 per cent of the girls, were 10 per cent or more underweight. One-eighth of the population, 7 per cent of the boys and 15 per cent of the girls, were to the same extent overweight. The differences between the sexes were not accounted for. The fact that almost twice as many children were underweight as were overweight suggests a problem of mal-nourishment which was not unexpected on account of the information at hand on the diet of many families.

The examinations for physical defects gave an even more informing picture of the health of the children. These examinations showed that less than one-half of the children of Upland Bend were free from some physical defect. Six of every ten of those with defects had only one, two of ten had two defects, and two had three or more. The measles epidemic, mentioned earlier, probably accounted for a good portion of the defects found. Throat, ears, eyes, and enlarged glands were the most common sources of trouble and these are the organs most commonly affected by measles. Roughly one-fifth of the children had very bad teeth, 15 per cent were obviously suffering from mal-nutrition, a few others were classified as anemic. Hookworm was reported for eleven children, all of them young, in grades one to three. Further light on the general health situation can be gotten from an analysis of the frequency of dental caries found during the examinations. The average school child had three unfilled cavities, 25 per cent had six or more, 5 per cent had ten or more, and only 14 per cent had none.

There was no difference between the sexes as to the number with physical defects. But the younger children consistently had more defects than did the older ones. Sixty-five per cent of the younger children, those in grades one to six, had one or more defects, while only 40 per cent of those from the upper six grades had any. Several possible factors may have been involved here. A part of the difference may have resulted from the measles epidemic. Many of the defects came as "after effects" of measles and measles in Upland Bend was very much a disease of young children. No attempt was made by the parents to prevent exposure to measles; in fact, many mothers deliberately exposed their children when they were young "to get it over with." Not all defects of the younger children were traceable to this source, however. More of them were undernourished, for example, and more had bad teeth than had the older children. Another factor which suggested itself was the work of the school in encouraging the correction of defects, but very little evidence was found of serious concern on the part of the school over the matter of health. The school had not even found it possible to follow up the examinations to see that the defects were corrected. A more plausible role of the school was in the gradual elimination of a relatively larger number of those children with defects. But another factor that was certainly involved was the custom of the people, probably found among most groups with limited medical facilities, to correct defects only after they have become serious.

The health nurse customarily held a pre-school clinic in the spring of the year for children who were planning to enter school in the fall. The clinic was held early in order that parents might take advantage of the examinations to correct any defects found before the child entered school. The most significant fact revealed from an examination of the records of the clinic held during the spring of the survey was the limited extent to which the parents took advantage of this service. The first grade at this time had an enrollment of 38 children, and there was no reason for thinking that the incoming class would be smaller than this;

consequently the clinic should have attracted at least this number of children. Actually only eleven children, considerably less than one-third of the number that might have been expected, were brought in for examination. Of this number only four were without defects, but four others were probably suffering from the after-effects of measles.

The facts presented in the pages above seem to justify the conclusion that the general health of Upland Bend was relatively poor. Some of the ailments were probably not preventable, others were not curable. But many of them were probably both preventable and curable. The necessary treatment was dependent, however, on adequate medical service among other things, and the amount of medical aid which the community had and was able to pay for was limited.

MEDICAL SERVICE

The organized health and medical service which the families received came from several sources. Medical care from doctors engaged in private practice was available; private hospital service while not very accessible was still within the reach of certain portions of the community; and the state made provisions through insane hospitals and a school for feebleminded to care for these two types of handicaps. In addition, the State Health Department, operating through the county health office, rendered certain general health services to the community. Nursing in many communities constitutes another phase of the organized medical service which is in the hands of experts, but in Upland Bend this was not the case. The families in general depended on neighbors and friends rather than on trained nurses for assistance in time of sickness.

Private practitioners in numbers sufficient to attend the sick were at hand. Three doctors, only one of whom was a resident, regularly served the community. The two outsiders came in, one from a neighboring community, the other from a nearby town. The only one whom it was possible to interview was the resident doctor. By far the largest part of the practice in the community was in his hands, however, and for that reason facts pertaining to him are of particular importance.

This doctor had lived in the community since he started the practice of medicine forty years earlier. He was a native of a neighboring community where his ancestors had been landowners for three generations. His early education came from the public schools of his community, after which he attended an Academy in the county seat for two years and then spent three years in the Louisville, Kentucky Medical School, where he received an M.D. degree at the age of 18. In 1896 he moved into Upland Bend where he had practiced medicine and farmed ever since. From his activities he had managed to accumulate quite an estate, a farm of 640 acres, estimated wealth aside from this land of $12,000, and $5,000 of paid-up life insurance. His annual income he placed at $2500. He was a member of the county and regional medical societies and of the American Medical Association. His medical library consisted of 75 volumes, more than one-half of which were published since 1900, and a subscription to the *Journal of the American Medical Association*.

The practice of this physician was not confined to the community but included outlying districts as well. Most of this practice involved making calls at the homes of the patients, although he did have an office in his home. A few callers came to the office but it served chiefly as the laboratory from which he filled his own prescriptions. His fees were $2.00 for an office call, $2.00 for visits within one mile, and $1.00 extra for each additional mile traveled on a call; but in cases of severe or protracted illness where many calls were made these prices were greatly reduced. The fees collected usually included also the cost of the medicines which he prescribed. Medicines of some sort usually were prescribed, for experience had taught him that collections were more difficult when a prescription had not been given. According to his reports, the ailments for which he most commonly treated adults were influenza, fevers, rheumatism, and pneumonia. For children they were dysentary, diarrhea, colitis, and measles.

Use of his services, or those of any other doctor, did not appear to be made very often by the people of the community. More than one-half of the families reported that they had not had the services of a physician during the entire year preceding the survey. Two-thirds of the remaining families reported that a doctor had called, or that they had visited his office, only once or twice. Ten families from some two hundred had required the services of a physician, either in the form of a call at the home or an office visit, more than five times within the period of a year. Six of these had "some one sick all the time" and had received many visits. In one family a doctor had called every day for more than a year. The number of visits made to or by the doctor varied somewhat for the occupational groups. The related tenants, the youngest group, had fewer visits than any other white group while the landowners had received most calls. But the most striking difference was between the negroes and whites. Some 30 families, a total of 181 negroes, who lived in the community had received service from a doctor only 13 times in the entire year. Three-fourths of the negro families had received no calls, only two families had received as many as three. Evidence presented earlier on the health of the negroes does not justify the inference that this scarcity of medical aid was entirely due to a lack of need for medical attention.

Upland Bend had no hospital. The nearest institution of this type was located in the county seat of Chehaw County, some 25 miles away. This fact and the limited incomes which were available, rather than the lack of need for hospital treatment probably accounted for the relatively small amount of institutional care which the people of the community received. Evidence on the amount of general hospitalization came from two sources. A question relative to the amount of "hospital care received by members of the family during the previous two years" was included in the general interviews. According to the family reports, some thirty persons, one member of every sixth family in the community, had received hospital treatment during a two year period. All except three of these cases were from landowning or related tenant families, two-thirds were members of the families of larger owners. The three cases from non-landowning families were from the white tenant group. Only one person from a sharecropper's home, and no negroes received hospital treatment during the two year period. The hospitalization which the people received appeared to be almost entirely for the purpose of performing emergency operations. One-third of all cases were appendectomies. Other operations were for gall stones, abscessed kidney, abscessed side, and "female troubles." One person had gone with a broken hip, one with a rupture, another for goitre. Two families felt that to classify the visit as "an operation" satisfactorily described it. Of those from tenant homes who had been in hospitals, two were cases of acute appendix and the third had gone for examination and observation after injuries resulting from a logging accident.

Most of the hospital patients were treated at the general hospital in the county seat, consequently the records of this institution were examined for information on those from Upland Bend who had been admitted during the year previous to the survey. Of the total number of patients all except one were members of owners' families, two-thirds of them were from large owners' families. The average length of stay in the hospital was six days, the average charge $30.00. None had been accepted as charity patients, all bills had been paid. All cases except one were for operations, this one for treatment after an accident. One-half of the cases were for appendicitis. All were sent in by the local doctor of the community but they were cared for by a physician of the town. The local physician in Upland Bend did no operating; consequently he commonly turned his hospital patients over to a "town doctor."

In addition to general hospital care, six people from the community had been treated during the past few years, or were being treated at the time of the survey, in hospitals for the insane. Four of the six were white, four were male. All of the cases except one were incurable. This person had been discharged the year before the survey. Two of the cases had been diagnosed as psychosis with pellagra, two as mental deficiency with psychosis, one as epileptic psychosis, and one as Huntington's Chorea. Aside from the two mentally deficient cases mentioned above, there were no institutionalized feebleminded persons from the community. As with most rural communities, the mentally deficient, unless they were very extreme and oftentimes even then, were apt to be cared for in the homes. Three cases located in the homes were definitely feebleminded, another the interviewers did not see but the parents reported him as "wrong in the head." Attending the school were at least three others who, although not extreme cases, were without doubt seriously feebleminded.

The final source of organized medical assistance which the people received came through the County Health Department which served Upland Bend along with other communities in Chehaw County. The health unit consisted of a health officer, who was an M.D., and two nurses. One of these nurses gave her entire time to work in the county seat, the other worked in the rural sections of the county. This nurse did the best she could in caring for the needs of 12,000 school children in addition to assisting with the collection of vital statistics, giving some prenatal care, inoculating adults, and conducting pre-school clinics. The closest contact Upland Bend had with the Health Department came through the school. The vital statistics, births and deaths, were reported by a member of the community to the Health Office in the county seat. Adults, and children too for that matter, could at any time get inoculations and certain free treatments by calling at the Health Office. But through the schools the Department did its most important work. The health nurse, rather than the doctor, usually visited the school at Upland Bend once, sometimes twice, yearly. At this time she conducted physical examinations of the children and gave inoculations to them and to any adult who requested it. If the visit was in the spring she also held a pre-school clinic for children who expected to enter school the next fall. The examinations of the school children were required and any defects found were reported to the parents who were urged to have them corrected. All inoculations were voluntary.

The nature of the physical examinations was commented on earlier. The immunizations, given free to those children whose parents consented, were for diphtheria, small-pox, and typhoid. The treatment for hookworm, too, was furnished free for children who were found to have it. The extent to which these services were used throws interesting light on the reactions of the people to such matters. Most of the school children had been vaccinated for typhoid. The percentage was more than 90 in every grade except among the boys in grades four to six, where more than 75 per cent had been vaccinated. Most of the younger children, those in grades one to three, had been inoculated for diphtheria. In the upper three elementary grades less than one-half, and for the higher grades, those above the sixth, less than one-fourth had taken this precaution. Small-pox vaccination, on the other hand, was extremely rare among the children. Less than 10 per cent of the total school population, and practically none of the younger children, those in grades one to six, had been vaccinated. Twenty-five per cent of the older girls and 50 per cent of the older boys had been vaccinated.

The County Health Department had an explanation for the difference between the amount of vaccination for typhoid and the amount for small-pox. They spoke of a willingness on the part of the people to cooperate in the health program, but felt that an active interest in health seemed to be dependent upon some "dramatic instance" which the community could see and understand. Certain incidents which they reported made their thesis seem plausible.

A few years prior to the survey one of the young women of the community, Mattie Sigler a sharecropper's daughter, returned from a visit in a neighboring county where she had spent the Christmas holidays. On January 1 she became sick with what was thought to be influenza. The neighbors went in to help the family, and as was customary, many of them ate and drank there. When the doctor was finally called the case was immediately diagnosed as typhoid. But the damage had been done. On January 15 two members of the neighboring Waddell family, the head of the household and a son, went to bed. Thirteen days later (the incubation period for typhoid is approximately two weeks), Mabel Howton, a girl who "helped out" at the Waddell's, was stricken, and on January 31 her father, Greely Howton, another contact of the Waddell's, became sick. Reatha Standifer and Mrs. J. C. Lawless nursed the Howton's and on Feb. 14, Miss Standifer and Mrs. Lawless' husband developed typhoid. Three of these seven cases had ended fatally. The community was very much upset by the experience, and the Health Department and local doctor did not hesitate to "play it up." The result was that it aroused considerable concern over typhoid inoculation. This interest was intensified the next year by the case of William Keene. Mr. Keene's family had all been inoculated. He himself had taken one "shot" of the series of four needed for immunization, but had refused to complete the treatment. He developed typhoid. The members of his family consisting of his wife and four sons, a sister-in-law, a nephew, and a neighbor, all of whom had been inoculated, nursed him. None of them developed it. Seemingly as a result of these cases, the amount of typhoid inoculation in the community had greatly increased.

The history of the hookworm treatment in the community illustrates the same point. The early attempts at eliminating hookworm were not very successful, oftentimes they aroused the active enmity of the adults. The nurse, Mrs. Banks, attacked the problem through the young children with a large box of stick candy, one stick for a feces specimen and one for taking the medicine (carbon tetrachloride). The children were interested, so much so that they began to bring pressure to bear on the parents, some of whom accused the nurse of attempting to poison their children. But Mrs. Banks persisted, and finally a picnic, with ice cream furnished by Mrs. Banks, for all children in the first three grades who upon examination were found to be free of hook worm resulted in almost complete elimination of hookworm for the time being. But such methods worked only temporarily. The difficulty was in maintaining interest. Little permanent headway was being made until the case of Marian Snider arose. Marian, a daughter of one of the prominent families in the community, was a high school student, but she was a poor one, failing in all her work. Mrs. Banks decided she had hookworm and persuaded her to take the treatment. Her recovery was phenomenal. By the end of the school year she was among the leaders of her class. The next year she was awarded a prize given by the local congressman to the "Best girl in the Best 4-H Club in the county." During her senior year in high school she won a college scholarship in home economics for the quality of clothes she entered in competition, and at college she represented her institution at some national meeting in Chicago. The community was extremely proud of her accomplishments, and everyone, including the girl, credited the hookworm treatment for her success. As the county health officer stated it, "Her case ran the hookworm campaign after that."

No organized nursing service was at the disposal of the community. The sick, when not seriously ill, were cared for by members of the immediate family. In case of critical illness it was the custom to depend upon relatives or neighbors for assistance. There were no trained nurses available nearer than the county seat twenty-five miles away, and these were rarely called in. The local doctor could recall no case in the past year where one had been in service. No one in the community did nursing for hire, but there were a number of women who were known as "good nurses", and their services were willingly offered to any family in need.

The following description of a "pneumonia case" reported by a local teacher to a member of the staff gives a fairly clear picture of the methods of caring for persons in cases of serious illness.

"On Saturday Mrs. Virgie Wheat went to bed with flu. By morning the Doctor had diagnosed her case as pneumonia. On Tuesday morning I went by on my way to school to inquire about her. I was directed to go to the kitchen door. From the kitchen, I was ushered into the living room, which was across the hall from the 'sick room.' There were about 20 women in the house. Some were in the kitchen, three were in the sick room, but most of them were crowded into the living room, where seats were at a premium. Some of these women were relatives or close friends of the family; most were neighbors who had simply come by 'to see if they could help.' The work was very well organized considering the number of workers involved. Some of the women stayed all day, doing the work of the household, cooking, cleaning, milking, helping with the nursing, and receiving the visitors. Most of them left at meal time, after which, if they did not return, their places were filled by others.

"The sick room was in the hands of Mrs. Beulah Oswalt a neighbor who was 'awful good at nursing.' She and Mrs. Lorrannie Going, who was also good, had taken Mrs. Wheat in charge from the beginning of her illness. One stayed at her bedside by day, the other throughout the night. While the patient was at her worst, only two other persons were allowed in the room with the 'nurse' at any one time. The visiting women 'took turns' at this duty. I was invited to go in but did not accept.

"When I inquired as to Mrs. Wheat the report was, 'She is doing as well as could be expected. She ain't reached the crisis yet.' Dr. Ashbough (the community's doctor) came while I was present. He went through the front door directly to the patient, but afterward came into the living room to speak to the ladies. He, too, felt that she was 'doing nicely.' He had been calling twice daily, and continued to do so for a total time of one week. He advised the women to act more natural when they went into the room with Mrs. Wheat, for, he said, 'She is certainly conscious and probably will live to tell you how you acted.' After he left Mrs. Cleary said, 'Doc's a case', but somebody else opined that doctors had to be that way if they were going to see sick people all day long."

The care of mothers and babies at childbirth was also in the hands of these local nurses. During the year prior to the survey there were in all 36 babies born in the community, roughly one to every fifth home. A child was born during the year to every eighth landowning family, one to every fourth white tenant home, one to every third white sharecropper family, and one to every fourth negro family. These babies were all delivered in the homes, the white children commonly with the assistance of the local doctor, the negroes with the aid of a mid-wife. One baby was delivered with no outside assistance, the members of the family handling the entire matter. Three of the white babies and all negro babies except one were delivered by negro mid-wives, of whom there were three in the community. No mother had the aid of a trained nurse during the period of confinement, depending upon the family, neighbors, and relatives for nursing. A few of the families of the larger owners did sometimes employ one of the negro mid-wives to assist the doctor during the delivery and to help take care of the mother and baby for a time after birth, but usually this latter responsibility was very quickly taken over by the family.

Such was the system of nursing on which the community was compelled to depend. Although the neighbors were always willing to help, in fact seemed to enjoy doing so, it can well be imagined that this manner of handling the problem did not always result in the best possible care for the patients. That it sometimes resulted disastrously for those rendering the aid, and for .their families, was well shown by the typhoid epidemic which was reported above.

MEDICINES IN THE HOMES

The limited extent to which professional facilities were available to the families of Upland Bend meant that many people depended upon home treatment for a great part of their medical aid. As in many other matters, here too, they were to a rather high degree self-sufficient. For this reason, the medicines which they had in their homes become a matter of some importance. As a part of the general survey, information on this subject was obtained from the families of the community.

In spite of the dependence on home treatment for many ailments the medicine chest of the typical family did not appear to be over-supplied. The average family had three different medicines in the home. Ten per cent had none, 20 per cent had more than four. The kinds of medicine found, the most common ones of which are listed at the conclusion of this section, throw light on the type of home treatment which ailing members of the family received. Slightly less than one-half of all medicines owned were patent medicines or proprietary drugs, a greater part were common unpatented chemicals that are widely used for medicinal purposes, and a few were obviously supplied by the doctors.

Turpentine and castor oil made up almost one-third of all the medicines found. Turpentine was by far the most widely found of all, and the indications were that it was just as widely used. It was made to serve, according to the reports, as a laxative, for colds, for indigestion, for sprains, wounds and burns, for sore throat, toothache, for sores, for rheumatism, and other aches. As one farmer put it, "turpentine is good for most anything." Castor oil was widely used, for not so many ailments, but by all members of the family "from baby to grandpa." Camphor, too, though not so commonly found served as a remedy for headache, tooth-ache, colds, rheumatism, for cramps and backaches, and for "general sickness." Aspirin was rather frequently found; 15 per cent of the homes had it. Only 5 per cent of the families reported either iodine or mercurochrome. Quinine, though it may have been an ingredient of certain tonics which were frequently found, was not common in its pure form. Only three homes reported it. Several of the homes that had babies reported Castoria, but only three had cod liver oil.

The two leading patent medicines found in the community were Vicks Salve and Thedford's Black Draught. These two items made up almost one-fourth of all the medicines found in the homes, and they were the only widely advertised medicines which were commonly owned. Black Draught was largely confined in its us-age to constipation and as a "tonic." But Vicks Salve served a greater variety of purposes. Although chiefly used for colds it had been found valuable for headaches, wounds, sprains, sores, and for rheumatic aches. Bromo-quinine, Ex-Lax, Listerine, Sloan's Liniment, Mentholatum, Nervine, all medicines which are fairly well advertised, were each reported by single homes only. Herb medicine and snake oil were others represented in individual homes. And one old man had a medicine which he found very useful called Life-Everlasting. It was made from hickory bark, cherry bark, mullen leaves and rabbit tobacco, by a receipt which he got from his Almanac. More popular in the community were the Raleigh products, medicines sold by itinerant salesmen who do house-to-house canvassing.

Drugs which appeared to have been furnished or at least recommended by the doctor were: Alcaroid, ephedrine, "green drops" (probably some barbital compound), "doctor's pills", paragoric, and strychnine. All except the last of these were reported from individual homes. Three had strychnine.

The medicines appearing in five or more homes were:

Medicine	Number of Homes
Turpentine	89
Castor oil	61
Vicks salve	54
Black Draught	49
Salts	45
Aspirin	30
Liniment	19
Camphor	14
Iodine	8
Calomel	7
Castoria	5
Magnesia	5
Mercurochrome	5

There were differences among the occupational groups with reference to both the number and kinds of medicines owned. The landowners had more medicines than other groups. The negroes and sharecroppers reported the most limited supply. Where the average owner had almost four, the latter groups had less than two. No negro and only three white sharecroppers had as many as five. This fact would be of less significance were it not for the fact that these people had been found to be the very ones with the most limited medical facilities of other sorts. In kinds owned there was some indication that the owners bought patent remedies while the tenants, negro and white, depended upon common unpatented medicines. Turpentine, castor oil and epsom salts, while frequently found in all homes, were relatively more common among the sharecroppers, negro and white; Vicks Salve and Black Draught were more common among the owning classes. Aspirin, one of the most common items found in owners' homes was found in only two sharecroppers' and in no negro's home.

The drugs which the people owned, like most other products which they bought, came from the local stores. This fact was indicated by an examination of the drug stock of one of the most popular stores in the community. But this examination also showed that for certain items carried in stock the turnover was not too rapid. Although most of the drugs which were found in the homes were included in this merchant's "line", a number of others which he had on his shelves were not reported from any of the many homes visited. The complete "drug list" from this store was as follows:

Calomel	Antiphlogistine	Dills Cough Syrup
Turpentine	Spirits of Camphor	Cold Tablets
Castor oil	Sloan's Liniment	Golden Medical
El-Ko-Hol	Nux Vomica	Discovery
Healing oil	Epsom Salts	Quinine Sulphate
Aspirin	Grey's Corn Pads	Boric acid
Penetrol	Sulphur	Tar compound
Thedford's Black	Alum	Allied Seven Leaves
Draught	Contabs Liver	Milk of Magnesia
Essotabs	Medicine	Four tubes of dental
Castoria	Cardui	cream
Sodium Phosphate	Colic Medicine	Two toothbrushes

This completes the description of the materials which were available on the health of Upland Bend. As a concluding note, a brief but unified view of the situation may be of use. It seems fairly evident that too many of the people were in poor health. When at any given time nearly one-tenth of a population, young and old, is gravely afflicted, and in addition, one-fourth of the school children are underweight and one-half of them have observable defects of a serious nature, the matter cannot be treated lightly. The fact that such conditions are to be found elsewhere rather than extenuating the problem in Upland Bend simply magnifies its general importance.

The extent to which this state of affairs was due to the constitutional make-up of the people or to the kind of life they were compelled to live is a matter for speculation only. The evidence does suggest, however, that a part of the trouble was the lack of adequate medical facilities, of health knowledge, and of proper concern over health. These phases, at least, are aspects of the problem susceptible to an amount of direct attack; but the limited economic resources, the amount and kind of education which the people received and the drainage of population from which the community suffered set rather definite limits to the progress that was possible through local initiative.

CHAPTER VI

THE HOMES

The home is the chief center of life in a rural community. The grown people spend most of their time in and around this center and so do the children except on school days, which in the country are limited in number. The surroundings in which people live influence greatly what they think and do. The home background thus becomes a matter of fundamental importance. For these reasons it is necessary to have a considerable amount of information concerning the physical and cultural environment that was furnished by the homes of Upland Bend.

DISTANCES

One of the significant features about the location of a home is its distance from other homes and from the routes of travel. Most of the homes with which we are concerned were situated along the highways. They were served daily by a mail route and during the school term by a school bus. Only three families in the community lived as much as one mile from a road of some kind, and five others were as much as one-half mile but less than a mile distant. Approximately 80 per cent lived within one hundred yards and one-third lived within twenty-five yards of a highway.

The roads on which the people traveled were graded and surfaced with a light coat of gravel. They were all passable except after prolonged rains. At the time of the survey the roads were in particularly good condition because of the repairs that had been made on them by relief workers. But in spite of this improvement every fifth home was on a road that was unsatisfactory for automobile travel. One of the roads, a loop that dropped in toward the river on which six owners and their seven tenants lived, was at all times practically impossible of use except by horse and wagon.

The community was served by two mail routes and these managed to pass near most of the homes. Sixty per cent of the people were within 150 feet of their mail boxes, and only four persons in the entire community were as much as one mile distant.

The greatest density of population was in the area surounding the school. Thus for many of the children the school was within easy walking distance. For those that lived more than two miles away there were busses, with the result that the average child was compelled to walk only a quarter of a mile to school. Ten per cent of them, however, were as much as a mile and one-half distant, and the children of two men walked two and one-half miles twice daily to get to school.

Neighbors were not too near. The average distance between houses was 700 yards. Only two families had neighbors within 25 yards, but 30 per cent had a neighbor within 100 yards. Twenty-five per cent were as much as a quarter of a mile away, and one family, that of a negro sharecropper, was as much as a mile from a neighbor.

Churches and stores were at a greater distance. The average family was two miles from the church which it regularly attended, and three-fourths of a mile from the store at which most of its purchases were made. Approximately one in every ten families was as much as four miles from the church and as much as two miles from the store. The stores had obviously been located on sites where their owners held lands rather than with reference to the density of population. Churches were usually located near the homes of influential members, the location having been determined in the first place by a gift of land. These gifts were not always made for reasons wholly altruistic. The deed of conveyance in such cases usually specified that the land together with all improvements should revert to the donor if it were no longer used for church purposes. With young and struggling congregations this contingency was not unlikely. Indeed it had already occured in at least one instance. As a result the owner had a good cow barn which otherwise he might have had to build at his own expense.

The occupational stratifications seemed to play a part in determining the differences in the locations of houses. The landowners, particularly the large owners, occupied preferred sites. The homes of these eleven men were located on the main roads, the roads weaving in and out in such manner as to serve all. Their mail boxes were within twenty-five yards of the house, and the eight of them who had children were within twenty-five yards of the school or of the route of the bus which took the children to school. More than one-half of all the owners lived within twenty-five yards of the highway. Tenant homes, on the other hand, were so located as to be accessible to the land; that is, they were scattered about over the farm rather than located on the roads. However, since the farms were small they were not far from the roads. The landowners and related tenants had neighbors nearer and even the stores were slightly nearer them. Only in distance to church were there no differences among the occupational groups.

The negroes who seemed to have located relatively close to one another, had developed a settlement of their own in the northern part of the community, so that not only did they have near neighbors but neighbors of their own race. Twenty-seven of the thirty negro families were located in an area of three square miles. The three remaining negro families were isolated from the mass of their people and from one another. They were situated in the southern part of the community probably because the women served in the homes of their landlords.

THE HOMESTEAD

The farm home commonly consists of a house and certain outbuildings, the number and nature of which vary with the needs of the family. The typical homestead in Upland Bend consisted of a house, a barn, a wellbox, and a privy. Approximately 40 per cent of the 200 householders had chicken houses; one-third had smoke-houses; 15 per cent had garages; and 8 per cent had shops. These outbuildings were of simple structure, all unpainted, and commonly built of small logs fitted closely but without chinking. In addition many of the homes, one-fifth of the total, had storm pits. All of the latter had been constructed a few years earlier following a cyclone which struck a neighboring community with great loss of life and property.

The layout of the homes of owners was much more complete than that of the typical place. Two-thirds of their homes had chicken houses; 40 per cent had smoke houses; 20 per cent had

A comfortable home, with adequate outbuildings, yard and trees, and sufficient room for a family of five. This home was typical of the better type of landowner's home in Upland Bend. But few were superior to it.

shops. And all of the garages except four belonged to them. Probably more readily available construction facilities accounted for the fact that most of the storm pits were found at the homes of owners. But the other pits all belonged to unrelated tenants. The related tenants, presumably, depended on their relatives, the landlords, for this type of protection. Only in the matter of privies were the sharecroppers at an advantage. Fifteen per cent of the owners and upper class tenants (cash renters and furnishing tenants) were without privies or other means of sewage disposal while only four white sharecroppers and no negroes reported a lack of these facilities.

Customarily a plot of ground surounding the house was set aside for a yard. But it was not commonly enclosed. Only seven enclosed yards, three of these the homes of negroes, were found. Every fifth house had no yard. These simply sat in an open field, the land around them being cultivated up to the very doorstep. Most such places were sharecroppers' houses, one-half of the negroes and one-third of the white croppers being so located. Ten per cent of the yards, most of them owners', were sodded, but usually not a spear of grass was allowed to grow, the yard being swept with a husk-mop, an old broom, or a bunch of switches.

One of the signs of good housekeeping was the regularity and care with which the yard was swept. Some flowering shrubs and evergreens were found in the yards of two-thirds of the owners, of one-third of the tenants. Shade trees were found about 80 per cent of the homes. These trees were usually chinaberries for the tenants, and hackberries and water oaks for the owners. There were fruit trees in more than half of the yards. Shade was not limited to the owning classes, but fruit was certainly more plentiful on their places, 75 per cent of their homes as compared with 40 per cent of the sharecroppers' having fruit trees.

The houses typically were one-story wooden structures. They were set on unenclosed foundations and covered with tin roofs. There was but one two-story house in the entire community. All were constructed of wood. Roughly one-half were frame houses, built of boards on a wooden framework and ceiled inside. Some were ceiled with dressed, some with undressed lumber. Only two houses, those of an owner and his son-in-law tenant, were plas-

This tenant's house, of boxed structure and clapboard roof, was more picturesque than livable. The chimney made of native stone was typical of many beautiful ones to be found in the community. The open well at the left not only furnished water for the family, but the mule and cow were watered here also.

tered. Most of the remaining houses were of a structure known·
as "boxed", which consisted of a single boarded wall of rough lumber with narrow strips nailed over the cracks. The third type of
structure found was of logs. Ten per cent of the total were log
houses. These were all old and very definitely represented an
earlier era of building. No house in the community had a base-
ment. Although the typical roof was tin, many of the older houses
had rough shingle (clapboard) roofs, and some of the newer ones
had a composition tar roofing. The owners, all but 14 per cent of
them, lived in ceiled frame houses while most of the tenants lived
in boxed houses. The log houses were evenly scattered throughout the community and among the occupational classes.

Paint and screens, often assumed to be essentials in house construction, were not the rule in Upland Bend. One-half of the
owners' and one-third of the tenant houses were painted on the outside and fewer were painted inside. Forty per cent of all houses
were screened. Among the owners this percentage was 60, and
with the sharecroppers it was only 20. Many of the houses that
were reported as screened had screening only on part of the doors
and windows.

The size of the houses varied. The average had four rooms, the
largest had ten rooms, and three houses were only one-room structures. Differences among the occupational classes were more than
the differences in the size of families would necessitate. The
average large landowner had six rooms, the average small owner
five. The average tenant had less than four rooms and the average negro had but slightly more than two. The rooms available
were variously used. One commonly served as kitchen and dining room, one as living room and bedroom, the others as bedrooms. In many houses one room served as kitchen, dining room
and living room.

PHYSICAL EQUIPMENT

Although no attempt was made to obtain an inventory of household equipment and furnishing which could be called complete,
the evidence at hand does give a picture that is fairly comprehensive and not without significance. The convenience, the comfort,
the health, and the esthetic life of a family are to some extent dependent upon the possession of such things as an adequate water

Wood chopped by father and son heated the house, cooked the meals, and often a cord or two was sold to supplement a meager cash income. Although most of the timber had been cut off, wood was still plentiful enough for fuel.

supply, proper heating facilities, labor saving equipment and a modicum of household furnishing. Concerning these matters some information is available.

Most of the water used for household purposes by the people of Upland Bend was drawn from open wells. Two homes, those of an owner and one of his tenants, had running water. The others depended on wells or nearby springs. The wells were usually located near the houses, and were operated by windlasses. Only three had modern enclosed pumps. One-fourth of the families had no water other than that from springs, and many of these were "under the hill" at a considerable distance from the house. Although the tenant families depended on springs for their water supply more often than the owners did, the fact is that 15 per cent of the owners, one of them around the largest in the community, carried all water from a spring.

Central heating was not found in the community. No furnaces were had, but all houses had at least one fireplace, many had two. This heat was usually supplemented by a cooking stove and every tenth home had additional stoves for heating other rooms. The fuel used in the fireplaces and the stoves was wood cut from the farm.

Labor saving household equipment was limited. There were four kitchen sinks, one washing machine, in the entire community. Two of the large owners had electric plants which were used for lighting purposes and three other owners had acetylene (artificial gas) lights. All of the remaining houses were lighted by kerosene lamps. No bathtubs were found. The two homes that had running water did not have bathrooms. Bathing, when not of the "short bath" variety, was done in a zinc washtub. Fifteen per cent of all of the homes, 30 per cent of the negro homes, had no time piece, watch or clock, in the place.

The furnishings with which rooms are provided give significant insight into living conditions. This part of the equipment in Upland Bend was very simple. Typically there were three or four beds in each home. In the rooms used for sleeping there were usually two, each large enough to accommodate two adults or three or four children. A limited number of wooden chairs, one of which was a rocker, a sewing machine, and two tables, one of which was used as a dining table usually completed the heavier furnishings. A large part of this furniture was homemade. Rugs were not very plentiful, only one-half of all homes had any. Most of those found were of linoleum. The inside walls of the houses were painted in less than one-fourth of the cases and only three houses in the community had papered walls. Hangings consisted of calendars distributed by local or nearby merchants, or else of unframed pictures that had been cut from magazines.

Typical of the supply of less durable equipment was this: the average family had one bedspread, one blanket, four pillow cases and two sheets per bed. Several families had no bedspreads or blankets; a few families had no pillow cases; and one family had no sheets. Only in supply of quilts were there signs of extravagance. The average home had seven quilts for each bed. Although such thinly built and poorly heated houses would demand plenty of cover on cold nights, one does have difficulty in imagining sleeping under this number of quilts.

The larger houses of the upper classes were more elaborately equipped: more beds per person, fibre or woolen rugs, wicker or upholstered furniture, pictures of the family and of relatives and friends, or pictures cut from magazines, framed and hanging on painted walls or standing on tables, and stacks of quilts. In beds and quilts, particularly, the owning classes were well supplied. One owner with a small family of three children reported ten beds in a seven-room house, and one woman reported a total of seventy quilts.

The following accounts chosen more or less at random from the notes of interviewers will help to complete the picture of the houses and their equipment.

An Old Owner's House

"Originally a log cabin. Enlarged by adding a living room, dining room, and porch across the front. New wicker living room suite. Buffet and dining room table belonged to his mother. Open fireplace in kitchen in addition to cooking stove. Calendars on all walls. Floors uncovered and unpainted."

A Young Owner's House

"Three rooms and sleeping porch. House painted green. Yard newly sodded, large flower garden to side of house. Living room large and furniture limited. New Seller's kitchen cabinet. Two iron bedsteads. Floors unpainted. Six or eight flower vases temporarily empty."

A Large Owner's House

"Eight rooms with a large hall running down the middle. Painted inside and outside. Needs new coat. Old fashioned piano in hall. Living room furniture bought by older daughter who was teaching before marriage. Fibre rug on living room floor. Chairs in bedroom rebottomed with sheepskin. Room of another daughter, a high school student, redone as a home-economics project, old paint taken off furniture and repainted, draperies, cover for day bed and chair covers, pictures bought at Kress'. Kitchen and dining room furniture homemade. Newly built homemade cabinets in kitchen."

A Tenant's House

"Three rooms, unpainted, only outside door entering kitchen. At entrance a large hall tree made by Mr. J. from a willow tree. Two rooms sealed, children's bedroom unsealed. Floors undressed lumber, no covering. In one bedroom a desk made at school by oldest son, nicely finished and varnished. Kitchen furniture all homemade. Kitchen walls decorated with three calendars."

A Young Newly-married Sharecropper's House

"Yard freshly swept. Two rooms. Flat roof covered partly with tin, partly with composition roofing, and recently patched in two places with boards. Uncovered front porch, several planks in it broken through. Kitchen furniture, wash stand, and table in bedroom made by Mr. C. Homemade mattress on bed. Cracks in walls stuffed and sealed over with strips of paper. Floors undressed, unpainted, and uncovered. Calendars on walls."

CULTURAL EQUIPMENT

The materials described above provided the physical background against which the general routine of daily activity was carried on. Scarcely less informing than these are the types of equipment which were available for activities of a more leisurely kind. How people think and how they entertain themselves are directly conditioned by the reading materials, musical instruments and play equipment which they have at hand. Due attention to these factors, therefore, is an essential part of the description of the homes.

Reading material, whether in the form of books, magazines, or newspapers, was extremely limited in Upland Bend. The books found most often were, in order of frequency: Bibles (146); Almanacs (76); Catalogs (41); Song Books (31); and Sunday School Quarterlies (18). These five types of books made up approximately 60 per cent of the total of 544 books found in the homes of the community. Seventy-five per cent of the homes had a Bible; 35 per cent had an almanac, and 20 per cent had a general catalog from one of the large mailorder houses. Song books were not found so often but those homes that did have them usually had two or three.

There were only 232 other books found and 42 of these were in the home of one of the local ministers. In other words, excluding the five types of books above named, the average home had one book. Actually there were 131 families, of 60 per cent of the entire number, that had no books other than these five and 20 per cent of all of the homes had only one book of any sort. The types of books found cause one to suspect that those available were read only to a limited extent. One-third of the 232 books were religious books with such titles as *Bible Sketches*; *Bible, Baptist and the Board System;* the *Christian Sabbath; Systematic Giving; A Young Man's Difficulties with His Bible*; and *How Baptists Work Together.* These were not concentrated in the homes of the ministers, but rather were scattered throughout the community. History was represented with such titles as these: *America's War for Humanity*: *The Story of Roosevelt; A History of the World War; The Life of Dan T. Moody; The Merrimac; The Johnstown Horror,* or *The Valley of Death; Woodrow Wilson, Great American;* and *The Galveston Storm.* These books suggest the work of clever book-agents who usually travel through the country during or immediately after some event of national moment selling a "special edition." Seventy-nine books of fiction were found. The works of Edgar Rice Burroughs and Zane Grey were most popular, O. Henry following. There was very little duplication of titles. The only books that appeared in more than one home were two copies each of Zane Gray's *Arizona Ames* and his *Call of the Canyon,* three copies of Milton E. Stine's *The Devil's Bride,* and two of Harold Bell Wright's *Shepherd of the Hills.* There were twenty-one children's books, all for the adolescent age. Seven dictionaries, four of them Webster's Secondary School Dictionaries, and five encyclopedias, a 1904 Britannica and others by Bufton and Chambers, constituted the reference materials. One book on etiquette, and two "success" books, *How to Develop Self-Confidence,* and *The Power of Personality,* were reported. The sole representative of recent best sellers was Durant's *Story of Philosophy,* and the only title that suggested radical social literature was a tract called *Socialism in the Test Tube,* of which two copies were found. The classics were represented by sixteen, philosophy by eight, and sociology by thirteen titles.

The books were seemingly all acquired incidentally as gifts, from pressure salesmanship, or as "bargains." There was no evidence of a definite buying policy on the part of any family. But two books, Edgar Rice Burroughs' *Square Deal Sanderson,* and Zane Gray's *Thundering Herd* were bought during the year of the study. Every fourth book was 25 or more years old and but three of every ten found had been acquired in the previous ten years. In addition to the books owned there were in the homes at the time of visitation a total of forty-one borrowed books. These books, mainly borrowed through the school library, were usually fiction. There were a total of forty-six library cards from the school library and ten cards from the county library which was located in the county seat some twenty-five miles away.

The differences in the number of books owned by the various occupational groups were not as great as the difference in income would lead one to expect. Although a few owners had many more books than any tenant, two of every three landowners had no books other than Bibles, Song Books, Sunday School Quarterlies, Catalogs, and Almanacs. For the tenant classes this ratio was three of every four. The median number of books in the houses of owners was three, and for the tenants was more than two. The negroes, too, seemed to have a fair representation. The number of books found in their houses was actually more than that found among the white sharecroppers. But borrowing facilities among the negroes were non-existent. No library, either in the school or county, was available to them. Some evidence of race consciousness was reflected in the literature owned by negroes. *The Life of Booker T. Washington; The Negro Year Book; The Origin of the Black Man;* and *Up From Slavery* were titles found. One negro sharecropper had the following very interesting collection: The *Bible; Steps to Christ; Spiritualism vs. Christianity; Socialism in the Test Tube; The Christian Sabbath;* and *The Other Side of Death.*

Magazines were relatively more plentiful than books. At the time of our visitation seventy-three different magazines were represented with a total of 323 recent copies actually in the homes. Most of these had been subscribed for. There were a total of 189 that regularly came into the community. One-half of the homes subscribed for one or more and every tenth one got four or more. Twenty-three of those found were single copies that had been bought from news-stands in nearby towns and forty-nine of them had been borrowed from neighbors.

Most of the magazines were of general interest, but farm journals, magazines on the home, and religious publications were rather common. The magazines appearing in five or more homes were as follows:

	Number of Homes
Progressive Farmer	62
Country Gentleman	41
True Story	26
McCalls Magazine	23
Saturday Evening Post	21
Ladies Home Journal	14
American Magazine	10
True Romance	10
Pictorial Review	8
Comfort	8
Southern Agriculturalist	7
Southern Farmer	5
Home Circle	5
Western Story	5

As can be seen from this list, the cultural content was not particularly high. Only two magazines which were rated by Morgan and Leahy as having high cultural content were found. These were the *National Geographic* and the *Literary Digest*. *Parent's Magazine* appeared in one home and one family subscribed for *Child Life*. On the other hand, there were 18 periodicals with a total of 61 different copies represented by such titles as: *True Story, Detective Stories,* and *Wild West Weekly.*

ADVERTISEMENT OF MAGAZINES AS FOUND IN A WEEKLY
COUNTY NEWSPAPER

Another type of magazine frequently found is represented in the accompanying advertisement reproduced from a weekly county paper. One hundred and seventeen of the subscriptions found in the community, more than 60 per cent of the total, are accounted for by the magazines listed in this advertisement. Seven of the magazines listed in *Group A* and ten of those from *Group B* were found in Upland Bend. These magazines were seemingly popular because of their price. The possibility of getting a year's subscription to six magazines and a weekly newspaper for $1.60 is certainly attractive. The religious journals represented the various denominations with titles such as *The Alabama Baptist, Christian Advocate, Herald of Holiness,* and *Minutes of the Church of God's Children.*

Differences among the economic classes were pronounced here. The average owner subscribed for a little more than two magazines; the renters and furnishing tenants had one and the sharecroppers, negro and white, had less than one-half a magazine per home. Only one-fourth of the landowners subscribed to no magazines while two-thirds of the tenants had none. The economic differences were not reflected in the cultural content. The "confessions" and the cheap general classification described above were found in the owners' homes just as often as in those of the white tenant classes. With the negroes, the general interest reading was confined to the "confessions" literature except for two Westerns and two copies of *Argosy.* Most of the negroes' magazines were farm journals, however.

Newspapers, too, constituted a form of reading matter found in many homes. Four of every ten of the homes of Upland Bend regularly received a daily paper and twelve received two. Homes that got one paper only invariably subscribed to the daily from the county seat, the second paper came from the state's metropolis, Birmingham. No one received a daily paper from any other city. The number of weekly papers taken was much more limited, only eighteen being reported from the entire community. Weekly papers were published in both Chehaw and DeSoto counties, but eleven of the weekly papers found were from more distant counties, probably being from counties where their readers had previously lived or had connections.

Availability of a newspaper was very definitely related to economic standing in the community. All of the eleven large owners and 60 per cent of all owners received one paper. The twelve homes receiving two papers were all those of owners. Only 30 per cent of the total tenant group and only one sharecropper received a daily paper. Among thirty negro families two papers were found. The weekly papers published nearby were subscribed to by the owning classes, but eight of the eleven weeklies from a distance were found in tenant homes, a finding consistent with evidence presented earlier to the effect that the tenants represented a more migratory group.

The educational and recreational implications involved in limited reading facilities are probably no greater than those that result from a scarcity of the materials for producing and enjoying music and playing games. Musical equipment, particularly of the more elaborate and expensive sort, was scarce in Upland Bend. There were 64 different musical instruments in the community: 22 victrolas (most of them portable), 16 organs, 14 pianos, 6 radios (one of these not working), 2 hand organs (accordions), 2 violins, and 2 guitars. It will be noticed that the number of instruments that need "playing" rather than "listening to" was relatively large. The scarcity of radios was in part due to the generally limited economic resources, but the unsatisfactoriness of battery sets, the only type available in the absence of electric power, was also a factor.

The possession of instruments was mostly confined to the owning groups and one-third of the total were in the homes of the eleven large owners. All of the radios, pianos, violins, guitars, and hand-organs were the property of landowners. But four victrolas and five organs were owned by tenants. The white sharecroppers' portion was one organ and one portable victrola. Although negroes are commonly thought of as having more interest in music than have white people, the musical equipment of the entire negro population consisted of one old organ owned by a negro sharecropper.

Equipment for playing games represents a much smaller cash outlay and was correspondingly more plentiful. In the community there was a total of 140 pieces of equipment. Sixty-one of these were sets of dominoes. Playing cards (26 packs), checker boards (21), and rook decks (13) came next in order. These four games, which accounted for 90 per cent of the total equipment, are purchasable from the ten cent stores in the county seat and that is probably where those found were bought. The cheapness of these materials doubtless accounted in considerable part for their popularity, but they are also sedentary games and as such were more congenial for old and young alike after hours of physical exertion in kitchen and field.

Most of the remaining equipment for play consisted of a few bags of marbles, horseshoes, baseballs, and kites. One might imagine that horseshoes would be a popular game in the country. In this community, however, nearly all of the horses were mules and many of them small at that. The initiated know, of course, that mule shoes won't do for the game of horseshoes. One might look for more baseball equipment. But baseball, even the "sand-lot" variety, calls for a number of players, experience in team work, a broad, level playing field, and some equipment. These are more difficult to find in the country. Six families had some tennis gear although the only tennis court available, located at the school, was weedgrown. One of the large landowners had a pool table, and another, a set of golf clubs. The landowners, as usual, were much better provided with equipment than the other families. Approximately 60 per cent of the owning groups and related tenants had some equipment, only 30 per cent of the unrelated tenants had any. Only six games were found in the thirty negro homes. However, the economic factor was not the only one involved in the scarcity of playing equipment. In five homes the reason for their absence was given as being "against our religion"; in another home the older daughter reported a deck of rook cards which the mother denied the existence of. This taboo was particularly strong against playing cards as one of the interviewers discovered when he asked an old sharecropper if he had any games. After some hesitation the old man replied: "Yes, we have a pack of playin' cards." His wife, who was listening in, was obviously shocked at this frank admission of questionable practice before a stranger. Recovering quickly, she put in sharply: "Now, pappy, you know we ain't."

In summary, the homes were found to be fairly well located with reference to roads, certainly not congested but not too isolated from neighbor, school, church, and store.

They were homes with some picturesqueness, but at the same time one who reacts to them in terms of the modern American setting is impressed with a certain physical unattractiveness, a paucity of equipment, and a cultural inadequacy. This was without doubt mainly because of an economic insufficiency. Among people with limited incomes one would not expect a great deal in the way of beautified surroundings, labor saving equipment or the materials of culture. That the economic factor was a fundamental one was shown by the consistency of the differences among the occupational classes.

On the other hand, there was some evidence supporting the assumption that qualitative differences were often not as great as the quantitative. In the matter of privies, of carrying water from springs, of kinds of equipment and furnishings, of quality in reading matter, superiority was not found commensurate with increased economic position. Perhaps the cultural patterns of the people, which involved limited concern with esthetic values and material conveniences, must be put alongside economic status as a contributing factor in making the homes what they were.

CHAPTER VII

THE CHURCHES

The first institution which the early settlers of Upland Bend felt they needed, when their homes had been raised, was the church. From that day until comparatively recent years the intellectual and cultural interests of the people have been centered very largely in this institution. At the time of the survey the life of the community was revolving, more and more, around the consolidated school. Even then, however, it was taken for granted that any grown person was a member of the church and toward it nearly everyone assumed an attitude of respect.

The oldest of the seven churches that existed at the time of the survey was the Shady Grove Missionary Baptist which was founded on a site of six acres in 1824. A few years afterwards the Tabernacle Methodist was established with eight acres of ground which proved to be very useful several decades later when the camp meeting became a favorite Methodist activity. In 1880 the New Chapel Free Will Baptists set up their church on a single acre to which later a second acre was added for the cemetery. The Mount Gilead Missionary Baptist Church for negroes was erected in 1892. Seven years after this the Good Hope Methodists had their beginning. After a series of meetings under a brush arbor Kellum's Nazarene Church was built in 1929. Finally the institution which we shall call the Church of God's Children was organized in 1933.

The religious needs of the community, it is thus seen, were being served by six churches for white people and by one for negroes. The attention of the reader will be directed first to the five oldest white churches. Between the several congregations marked differences existed as will be shown. On the other hand it was feasible to treat these five institutions as a group because their practices were similar in many ways and all belonged to well-known, traditional denominations. The discussion of the Church of God's Children will be reserved for a later section for reasons which will there be explained. After this consideration will be given to the church for negroes.

MEMBERSHIP AND MATERIAL BACKGROUND

One of the first questions to raise about an institution is—who belongs to it? The place of the institution in the community, the nature of its contributions, and its influence are all illuminated to a considerable extent by analysis of its constituency. The five chief white churches with which we are now concerned had a combined total of 654 names on their rolls. Most of the institutions served adjacent communities as well as Upland Bend and some of the names belonged to people who had moved away. Approximately three-fifths of the total number of names, however, were identified as those of people then residing within the community.

Analysis of the combined membership yielded a number of interesting facts concerning sex, age, and denominational affiliation. Women and girls constituted 58 per cent of the membership as compared with 42 per cent for men and boys. Of the total number 74 per cent were adults while only 26 per cent were under 21 years of age. Of the younger group 67 per cent were females and 33 per cent were males. Grown women, it is clear, constituted the numerically predominating element. Men were present in substantial numbers, but young men and boys were compartively few. The tendency of the young, and especially of the young male, not to come into the fold was more marked in the two older and larger churches in which the more fortunate economic classes were most heavily represented. The denominational choices were overwhelmingly Baptist or Methodist. More than a majority (54 per cent) of the total number of communicants were Baptists. Most of the remainder (43 per cent) were Methodists, but 3 per cent were Nazarenes.

The facts above given are supported by the returns from the canvass of the entire list of Upland Bend families. Three-fourths of the householders, white and colored alike, reported that they were members of local churches. Some of the remainder were affiliated with churches outside of the community; but their attendance was probably very irregular on account of the distances to be traveled. The housewives belonged in decidedly greater numbers than their husbands; only a handful of the former (5 per cent), in fact, had not joined. Nearly all of the church people were Baptists or Methodists. A small number were Nazarenes

Churches have played an important role in the life of Upland Bend. The history of the congregation housed in this attractive building dated back to 1824.

and two or three were Presbyterians or Christians. Usually, but not always, the members of a family belonged to the same church. When they attended they went to the church to which they belonged. There was, on the other hand, a considerable amount of visiting around, especially on the part of the owning families. Any person who wished to attend regularly, indeed, was forced to visit other churches than his own because none in the community had a congregational meeting every Sunday.

The largest of the five churches was the Tabernacle Methodist which had 241 members. To it belonged one-half of the owning families of the community, including several of the large owners and one-third of the related tenants. The Shady Grove Baptist church which enrolled 220 members also enjoyed substantial support from the owning groups. The New Chapel Baptist with 130 members drew its strength about equally from the owning, related, and unrelated tenant classes. The two remaining congregations were small—there being only 40 names on the roll of the Good Hope Methodist, and 23 at Kellum's Nazarene. Neither of these congregations included more than two or three owning families. Three only of the five churches enrolled more than 100 members. But more than 90 per cent of the total membership was concentrated in these three. The numerical weakness of the two small congregations was so marked that it was difficult to envisage anything for them but a grim struggle for existence.

It is worth while to know what families directed the activities and controlled the organization of the churches. This question was readily answered by examining the lists of congregational officers including deacons, stewards, trustees, and Sunday-School superintendents. Four-fifths of these officials, it was found, were residents of the community which meant, doubtless, that the Upland Bend people exercised the predominating influence. Of the officers who lived in Upland Bend two-thirds were representatives of owning families. The remaining one-third came from tenant families but most of these families were related to owners. So it is safe to say that the control of the churches rested in the hands of the owning groups. The smaller institutions in which owning families were scarce were not exceptions to this rule. All of the congregations, it appeared, had been built around families that owned land.

The younger struggling churches have to be satisfied with such simple buildings as this, weatherboarded, with tin roof, and unceiled. The picture, taken during services, shows that many people, particularly young men, "stood around" outside.

The material equipment and financial support that were available to the five white churches conditioned substantially the work they were able to do. All of the houses in which they worshipped were one-room frame structures which were covered with weatherboarding on the outside. In size they ranged from 30 x 36 to 40 x 60 feet. With the exception of the Nazarene building all were ceiled and painted inside and out. A belfry crowned the Shady Grove Baptist structure.

On the inside there was a platform and pulpit but only the three largest institutions had special chairs for the platform. For music the larger Methodist and Baptist churches had pianos while the others used foot-power organs. The number of song books per congregation ranged from twenty-four to sixty. Lighting was supplied by one to three gas or oil lamps and heating by one or two wood stoves. The aisle and platform of the old Methodist church were covered with carpet.

The annual salaries assigned to the pastors were—$350.00 by the Tabernacle Methodists, $125.00 by the New Chapel Baptists, $100.00 by the Shady Grove Baptists and $50.00 each by the other two. These amounts were not always paid in full. In every case part of the salary, in some more than one-half, was paid in eggs, chickens, meat, corn, syrup, potatoes, and quilts. To round out a living each of the pastors served from one to four other small congregations or drew support from the denomination at large. But even this was not enough, for four of the ministers followed other vocations. Only one pastor, he who served the best-paying congregation, was a full-time professional man and he alone resided in the community.

Expenses for maintenance were on an even smaller scale than pastors' salaries. Nothing was set aside for insurance which is comparatively expensive in the country. When a building burned the congregation simply started again from scratch. Janitorial service cost nothing because it was done without charge by devoted women who lived nearby. They were the ones that changed the pulpit linen, washed the windows, and swept the floor. When the wood pile ran low a landowner cut up an oak tree that had blown down and donated it to the church. When the lamps burned low a free will offering was collected at Sunday School to buy a few gallons of oil. By these means cash outlays for current expenses were kept at a minimum.

CHURCH SERVICES

Regularly scheduled hours of worship, which the entire congregation is expected to attend, constitute the most traditional activity of Protestant churches. A large part of the work of the grown people is done in connection with these services and most of the instruction particularly designed for adults is given there. The number of services offered is determined, largely, by the proportion of the minister's time which a congregation is able to command. The average pastor's salary of the five chief churches in Upland Bend was $135.00 per year. For this compensation not many services could be obtained. None of the churches had a regular congregational service every Sunday. The total number of such services per congregation ranged from two to four a month, but these were concentrated on either one or two Sundays. The Tabernacle Methodist Church, which was the largest and whose membership had most wealth, for example, held one service every second Sunday and two services every fourth Sunday. Kellum's Nazarene held only two "preachings" per month both of which fell on the second Sunday. In addition to the Sabbath Day services two of the churches, the Tabernacle and Kellum's, held prayer meetings during the week. These regular services were supplemented by revivals which usually lasted from ten days to two weeks and were conducted by a visiting preacher or by a revival specialist. One such meeting a year met the needs of the Baptist and Methodist churches but two or three a year were held by the Nazarenes.

The hours of worship of the several churches, it so happened, were distributed in such a way that a service was available somewhere every Sunday. Any person who so desired was able to hear a sermon every week if he was willing to attend another church than his own. The fact that the pastor was away much of the time forced the members of each congregation to rely much on themselves. On this account leadership was developed and talents were cultivated that otherwise might never have come to fruition.

The order of service was much the same in the several congregations. The meeting that was held one Sunday morning in March at the Shady Grove Baptist Church will serve as an example. The service opened with the song, "Rescue the Perishing." After prayer by the pastor a second song, "What a Friend We have in Jesus", was sung. The Scripture lesson, which consisted of the second chapter of Habbakkuk, was then read. When the collection had been taken a visiting minister offered a second prayer. After this the pastor launched into the sermon, the entire second chapter of Habbakkuk serving as his text. At the conclusion of the sermon "Jesus is Calling" and "Dwelling in Beulah Land" were sung. Finally the benediction was pronounced by one of the laymen who was a physician. The singing, which was led by an informal mixed choir of a dozen voices or so, was accompanied by a piano that was played by one of the women of the congregation.

The central feature of the Protestant congregational service is the sermon. In this discourse the minister finds his chief opportunity to instruct the people in the principles that are regarded as fundamental. The value of a particular service is judged by the layman pretty largely in terms of what he thinks of the sermon. Realizing this to be the case the minister to some extent undoubtedly tries to incorporate in his discourse what he thinks the people want as well as what they need. Sermons, for these reasons, give significant indications of the quality of the cultural patterns which prevail in religious circles.

The titles of sermons, taken by themselves, yield important clues. During the survey sermons by the following titles were preached by the pastor of the Tabernacle Methodist Church: "Render unto God that which is God's", "The Church as a Divine Institution", "Christ's Mission", and "The Power of the Gospel." These themes are conservative and neatly based on Scriptural passages; yet they are definitely evangelical. The language in which the titles were couched bears evidence of intellectual polish and it is rhetorically correct. The author of the titles had more courses in a theological school in his training than the other ministers and his form of worship was the most restrained.

The following titles are those of sermons which were preached by the minister of the New Chapel Free Will Baptist Church: "The Dedication of the Will", "Christ must Increase but I must Decrease", "By the Grace of God I am what I am", "The Wages of Sin versus the Wages of Christ", "To Know Christ in the Power of His Resurrection", "A Divine Savior", "One Who can Understand our Errors", "The Race is not always to the Swift", "He that Endureth to the End", "The Many Mansions", and "Reviving old Customs." These themes are Scriptural and evangelical like those above. The ideas that were developed around them included, among others, the necessity of religious self-discipline, the destructive results of sin, Jesus' redeeming power, strength through faith, blessings in the future for those now unsuccessful, and great rewards for resistance to worldly temptations. By minister and congregation alike discourses on such ideas as these, it may be safely assumed, were considered both profitable and appropriate for the people who came to church.

In the Nazarene Church sermons were preached on the following topics: "The Need of Sanctification", "The Power of the Blood", "Young People on the Primrose Path", "The Judgment Day", and "Hell and its Horrors."

To extend further the reader's understanding of the nature of the instruction which the ministers delivered to their congregations it will be helpful to go beyond the titles and examine the digests which it was possible to make of several sermons. The full thought and spirit of the preacher cannot be captured completely in a form of reproduction as compact as a digest. It does, however, afford a record of the main points that were made as these were taken down from outlines provided by the minister.

The sermon that is presented first, "Reviving Old Customs" was preached by the minister of the Shady Grove Baptist Church on Homecoming Day. Homecoming was an annual feature of the worship of the older churches. On the Sunday that was designated for this purpose former members and relatives and friends who had moved away from the community came back to visit their families, decorate the cemetery, and worship at the old church in which they were reared. The crowd was swelled further by many visitors from other churches within the community. These were happy occasions and the church in which the meetings were held was usually filled to overflowing. The sermon, "Reviving Old Customs", therefore, represented a strong effort on the part of the minister to prepare a discourse aptly fitted to a special occasion.

Reviving Old Customs

"The text tells us that Isaac digged again the wells dug by his father, Abraham. (Genesis 26:18) In the wilderness where Isaac lived a well was a blessing to the traveler, it enriched the land and made things grow, and tents were built about it. A well was as great as a castle or a pyramid in that land and time.

"God, who is our salvation, is like a well to us. The Christian will trust and not be afraid who understands that the Lord Jehovah is his strength, his song, and his salvation. (Isaiah 12:2-3) Isaiah saw what was to come in modern times. You are too busy amassing fortunes and seeking fame. You have lost God and what makes for character. Today men have no song, no strength, no joy. You should ask yourselves what is your strength, your song and your joy.

"At another ancient well, that of Jacob, Jesus was sitting one day about the sixth hour when He was weary of His journey. (John 4:6) A woman who was bad came unto Him and He gave her water that cured her thirst forever and told her all she ever did. The Old Testament Law was the best well of water they had in those days. It was a covenant between men and God. In the old law the Sheep died for the shepherd. The day this law was given 300 souls were slain. The new law is that of Grace.

In this the Shepherd died for the sheep. When this law was given 3000 souls were saved. (Acts 2:41) We enter into the new law by faith in its works.

"This day of homecoming in our church is the time for us to dig a well from which we can drink the water of friendship. We need a closer approach to God, a greater fellowship with his children, and a greater desire to please Him. Let us gather around this well and record our vows that we will say goodbye to selfishness, thoughtlessness, and sin of every sort. Let us leave failure and set our faces toward Christ and drink of the water that He giveth. Let us go back to the Bible and bubble up for Him like an artesian well. (Genesis 25:11)

"Abraham gave the wells he dug a special name that meant the well of Him that liveth and seeth me. It is good for us to remember today that God sees us. (Genesis 22:19) Beersheba was the well of the oath or covenant between God and man. After his death Abraham's wells were filled up by his enemies. (Text requoted) Let us, like Isaac, dig up the old wells anew and blaze away for a greater church and a greater faith. Even in our failures Jesus loves us, for once when He found His disciples asleep, He explained that their eyes were heavy. Our wells have failed in the past because of strife and hatred which we must forsake for God's plan of salvation on which we cannot improve.

"Let us then contend for the faith once delivered to the saints. Let us dig anew the wells for our homes, better church attendance, better living in business, and better representation of Christ. He will give unto us of the water of life freely. The enemies of Christ are trying to fill up His open side. But you should seek the Lord while He may be found. Today if ye hear His voice harden not your hearts."

The two remaining sermons were preached by the pastor of the New Chapel Baptist Church. "Ruth's Resolution" was a vigorous call to sinners to forsake the paths of sin and the terrible future that awaits them in order that they might take this stand with the people of God before it is too late. "A Divine Savior" was more of a doctrinal discourse in which the effort was made to set forth the necessity of accepting Jesus. In this sermon there is an incidental but powerful denunciation of the religious position of the

Jewish Church. The young man who took this stand in the pulpit was sweet in disposition and tolerant in personal relations. It is difficult to believe that he ever had or ever would behave in an unkindly way toward any member of the race whose religious tenets his conception of God and of Salvation compelled him to condemn.

Ruth's Resolution

"Ruth asked her mother-in-law, Naomi, not to entreat her to return to Moab. Whither Naomi went she herself desired to go. But Orphah followed Naomi's entreaties and returned to her native land. (Ruth 1:16).

"This story is included in the Bible because the Holy Ghost took notice of Boaz and Ruth. From their loins sprang the Savior of the world. And the Bible is the story of Christ, their descendant. This story, moreover, seems to be typical of the calling of the gentile church and, likewise, of the conversion of every believer. For Ruth forsook her own people and their idols to join Israel and she became the mother of Jesus. Every true Christian, in the same manner, is the mother of Jesus. (Matt. 12:50) All true believers, like Ruth, must forsake their relatives and country.

"Ruth and Orphah represent two different sorts of professors of religion. Both told Naomi they would go with her. Orphah, however, returned after going a little way. Thus some professors start well and fair at the beginning but do not last. Ruth, on the other hand, was sound, sincere, and steadfast. (Text requoted) She received her reward in natural and spiritual things. For God raised David and Solomon from her seed, and Jesus. (Ruth 2:11-12) Thus through her all the families of the earth were blessed.

"You have a right to the same blessing. Those who have accepted Christ are anxious for you to follow them. Decide now with whom you are going to live. (Text repeated) When those with whom we live are turning to God and joining His people it ought to be our firm resolution that we will not leave our people and God. With our neighbors and friends of enlightened mind we ought to leave the tents of wickedness and dwell with God and His people. There is a great difference in those about us. The children of God are citizens of Zion and happy. The others are enemies of God and miserable. They are condemned to Hell. We must deside which we will be.

"The God of the children of Israel is a glorious God. There is none like Him in glory and excellency. He is kindness, the King of Glory, a strong rock, a high tower. In His hands He hath all things but He delighteth in mercy. His race is infinite and endures forever. Such is the God of those that have forsaken their sins and have received forgiveness. They have exchanged sin for God. They have a savior, the only begotten Son of God who was sacrificed for them.

"Their people are excellent and happy people. (Prov. 12:26) They are children of the King and more excellent than their neighbors. God is for them; who can be against them. As the mountains are around Jerusalem so God is around them—a shield and a rewarder. Happiness is nowhere to be found but in God and His people. He is the God for calamity and for a broken, sinful heart.

"Can't you see by the example that the call is for you? You ought to be fixed and strong. Whosoever of you that forsaketh not all he hath, he cannot be my disciple. (Luke 14:33) You need to go out, letting God show the way. Ruth did this and she became a strong person. She left all for God. You who are Christians have gone under the same roof with God. You who are sinners look to the Rock of Ages, consider your souls precious and immaterial. There is a great gulf, as between the rich man and Lazarus, as wide as right and left, between those who rise to God and those who go down in contempt to Hell."

A Divine Savior

"Jesus knew that His life was almost over. His disciples were worried about the future. He realized that they needed a conception of His coming to earth. So He asked the disciples what men said that He was and then He asked the real question "Whom say ye that I am." And Peter answered "Thou art the Christ, the Son of the living God." (Matt. 16:15-16) Which is our text today.

"Many verdicts concerning Jesus were passed by various men as reported in the Scriptures. They called Him a mystic, a winebibber, and a friend of publicans and sinners. John the Baptist said He would be a healer and require repentance of those who

would be saved. Some discerning the sorrow on His face said He
was Jeremiah. Others, that He was another prophet preaching a
new faith in God. None of these people had the New Testament.
Having this, we can know more about Jesus than they did. Yet
many men today believe the same things of Jesus that His contem-
poraries did.

"The Jews do not accept Jesus now, as they did not then, for
what He said He was. (John 8:58) He was not a deceiver; it is
blasphemy of them not to believe Him. It is also said in the Scriptures that he that honoreth not the Son honoreth not the Father.
The Jews killed Jesus for claiming that He was equal with God.
This was right by their law. They say He is dead and they will
not worship a dead Christ. Their hearts are carnal and they have
no hope in the next world.

"But Peter said, 'Thou art the Christ.' Jesus told him that God
had given him this insight, not flesh and blood. This is faith. The
Spirit called Peter. If we will study His deeds and character we
will confess like Peter and this will increase our personalities.
Christ was not just a pure, noble, and pitiful man but He was the
Infinite. If you are in doubt let the divine Savior talk to you and
tell you what God said. Christ gave men the privilege of worship-
ping Him. If we believe Christ is the Son of God let us go forth
and worship Him all the days of our lives. Let us not go to Hell
but keep the broad way which He marked out."

The titles and digests of sermons, as reported above, give significant indications concerning prevailing patterns of religious
thought. The Scriptures, it is clear, overshadowed everything else
in the sermons. Of an inclination on the part of the preachers to
remind their hearers of the vast body of secular learning there was
little evidence. Interpretations of the Scriptures were conservative. Improvement in the lives of members was sought along or-
thodox lines. It was as individuals that the people were urged to
leave off sinful things, to depend on Jesus, and to take a stand for
God. Personal salvation was at stake.

OTHER ACTIVITIES

Like other churches those in Upland Bend had found it expedi-
ent to organize other types of religious work to supplement that

of the regular church service. These additional activities were intended to provide more effective opportunity for certain readily distinguishable elements of the congregation such as the children, the young people, or the ladies.

The Sunday School was designed originally for the instruction of children. Although classes are now organized for adults and the leadership is supplied by adults the Sunday School still represents the most substantial effort of religious bodies to train their young in the principles for which they stand. In Upland Bend this work was even more important than the above would indicate because, unlike the congregation, the Sunday School met every Sunday and every church maintained a Sunday School. The bulk of the responsibility for this work, moreover, rested on the laymen as the pastor was seldom there. Those who participated had opportunity to gain valuable training and many, who otherwise might have had little to do, were thereby developed in religious experience. The level of this experience, however, might have been raised materially if the laymen had had more ready access to professional counsel.

The enrollment of all five Sunday Schools taken together was 298. The Tabernacle Methodist was the largest with 96 members and Kellum's Nazarene was the smallest with 38 members. In the two younger and weaker churches, in which congregational services were less frequent, the Sunday School enrolled approximately as many members as the church itself. This was not true of the older and larger institutions where many of the parents believed, it appeared, that the Sunday School was better for the children than it was for adults. Like the church, however, the Sunday School was more attractive to girls and women than it was to boys and men.

Each of the Sunday Schools maintained classes for members of different ages but the classes were not divided according to sex. In the Tabernacle Methodist School, there were six classes: two for adults and one each for the seniors, intermediates, juniors, and "picture cards." In the Nazarene School, however, there were only three classes, one each for adults, older children, and primaries. The officers included a superintendent, a secretary-treasurer, a pianist or organist, a song leader, and a teacher and secretary for each class. The superintendent was usually a man but most of the other officers were women or girls.

The services of the Sunday Schools usually began at 10:00 o'clock and lasted about an hour. In all cases the procedure was about the same. As an example that was typical we can take a meeting of the New Chapel Baptist Sunday School that was held one Sunday early in March with seventy-five persons present. The services opened with the song, "When the Love Waves Reached My Soul." After a prayer by one of the older boys the following songs from the Hartford Music Book were sung by all: "When We Sing the Morning by the River", "We'll Sing Again", and "I'll Let the Hallelujahs Roll." A second prayer was offered by one of the women which was followed with the song, "Remember Me." The five classes then adjourned to their several places for the discussion of the lesson. During this time the collection, which amounted in all to 75 cents, was taken. When the classes had reassembled the secretaries reported on attendance and collections. Certain announcements were then made by the superintendent whereupon the pastor pronounced the benediction.

Young People's Societies are a comparatively recent development in the history of the Protestant Church. Their chief function is to give adolescents actual experience in religious work. Instruction is offered, but activity on the part of the youngsters themselves is what is expected to be emphasized. As far back as 1915 the value of this work was recognized at the Tabernacle Church and in 1927 organizations were formed at the Baptist churches. Weekly meetings that lasted about an hour were held every Sunday. Every few weeks there was a "social meeting" at some member's home at which candy was pulled, popcorn was roasted or games were played. Each of the societies sent delegates to the occasional district meetings. In this way the local youth made contact with those of other communities—an experience of a broadening nature that was especially valuable to young people in the country.

The total number of members in the three societies was 129, boys and girls being represented in approximately equal numbers. More than one-half of the membership, however, was concentrated in the very active League of the Free Will Baptist Church. The officers included a president, vice-president, secretary, treasurer,

Bible quiz leader, song leader, accompanist, and two group captains. The duty of the latter was to arrange and direct the programs on alternate Sundays with the assistance of the members of their groups. This wide distribution of responsibility encouraged extensive participation. To see that these opportunities were used to good advantage was the responsibility of a few interested adults.

The chief activity of the societies, as indicated above, was that of the Sunday evening meeting. What was done on these occasions, determined in large measure the worth of the contributions which the societies made to the religious training of their members. With the intention of aiding the reader to form an opinion on this subject brief descriptions will be given of several programs as these were observed by members of the staff.

"Shady Grove Baptist Young People's Union"

Ages 16-21—March 18, 7:00 P.M.—16 present

Opened with a song
Scripture lesson: John 1:1-14 (Read)
Sentence prayers by several members
Short talks by members on the following topics:
"Christ is Eternal"
"The Scriptures Teach that the Child is the Medium of Creation"
"Through Him the Physical Universe was Made"
"Through Jesus Christ Life was Created"
"Christ is the Creator of Spiritual Realities"
Dismissed with prayer

"Shady Grove Junior Baptist Young People's Union"

Ages 6-15—March 11, 7:00 P.M.—12 present
Opened with a song
Subject: "A Miracle on a Mountain Top"
Scripture lesson: John 2:5-15 (Read)
Short talks by members on the following topics:
"Elijah Starts back to Samaria"
"When Obadiah Met Elijah"
"Ahab Talks to Elijah"
"Elijah Proposes a Contest"

"The Prophets of Baal Fail"
"Elijah's Preparation"
Dismissed with prayer by older woman

"Free Will Baptist League"

Ages 8-21—March 18, 7:00 P.M.—45 present
Opened with a song
Subject: "How Jesus Deals with Sinners"
Scripture lesson: John 4:9-26 (Read)
Introductory prayer
Song
Collection
Short talks by members on the following topics:
  "The Awakening of a Soul"
  "The Satisfying of Soul Thirst"
  "Introducing a Delicate Subject" (The woman of Samaria)
  "A New Question Raised"
Prayer
Quartet: "On the Road to Jericho" (4 boys)
Dismissal

The young people obviously enjoyed the social and the musical parts of the programs.

The Ladies Aid Society was not a prominent feature of church life in Upland Bend. Only one society, that of the New Chapel Baptists, was in operation. The explanation of the scarcity of distinctively feminine organizations was to be found probably in the fact that the energies of the leading women were already heavily engaged in the other divisions of church work. The one society that existed, however, was quite active. It met monthly on Thursday afternoons from 1:30 to 4:30 at the church in the winter and at the homes of members in the summer. The Scriptures were read and prayers were offered at these meetings but most of the time the ladies were very busily engaged making quilts for the pastor or for the orphans or to be sold for funds with which to beautify the cemetery. Reports were made on visits to the sick. Dues of 5 cents per month were asked of the eighteen members but none needed to be embarrassed who was unable to pay. There was $7.95 in the treasury.

COMMUNITY SINGINGS

Community singings were a very important side of the religious life of Upland Bend. Several of the churches, the three younger and smaller ones, held a singing on a designated Sunday every month. This practice had been discontinued by the two older and larger institutions, but their people especially the younger ones freely attended such meetings at the other churches. In one church, the Free Will Baptists, music was cultivated with unusual elaboration. In this congregation there were four quartets, mainly of young people, two of the groups being of male and two of female voices. Two young women and two girls sang duets and one young man was a soloist. All of these participated actively in the singings held at their church. Religious songs and hymns made up nearly all of the music.

The direction of the singing at a given church was in the hands of a relatively permanent leader. This individual was a man, ordinarily, who had had the benefit of a short summer-school course of instruction in religious group-singing. The songs he knew by heart. With all the musicians and singers in that vicinity he was well acquainted. Usually he was a hale and hearty fellow who was good at managing a rural company. The "seven note" music, as distinguished from the "four note" or Sacred Harp music, was employed in the singings at Upland Bend.

The atmosphere about a singing was good humored and informal. Men, women, young people, and children were all equally welcome. Some came dressed up but others wore everyday clothes. Everybody was invited to join in but his ability to do so, especially in the case of less familiar songs, was limited by the scarcity of song books. People came and went as they pleased. When they were tired little children fell asleep in their parents' arms or under the benches where they had been playing. The county politicians, some of whom were good singers themselves, did not fail to recognize the importance of these musical occasions, for they were among the favorite haunts of the seekers-for-office.

For further details concerning singings the reader will be invited to follow the observations of a member of the staff who attended an occasion of this nature at Kellum's Nazarene Church. The account reads as follows:

All-Day Sunday Singing at Kellum's Nazarene Church

"The third Sunday in April was a bright, sunshiny day. The air was fresh and cool. The birds made sweet music in the trees. It was a good day to attend the singing at Kellum's Nazarene Church. By 10:00 o'clock about 200 people from all over the community and thereabouts had assembled. There they would remain until 4:30 that afternoon. On the outside about twenty people were sitting in vehicles or standing around in small groups, talking. Eight or ten men stood in the door and about as many were leaning against the wall in the back. Most of those inside were sitting on backless benches of undressed lumber.

"On the pulpit platform the pastor, the Reverend Earnest Ancell, was seated. In the chairs behind him sat five men including one of the leading politicians and singers of the county (Mr. John Etheridge), a visiting Nazarene minister (the Reverend Holley Boyd), and three of the leading members of the church. The organists and the chief singers, some of whom came from other communities, were grouped about the ancient organ which furnished the music and which stood at the right of the platform.

The pastor, suddenly rose from his seat, rapped hard on the pulpit, and, when the hum of voices had died down, spoke out in a cheerful, strong voice: "Now, folks, I know you have come here to worship the Lord. Let's get going right away. We can't do no better than start on that grand old standby, the 'Glory Land Way.' Everybody stand and let's go to it." With this the organ started, the pastor waved both hands, and began to sing powerfully from memory. The expectant audience joined in with a will and everybody seemed glad he was there. When the last verse had been finished Brother Ancell called on Brother Boyd, the visiting minister, to lead in prayer.

"Then Mr. Ancell said, 'Folks, we have a real treat today: the Ramah Quartet will sing for us.' The leader of the four young men, who were from a neighboring church, then rose and announced they would sing "Going Home." This they did with vigor to the accompaniment of their own organist, a young lady. When the quartet sat down the pastor announced that Mr. Ted Capley would lead two songs, "I want to Go over There" and "I'm So Glad." The audience did not manage these very well. At the conclusion of the second song Mr. Ancell, evidently seeking to arouse greater enthusiasm, said, 'I'm going to ask Mr. Capley to sing that first verse again. Pick up now, folks and let's don't slip up on this song.' The visiting minister yelled, 'Thank God! I'm so glad! Praise God!'

"Mr. Ancell then asked Mrs. Mayme Hayes (about 23 years old) to sing. Mrs. Hayes rose quickly, announced the number of "Death will Never Knock on Heaven's Door", and began timing the music with short, snappy movements of the right hand. The audience sang loudly. At the end Mr. Boyd shouted, 'Thank the Lord.' Mrs. Hayes then announced "Happy in Jesus." This having been attacked with tremendous enthusiasm Brother Boyd shouted, 'Thank the Lord! I'm Happy!' Miss Amanda Johnson (about 14 years old) was called next. She moved out promptly and said, 'We will sing "Step out and Try God's Love",' which they did with a will.

Mr. Ancell then invited Mr. Robert Fitzpatrick to take the lead. Mr. Frank Caffee relieved the musician at the organ as Mr. Fitzpatrick announced his first song, "In the Shiny Way." This the people did not know very well. The first verse of the next song, "Shouting on the Hills of Glory Land" was also sung with little spirit. This aroused John Etheridge, the famous county singer who was sitting on the platform. Up he jumped, shouting commandingly, 'Come on, folks, come on! Let's help the man sing!' With this encouragement Mr. Fitzpatrick attacked his song with renewed vigor and Mr. Boyd clapped his hands to stir things up. But even this did not help much, for the audience seemed to be tired throughout the remaining verses.

"Sensing the condition of the crowd the pastor came forward and said, 'It's getting pretty close to the noon hour, something inside tells me, and you sang that last song, folks, like you knowed it too. You'll be glad to hear this announcement. We are going to call the Ramah Quartet again to perk us up. After they sing "Crossing the River", dinner will be spread outside. Everybody is invited to partake of the food.' Following this announcement Mr. Boyd called out, 'Now is the time to get blessing. Say, Praise the Lord, once in a while.' When the quartet, having finished its song, was about to sit down, Mr. Boyd said, 'Let's ask these brothers to sing the first and second verses again. Thank God we've got people to sing like them.' As they started singing again Mr. Boyd arose, waved both arms up and down with the music, and shouted, 'Hey, Praise the Lord, Amen! Amen! Listen to that. We'll all have to cross that river some day.'

"At the end of this number Mr. Boyd was asked to dismiss the company with prayer. After that Mr. Ancell spoke up, 'Everybody leave the house quickly so that the men folks can take the benches outside. And, one other thing, as we spread the dinner let's please step up and get something and get back. Let's not throw anything away. When dinner is over let's bring the seats back quickly.'

"With many ready hands helping, the benches were soon removed and a long table was made by placing two benches together with their backs outside. Boxes of food, small trunks in some cases, were brought from the cars and wagons by the men and boys and spread by the women on the improvised table. The pastor called on Brother Boyd to ask the blessing at which the men removed their hats and all heads were bowed. This done everybody rushed for the table. Several had brought plates but everyone ate with his fingers in picnic style.

"As they finished eating small groups sauntered over to Mr. Kellum's home, where, at the well, a bucket of cold water and a gourd dipper were waiting. When all had drunk and otherwise refreshed themselves the pastor sounded the recall by clapping his hands. The benches were soon carried in and the people followed. Everybody took his place and the service was resumed for the afternoon."

After reading the narrative above it is clear that the singings constituted an attractive type of community enterprise. They cost little. They could be carried on successfully even in the absence of the pastor. To many they opened socially approved and wholesome avenues of skilled expression that otherwise might have remained undeveloped. Attracting young and old alike they tended to promote sympathetic understanding between youth and maturity. Drawing from all congregations, as they did, made them a force in the reduction of denominational division in the community.

THE MINISTERS

The position of the churches in Upland Bend, the quality of their work, and the future that lay before them depended in large part on the character of the pastoral leadership which was at their disposal. Understanding of this aspect of the situation will be furthered by examining the educational equipment which the ministers brought to their service and the conditions under which they labored. Their views on various questions, likewise, will be useful. Four of the five pastors contributed a considerable amount of information along these lines. About the fifth less was known.

The four ministers of whom most is known were married men with children. In age they ranged from 30 to 49 years. They were born and reared in Alabama or in nearby southern states. Their libraries consisted of from twelve to one hundred books and pamphlets, mainly of a religious nature. In addition they took from two to five magazines of denominational or farming interest.

Two of the ministers had graduated from high school. The pastor of the Tabernacle Church, after this, had taken two years and some summers of general and ministerial training in Methodist colleges. His was the most extended academic background and he alone worked at the ministry full time. He was also a Mason. The second of the two, the pastor of the Shady Grove Baptist Church, entered the ministry soon after he finished high school. The son of a large landowner in the southern part of the community, he made his living from farming and preached for two small churches on the side. The third minister, who served the Good Hope Methodists, after an informal secondary-school education took several correspondence courses on religious subjects. Most of the money he drew from preaching came from another church than that at Upland Bend, but this was supplemented with an income from farming. He belonged to two fraternal and one farming organization. The Nazarene preacher entered the ministry at an early age after two years in a rural high school. His living came from the trade of painting which he pursued at the county seat.

The fifth minister of whom little detailed information is available served the New Chapel Baptist Church. He was the unmarried son of one of the large owners. Having graduated from the local high school he entered a standard academic college. At the time of the survey he had reached the junior year. The small salary which he received for ministerial labors helped materially in meeting the expenses of a college education.

The views of the ministers on various subjects are worth examination because the positions they held enabled them to affect substantially the thought of the community. The weight of their influence in Upland Bend had not been diminished seriously by such counter attractions as the radio and picture show which compete with the church for the attention of the people in urban centers. For these reasons members of the staff invited those ministers who were accessible to give consideration to a number of questions that pertained to the situation of the churches which they served.

Indifference to religion, lack of appreciation of the services, and drinking liquor were each mentioned by three of the four men as "the worst faults of the people that the church can correct." Failure to contribute financially was also mentioned by the pastor of a church that paid $50.00 a year.

On the question, "Are the young people being reared properly in the Christian life", uniformly pessimistic views were expressed. It was difficult, they said, to keep the young people away from Anti-Christian influences such as the movies, dances, swimming pools, cards, and association with transients of lower morals. The tendency of children was away from the church and toward sin and worldliness. Church services were dull and dry to most boys and girls and the young people's societies were not very effective. Parents themselves were often indifferent to the Christian life and failed to set the proper example.

The religious attitudes which they were trying hardest to cultivate, the ministers said, included getting the young people reestablished on the old fundamental principles. One of them told about the organization last summer of a young people's fellowship club "To live without sinning." After a short time discouragement set in and the club disintegrated. The older people were being urged to abstain from liquor, to give fewer parties, to attend the services more regularly, to support the church financially, and to pray more.

"The worst handicaps against church work in Upland Bend included petty jealousy and rivalry between denominations, a larger number of churches than could be properly supported, and lack of trained leadership. The pastor of one of the weaker churches bemoaned the fact that most of the leaders belonged to other congregations.

The next question was, "What things were most needed to improve the community? Consciousness, on the part of the ministers, of the need of greater material resources loomed largest in their answers to this question. More money crops and getting out of debt were mentioned more frequently. Better roads, electric power lines, a library, and a new school building were also considered important. More community spirit also was needed, in the opinion of two of the pastors. Such a spirit, as has been seen, had already been rallied around the consolidated school which held the community together. The church, being divided, did not work strongly in this direction.

"Was it desirable or practicable for the churches to be consolidated into one strong church?" This indeed had been done in the case of the school. It would be a "fine idea" for the church as well, three of the ministers agreed, for only one institution could be supported properly. But it was impracticable, they all thought, on account of denominational prejudice. This attitude, one of the ministers observed, had very recently resulted in the organization of the Nazarene Church largely as a split-off from the Free Will Baptists.

THE FUTURE OF THE CHURCHES

The ideas above set forth bring one face to face with the question of the future of the churches in Upland Bend. This problem was raised with the ministers. Most of them felt deeply and had thought seriously on the subject already. Three of them were far from hopeful. "Going down", said the pastor of the Tabernacle Church. "We have lost too many members already on account of an unavoidable overemphasis on financial matters. If the small churches do not unite they will be forced out of existence." "On the decline", replied the Shady Grove man, "Interest is lacking and the young people are not growing soundly in the Christian life." "It looks dark to me", said the New Hope minister, who during the last quarter had made three forty-mile trips to preach at this church for which his compensation to date had amounted to 75 cents and a gallon of molasses. At this rate, he said, he at least could not last long. Only the Kellum's pastor felt that progress lay ahead. To bring this about he was counting on the appeal of the singings to the young people.

Was the future of the churches as clouded as their pastors believed? Their views may have been colored unduly by the meagerness and uncertainty of their compensation and by the apparent indifference of some of their clientele. Even as unselfish and as devoted a profession as the ministry could not be wholly unaffected by such considerations. But poor pay and indifference boded good no more for the institution than for the men who served it. Small memberships, likewise, were an ominous sign. Rural churches with less than 150 members, previous studies have shown, had only a 50-50 chance to grow. Only two of the churches had more than 150 members. The landowning families, who constituted the backbone of any community enterprise, were not committed to the service of the church as wholeheartedly as once they were. In former years the church was able to command the best energies of the leading citizens. Now only two or three of these men were very active in church affairs. The others were engrossed in politics, the school, or the management of their own affairs.

The outlook for the Tabernacle Methodists and the Shady Grove and New Chapel Baptists was more favorable than that of the others. These three institutions were larger and more deeply rooted in the customs and traditions of the people. Their buildings and equipment appeared to be reasonably adequate. In their membership the landowners were concentrated. Church services were held more frequently and societies had been organized for the young people. Even the smallest of the three, the New Chapel Baptists, seemed to be comparatively secure. Their location was about five miles distant from the other Baptist church. They enjoyed the very active support of a large owning family with numerous connections. The pastor, one of the younger sons of this family, was energetic and attractive. Large numbers were drawn to his services, which were materially aided by the musical accomplishments of several members. This church also profited from the work of the only Ladies Aid Society.

As for the two younger and weaker institutions, the Good Hope Methodists and Kellum's Nazarenes, it was difficult to see how these could be kept alive except as missionary enterprises supported by the general extension boards of their denominations. Thus the number of institutions, for which continued existence was likely, did appear to be on the decline. The forces of consolidation, moreover, had already demonstrated their beneficient effect on the community's educational activities. In response to similar pressures it is possible that the church, likewise, was moving slowly in the same direction.

The Church of God's Children

There remains for description a sixth congregation of white people which we have called the Church of God's Children. Having been "set in order" only the year before the survey was made this small church was the youngest of the community's religious institutions. To include this sect in the discussion of the older denominations was impracticable because its activities were very different from theirs and it was far from being typical of the religious life of Upland Bend. To some of the more thoughtful citizens, indeed, it was a problem of considerable concern. But it was a part of the life of the community and, as such, is rightfully a part of the picture.

The people who belonged to the Church of God's Children lived in an isolated section about a half-mile square which was almost completely surrounded by woods. Two or three of the families owned land but their homes, like those of the others, were small and crowded in the main and often untidy. With other people they had little to do. Indifference toward sending the children to school was characteristic because they did not "think much of these here schools we have in this day and time", and "Jesus didn't have to go to school to have some sense." One of them said frankly that he believed "in keeping his children at home and working them and not letting them run around to parties. If they run around and kick up their heels all the time you can't do nothin' with them." The result of this attitude was that the youngsters dropped out of school soon after they entered at the beginning of the year. Lax enforcement of the attendance laws permitted them to remain away. Few of these children, as a consequence, had been able to advance much beyond the first or second grade.

The denomination at large, according to the minutes book which the Clerk of the Upland Bend church permitted to be examined, had congregations in thirteen states all but two of which were in the South. The total membership throughout was less than 3000 persons. In Alabama there were nineteen congregations, all of which were small.

In Upland Bend the Church of God's Children, with a membership of thirty-seven, was very active. Meetings were held every Sunday from 10:00 in the morning to 1:00 or even to 4:00 in the afternoon. They met again on Wednesday from dark to 10:00 or 11:00 o'clock and on Saturday at the same hours. During the winter season services were conducted in the homes of members; in the spring they adjourned to a brush arbor. Two revivals were held last summer, one in July and one in August. On these occasions the congregation met every night from dark till past midnight for two or three weeks until they became worn out physically—according to their own report.

Collections were taken at church services only when the pastor, who lived in a nearby town, came to preach. These free-will offerings usually yielded something like 85 cents which were given to the pastor. Sunday-School offerings ranged from 6 to 23 cents. These were sent to the headquarters of the denomination to pay for the weekly Sunday-School leaflet. Further light on these aspects of its work may be obtained by examining three excerpts from the records of the Church Clerk.

november 12

Taken up a free will ofern_____ 86c
Paid pastor_____ .50   50
                                                                                          —
                                                                                          36
Taken it and bought note book until got a Church C   36
                                                                                          —
                                                                                          00

december 19

We sent in a church report fill ought by the pastor and clerk. Sent in a $1.00 fore the dear little messinger paper which is in debt so much $1.00

The church exhorter are clerk sent in a church report nov. 5 with $1.25 for the old debt

january 3

Come in church jan. 3

Bro Oscar Carr
Bro Ruben Cox
Bro Earl Day (feb. 5, pd 39c)

One more excerpt will be given. It appeared originally in the proceedings of the last general convention of the church and had been copied by the Clerk on the minutes of the local institution. Set forth in this excerpt was a conception of the mission of the Church of God's Children which impressed the local officers sufficiently to cause them to spread it on the minutes of their own congregation. It read as follows:

"We have met at this convention at one of the most neediest times on the pages of history. There is more resting on the shoulders of the ministry of "The Church of God's Children" today, than ever has at any previous time, since the days of the early church. There is more opposition against the truth today and the true teachings, dicturns, and government of the true church of God than at any previous time.

"As false doctrines, heresy, false manifestations, Spirit of leadership, independency, are invading our land, as never before. All of the above and a hundred other things, the true ministers must come in contact daily, as they fill the pulpits of the various churches."

The members of this church believed in "divine healing." Instances in which individuals in their own congregation had recovered from illness through the "power of prayer" and without the aid of physicians were freely described by the leaders. The beneficiaries in every instance were women or children. A few of these cases, as they were recounted to a member of the staff, will enable the reader to appreciate the significance of this experience.

Evie Estes

"One night last August during the revival meeting, we come home about 1:00 o'clock from services. I was tired and hot and

I stepped out to the well to git me a drink of water. When I come back in the house I felt queer and fell on Annie. I lay on the bed over a hour and knowed nothing. They went off and got all the people to come and help pray for me. I woke up and felt good and shouted praises to God for letting the Holy Ghost in me save me."

Annie Estes

"Dr._____said I had appendicitis and to take me to Shallow Ford for an operation at once. We don't believe in that so they took me to a healing doctor in_____County. He felt my pulse and said there is a pulse in a person's arm for every organ in the body. So he knowed I had appendicitis. We come back home and they prayed for me. Soon I got up and walked and shouted and I ain't been bothered since."

Cleo Barger

"She had trouble with her leg when she was young. The doctor at Chocco operated on her leg and she still didn't git well. At the same time she took diptheria on one Tuesday and got worse and worse. The next Sunday morning about 7:00 o'clock we started praying over her. Big drops of sweat dropped from her. At 3:00 o'clock that evening she got up and went to playing with the other children. She took tonsilitis last Saturday and after praying for her Sunday night she got well."

Semmie Sartain

"This child had the measles and took pneumonia with them. We prayed for him and all at once he looked up and said, 'Give me some water. Now get me a potato and some milk and bread.'"

Esther Sartain

"Esther got sick with pains running up and down her back It was the devils trying to get possession of her. We prayed and ran him out and she was not bothered any more."

In the services the more fervent members of the congregation, when they were thoroughly aroused, as was the case much of the time, were accustomed to make free and fluent use of what was called "the unknown tongue." This consisted in a vigorous repetition of exclamations which sounded like I — see — la, I — see — la. Comme — see — ma — la — see — ma la. La — see — ma — comme. O - a - a - a - a - a. Har — po, har — po, etc. In using these expressions they believed they were following the practice of the early Church and they felt that they were "saying things to God which no other living man knows what it is." When they tired of "the unknown tongue" they fell back on exclamations which are much more familiar such as Praise God! Hallelujah! Praise Jesus! Glory! Praise Him! Love Him! Bless the Lord! Bless Jesus! Glory, Glory, Glory! and Amen!

Further to understand the work of this church it will be helpful to follow the observations of a member of the staff who attended a meeting that was held one Sunday morning in April.

"Stopping at Mr. Munroe Bean's to inquire about the meeting place I met the Reverend William Baugh, the pastor, who had spent the night with Mr. Bean. Mr. Baugh gave me a cordial invitation to attend the services. He told me that he had been reared in a Free Will Baptist home and had preached for that denomination for a short time. The Church of God's Children, he said, believed every word in the Bible, they wanted to make all people children of God, and they were glad to have folks of any faith hear their preaching. On the way to the Estes' home where the meeting was to be held, Mr. Baugh remarked, 'Brother Bean, I see that you have plenty of cows.' 'Yes', said Mr. Bean, 'my landlord has been a blessing to me. He give me two cows to milk.' 'That goes to prove, Brother Bean', Mr. Baugh replied, 'that the Holy Ghost is with you. You have already been hit by it or you would not have been blessed.' To this high explanation Mr. Bean, who had once been a Free Will Baptist, found no other answer than, 'Yes.'

"On approaching the house I heard the organ playing and a young man and woman, Annie Estes and Earl Day, singing. They stopped just before we entered. I followed Odis Pearson in. He walked up to Earl, both hugged, kissed, and said, 'God bless you, brother, I'm glad to see you.' Odis called Annie, "Sister", and shook hands with her. Mr. Baugh and Mr. Bean followed Odis in the same manner. During the next twenty minutes men, women, and children came in, two or three at a time. All used the same affectionate mode of greeting and all kissed the babies on the mouth.

"About 10 :00 o'clock Mrs. Bertie Redd appeared with a baby in her arms. She shook hands with Mr. Baugh, closed her eyes, bowed her head, frowned and began to speak strongly in 'the unknown tongue.' Jerking her shoulders back and forth over the body she staggered across the room and back still holding Mr. Baugh's hand. Disengaging herself but still pressing the baby to her bosom, she began running up and down the room, sharply stamping her feet for emphasis, as she shouted many times, 'Praise God! Hallelujah! Praise God! Hallelujah!' Finally she sat down winded. Everyone was quiet for a moment until Mr. Baugh started laughing and began 'Brothers and Sisters, it's time to go, the Spirit has done hit me.' Without more ado he launched into the song, "Precious Love of Jesus." Everybody, including the small children, joined in from memory. Closing their eyes they clapped their hands and stamped their feet in time with the music. Annie played the organ.

"When the song was finished Mr. Baugh led off again, 'We have come here, Brethen and Sisters, to praise God. We will do that now in our Sunday School.' Immediately the children ran to a bench in the rear of the room where Annie Estes took charge of them. The adults remained on the front benches. Clarence Fikes who was the teacher of the adult class asked the pastor to take charge of them.

"On the back row Annie told the children to believe everything the preacher said, and likewise, what their fathers and mothers told them, but they should believe no one else. After giving them this and other admonitions she called for the offering. Three or four youngsters gave a penny apiece. To each child Annie then presented a picture card which pertained to next Sunday's lesson. This having been done she dismissed them to play outside. In the meantime the adult class had been scanning the Sunday-School leaflet. Each member of the class in turn read aloud a verse in the Scripture lesson whereat the pastor read the corresponding paragraph of 'explanatory notes.' For most of the members getting meaning from the printed page was a tedious and difficult process—in some cases, quite uncertain. Few voluntary comments were offered. At the conclusion of the lesson Clarence

Fikes took the collection and distributed leaflets for next Sunday's lesson.

"While the grown people remained in the room Mr. Baugh went to the door and called the children. As soon as all were settled Mr. Baugh suddenly jumped to his feet and, jerking his left side, shouted ' ! ! ! ! ! '([1]) Then he began, 'I see a house on a hill. I'm going there some day.' At that everybody joined him in singing, "I See a House on a Hill." At the end of the song Mr. Baugh exclaimed ' ! ! ! !. It feels good to be praising God again, doesn't it?' ' ! ! ! ! ! ' followed from the congregation([2]) who were all beginning to squirm and jerk in their seats. Continuing the preacher said ' ! ! ! ! Everybody get the Holy Ghost now. ! ! ! ! Have you been baptized with it? ! ! ! ! I can baptize you only with water. ! ! ! ! God can baptize you with the Holy Ghost and fire. ! ! ! ! Everybody give yourselves up to the Holy Ghost in you. ! ! ! ! Let God take this meeting over and run it. ! ! ! ! You can't save yourselves. I can't ! ! ! !. I'm just a representative of God. The Holy Spirit is in me. ! ! ! !. I just want to tell you how to get the Holy Spirit and keep it. ! ! ! !. Deny yourselves all pleasures and the Holy Spirit will come to you. After it comes to you let me baptize you with water so you can keep it. ! ! ! ! Our church is the Church of God's Children. ! ! ! !. In it is founded all law and government. ! ! ! !. You shall be led only by this teaching and the Holy Ghost and not by the new kind of leadership that we have here of men. ! ! ! ! The more you suffer in this life the better you will live up yonder. ! ! ! !'

"Sisters make sure that you get ready for the man of God, the representative. ! ! ! !. God is the same as in the days of Elijah and always will be. ! ! ! !. He sends out his representatives just as he did then. ! ! ! !. There was a woman that heard of Elijah and told her husband that she was going to make ready for him. ! ! ! ! She didn't fix for him in the chicken

---

(1). Hereafter the four exclamation marks, ! ! ! !, will be inserted to mark the use by one or more persons of expressions of "the unknown tongue" and/or of the more familiar expressions, Glory to God! Praise God!, etc. which were described above as frequently employed in the services of this church.

(2). Whenever the preacher shouted ! ! ! ! the congregation responded in kind. After nearly every statement he made they yelled ! ! ! !.

house, the smokehouse or the barn. No, she even put him above her and her people. ! ! ! ! She went up in the loft of her house and fixed a bed and put clean sheets on it. Then she went out on the road toward Jerusalem every day and looked for the man of God. ! ! ! ! Finally she brought the man to her house and carried him up in the loft. ! ! ! ! She was over age, but listen, dear Sisters, she had the Holy Ghost and He gave her a son in her season. ! ! ! ! This son growed up and died the day he was twenty years old. This good woman again went out looking for the man of God. ! ! ! ! Elijah came and went up in the loft where the boy was lying on that same bed stretched out on his back. Elijah got down over him, put his hands over the boy's hands, his mouth on the boy's mouth, his feet over the boy's feet, and breathed into the dead boy. ! ! ! !. The second time he breathed into the boy's mouth, the boy moved and sneezed nine times. ! ! ! ! Them nine sneezes represented the nine iniquities of the church.'

"In the same strain and manner the sermon continued until about 12:15. At this time several songs were sung including "Only Give Me Jesus Night and Day", "What Little Light I Have I'm Gonna Let it Shine", "When the Lord Shall Come Again", and "If you Meet the Holy Spirit you'll Walk the Golden Street." Then came about a half-hour of testimony on the part of individuals which was broken now and then with a song. The pastor invited all who wished to bear witness to the power of the Holy Ghost in their own persons to stand up and do so in the way the Spirit would make known to them. About two minutes time was enough for most of the witnesses but in three instances the demonstration lasted as long as ten minutes.

"Odis Pearson was the first to testify. He marched rapidly up and down the room, with his eyes half closed, raising high over the head first one hand, then the other and shouting ' ! ! ! !. He's done so much for me. ! ! ! ! He's done so much for me. ! ! ! !' The crowd responded ' ! ! ! ! ' vigorously to him, as they did to all that followed. After Odis came Lawton Estes, who did not move from where he stood, but with eyes closed and head bowed delivered short and jerky punches against an invisible opponent as he yelled ! ! ! ! Mrs. Evie Estes then took the floor, and danced about frantically jerking herself all over and

shouting in words that could not be made out. ! ! ! ! After
her Mrs. Bertie Redd made a prolonged demonstration. Closing
her eyes and dropping her head she hopped spasmodically from
one side of the room to the other. On one movement she bumped
into her own little boy, who was standing on the floor watching
his mother's excited movements, and knocked him down. The
child cried out in surprise but his mother left him to be picked
up by some one else as she began falling and rolling on the floor
shrieking ! ! ! ! at the top of her lungs. Mrs. Foster Sartain
followed Mrs. Redd with a long exhibition of much the same
nature. Next Earl Day rose. Closing his eyes apparently and
holding both hands high above his head he strode swiftly but
gracefully about the room moaning ! ! ! ! whenever he reached
the far side. Annie Estes, who had been found singing with Earl
before the service, followed him and danced around in an energetic, staccato style without covering much ground but calling continually ! ! ! !. Clarence Fikes jumped up and down where he
stood and said that he was on his way to Heaven. He didn't care,
he said, whether his wife or children or anybody else got there but
he was going to be sure that he did. Bertie Redd then put on a
long dance and roll just as his wife had done. The last of the
witnesses was a frail little woman who danced slowly around the
room once, with both hands straight to the front, smiling and
muttering ! ! ! !.

"While all this was going on, two little girls unconcernedly
played dolls with balls of crumpled paper in one corner of the
room. Occasionally they walked about in the crowd quite naturally without noticing the uproar. Boys and girls five years old
and up joined enthusiastically in the shouting and singing. The
only exception were two young couples who sat on a bench in the
rear of the room. As far as one could see they were almost completely detached from the proceedings, for they spent the whole
time laughing, talking, and flirting with each other. All of the
witnesses, except Earl Day and Annie Estes, were grown men
and women who were married.

"When no one else seemed moved to testify Mr. Baugh called
for prayer. The children quickly huddled down in the middle of
the room. The grown-ups fell on their knees around the children.
All then raised their hands and, at a signal from Mr. Baugh, be-

gan moaning and yelling ! ! ! !. Having done this for some time the preacher shouted an unusually loud Amen that brought the service to a close."

Reports of the activities of the members of the Church of God's Children did not fail to reach the ears of their neighbors who belonged to other communions. What the neighbors thought about them was not difficult to learn and it constitutes an important detail of the picture that has been drawn. "All of them are a bunch of damn fools", said one. And another, "It looks like to me they are an impossible case." A third suggested, "Something should be done to scatter these people, because they are raising too many children who are mimicking them like a bunch of apes." The last man was puzzled, for, said he, "I have thought about these people quite a bit. Frankly I don't know how they can be helped, for they refuse to associate with better people or to listen to outsiders. They are steeped in ignorance and poverty and, being in that condition, they have become insane in their religion."

THE NEGRO CHURCH

The Mount Gilead Missionary Baptist Church for negroes was located in the northern part of Upland Bend where most of the people of this race lived. The building in which the congregation worshipped was much like those of the better white churches and about the same size. It was a weatherboarded frame structure painted white on the outside. At the front an imposing, though somewhat awkwardly proportioned tower, with a belfry and bell at the top rose from the ground to reach above the roof. There were four windows on each side of the building. Leaning against it at the right was a long ladder which was intended for protection against fire. Inside there was a platform and pulpit but no organ. The ample grounds were pleasantly shaded. The contrast between the church and the poor one-room unpainted structure that housed the negro school was most striking.

The outstanding leader of the church was Robert M. Jackson, a fine old negro landowner who was seventy-three years of age. He had helped erect both the old and the present building. In this enterprise he had the advice and encouragement of a white friend among the landowners who lived nearby. Robert was

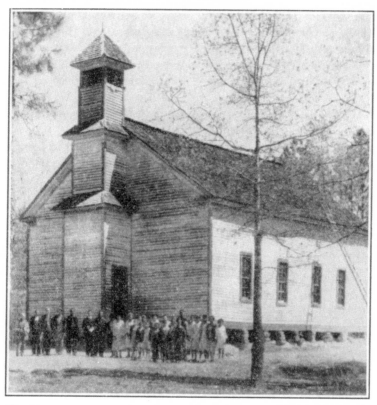

The Negroes were proud of their church. This building, built with the support of their white neighbors, was in marked contrast to their school.

afraid that the church would not be kept up when he died. "I think we've got too many churches", he said, "but I sho wants mine to stand." The young people were not as faithful to the church as they once were, he thought, because "they don't put the hickory to the children like they used to." Robert and two other landowners were the backbone of the church. One of the latter read the Bible "the first thing after I gits up every morning."

The church was a larger factor in the lives of the negroes than of the whites because many activities, which were available to the latter, were closed to the negroes. A great majority (87 per cent) of the householders of the thirty negro families belonged to the same church. The women belonged in even larger numbers (93 per cent). All but two were members of the Mount Gilead Church. This notwithstanding, most of them visited two or three other negro churches from time to time which they could easily do as there were several congregations in adjacent communities. A large part of the social life of the negroes was secured in this way.

With this description of the situation in mind and with the intention of gaining further insights into the nature of the worship of the negroes the reader is invited to follow the observations of a member of the staff when he attended the weekly Sunday-School service of the Mount Gilead Church.

"The last Sunday in April about 10:00 o'clock I reached the pleasant, well-shaded grounds of the Mount Gilead Missionary Baptist Church. Standing around talking under the trees were about seventy darkies—men, women, and children being equally well represented. As I entered the building the Reverend Sam Maxwell, the minister, who resided outside of the community, left the two men with whom he was talking and approached to welcome me.

"Having courteously shown me to a seat Sam went to the door and shouted: 'All right, everybody come in and let's get started.' When the congregation was seated without announcement and without book or musical accompaniment (for this sect does not allow instruments in church) the minister led off in a rich baritone voice with the song, "Oh, How I Love Jesus." All of the grown people and nearly all of the children followed with enthusiasm. The singing was slow in tempo but vigorously rendered in perfect time. The different male and female voices blended in beautiful harmony.

"The song was followed by a prayer, the conclusion of which was marked by a chorus of amens from a number of the more articulate men and women.

"Then the minister got up from his knees and said: 'Brothers and Sisters we are glad to see all of you out this morning. We are going to review this quarter's work today as our new Sunday-School books have not come in yet. This is your review, now. I will ask some questions and let you answer them. If any of you teachers would like to lead the discussion I would like for you to step up and take charge.' No one moved so he proceeded: 'We will start back with the first lesson now and discuss each one briefly.'

" 'The subject of the first lesson is faith in Jesus. Will some one explain what he thinks about this.' Mose Franklin, a white-haired old man rose and said: 'Mr. Superintendent, I look at faith as a three-wheeled wagon. We all know a wagon just can't run with only three wheels. I calls the three wheels repentance, confession, and forgiveness. The fourth wheel is faith.' 'That's a good description, Brother Franklin', said the minister.

"About this time the whispering and giggling of a group of boys aged around eight to twelve had become disturbing. Turning in that direction the minister rebuked them sharply saying: 'Boys, now boys, be quiet now. We're talking about Jesus Christ now and let's be quiet. He don't like noise in church.' At that the boys were subdued to the point of causing no further trouble.

"After several other topics the lesson on temperance was brought up. No one having volunteered, Sam, the minister, observed: 'When we talk about temperance most of us think about liquor. But there are other things that we ought not to forget. If I eat enough to make my stomach sick I have done wrong just as I would if I drink too much whiskey and get drunk. When a man gets enough liquor in him to make him fall about from one side of the road to the other, that's going too far. It's all right to take a little drink but don't get drunk. We ought to take it as medicine.'

"The next topic was the ten virgins. This, too, the minister had to tackle which he did as follows: 'We read that five of these virgins were wise. They put oil in their lamps and were allowed to go into the house to see the wedding. The other five were foolish and did not oil their lamps. The best way I can explain that is to say we have lots of unmarried girls who are virgins. Some of them have good characters and some of them do not. Some are like the five foolish ones. They are called virgins but they are not.' At this, eight or ten young girls giggled; two or three, out loud. Turning toward them the minister said with dignity, 'Let's be quiet, please.'

"Then came several songs including the "Way of the Cross Leads Home", "Where He Leads Me I Will Follow", and "Precious Name"—all of which were led by the minister from memory.

"About 12:00 o'clock the minister said: 'We are glad to see all of you here. We are especially glad to see our white visitor, too. We will now ask him if he has something to say.' Responding to the invitation I thanked the minister and briefly expressed the pleasure I had had in listening to the service and in noting the interest with which they discussed the great moral problems that concern us all. When I sat down the minister replied, 'We appreciate the good words of our white friend about our work. We want him to come back when the classes are divided. We love our church and want him to know we take a big interest in it.'

"The congregation then proceeded to elect, one at a time, three girls and one boy as delegates to attend the Sunday-School Convention, which was to meet in a neighboring county the second Sunday in July. The nominator would rise, address the minister as Mr. Superintendent, and name the nominee. The nomination having been seconded the minister would pronounce the name and say, 'Question.' To this the congregation responded in unison, 'Question.' Whereupon the minister said, 'All those in favor raise your right hand and say yes', and then, 'Those who have any objections voice them.' This having been done a committee of four was elected in a similar manner to solicit the members for money to pay the expenses of the delegates.

"When the final prayer had been offered the minister asked them 'to tell everybody about our meeting here the second Saturday.' At this the Sunday School adjourned without formal dismissal—the time being about 1:00 P.M."

One of the great missions of the church is to sustain and comfort men in the presence of death. One May morning a young negro in Upland Bend was shot and killed by another negro. Both belonged to the Mount Gilead Church. Some insight into the effect of a tragedy of this kind on the minds of the negroes and into the nature of the effort of the church to deal with it can be had by going with a member of the staff to witness the burial which occurred the day after the shooting.

"About 9 o'clock in the morning a wagon bearing the coffin came in sight down the dusty road. Two men rode in the driver's seat, one on each side, and two in the rear of the wagon. Behind and on foot groups of five to ten persons followed some distance apart. At the grave, which early that morning had been dug by volunteers with picks and shovels borrowed from nearby white families, the wagon stopped. Leaving the mules hitched the riders jumped down and joined the little knots of people who were standing around the cemetery. One of these, a group of women, was discussing the murder. A number of older men talked about their crops. A mixed crowd chatted gaily over the details of a recent party. A group of young men were engaged in a lively discussion of baseball. One young man argued that he was a better pitcher than the other—to which the latter replied in the same vein. At this juncture a third broke in saying, 'You all can't prove who's the best pitcher, let's see you prove who is the best rastler.' At that the two contestants removed their hats and started toward each other grinning good naturedly. Within ten feet of the corpse they wrestled four or five minutes while the bystanders looked on without a suggestion of rebuke. In the meantime other groups sauntered up, including the mother and sister of the deceased, until approximately 150 people had assembled.

"About 10 o'clock the minister, the Reverend Sam Maxwell, came up dressed in white coat and vest with black tie and pants. Having left his spectatcles at home he borrowed a pair from one of the bystanders and leaning against a tree, he began hunting for a suitable passage of Scripture. This found he straightened up and asked a relative of the deceased if they were ready to begin. Being assured on this point the minister launched into the hymn, *I'm Bound for the Promised Land.* During the singing the crowd gathered closer about the grave but only a few sang. To the minister's call for pall bearers six men responded. When they reached the grave with the coffin they became involved in a vigorous argument as to the direction in which the head should lie. Twice in the course of the discussion they turned the coffin around until the minister stepped up to settle the question by saying, 'Now boys, you know the head should always be pointing to the West.'

"When the coffin was lowered partially, the men held the supporting ropes, the minister read a few verses from the Bible, and began: 'Brothers and Sisters, I wants to take this opportunity to say just a few words concerning our deceased brother. He is not the first one brought here just like this. As you all know this brother was shot with a gun. We are told a little argument caused his death. We ought to let this be a lesson to all of us. This is the thirteenth person laid here because of murder. We know that this man had no reason in the world to kill this boy. I have never heard anything that this boy ever did to harm anybody.'

"By this time several of the women were in tears and the mother and sister of the deceased were crying hysterically while the others looked on with quiet respect and awe. Changing from a natural voice to a rhythmic chant the minister continued to the effect that the dead boy had been baptized, joined the church, was one of God's children, had been kind to his neighbors, and that he hoped he was now resting in peace in Glory. At the conclusion of the talk he announced, 'We will open the coffin now and let you take a last look at our brother.' Slowly the crowd filed by viewing the body that, save for the head, was covered simply with a sheet.

"This done the lid was replaced and the coffin lowered to its resting place. While the minister and several others sang *At the Cross* the grave was filled. When the song ceased the minister spoke as follows: 'One other thing before you go. You all know the white folks have been good to us. The county officers gave us the coffin. They always help us when we go to them for help. One white man offered to take his truck and go to town to get the coffin for $4.00 (a round trip of 50 miles). He said that $4.00 would pay for the gas and oil for his truck and that he would give his services free. We have made up $1.75 of that money. We need $2.25. I want to ask two or three people to pass their hats around and let's chip in and pay this debt. We owe it to our brother to do this.' The collection having brought in only $1.05 the minister, said, 'We still need $1.20. Let's remember this and bring an extra nickle next meeting day.'

"When the matter of the collection had been disposed of the minister offered a concluding prayer in which he asked God to help everybody realize the seriousness of the mistake that produced this occasion and to make a lesson of it so that he would live right in the future. At the conclusion of the prayer the crowd dispersed."

THE FORCES AT WORK

Before leaving the subject of the churches it is desirable to get a glimpse of the broader forces that were affecting the religious life of the community. The people of all denominations and of both races were seeking security and peace of mind on the great issues of life and death. According as they lacked these things here they hoped to find them in the Hereafter. Those who enjoyed the greater material prosperity, the larger owners, were less zealously committed: they had largely turned the church over, it appeared, to the smaller owners and tenants. The men tended to turn it over to the women. And the young people felt the drawing power of other attractions.

Powerful forces of division were at work and had been from the beginning. One or more new churches had been set up every generation or so. These appeared to result from the disaffection of small groups of owning families or from the desire for more satisfying modes of self-expression on the part of culturally retarded minorities. The latter especially seemed to explain the origin of the Nazarenes and the Church of God's Children. The members of these congregations could not have been happy under the eyes of their superiors, the landlords, or with a quiet, conventional form of worship which "cramped their style." Nor is it likely that they would have been accepted very cordially by the members of the traditional denominations.

The efforts of these submerged elements to establish churches of their own were not too likely to succeed, however, in a community that was so largely dominated by the owning group. These unfortunate elements of the population had only the smallest means of their own. Capable leadership they lacked also. And the unconventional forms of worship which they used could but alienate the sympathies of those who, otherwise, might have helped them. A long continued existence of their congregations was doubtful at best. Yet the forces that impelled them to organize were deeply rooted in the reactions of human nature to the environment in which they lived. Of these conditions no early end was in sight.

The older and larger congregations, whose future was better assured, had demonstrated considerable power of adaptation to changing conditions. Being unable to hold church services regularly, they emphasized the Sunday School. For the young people they had given the special opportunities that were recommended by their denominations. Good use of the old singings was still made. The condition under which their ministers labored, however, were such that other and even more essential adjustments were difficult to make. Certain forces appeared to be moving slowly in the direction of consolidation. This was the final and possibly the most needed of the adjustments that might be envisaged. But the forces that hindered consolidation were strong and not soon to be overcome.

CHAPTER VIII

THE SCHOOLS

The institution in which the people of Upland Bend had greatest pride, the one in which their chief hope for the future lay, was the school. Around it a large part of their communal life was built and through it learning superior to what they themselves had enjoyed was assured for their children. Among the leaders and the women especially there was an implicit faith in education, in the kind of education which their school gave. With the negroes and small groups of whites education was yet subsidiary to religion, but many things indicated that schools rather than churches were on the ascendancy in Upland Bend. In this chapter it is proposed to examine the educational facilities of the community, the children who attended the school, and the extent to which they profited from this training. Attention will be directed first to the white schools and then to that for the negroes. Finally consideration will be given to the program of adult education.

The white population was served by an educational institution known officially as a Consolidated Rural School. This school was housed in three buildings, offered instruction in twelve grades, had a faculty of eleven teachers, and was served by six buses which transported children from Upland Bend and neighboring communities. The annual cost of operation was approximately $11,500. Instruction was organized around an elementary school, where grades one to six were taught, and a junior-senior high school offering work in grades seven through twelve. The total enrollment was 345 pupils, of which number 220 were in the elementary school and 125 in the high school.

THE SCHOOL PLANT

Situated on the top of a hill, at almost the exact geographic center of the community, on a tract of land containing fifteen acres, the Upland Bend school was the most imposing collection of buildings in the community. The site was located at the forks of two of the community's important roads, one running north and south, the other east and west. The east-west road in fact cut through the school grounds, separating one of the buildings from the others. Although rather well supplied with acreage, the grounds were too rolling to provide adequate outdoor recreational facilities for the children. Some play space had been made through grading a part of the grounds. On another part an attempt had been made at terracing, but heavy rains had destroyed the terraces before they became well-sodded and they had not been replaced. The fifteen acres had only two trees on them. The landscaping consisted of shrubs which had been planted around three sides of all buildings. Most of the soil was worn bare from the tramping of many feet; isolated and inaccessible parts were weed-grown.

Of the three major buildings constituting the plant, one housed the elementary school, another the general high school, and the third the vocational work. The elementary building like the others was a frame structure. It consisted of two stories, three rooms and a hall on each floor. One of the rooms was used as a high-school laboratory and classroom, one as a storeroom; the other four accommodated the groups into which the six elementary grades were divided. This building had originally contained four rooms. An addition at the middle of the back added two rooms, but at the same time subtracted greatly from the light available in the original rooms. The building, in addition to having unsatisfactory lighting and poor ventilation, undoubtedly represented a fire hazard of some magnitude. The cloak rooms were inadequate in number and size, inconvenient and unlighted. There was none on the second floor, two of the three on the first floor were located under the stairways. The desks were dilapidated and too large for young children. Most doors did not fit tightly, panels were cracked, and locks off. Several windows had broken panes, in the storeroom the lower sash was completely gone from the window. A State Department of Education Survey, made three years prior to this study, had recommended the abandonment of the elementary building as soon as possible. It was still in use, however, and no repairs had been made since the recommendation.

The high school, located across the road from the elementary building, was housed in a more substantial structure, but a building more inconveniently planned for school purposes could scarcely be imagined. It consisted of an auditorium-gymnasium, a library-study hall, and three classrooms. Two rooms were located at either end of the auditorium. These were not joined with a hallway with the result that movement from one end of the building to the other, which was necessary every time classes changed, was by way of the outdoors in good weather but through the auditorium in bad. In addition to these the space included one cloak room, three small closets for storing teaching materials and books, and one drinking fountain located in a tiny hall cut off from one of the classrooms. There was no office for the principal.

The auditorium-gymnasium was perhaps the most satisfactory unit in the plant. It would seat on folding chairs approximately 300 people and when cleared was large enough to serve as a basket-

In their school the people of Upland Bend had great confidence. The high-school building was the most imposing structure within the community. Whether the school actually met the needs of the youth it served is another question.

ball court. In addition it had a stage which, though not large, was adequate for the plays which the school produced. The library-study hall had bookshelves the length of one end, a counter from which the books were issued, and four large reading tables with chairs. The desks and blackboard space in the classrooms were much more satisfactory than those in the elementary school.

The vocational building was by far the most adequate one of the three. It consisted of five class or work rooms, each with a locker room, and an office which was used by the teacher of vocational agriculture. Three of the rooms served for the work in agriculture, one being a blacksmith shop, one a wood shop, and the third a classroom and library. The other two rooms housed the home-economics department, one serving as a sewing room and the other as a kitchen-dining room. This building was in better repair and was much more completely equipped than were the other two.

The equipment for teaching purposes was in general limited. The high-school library, which is described in some detail in Chapter IX, contained something over 400 volumes, and to these additions were being made at the rate of about $150 worth of books annually. The 12 magazines subscribed for were of a relatively high quality, the two newspapers received were state dailies. Some idea of the sufficiency of the library can be gathered from the fact that it contained one dictionary, 13 volumes on music and fine arts, 7 volumes on science, and 17 biographies. The vocational department maintained a library of its own which included almost 300 volumes, more than one-half of which were government bulletins. This library regularly received 16 magazines. The elementary school had no central library, each room had a dozen or so books most of which were circulated from the office of the County Superintendent of Education, and no magazines suitable for young children. The classrooms had no equipment except blackboards and chalk. Maps, globes, dictionaries, and other teaching materials were lacking. The high-school science laboratory was one in name only since it failed to meet even the minimum requirements set by the State Department of Education for rural high-school laboratories. The gymnasium had a basketball and basketball goals, nothing else. The girls' athletic association, one of the student organizations, did own a volley ball, a soccer ball, and three baseballs and bats. The shops used by the agriculture department were better equipped but even their layout was meagre. One set of wood-working tools served the entire department. The blacksmith shop was scantily furnished. Tools for farming were of the simpliest sort, and the agriculture teacher complained that his students never saw modern farming machinery. The home-economics department had the most complete equipment. Four cooking units, two coal-burning and two oil-burning stoves with the necessary implements, a complete dining room set, four sewing machines and a fitting mirror furnished the materials with which these courses were taught.

The three buildings were equipped with lighting, water, and heating facilities. The lighting came from a Delco system, the engine for which was housed in a small outbuilding on the school grounds. The water supply was pumped by the same Delco plant from an open spring, which was located on the school property, to a tank placed well above the ground in the rear of the high school. From here it was piped to the various buildings. The elementary and high-school buildings had one drinking fountain each but the vocational building had none. The home-economics cooking room had a sink with water, but neither of the two agricultural laboratories nor the high-school laboratory had water, and lavatories were not provided in any building. Toilet facilities consisted of two outdoor structures, one for boys and one for girls, located along one edge of the school property at a distance of approximately two hundred feet from the elementary school and more than twice that distance from the high-school building. The rooms were heated with coal-burning stoves. Those in the high school were jacketed so as to get a somewhat even distribution of heat, in the other two buildings they were unjacketed.

PERSONNEL

The kind of physical plant which is provided is one factor involved in the learning of school children. Another even more important one is the staff in whose hands the pupils are placed. The personnel of the Upland Bend school was composed of eleven teachers, one of whom also served as principal, and six bus drivers who had responsibility for the safe transportation of the children. Of the faculty seven taught in the high school and four in the elementary school. The four elementary teachers were unmarried women. All were graduates of a nearby two-year normal school, one had done a year's college work beyond this. Three of the four were local women, daughters of large landowners. The youngest in teaching experience had taught for seven years, the oldest twelve. All had taught in other communities although only one had had experience outside the county. They had been teaching in Upland Bend for from four to seven years.

The high-school teachers were a more cosmopolitan though much younger group. Three of the seven were men, two of whom were married, one being the husband of one of the women teachers. All but one had graduated from college and the one who had not lacked less than a semester's work. Their experience ranged from one to nine years, four were teaching their second term. All had had experience in other counties; one, the principal, had taught in another state. The home-economics teacher, in addition to her teaching experience, had served as a county home-demonstration agent for three years. None had taught in communities other than rural or small town, however, and all came from farming communities and homes very similar to those found in Upland Bend. None was a native of the community. Five were teaching in Upland Bend for the first time, and the longest period of service in the school for anyone was four years. This heavy turnover in the high school was typical. The salaries paid were such that the teachers were constantly on the lookout for other jobs.

In the elementary school the four teachers cared for an enrollment of 220 pupils, although as will be reported later the regular attendance was much less than this. One teacher taught the first grade, one taught the sixth, the other two taught two grades each. In the high school, the man who served as principal taught all the mathematics. Another taught science and physical education and coached the boy's athletic teams. A woman taught history and the social studies. The English was divided between two other women; one of these handled, in addition, the girl's athletic program, while the other also taught the courses called occupations-for-girls and served as librarian. The agriculture work was done by a man. His wife had charge of home economics. All of the teachers except those handling the English courses were working in the fields for which they had been trained. The English teachers had had only Freshman and Sophomore English in college. One had "majored" in physical education, the other had been trained in home economics.

Most of the teachers lived on the school property where two teacherages had been built for their accommodation. The three women who were natives lived with their families. The science teacher lived with his wife on a small farm nearby. The agriculture teacher and his wife "kept house" in one of the teacherages. The second teacherage in which the others lived was operated as a boarding and rooming house, for teachers only, by the wife of a local farmer.

The salaries paid the teachers were not high but they were among the highest paid in rural schools of the state. For their services those working in the elementary school received from $60 to $70 per school month, depending upon the number of years of experience. This salary they drew for a maximum of seven months which meant their annual income was less than $500. They were constantly faced with the possibility of receiving even less than this because of a shortened term. Three of the four terms prior to the survey had been for less than seven months. In the high school, the academic teachers received from $70 to $80 and the home economics teacher $90 per month for nine months. The principal got $110 a month, a total of $990 for his year's work. Only the agriculture teacher, whose salary was in part paid by the Federal Government, was on a twelve months basis and his monthly income of $140 was the highest in the system.

The transportation of the pupils was done by six private buses which daily carried from 25 to 58 pupils each. The length of the runs varied from 12 to 26 miles, three children actually rode the full 26 miles to school. This service was contracted for by the County Board of Education with the approval of the local trustees. The routes were let to the lowest responsible bidder. The contractors during the year of the survey received from $70 to $85 a month, depending upon the length of the route and the number of pupils transported. Out of this amount they had to furnish, maintain, and service the buses. The work was part-time, however, since the drivers were on duty only before and after school. The drivers were all young men. Three were high-school students whose fathers held the contracts for routes. The others, sons of large landowners, were recently out of high school and the "bus routes" served to fill out days which otherwise were spent on their fathers' farms.

The buses with one exception had homemade bodies built on cheap chasses. In spite of this they had been operated for several years over roads that were not too good without serious accident. During a year only one bus had failed to deliver its load daily. The homemade buses opened only at the rear with the result that the driver was separated from the children and therefore had little control over them enroute. Discipline was maintained while the buses were in transit by a system of pupil captains. These captains reported to the driver, and he in turn to the principal, any misbehavior on the part of the riders. Both the children and the school authorities felt that the success of this plan depended upon the character of the captain. Only a few discipline cases were reported annually.

Costs of Operation

Examination of the cost of operation will explain the inadequacy of the plant and the meagreness of the salaries. The funds available for operating the school throughout a year amounted to approximately $11,500. This money was spent for teacher's salaries, for transportation, and for servicing, lighting, and heating the buildings. No provisions were made for building depreciation, although the buildings represented an investment of approximately $25,000. Nor was provision made for repairs or for replacing equipment. Slightly more than two-thirds of the operating cost went for teacher's salaries, most of the remainder was used to finance the transportation system. Only $400 was required for janitorial service, heat, and light. Janitors were pupils in high school, coal was bought from mines in nearby communities, and the light plant was not expensive.

At that the cost of operating the school represented a financial outlay which would have taxed the resources of the community to the limit. It was fortunate for Upland Bend that support was not entirely from local funds. Most of the financing came from county and state taxes of which the community, of course, paid a proportionate amount. In addition, the school district which included surrounding communities had voted a special three-mill property tax which was used entirely for the school. The revenues from these sources, however, were not sufficient for maintenance, consequently it was necessary to supplement them locally. This supplement, which usually amounted to about $1500 a year, more than 10 per cent of the total, came through fees which the children were required to pay, through entertainments which the school gave, and from an occasional donation that was made usually by a county politician. The annual fees paid for each child in attendance were $1.50 for the elementary school, $5.00 for the junior high school, and $10.00 for the senior high school. These amounts though small meant that education was by no means free. For many families with limited incomes and numerous children the fees set an economic hurdle which was impossibly high. The result was that in the high school particularly the school population was limited almost entirely to the more fortunate economic groups, a fact which will be examined at greater length later. Funds raised from entertainments sponsored by the school played an important part in the financial program. The basketball games, plays, parties, dinners, and rallies which the school together with the P.-T.A. conducted constituted the chief source of entertainment which the community had, and were as a result well attended. Although the prices of admission were usually small, 5c, 10c or at most 25c, the accumulation of such amounts helped to buy school equipment, heat the buildings, pay the student-janitors, sometimes even supplement teachers' salaries.

The cost of operating a school is commonly translated into terms of *cost per pupil enrolled.* The annual cost per pupil in Upland Bend, if building depreciation is ignored, was approximately $33. Of this amount about $21 went for instruction, more than $10.00 for transportation and less than $2 for service and maintenance of the plant. The service and transportation costs per pupil were approximately the same for high school and elementary school. The cost of instruction in the high school was $55.64 per pupil while that for the elementary school was $8.27. This latter figure is less than the cost of transportation reported just above. But the transportation figure was based upon all the children enrolled and not all of those rode the buses. Those who lived nearby walked to school. Actually, if one considers only the children who were transported, the cost of transporting a pupil was $14.75. Yet if this child was in the elementary school the cost of instructing him after he got to school was but $8.27. Almost twice as much for transporting him as for educating him! This probably did not mean that the transportation costs were too high. Rather the cost of instruction in the elementary school was abnormally low even in a state where educational expenditures are less than in most.

THE COURSE OF STUDY

The work which goes on in a school is in some measure determined by the program of studies which is planned for the pupils. The curriculum to which the children of Upland Bend were exposed was mapped out by the State Department of Education and was the same one that could have been found in hundreds of other schools in the state. The course of study in the elementary school, except for some juggling necessary to make a schedule by the teachers who taught two grades each, was the state approved program. Although it had certain "fads and frills" in the form of music, art, and physical education, the emphasis was where it had been for generations in American schools, on the tool subjects of reading, writing, and arithmetic. The daily programs for the first grade and for the combined fourth and fifth grades which are reproduced below were typical:

First Grade Program

8:40	Opening exercises
8:45	Reading (Section A)
9:15	Reading (Section B)
10:00	Recess
10:15	Language and writing
10:35	Writing and spelling
11:00	Music, two days per week (Art three days per week)
11:35	Health one day per week (Reading four days per week)
12:00	Lunch
12:30	Rest period
12:35	Number work
12:50	Reading (Section A)
1:10	Reading (Section B)
1:30	Physical education
2:00	Rest period
2:05	Social study
2:20	Nature study
2:40	Dismissal

Combined Fourth and Fifth Grades Program

8:40	Opening exercises
8:45	Reading 4*
9:10	Arithmetic 5*

```
 9:40  Writing and spelling 4 and 5
10:00  Recess
10:10  Arithmetic 4
10:35  Language 4
11:05  Language 5
11:30  Music 4 and 5 (two days per week, Art two days, Health one day)
12:00  Lunch
12:30  Rest period
12:35  Reading 5
 1:00  Reading 4
 1:30  Physical education 4 and 5
 2:00  Geography 5
 2:30  Alabama History 4
 2:55  Civics 5
 3:25  Dismissal
```
*Numbers refer to grades.

The high-school program, too, followed very closely the minimum course of study set up by the State Department of Education for rural high schools.

It was divided into junior high (grades 7 to 9) and senior high (grades 10 to 12) programs. In the junior high school only one curriculum was offered and because of the limited number of students no electives were available. The curriculum included no work in agriculture, none in home economics, very little in community problems. General science had been introduced the year of the survey. Courses called occupations, designed to help pupils in their vocational choices, were offered separately for boys and girls for two years. English, mathematics, and physical education were the constants. The subjects carried in each of the three years of this school were as follows:

Junior High-School Program of Studies

Junior I

Geography
Mathematics (Arithmetic)
English
Science
Study of occupations
Physical education
Current events (1 hr. per week)

Junior II

Occupational study (double period)
English
Science
Mathematics (Arithmetic)
History
Physical education
Current events (1 hr. per week)

Junior III

    Civics
    English
    Mathematics (Algebra)
    Business training (½ yr.) and
    Commercial geography (½ yr.)
    Physical education
    Current events (1 hr. per week)

The curriculum in the senior high represented a far departure from the traditional classical course of study. The boys were all required to take agriculture, the girls home economics for three full years. The other required subjects were continuations of their English and physical education. Foreign languages, either ancient or modern, had completely disappeared from the course of study. Mathematics had become an elective. The electives available each year were limited to a choice of two from three different subjects, usually mathematics, science or history.

The subjects of study for the three grades were as follows:

Senior High-School Program of Studies

Senior I

Required
    Agriculture (Animal husbandry) or home economics
    English (Composition and rhetoric)
    Physical education
Electives (2 of 3)
    Plane geometry
    World history
    Biology

Senior II

Required
    Agriculture (Horticulture or farm crops, in alternate
        years) or home economics
    English (American classics)
    Physical education
Electives (2 of 3)
    Solid geometry
    American history
    Physics or chemistry, in alternate years

Senior III

Required
    Agriculture (Farm crops or horticulture, in alternate
        years) or home economics
    English (English classics)
    Physical education
Electives (2 of 3)
    American Democracy
    Industrial history (½ yr.) and
    Business law (½ yr.)
    Chemistry or physics, in alternate years.

It seems rather obvious that some one had been concerned with planning a program of study which would to some extent serve the needs of life in a community such as Upland Bend. Yet it is still difficult to see why the students were compelled to take certain courses. One cannot generalize too much from the title of a course as to what the curriculum actually was, but it does appear that there were fields of study that would serve a greater function in the life which these boys and girls were almost sure to lead than would so much higher mathematics. One would need to justify these courses in mathematics either as mental training or as college entrance requirements. The small number of pupils who would ever enter business leads one to question the wisdom of giving courses in Business Training and Business Law, unless these dealt largely with the business of home or farm. One would imagine that a course in the history of agriculture would have more meaning and play a more significant part in their lives than industrial history. But the most serious criticism of the program seemed to be the postponement of all work in agriculture and home economics until the senior high school. As will be shown later most Upland Bend children never reached these grades, consequently the very courses that would serve them most directly were limited to small numbers.

Instruction in the classrooms except that in agriculture and home economics followed conventional lines. Assignments were made by announcing the number of pages or the chapters that would be discussed at the next meeting. The teacher asked questions and the pupils answered as briefly as possible what they remembered from the textbooks. In the higher grades the teachers "lectured" on the assignments for a part of the period at least. Tests were given often and they commonly dealt with memory for factual material. In the elementary school reading was largely oral, the pupils taking turns at reading. Spelling and arithmetic were mostly written work. In mathematics each pupil usually "worked a problem" at the board and when all were finished the class listened while each explained his work. In occupations the pupils were engaged in "filling out" a workbook which asked questions concerning various callings. Information on this subject was obtained chiefly from an encyclopedia. In English considerable writing was done, in many other courses term papers were prepared, but the teachers were so busy that most of the papers were not returned to the students. The work in agriculture was organized very differently. "They didn't really have classes" most of the academic teachers thought. The instruction was organized about problems of the farmers and the pupils commonly read about the subject, most often from government bulletins, then tried out in the shops or on the farms some solution which they found. A considerable part of the time was spent in the shops or outdoors, the boys oftentimes working independently on different problems. The home-economics work represented a compromise between the traditional method of teaching and the informal method used by the agriculture teacher. The period was definitely broken into two parts. The early part of the period was devoted to a lecture, discussion, and quizz on the assignment. Later the girls tried out or the teacher demonstrated the work studied formally during the first part of the hour.

The school experiences of the young people were not confined to the regularly organized course of study. A very important part of their activities in the high school was concerned with what has

Playground equipment, which was very limited, was all homemade. These children consented to leave the seesaws to pose for a picture. Notice the prevalence of overalls. When the young children in the schools were asked to draw a picture of a man they invariably put him in overalls.

come to be called the extra-curriculum, the various organizations that have grown up in the school to give children experience in living and working together. The organizations which the Upland Bend school had were: a student government, whose officers constituted a council, six class organizations, two athletic associations (one for boys and one for girls), four clubs (Home Economics, Girls 4-H, Roosevelt History, and the Willing Workers, a charity club), a Junior Safety Council, the Future Farmers of America, and the Girl Scouts.

Some of these organizations were very active. The girls' athletic association for example had raised money enough during the year to buy gym suits for all girls in the school. The Home-Economics Club sent a dozen girls to an "Inter-high-school state meet" where a member of the club won first place for the quality of her "Personal Account Book." The Junior Safety Council had a representative in each class and on each school bus to promote safety. The Willing Workers sent fruit, clothing, and toys to needy children of the community and they had a standing Committee on Investigation whose task it was to decide on the children who needed aid. The student council met four times a month for a period of one hour. In addition, they commonly had charge of one assembly exercise each month. The following program will serve as a sample of those prepared and administered by this organization for assemblies:

Song—America
Bible Reading, Comment and Prayer
Song—The Last Roundup
Music Selection—French Harp
Reading—Laxatives (humorous)
Reading—Safety (read from Encyclopedia)
Style show (Four girls walked across the stage in dresses which they had made in the home-economics classes)
Declamation (Given by a girl who had won the county declamation contest)
Announcements (by the teachers)
Dismissal

Other organizations such as those of the various classes, the history club, and the 4-H Club met only once a month or less often and for briefer periods of time. These had no program, no committees, and a very loose organization. The boys' athletic association was purely honorary, made up of all letter men from the school teams.

With the exception of the student government organization, to which all pupils belonged, the membership of the groups was usually small, the range in numbers being from six to fifty. All of the societies had officers; many of them standing committees; and all but the class organizations reported the keeping of minutes. The dues and other receipts collected by eight societies amounted to $90.00 for the year, the greater sums being raised by the senior class and the athletic associations.

The quality of work of the organizations varied greatly because the teachers who supervised them were new at such duties and heavily burdened with other responsibilities. The management of the school, on the other hand, considered actual experience, on the part of youngsters, in the administration of social enterprises as an essential part of a practical program of education for citizenship. And the indications were that persistent attention would continue to be given to the improvement of this side of the school's life. But even at the time of the survey the pupils then enrolled had far richer opportunities for obtaining social experience than were available in the separate little schools of previous generations. The provision of such facilities, indeed, was one of the greatest of the advantages that proceeded from the recent consolidation.

THE SCHOOL CHILDREN

The total enrollment of the school during the year of the survey was reported earlier as 345 pupils, 220 in the elementary and 125 in the high school. This number was never in attendance however. The fact was that during the month of March, the sixth month of the school term, the enrollment was only 272 of which number 166 were in the elementary and 106 in the high school. One-fourth of the elementary pupils and almost one-fifth of those in the high school had dropped out during the year. The enrollment decreased with successive grades. The elementary school enrolled more than the high school, and the junior high more than the senior. Within these schools the lower grades had the heavier enrollment. The first grade had the heaviest enrollment of all. Nearly twice as many were in this grade as in any other. This heavy enrollment in the beginning grades was in part due to the fertility of the population with a consequent preponderance of young children, but a more important factor seemed to be a high percentage of failures which caused many to repeat their work and thus swell the numbers in the early grades.

Although the buses transported children from several adjoining communities, particularly to the high school, most of the pupils came from Upland Bend homes. In the elementary school three-fourths of the enrollment was drawn from local families. In the high school, though it was the only one for miles around, more than one-half were sons and daughters from the community. Those in the elementary school were drawn from all homes within the community, in the high school they came largely from the homes of landowners. The sexes were equally represented in the elementary school. In the high school girls outnumbered the boys, 55 per cent as compared with 45. As with the adults, so among the youngsters the tendency was for the females to get more education than the males did. Most of the children had received all their training in the Upland Bend school. Twelve children, about 5 per cent, had moved into the community after having started their schooling elsewhere. The parents of ten of these were tenants, the other two were children of the local Methodist minister who had but recently been assigned to the Tabernacle Church.

The achievement of the children in their school work was investigated by means of standard tests. In connection with the survey a number of such tests covering various subjects of study were administered to those children in grades 2 through 9 who were in school during the month of March. The subjects tested included reading, arithmetic, spelling, language, literature, history and civics, geography, and hygiene. Because these tests have been given to many thousands of children throughout the country, they made possible a comparison of the learning of Upland Bend's pupils with those elsewhere. The results of this testing will be summarized rather than reported in detail.

When the combined scores on all tests were considered, grades 2 and 3 were at the norms, that is the scores were the same as those of average children the country over in these grades on the same tests. Grades 3 and 4 were about a half year behind the norms. The grades above these were one full year behind. The children in all grades were better in arithmetic than in any other subject. In this subject they did as well as average children enrolled in these grades elsewhere. In the mechanics of reading,

too, they compared very favorably with children from other parts
of the country. In spelling, language and hygiene they were
usually about a grade behind. In history, civics, geography, and
literature the greatest deficiency in their work was found. In
these subjects they were usually two grades behind the norms;
that is, 7th graders scored about what average 5th graders do, 9th
graders what 7th graders do, etc. The best achievement in the
school was in the tool subjects, reading and writing and arithmetic.
The poorest was in the social studies.

This performance should be interpreted in terms of at least two
factors: the ability of the children to learn and the length of their
school terms. Whether children in a particular school do as well
as, better than or worse than normal children is in part at least determined by their ability to do school work. If children are slow
or do not learn well, one cannot demand too much of them; if
they are bright or learn quickly, more may be expected in the way
of school achievement. The so-called intelligence tests help here.
These tests, though they probably do not measure native ability
independent of environment, have been found useful as indica-
tors of what may be expected in the form of school work. The
evidence obtained from the administration of such tests indicated
that the Upland Bend school children were about normal in ability
to learn. An average I. Q. (intelligence quotient) of 98 was
found for the children in this school who were in attendance during
March. This is but slightly lower than the 100 which is commonly
considered normal. The school terms however were very short.
The average length of term in the Upland Bend elementary school
was less than seven months, that of the high school eight. The
average throughout the country on the other hand was almost
nine months. One would not expect Upland Bend children to
learn as much in seven or eight months as normal children elsewhere learn in nine months. But during the three years prior
they had had considerably less than this and during one year the
schools had been in session only three and one-half months. Their
learning in the tools subjects, then, which was only slightly below
normal, represented a creditable achievement, but the low levels
which they consistently reached in the social studies represented
poor accomplishment. One could scarcely demand a well-rounded
development with a school year of such length, yet it does seem

unfortunate that these subjects so essential for citizenship in a democracy were neglected.

Further investigation suggested that the children paid an even higher price for either the short terms or other educational limitations. Not only because of what they knew at a given grade level, but through having to take a longer time to attain a given grade they suffered. A study of the grade placement indicated that the Upland Bend children moved very slowly through the school system. Usually a child in this state enters school between six and seven and is expected to make a grade each year. By examining the age of the children in a particular grade one may determine the number that have progressed normally, the number that have moved slowly and as a result are over-age, and the number that have progressed more rapidly than the average and in consequence are under-age. Seventy per cent of the entire elementary school population was over-age for their grade, indicating that they had not made normal progress through the school. In many cases the amount of over-ageness was extremely large. Ten per cent of the children were three years or more older than was normal for their grade. The normal age for entering the fourth grade, for example, would be somewhere between 9 and 10, but in the Upland Bend school more than 15 per cent of the children in this grade were 13½ years or older at entrance. On the other hand, one expects some of the children in a school to be under-age, through skipping a grade, or getting extra promotions; but of 220 children enrolled in the school only one was younger than would be normally expected. This child entered the sixth grade at the age of 10½ when the average child is eleven at entrance to this grade. The enrollment in the six grades of the high school showed the same tendency. Of the 125 pupils in these upper grades sixty per cent had not progressed normally through the school. Ten per cent were three or more years over-age. Slightly more than one-third had made normal progress and as few as 5 per cent had advanced more rapidly than a child normally does. Except in the tool subjects, the children in a given grade knew less than average children in the same grade, and it took them an abnormally long time to reach this level.

Who Went to School

The tendency is to evaluate a school in terms of its graduates, or at least in terms of how well it succeeds with those who are in attendance. It was in such terms that the Upland Bend school was appraised in the preceding section. In doing this, however, a potentially large group, those who are dropped by the way, is ignored. In a democracy education has been assumed to be a prerogative of all. In America the position has commonly been taken that it is the function of a public school to train every child. But informed persons have long realized that the physical proximity of a school does not mean necessarily that all of the children thereabouts are being educated. It is the purpose here to look at the young people, those of school age, to ascertain the extent to which "all the children of all the people" were being educated.

The number of children of various ages who were in school and the number who were out tells the story. The information was obtained by checking family reports on children of various ages against the school records. From a total of 406 Upland Bend children of the ages 7 to 21, that is of school age, 228 (56 per cent) were in school. Most of the younger children those from ages 7 to 13 years were in attendance, but even with these groups only three-fourths were. For the ages above 13 the proportion in school was much less. Slightly more than one-half, 57 per cent, of the children from 14 to 17 years old were in school, and for the next age group, those 18 to 21, less than one-fifth were enrolled either in Upland Bend or elsewhere.

There were very pronounced differences among the occupational groups with reference to the extent to which their sons and daughters were in school. This was true even for the younger children. Of the landowners' children between the ages of 7 to 13 years, 84 per cent were in school. Among the unrelated tenants 63 per cent were, but this percentage dropped to 58 for the children of this age from sharecroppers' families. When we consider the older ones the differences are greater. Two-thirds of the landowners' children who were between the ages of 14 and 18 were in school, but less than one-half of the unrelated tenants' and only one-third of the sharecroppers' were. More education was being obtained by landowners' children of all ages but at the higher ages the chances were twice as great that a son or daughter of a landowner would be in school. Education above the age of thirteen or so was in large measure limited to the upper divisions of the economic system.

Most of the tenant children who were in school, even the older ones, were in the elementary grades. This was particularly true among the sharecroppers. There was some suggestion that share-croppers' children unless they were unusually bright ended their school careers with the elementary grades, the sixth grade or before, the children of renters went on through the junior high school, while the owners' children went to senior high school, even graduated. But only the sons and daughters of large owners got to college, and among this group very few did. Sharecroppers although they had 49 children between the ages of 13 and 21, had only five enrolled in the entire high school, junior and senior. Of these, four were in the junior high whereas only one was in the senior high school. Among the renters, 13 of 30 children aged 13 to 21 were in the high school, but 10 of the 13 were in the junior high. More than one-half of the owners' children of these ages and three-fourths of those of large owners' were in school. Most of them were in high school and about as many were in the senior as in the junior high school.

Many factors were probably involved in causing large numbers of children to leave school. The differences among the occupational groups at once suggested an economic factor. What is known concerning the income of the people makes such an explanation readily acceptable. The charges for tuition which the school was compelled to make undoubtedly contributed its share. How a sharecropper with an annual cash income of $150.00 and a family of six to support could pay a fee of $5.00 or $10.00 and buy the necessary clothes and books is hard to see. Rather the labor which a son or daughter of thirteen or more years could contribute to the making of a larger crop of cotton was a welcome addition to the funds available for buying the necessities.

But the problem was not entirely an economic one. The school itself appeared to be involved. Mentioned in the previous section was the slow progress the pupils made through school. That is, large numbers were refused promotion, were made to repeat grades, often time and time again. Constant repetition of grades discouraged the children and their parents. The relatively high standards which the school set gradually drove out those less able to do the kind of work which the school demanded, which in the lower grades involved chiefly a mastery of reading and arithmetic. That this point is not surmise is borne out by two findings. During the first six months of the term 74 children withdrew from the Upland Bend school. Of this number none was under-age for his grade, only 3 were normal, all of the others were over-age, that is they had made less than normal progress through the school. The second fact was that those who left were the less intelligent, that is they made lower scores on an intelligence test, and in consequence were less able to do the type of academic work which the school emphasized in the lower grades. Examination of the records from an intelligence test which had been administered in the school at the fall opening revealed that the average I. Q. of those children who withdrew was 11 points lower than was the average of those who remained. Not all of the children took this test, but of the 54 who did and then withdrew from school only six had the normal I. Q. of 100 or above. On the other hand, the average of those who remained was 98 and more than 40 per cent had an I. Q. of 100 or more. The children who left must have been those who were not able to cope with the curriculum which the school furnished. The school was not fitted to the children, rather standards of work were set up which they could not attain. The only basis for justifying such a procedure would seem to be the doubtful assumption that there was no learning of a worthwhile nature which these children could do. The tragedy was that the children who had most need for some training, those from the lower economic brackets, were the very ones being denied the opportunity.

THE NEGRO SCHOOL

The negroes of the community along with those of a larger community to the south of Upland Bend were served by the Mt. Gilead one-teacher school. Their building was a poorly constructed one-room wooden structure. It was built up on loose stone pillars in such fashion as to create doubt in one's mind as to its ability to withstand a strong wind. Set in a "cut-over" field, the only tree left by the woodmen had been recently cut. The building had windows on three sides, five small windows in all,

A one-teacher school served the Negroes of Upland Bend. This building, neat and clean inside, was located in a cut-over field. The children were mostly young, it being the custom for them to stop school as soon as they were large enough to "make a hand" on the farm.

and was heated by an unjacketed wood-burning stove. It had a few modern double desks in it, but most of the seats were long benches. Some of these had no desks in front of them so that the children were compelled to "write on their knees." The room at the time of the visits made to it was extremely clean, the walls had several unframed pictures pinned on them and the windows, although they had no shades, had clean cotton half-sash curtains.

The teacher was a woman of 34 years with 15 years teaching experience. She started teaching in 1918 after having finished the elementary school, but during the interim had attended the state teacher's college long enough to finish a high-school course and to do one-third of a year's work at the college level. Her salary was $40 per month for the seven months that school was in session. From this she supported herself and two children whose father had left them and from whom she had obtained a divorce. In addition, she was paying for the education on which she was still working during the summers.

At the time of the survey only the first four grades were being offered in the Mt. Gilead school but when there was demand for it work up to the sixth grade was done. The enrollment for the year was 69, but the attendance was irregular so that there was never anything like this number in school. The average daily attendance was only 41, and by the end of the term 29 (40 per cent of the total) had definitely withdrawn. None but a single child in the entire school had a perfect attendance record for the term. On a day early in spring when the school was visited only 27 children were present. Many factors were involved in this irregular attendance, some of which were identified. The distance to school was great for many children. The average child lived two miles away, but 20 per cent lived three or more miles and 7 per cent lived as much as five miles away. With children living at such distances and no transportation furnished weather was an important factor in attendance, but illness seemed to be even more important. More than 80 per cent of the children had missed some time because of illness. This may have been abnormally high because of a serious measles epidemic in the community, but, the teacher explained, "It seems like my children are always out on account of sickness." Nine of the older children were absent from school a great deal because they had to work at home. Ten others having no clothes suitable for cold weather came only when it was fair and warm.

One-half of all the pupils were enrolled in the first grade. In this grade were children ranging in age from five to thirteen years. Five of them were younger than the legal age of entrance. Six were more than ten years old. More than 50 per cent were over-age for the grade. In spite of this, in the opinion of the teacher, exactly one-half of them did not do work of a quality sufficient to justify promotion, consequently if they returned the next year it would be to study in the same first grade.

Facts for the other grades were similar. Three of the children in the second grade, one in the third, and one in the fourth were of normal age for their grades, all other were over-age. The range of ages in the fourth grade was from 9 to 16 years. According to the teacher, however, more of the children in these upper grades were to be promoted.

The curriculum of the school was the traditional one: reading, writing, arithmetic, and drawing in the first grade, language was added to these in the second, geography in the third, and Alabama history in the fourth. Music was not formally included in the course of study, but as is apt to happen, the teacher was the one who actually determined the curriculum and musical development was not neglected in Mt. Gilead school. According to the teacher, group singing was the part of the school work which appealed to the children most. Certainly the exhibition which they gave for the benefit of visitors was entered into with enthusiasm. The other school work appeared to be entirely a matter of memorization. The children, seemingly parrot-like, repeated answers which had no meaning to them other than that they brought a rewarding smile from the teacher and from the guests. And the teacher made no effort to clarify or elaborate on the words of the textbook. The children certainly showed some mastery of reading, perhaps writing and figuring. Yet it was difficult for the visitors to imagine that anyone had selected the materials which were being studied because of their usefulness in living the life which was to be the lot of those negro boys and girls.

The limited number of children of school age who were actually in school may have been in part a result of this curriculum. Factors, however, such as those mentioned in dealing with the extent to which white children went to school also probably were involved. For whatever reasons, only 36 per cent of the negro children reported from Upland Bend homes as being between the ages of 6 and 21 years of age were in the school and all of those in attendance except one were less than 13 years old. Of the children between 6 and 12 years, 56 per cent were in school; but of 27 children in the community who were between the ages of 13 and 21 only one was enrolled and this boy, the son of a sharecropper, entered the fourth grade in September but attended school only 20 days during the seven months term. Education for most of the negro children ended at 12 or earlier. In fact only for the ages below 10 were there more children in than out of school.

ADULT EDUCATION

Not all of the education work of the community was directed toward the children. Informally through entertainments, plays, games, and other community gatherings the school educated as well as entertained a large part of the white population. In addition, direct instruction was available to adults in the form of two evening classes, one in agriculture for men, and one in home economics for women, and through a home-demonstration club for women. The evening classes were sponsored by the local high school and had been in existence for seven years. The home-demonstration club had been organized fifteen years before by the Chehaw County home-demonstration agent. Eighteen white farmers were enrolled in the agriculture class which met twice a week during the months of February and March under the tutelage of the local agriculture teacher. The men were entirely from the community, although the school presumably served a much wider area, and they were mostly landowners. Only one unrelated tenant attended and he was a renter not a sharecropper. In fact the instruction was directed toward the problems of landowners. In connection with the course the members of the class were expected to carry out some farm improvement project such as the "development of hay crops", "planting of winter legumes", "terracing of the land", or the "breeding of stock to pure-bred animals." At the time of the survey they were working on the subject of diversified farming. But during the month just prior a rat control campaign had been conducted through the cooperation of this class and the senior high-school boys who were studying agriculture. Every farm whose owner was willing to pay 30c was included in the "rat killing" which was done by means of poisioned meat prepared from a steer which the members of the evening class furnished and the boys butchered, ground, and mixed with "red squibb." This bait was placed at strategic places by the farmers, and the reports were that it practically "cleaned out the rats." The outstanding achievements of the agriculture work were considered to be the terracing of the hill land and encouragement of the use of winter cover-crops. The use of these two soil conservation measures was very general in the community and it was commonly recognized as a contribution made by the school.

The homes-economics evening class attempted to do for the home what the agriculture class did for the farm. It enrolled 28 women most of whom were wives or daughters of the men who attended the class in agriculture. The class met at the same time the men's class did and was taught by the home-economics teacher. The work at these meetings was rather rigidly broken into parts, a theoretical lecture and a practical demonstration. At the time of the survey the work was concerned with cooking. During the year they had treated the preparation of bread, potatoes, salads, pastries and pies, and club refreshments. Sewing, home management, gardening, chicken raising, and child care were other problems that the classes had considered. Typical of their programs was the lecture on "preparing cleaning materials at home" which included: how to make soaps, water softners, silver cleaners, and cleaners of other metals. This lecture was followed by a demonstration of "soap making without boiling."

The Home Demonstration Club, although one of the men of the community felt that it "was mostly for eating and gossiping," actually represented the pioneer attempt at adult education among the women of Upland Bend. The club enrolled 49 women all except one of whom were married. One of the local elementary-school teachers had been admitted as an "honorary member." As with the men, the enrollment was made up entirely from the community and mostly from the landowning groups. One-half were wives of large landowners who had tenants. Only four members were from unrelated tenant families, only one of these was the wife of a sharecropper. Meetings were held in the homes of various members "every third Thursday afternoon from 1:30 to 5:00." As will be seen from examining the minutes of the March meeting, the club did not confine its activities entirely to instructional matters.

Minutes of the March Meeting

"The Ladies Home Demonstration Club met in the home of Mrs. Frank Hosmer with Mrs. Hosmer and Mrs. Annie Appleyard as joint hostesses.

"A lesson in the study of poultry was lead by Miss Mamie Snow (the home demonstration agent). We learned:

1. Pure bred farm flocks are necessary to make money in poultry
2. How to start:
   Cull flock and sell all but ten hens. Buy baby chicks with the money and start the type breed you like best.
3. Hatch early to avoid diseases.
4. Care of hen just before hatching.
   To keep lice and mites down put 1 to 2 drops of black leaf 40" under each wing of hen 12 hours before putting chick with her.
5. Feeding:
   For 100 chickens it takes:
       200 pounds feed to raise to 6 weeks.
       200 pounds feed to raise to 12 weeks.
       500 pounds to 750 pounds to raise to 24 weeks.

"Dues were collected from the members present to help finance the Federated Club. Dues were 5c each.

"Refreshment of fruit jello, cake and cocoa were served by the hostesses at 4:00 and a social hour was enjoyed.

"The Club meets in April with Virginia Fisher, Edna Rainey, and Mallissa Tubb as hostesses."

Although the adult educational program may have combined entertainment with instruction, the practical nature of the work, along with that done in the high school, was appreciated by many farmers and its influence on the life of the community was evident. This was particularly true for the work in agriculture. The methods of farming had been changed and as a result the incomes had been increased while the fertility of the soil itself was improved. In many homes, too, life was undoubtedly more complete because of this work. The unfortunate part of the program was the limited extent to which it touched the lives of the tenant groups. No negroes and very few white tenants had any contacts with the program. As in the high school, so with the adults, education was not universal but rather tended in practice to serve least those who needed it most.

PARENT-TEACHER ASSOCIATION

No description of the Upland Bend schools would be complete without including the Parent-Teacher Association. Through this organization public relations were kept up and a high order of educational morale was maintained. Not only this but considerable financial assistance was given to the school and the recreational, social, and informal educational life of the community was promoted. The P.-T.A. was a very active organization. It had been in existence for ten years, held evening meetings twice a month throughout the school year and in addition to the usual officers had four standing committees, on membership, publicity, hospitality, and programs. The active membership included almost as many men as women. At the time of the survey 61 members had paid their annual dues of 25c and of this number 34 were women and 27 men.

The regular meetings were well attended. Time was given for reports from committees and for planning ways and means of raising money but most of the evening was devoted to a program of entertainment or instruction. These were usually the work of various groups of children from the school but often a speech by one of the teachers or an outsider was included. The following excerpt from the minutes for the meeting of April 3rd as written by the secretary, who was a teacher in the elementary school, represents a typical evening's program.

"The P.-T. A. opened at the usual hour 7:30 o'clock for its monthly meeting. The house was called to order by the President. The meeting opened by singing songs "Come Thou Almighty King" and "Swing Low, Sweet Chariot." The singing was led by the Secretary. The President read from the Scripture the 100th Psalm, followed by the Lord's Prayer in unison. The secretary read the financial report. The amount in treasure is $77.66.

"The Principal announced that Dr. Blackman would visit the school at an early date to make an examination of the eyes and ear. He also announced the summer round-up examination for pre-school children to be April 25. He announced a plate supper and political rally on April 9, which is on Monday night. The President appointed a committee (of three women) to secure donations of foods to be used in the supper.

"Program of the evening was put on by the sixth-grade children and was arranged by their teacher.

1. Quartette 'Just Before the Battle, Mother,'
2. Recessional, Recitation
3. 'Happy Am I' by the quartette
4. 'Who Hath A Book', Recitation
5. 'Old Ironside', Recitation
6. 'The Wind', Recitation
7. A one-act comedy by the 6th grade—Title, 'An Operation'
Adjourned at 9:00 o'clock to meet April 17th."

Some project usually involving financial aid to the school was carried on each year and varied means of making money were resorted to. It was as a by-product of these money raising efforts that the greatest service to the community was made. Experience had taught them that the easiest and surest source of money was through entertainments, consequently a great part of the community's social life was sponsored by the P.-T. A. The following program for the second semester, submitted for the approval of the group by the program committee at the December 13th meeting, gives some idea as to the extent and nature of this activity.

"P.-T. A. Program for Second Semester"

"Jan. 5. Mock Trial. Admission 10c and 15c.
Jan. 12. Negro Minstrel. Admission 10c and 15c.

Jan. 26. Newspaper wedding. Admission 10c and 15c.
Feb. 1. Plate Supper and Political Rally. Plate 50c.
Feb. 16. Valentine Domino Party. Admission 10c and 15c.
Mar. 9. Tacky Party. No charge.
Mar. 30. Program by Agriculture and Home Economics De-
          partment. Admission 10c and 15c.
Apr. 13. Musical Program. Admission 5c and 10c.

Other dates open for other entertainments and senior play."

Considerable sums of money were raised through these varied
activities. The amounts collected during a year were usually only
slightly less than $200. The following report on collections, taken
from the annual financial statement, was somewhat larger than
usual because it included returns from two political rallies. As
was reported in the chapter on CIVIC LIFE, these rallies represented unusual opportunities for money raising.

Dues	$ 15.25
Domino Party	14.14
Fiddler's Convention	31.00
Halloween Party	12.21
Box Supper	13.15
Mock Trial	7.08
Plate Suppers	144.97
Tacky Party	3.90
Total	$241.70

Although it was spent cautiously and the officers jealously
guarded an adequate balance, most of the funds eventually went
into much needed additions to the school's equipment. The financial statement from which the above collections came reported
total expenditures of $136.68, leaving a balance at the end of the
year of $105.02. The year's expenditures were listed as follows:

Books for the library	$ 88.00
Newspaper and magazine subscriptions for library	15.28
Equipment for home economics	10.00
Transportation of delegates to county meetings	8.50
Christmas decoration for school	2.90
Reporter	4.00
Flowers	8.00
Total	$136.68

Although its enrollment exceeded somewhat that of other adult school organizations, the P.-T. A., like the others, was limited in the extent to which it touched the various homes of the community. Perhaps because their children were more actively associated with the schools, the landowners of Upland Bend and their wives were the ones who mainly supported the organization. Only five representatives from tenant homes were members. And, although, almost one-half of the enrollment of the school came from neighboring communities, three parents represented this entire outside population. The organization was rightly called the Upland Bend Parent-Teacher Association.

In Conclusion

As a means of training many of its young, for its contribution to the education of numbers of adults, and as the center about which a large part of the community's group life was organized, Upland Bend rightly valued its school Because of its existence the community was clearly a better place in which to live. Direct influence of the school on the actual living of the people could be seen through the work in agriculture and to a lesser extent in home economics, and particularly through the recreational program which not only served individuals, young and old, but was the major integrating factor in the community's life.

The achievement of the children who passed through the school system was only fair. From an institution which operated for short terms on a limited budget, with a plant that by many standards would be called totally inadequate, and with a staff of young and relatively inexperienced teachers one could not demand too much; but the matter seemed to be partially one of emphasis. In the tool subjects, particularly in arithmetic, the quality of work being done in the classrooms was surprisingly high, in others such as the social studies it was extremely low. The fact that the curriculum with few exceptions was one that emphasized the 3 R's and such cultural subjects as higher mathematics and formalized science, was not the fault of the school, however, since it was but following patterns that were laid down by the State Department of Education and that had been given the teachers at state training institutions.

Recognizing the situation as one that was largely beyond local control, attention is called to a fact that will become clear to those who complete the reading of this report. Aside from the influences mentioned just above, the school did not appear to play a clear-cut role in modifying the ways of living which the people had. The descriptions which are presented elsewhere of the cultural level of the homes, of the health of the community, of civic life as it actually functioned, showed little or no effects of the school's work in the arts and literature, or in the natural or social sciences. For those who feel that education is maintained by society to aid in the struggle for a more abundant life the Upland Bend School did not appear to be taking full advantage of its opportunities. Perhaps the cue to the solution lies in the attack which the agriculture teacher made on his problems. He saw a need in the community, attacked it through both children and adults, forgot formal assignments, quizzes, and grades but measured results in terms of changes in the way things were done. Would the reading habits of the community change in the hands of English teachers who made the same attack? Would the health of the people improve? Would the treatment of the ballot be different? Could social problems of even greater significance be similarly tackled? Such questions involve speculation but they are worthy of consideration.

One of the larger social problems of the community the solution to which might be attempted through some such means was that of the limited extent to which the school served "all the children of all the people." Just as great inequalities have been found in the economic realm, in the cultural, social and civic realms, so too in the school opportunities in no real sense were equal. If Upland Bend is to serve the democratic way of life then not only facilities for education but the means of its attainment must be made available for all.

Chapter IX

HOW THE PEOPLE SPENT THEIR TIME

Human activity whatever its nature, involves the expenditure of time. How the people of the Upland Bend Community employed their time therefore is inevitably disclosed, if not emphasized, in several other chapters such as those pertaining to the home, making a living, modes of leadership, and the work of the school. Our purpose here is to describe a number of activities which represent important areas of behavior that require more extended treatment than could be given incidentally. Most of what follows is concerned with the doings of the grown people. In the last sections of the chapter, however, consideration will be given to certain activities of the children.

THE FAMILY'S WEEK

The hours of rising and of retiring determine the duration of the waking portion of the day. These are salient facts in the distribution of a people's time. The observations, which are to be reported on this score, were made during the spring months of the year. At that time the usual hour of rising in the community for all classes was between 4:30 and 5:00. On Sunday they rose about a half-hour later. The hour of retiring on weekdays ranged from 6:00 to 10:00 but 7:45 was the usual time. On Sunday they stayed up a little longer.

Where the people were and what they did during the day was ascertained by interviewing a sampling of accessible white families every day for a week during the months of March and April and inquiring about the hourly activities of every member. The majority of the families that were accessible for this purpose were landowners.

The average householder usually distributed his working day approximately as follows. Eleven hours were given to work or

Two mules, a good plow, and a sunny spring morning made his work
a pleasure, according to this young farmer. Rolling hills and cut-over
timber land were characteristic of Upland Bend.

routine chores. Of this time 2.5 hours were spent in the house
making fires, dressing, and eating; one hour, about the barn feeding the stock, drawing water, and milking; and 7.5 hours working
in the field, woodlot, smokehouse or garden. Talking or playing
with the family, reading, visiting, and resting took 2.5 hours. One
and one-half hours were spent in business away from home or in
going to town, and a half-hour in attending meetings or working
for the church. Sleep claimed 8.5 hours. On Saturday the householder saved several hours from work which he used in transact-
ing business off the place, in going to town, or in visiting about
the community. Sunday was much like Saturday except that religious services might be attended and more time was given to
reading and to visiting, the sick especially, and to being with the
family.

Like her husband, the housewife usually put in a full working day. Of the 11.5 hours thus employed 7.5 were spent indoors, five being given to dressing, eating, cooking, washing dishes, and cleaning and 2.5 to churning, washing and ironing, sewing or waiting on the family's sick. Four hours were spent outdoors feeding the stock, milking, curing meat, making soap or working in the garden, orchard or field. More than two-thirds of the housewives in fact, at certain seasons of the year especially, were accustomed to work in the fields either occasionally or regularly. Those who did not, for the most part, were members of the owning families. To talking, singing or playing games with the family, reading, visiting, and resting 3.25 hours were devoted. Public meetings or religious activities claimed 0.75 hours and sleep 8.5 hours. On Saturday considerably less work was done especially outside the house. The time thus saved was used in resting and visiting. Sunday was much like Saturday except that there was more reading and more time with the family; church might be attended, and much more visiting was done especially with families that were burdened with sickness.

Information as to "how *last* Sunday was spent" was obtained from the entire population. In the morning about half of the families, both white and negro, were at home. One in every three or four was at Sunday School or church, where services were available to a congregation once or twice a month. The rest of the people were visiting around in the neighborhood. But one family was outside; they were landowners attending the funeral of a distant relative in a nearby town. The afternoon, likewise, found most of the families at home. The others were visiting or attending a "singing" at one of the churches except for a few tenants who were hauling wood. All of the negro and nearly all of the white families were at home in the evening.

Further light is to be had on the family's week by examining the details presented in the three cases that follow. The first tells what a sharecropping family did on a Monday in April as it was given to the interviewer by the housewife herself. The second describes what was done one Saturday in March by a small landowner and his family. The third gives the activities of the family of a large landowner with tenants one Sunday in the same month.

ACTIVITIES ON A MONDAY IN APRIL, OF A YOUNG SHARECROPPER,
HIS WIFE, AND FIVE CHILDREN

Hour	Householder (32)*	Housewife (32)*	Children
(A.M.) 5- 6	Made fires	Cooked breakfast.	Elaine (8)* and Elsie (10)* set table. Samuel (12)* brought fresh water from the spring.
6- 7	Ate breakfast and went to the field.	Milked and fixed school lunches.	Aubrey (15)* went to plow.
7- 8	In the field breaking land.	Washed dishes and swept kitchen.	The children left for school.
8- 9		Made the beds and cleaned the house.	Abner (3)* played in the house.
9-10		Planted tomatoes and onions in garden.	Abner went with his mother.
10-11		Made fire in stove, started dinner. Mrs. R. came and stayed almost an hour.	
11-12	Came in. Fed and watered mules. Ate dinner.	Finished dinner.	Aubrey came from the field. Ate dinner.
(P.M.) 12- 1	Rested.	Washed dishes.	
1- 2	Caught mules and started plowing again.	Patched Aubrey's pants.	Aubrey went back to plowing. Abner played outside in sand. Abner went to sleep.
2- 3		Hoed young turnip greens and mustard.	
3- 4		Drew fresh water. Carried it to the men in the field and helped Aubrey clean up some land.	Children came home from school. Got something to eat in kitchen.
4- 5		Swept the kitchen floor.	Samuel went to field, raked up and burned some trash. Elaine and Elsie played house.
5- 6		Fed chickens and hogs, gathered eggs, made fire and started supper.	Elaine and Elsie gathered flowers and brought in wood and water.
6- 7	Came in from the field. Fed and watered the mules.	Milked the cow. Finished supper.	Elaine and Elsie set table. Aubrey and Samuel came in.
7- 8	Ate supper, played dominoes.	Ate supper, played dominoes.	Ate supper, played dominoes.
8	Sleep.	Sleep.	Sleep.

ACTIVITIES ON A SATURDAY IN MARCH OF A SMALL LANDOWNER, HIS WIFE, AND FIVE CHILDREN

Hour	Householder(49)*	Housewife (43)*	Children
(A.M.) 5–6	Helped cook and ate breakfast.	Ate breakfast.	Lorene (17)* and Lois (15)* cooked breakfast.
6–7	Fed the mules and hogs and started the hands to plowing.	Milked three cows, strained the milk and fed little chickens.	Lorene and Eugene (13)* washed dishes. Lois made beds and straightened the house. Eugene brought in wood.
7–8	Went to town. (Carried a "mad dog" head to be sent to the State Laboratory for testing).	Swept the yard and carded bats for a quilt.	Eugene went to the river to fish. Malcolm (22)* and Lois went to town to get their teeth fixed. Edward (10)* shucked and shelled corn for the mill.
8–9		Started quilting.	Lorene swept the floors, cleaned and dusted.
9–10		Mrs. R. came in. Talked about the sick sister. Quilted.	Lorene sewed on a cooking uniform.
10–11			Lorene washed cabinet shelves in kitchen and mopped floor.
11–12		Fixed small dinner.	Lorene helped with dinner and washed dishes.
(P.M.) 12–1		Finished the quilt.	Lorene read a book until she was sleepy and then took a nap.
1–2–5		Several ladies came in for the afternoon.	
5–6		Gathered eggs, fed hogs, chickens, and stock. Had supper.	Lorene cooked supper. Edward milked.
6–7	Came home from town and had supper.		Malcolm and Eugene came home, had supper and the girls washed dishes.
7–10	Went with wife to see her sick sister.	Carried oranges, grape juice, and ginger ale to her sick sister.	Children stayed home. Lois played piano, sang, and told the children about the picture show she saw in town.
10	Came home and went to bed.	Came home. Found all the children in bed and asleep.	Sleep.

*Age in years.

ACTIVITIES ON A SUNDAY IN MARCH OF A LARGE LANDOWNER WITH TENANTS, HIS WIFE, AND CHILDREN WHO WERE AT HOME

Hour	Householder (55)*	Housewife (49)*	Children
(A.M.) 5– 6	Not feeling very well so called Clyde to build fires.	Breakfast.	Clyde (11)* called Jimmy (14)* to make fires. Jimmy and Margary (18)* cooked breakfast.
6– 7	Fed and watered mules and hogs.	Milked and fed chickens.	Margary and Jimmy washed dishes. Cecil (23)* helped feed mules and hogs. Clyde turned out the cows.
7– 8	Rested. Didn't feel well enough to go to Sunday School (so children stayed home also).	Churned, molded and put butter away.	Hazel (21)* dressed to catch a train back to the Teachers College. Cecil carried her to the train. Margary and Jimmy made beds and swept floors.
8–10	Sat before the fire. Talked and played with children.	Talked and played with children.	
10–11	Talked with wife.	Talked.	Margary and Jimmy started dinner. Nancy (6)* and Clyde played marbles. Sybil (16)* stayed in bed. The girls finished dinner.
11–12			
(P.M.) 12– 1	Ate dinner.	Ate dinner.	Margary and Jimmy washed dishes.
1– 2	Went to the field to see how the hands had been carrying on the work.	Went to Mrs. B's to hear the radio.	Margary with her beau and Jimmy went to a singing. Nancy and Clyde went with their mother to play with Mrs. B's children.
2– 3	Talked to Mr. G. on Farm Bureau Business.		
3– 4			Margary and Jimmy came home and studied their lessons. Cecil came home.
4– 5	Mr. H. and Mr. R. came in to talk about school business.	Talked with Cecil.	
5– 6	Talked to visitors.	Milked cows.	Cecil fed mules, cows, and hogs. Margary helped her mother.
6– 7	Ate supper.	Made sandwiches and poured milk for supper.	
7– 8			Jimmy studied. Sybil was breaking out with German measles. Margary had another date.
8– 9	Talked with wife and read.	Talked and read.	Sleep (Margary went to bed at 11).
9	Sleep	Sleep.	

In concluding the discussion of the family's week it is pertinent to observe the extent to which "hired help" was employed to assist in dispatching the large amount of work that was inevitably the lot of the average white farming family of six to seven members. Full-time servants were available for the relief of the housekeepers in only four homes. Part-time servants were found in nine homes. The latter, in several instances, helped only temporarily—in cases of childbirth or of prolonged illness. For the most part the servants were colored women and their mistresses were all of the landowning class. To assist the householders with their work there were only five hired hands three of whom were white men. All of the hired hands were retained on farms of substantial acreage. When they needed assistance both the housewife and the householder called on their children. Everyone who was old enough lent a hand. Thus we see the families generally did not depend upon outsiders: they did their own work.

THE MAIL

Another way of spending time, to which occasional reference has been made, is that connected with receiving and sending mail. To people in the country, the rural free delivery offers a convenient means of conducting social relations and of making contacts with institutions outside of the immediate environment. The cultural level of a family—including the frequency of its indirect contacts with outsiders, the extent to which it is considered available as a market for goods, and the practical effectiveness of its educational advantages—is measured in some degree at least by the volume of mail which it handles. In Upland Bend the postman's arrival was an event of considerably moment as shown by the fact that many of the people, including some men, were accustomed to stop work for a half-hour or more to see what he had left in their boxes. The volume of mail that was actually delivered to the homes of the community during a typical week in April, including all classes of postal matter, amounted to a total of more than 1100 pieces. This is an average of nearly six pieces per family.

Newspapers and magazines, "second class mail", constituted the great bulk of the material. Nearly one-third was "first class", letters or postcards. Most of the remainder was "third class", that is mail-order catalogs, almanacs, circulars or small parcels weighing eight ounces or less. The very limited representation of this type of material in a weeks' mail would lead one to believe that few of the families were on the regular mailing lists of many commercial or other organizations in the nearby towns and cities. Only a few pieces of parcel post matter, that is, merchandise, factory products, seeds, etc., came in during the week. This fact offers further support to the conclusion drawn elsewhere that the volume of trade by mail was small.

The landowners' boxes took nearly three-fourths of the total number of deliveries; most of what was left went to the tenant whites, the negroes receiving the remainder. Twenty-one pieces went to the average large owner; eight pieces to the small owner; three to the tenant; and two pieces, to the negro. One in three of the entire number of families, including some owners, received no mail at all during the week. This is a fact of capital importance and more will be said about it later. To a majority of the families it is clear, none the less, that the rural free delivery was very useful and that a considerable amount of their time and attention was given to it.

The subject of "first-class" mail is worth pursuing somewhat further. This class of postal service requires of its beneficiaries a minimum competence at least in the arts of reading and writing, a strong desire to keep in touch with people who are out of sight, and the mobilization of time and energy to that end—all of which are important indications of social adequacy.

When the families of the community were interviewed the housewife was asked how many letters both of a business and social nature had been received and sent "during the past month." This having been estimated to the best of her ability, she was asked what members of the family were accustomed to write letters.

The returns to these questions showed that the average white family received 7.7 letters and the negro family 1.0 letter during the month, returns which jibe closely with those reported above for one week's mail. Most of the letters were of a social nature —from friends, married children or other relatives in the county or state. The average number of such letters was 5.1 for the white and 0.5 for the colored family. The landowners received twice as many as the tenants; but fifty families, including eleven owners received none. The volume of business letters received was about one-half that of the former but to 114 families, including one-half of the owners, not a single letter of this character was delivered.

The number of letters written was somewhat smaller than that received. Social letters were written three times as often as business letters. The landowners wrote four of the latter to every one of the tenants. Fifty-two families wrote no social letters but 131 wrote no business letters. The smaller volume of letters written is due in part to the fact that commercial houses ordinarily send more mail than they receive from their customers. Perhaps also the more recent schooling of the older children, who had moved away from home, enabled them to write with greater readiness than their parents.

The housewife wrote the social letters in one-half of the families. In half as many cases they were by the husband; in the remaining cases, by one or more of the children. The tenant husband took to pencil and paper much less frequently than the owning husband. Even business letters were written more commonly by the housewife except in the landowning group. In forty-four families, one-half of them owning their land, an older child generally wrote the business letters.

On reading the paragraphs above one cannot escape the observation that to a considerable number of the grown people, especially, the facilities of the United States mail meant very little if anything at all. The data at our disposal do not disclose with certainty why this condition obtained. Was it that some of them had not mastered sufficiently the fundamental tools of learning? Had they lost track of relatives and friends who lived elsewhere? Were there no stamps or tablets in their homes? Did no business concern consider them worth "selling"? Were their fingers too clumsy after the day's labor to hold a pencil? Or was it, as some of them said, that they "just didn't have nothing to tell"?

VISITING

In the paragraphs above visiting was mentioned several times. Each of the approximately 200 families in the community answered a number of questions on this subject. The facts disclosed are as follows:

"During the past week" members of the average white family either made or received seven daytime calls from friends or relatives in the neighborhood. The average negro family reported four visits of this nature. Twice during the week for the whites and once for the colored meals were served to visitors or members of the family "took a meal out." Once during the week some member of the family spent the day out or had visitors for the day. After supper the calls by members of white families were fewer—the probable explanation being that they went to bed soon after the chores were done. The negroes, on the contrary, called nearly as often in the evening as in the daytime because only then were many of them freed from the supervision of the landlord. There was more visiting on the part of the large owners and of their free related tenants than of other groups. The difference was most notable in the matter of receiving visitors for meals or for the day. These families had larger homes, better stocked pantries, a little more leisure possibly, and certainly more social prestige—all of which enabled them to dispense hospitality with greater convenience and acceptance.

A considerable number of families, including some of the smaller owners, reported very little or no calling at all. In a community in which the volume of visiting was substantial this is a fact of capital significance. For a number of the people visiting may have been difficult during the months of February, March, and April when their reports were made, on account of impassable paths and roads or the lack of clothing suitable for inclement weather. On the other hand, it is probable that some of the families, for reasons not here explained, kept much to themselves and suffered to a serious extent from the ills of social isolation

Trips to nearby towns were made by members of the average white family four times "during the last month." Only one trip was made by the average negro family. A few families, mostly owners, reported from ten to twenty trips. The owners, related tenants, and renters—who owned all of the automobiles and most of the mules—"went to town" much more often than the unrelated sharecroppers. The latter, when they went, had to go with the owners of transportation. These would not much mind "taking along" a sharecropper who was white. The negro sharecropper, on the other hand, would be less welcome in their vehicles. This difference of attitude explains partly at least the fact that one-half of the negroes, compared with one-fourth of the whites, had not been outside of the community at all for a month.

Longer trips than to nearby towns were events of comparatively rare occurrence. "During the past year" members of only thirty families had made trips of this extent. These had made a single trip only as a rule, though a few had made three or four. More than three-fourths of the owners even had not been this far from home. The men, especially those of the sharecropping families, went a little more often than their wives. In some cases the entire family travelled together. Limited means, animals to be cared for, and the scarcity of motor cars probably accounted for the tendency not to go far away.

The average duration of the trips taken by members of owning families was ten days, related tenants, six days, and sharecroppers two days. Four tenants had been away several weeks "making some cash money" at carpentry, logging or "working in a store." Three-fourths of the journeys were confined to the State of Alabama; the remainder, with one exception, were to adjoining states. It was the owners principally who had ventured across the state line.

In this connection one might well inquire how widely the people of the community had traveled during their entire lives. Information on this point will throw light on the degree of mobility; the variety of experience, and the extent of available income, among other factors. Never in their lives had one-third of the white and one-half of the negro householders been outside of Alabama. Those who had crossed the state line usually confined the visit to one or two adjoining states though several had been in three or four southern states. Nine-tenths of the white men had never visited a northern state. Most of those who had visited in the North had seen one or two. One of the large landowners, however, had passed through several states on a trip to Chicago with his family to see the Century of Progress. One man, who was a baseball player, had been all over the country. A third of the negro men had been in the North—chiefly in the lush years from 1920 to 1929. In all ranges of travel the owners, especially the large ones, went away more often and went farther than the others.

The women of the community have not travelled as often or as far as their husbands by a good deal. Sixty per cent of them had never been outside of Alabama; ninety per cent had not gone beyond the South. As with their husbands the more fortunate economic classes had travelled most. The attitude of some elements of the population toward travel on the part of women was not inaptly expressed by a negro man, who when asked about the trips his wife had taken, replied, "Aw, she ain't never been nowhere 'cept to Prude's store. She's a country gal."

READING, MUSIC, AND GAMES

Long hours of manual labor, we know, were the order of the day for the people of this community. They were able, nevertheless, to save a considerable amount of time for more leisurely pursuits such as visiting and writing letters, as has been seen. Consideration must now be given to what they did in the way of reading, music, and games. The equipment which they were able to command for these purposes having been described in the chapter on the home, the use made of it is our concern here.

The books which the families owned were so few in number that the housewife had little trouble in telling which had been read "during the last year." The Bible, the one book they owned in many cases, was read far more often than any other volume. Husbands consulted it as often as their wives. One old man, indeed, read the Bible every morning while his wife cooked breakfast. Comparatively few of the children were Bible readers. Two out of three adults, for that matter, had not read the Scriptures during the past year. The family records were often kept in the Bible, the interviewers discovered when they asked for vital statistics. Other religious books and almanacs tied for a poor second place. Song books, which were mainly of a religious nature, were consulted occasionally as were the mail-order catalogs. The little remaining reading was of books on farm work, carpentry, etc., by some of the men and of fiction by the women. In general the books in the home were read by the adults. Few indeed were suitable for children, who, as shall be seen, found the school library far more to their liking. To a majority of the grown people books were a very minor interest.

To the magazines that were in the home much more time was given than to books. The farm and home magazines such as the *Progressive Farmer, Country Gentleman, McCall's,* and the *Ladies Home Journal* were by far the most regularly read by men, women, and children alike. Next in popularity, especially with the women and girls, were *Love Stories, True Stories,* and *True Confessions.* Several men, women, and boys mentioned western, detective, and movie periodicals. Such periodicals as the *Literary Digest* and the *National Geographic* were not mentioned often. Nearly one-half of the families including some of the owners, reported no magazines read regularly.

When a man, white or black, picked up a magazine he usually searched for an article on farming or for a story. If these were not convenient he hunted for something on politics or religion, or on prominent people. Descriptions of new inventions often caught his eye. The landed men read "serious things" more and stories less than the others. The attention of the negroes was confined to the farm, religion, and stories. More women, especially those in the tenant families, read magazines than men. The women enjoyed the stories most of all but they liked articles on housework nearly as well. They read about religion and prominent people almost as much as their husbands. They were interested in farming also but not many of them cared for politics.

Newspapers were read in the community about as much as magazines. When a man tackled his newspaper he looked first for the headlines about politics. Sometimes he would read the editorials also. After politics he wanted the market reports. Stories of crime came next, especially if it was a tenant who was reading. After this he would examine the "funnies", the sports page, advertisements, and sometimes foreign news. A few claimed that they read every word in their papers.

More women than men read newspapers, but fewer of them read newspapers than magazines. Articles on housekeeping, then the "funnies" and stories were what caught the women's eyes. Next they would read about crime and the doings of society. About a fourth of them regularly examined the advertisements, editorials, and articles on politics. A few, mainly of owning families, paid attention to market and foreign news. A very large number of the women, as was the case with the men, however, read regularly no newspaper at all.

Music is another of the fine arts to which men everywhere have turned when the day's work was done. Opportunity for the enjoyment of music in Upland Bend was limited probably by the costliness of the instruments that produce it. Those who owned instruments in the community, however, were very generous in sharing their benefits with others. Much of the visiting was motivated by the desire to enjoy music in a neighbor's home. Oftentimes a whole family would gather about the organ or piano to sing hymns together. The music for dancing, when dancing was done, came from outside. The scarcity of radios withheld from the people much enjoyable entertainment and deprived them of not a little current information which, as citizens and farmers, they could have used to good advantage.

The fact that a large proportion of the instruments they used were organs, pianos, violins, and guitars is not without significance. These instruments demanded vigorous performance on the part of the players. They required persistent application, some knowledge of music, and active effort to give enjoyment to others. To the extent that they used these exacting tools the people of the community were culturally richer. They produced their own entertainment.

The games that the people played were mostly of the quieter sort, like dominoes, cards, checkers, and rook. Having worked all day standing up they preferred to play sitting down. Expensive sports such as tennis, golf, and pool were left to a handful of the large owners. Games that cost little such as dominoes, the most popular of all, fortunately can be as entertaining and as wholesome as any.

SOCIAL GATHERINGS

The social gatherings of the community constituted an important aspect of its life. Many gatherings were purely recreational in nature. Others mixed pleasure with more serious purpose. Sometimes the participants were invited more or less formally; at times they came spontaneously; sometimes institutions lent their sanction. A few descriptions of these occasions will help the reader to appreciate their significance.

Two of the events selected for this purpose took place under the auspices of the P.-T. A. (Parent-Teacher Association). One, a "tacky party", was given on a Friday evening in February to raise funds with which to purchase equipment for the science department. The party was held in the gymnasium. Seventy-three people paid the admission fee of five cents. The program, which was managed by two of the teachers and the wife of a large owner, included the following numbers: (1) A "Scrambling March" (for the selection of partners), (2) "I see you" (a singing game) and "Post Office", (3) "Passing the Ball" (to music—if caught with the ball when the music stopped a player had to sing, dance or recite a poem), (4) "Singing competition" (two groups sang "Old Black Joe"), (5) "Dramatic Contest" (groups competed in playing "Three Little Pigs"), (6) "Grand March" (in which the "tackiest dressers" were selected). The two winners were members of large owning families.

A "Plate Supper and Political Rally" was given by the P.-T. A. on a Thursday evening in March to raise funds with which to extend the term of the elementary school to seven months. Teachers and the wives of landowners constituted the committee in charge. They served 106 fifty-cent suppers, held a "most popular girl" contest with votes costing one cent each, auctioned several cakes, and sold peanuts and candy—all to realize the sum of $93.58. The master of ceremonies, a well-known county politician, presided in a vein of humor very acceptable to the company over a program that consisted chiefly of short talks by candidates for state and county offices interspersed with songs, amusing recitations, readings, and dances by school children. The occasion had taken the form of a political rally because, at that time, an unusually full field of candidates were ranging the country-side with lots of small change in their pockets which they were prepared to use freely in such ways as were calculated to draw favorable attention to themselves on the part of the voters.

To show their appreciation of the work provided for the community by the CWA (Civil Works Administration), an influential group of the landowners called a big meeting at the home of one of their number one afternoon in March. About 500 people attended including most of the adult residents of the community and the politicians of the county. The foreman of the road work was master of ceremonies. All of the candidates and lawyers present were introduced for short talks. After this the ladies served a free supper in the open air. Those who so desired, a small number of landowners, their older children and a few visitors, remained for a subscription dance.

"Quiltings" and "Barnraisings" were given from time to time. The Ladies Aid Society of the New Chapel Free Will Baptist Church organized one of the former, at the home of an unrelated sharecropper, to make a quilt for the pastor one day in April. Seventeen ladies, representing all of the economic classes, came. Each brought a picnic lunch which was "spread" at noon. Coffee was provided by the hostess. So busily did the workers ply their skill that before dark they had finished a quilt for the hostess in addition to that for the pastor.

A "barnraising" or "public working" and a "quilting" were organized at her home one March day by a middle-aged widow who was a landowner with tenants. Eight men, including owners and tenants, brought their tools. The foreman was a furnishing tenant who was also a carpenter. Before dark they succeeded in raising a 12 x 14 foot crib with a hayloft above and a shed with stalls for the mule and the cow at the side. While the men worked on the barn their wives quilted. Two competing groups worked in separate rooms. By sundown each had finished its quilt. At noon all were refreshed and strengthened against the labors of the afternoon by a substantial chicken dinner with four vegetables, peach and cucumber pickles, cornbread, biscuit, and coffee which was prepared by the widow with the help of a negro woman who had been engaged for that purpose.

Parties were given not infrequently to break the routine of work and chores. The most popular diversion on such occasions was the game of dominoes. One group of eight to twelve men, mainly landowners, played this game regularly Wednesday evenings. A family, now and then, had a party chiefly for its own members. One afternoon in March, for example, a large landowner and his wife put their married and unmarried children and a neighboring youngster or two, thirteen in all, in the old Ford truck and drove down to the river. The boys set out a trot line with the aid of a flat boat. The father, mother, and girls fished with worms and poles. The fish were "too smart to bite before sundown." Fortunately, an ample picnic supper had been brought along against this very contingency. The provender having been properly disposed of, a fire was built around which the men and boys edified the company with "fishing stories." At twelve o'clock the head of the family and its feminine members left for home. During the night several runs of the trot line yielded eighteen pounds of cat fish and two big eels which the hungry boys brought home for breakfast early the next morning.

Fox hunting was a favorite pastime with several groups of men. One of the most enthusiastic hunters was a large landowner who kept the finest pack of dogs in the community. One Tuesday night in February he invited a group of outside hunters and a number of landowning and tenant friends to a big chase after an old grey fox that had been giving the dogs great runs all winter. The outsiders' "brag pack" included two red hounds named Dallas and Alice, Sam, a "black spotted", and two young dogs, Trixie and Hump. Four of the local hunters brought their packs. One had two black and white "Walker gips"; one brought Mollie, a lemon and white spotted "Walker" hound; a third had "his famous" Guy and a black dog "on the order of an old pot licker" and Maxie, a white dog. The host brought his whole pack including Bollie, Raider, Long Boy, Joe, Fan, and Frank, a red and white "Trig" dog. At 7 o'clock the dogs were turned loose at Jim's place. And here follows the story of the hunt as it was told by the old sportsman himself. It is impossible, unfortunately, to reproduce precisely the language he used.

"In a short time Dallas struck the fox about a quarter of a mile from Jim's place toward the river. The sly old rascal knew the hunt was called, it seemed, and came close by to challenge us. Getting all the dogs bunched he took fast down the river for his famous hole on Willet's place, near a pond in a thick grove of pines. He had the dogs guessing; but there were too many for him to hide there long, so he slipped down the Still Branch toward the old wash hole where he held till they almost got up on him.

"Then the race was on in full cry. Round and round the pond and branch they ran for all of a half-hour until the wise old boy hied south for the pocket of the river. All round the bend the bluffs are high and here he ran for at least an hour and a half.

"Being unable to throw the pack there he slipped back through the pocket to the fields of Pink's land. Failing again he shot down the steep hollows and bluffs to the river. The pack continued to crowd him so he pulled out over an open field and headed for the three-acre pond.

"After realizing his mistake in taking to the open, he turned back to the thick hollow between Hollis' and Willett's farms, then back to Jim's pasture near the old barn. Finding this too hot the old gentleman lit out for the burnt woods. But the pack passed on through and almost trapped him on the other side. Hustling out of there over an old road he whirled by Uncle Bill's place, then on to Jim's barn again.

"Unable to lose the dogs here he turned north to Bob's place down by Kizziah Creek bluffs. Having already tried all his slick tricks and rough places with the pack still after him, he went to earth in the bluff about two o'clock in the morning."

During the entire time the chase lasted the hunters did not leave the vantage point from which they had chosen to follow the race. The long hours of the night passed as quickly for them as they did for the fox and the dogs. While the latter "ran their heads off" the men squatted around the fire listening to the "music of the pack." Each dog was known by "his cry." In that familiar country the hunters' keen ears told them precisely where the race went. They boasted about the prowess of their own dogs and "ribbed" the others about the "oneryness" of theirs. Now and then a roasted sweet potato was raked from the hot coals while cups of steaming black coffee made the rounds. It was a great hunt. There must be another one soon, they all agreed, as they dispersed for home and a short nap before getting up to feed the mules at sunrise.

Dancing, although it touched directly only a minority of the population, constituted an important form of recreation. Between the World War and the Depression of 1929 there was very little indulgence in this pastime. Prior to this period, square dances were not uncommon. At that time the music usually came from a single violin. The master player, however, was assisted by a second musician who kept time by beating on the strings of the violin with two stout straws which produced a drum effect. "Seconding the Fiddle" it was called. During the years following the Depression square dancing and round dancing both "came back." They needed this form of entertainment, some of them said, as a relief from the nervous strain of those hard years. Orchestras of three or four men from nearby towns had displaced the earlier and simpler provisions for music. If the players came from the county seat they received $3.00 each for the evening; if from towns nearer by their wage was $1.00.

Sentiment on the subject of dancing was divided. Many of the leading church people especially felt that dancing was doubtful in itself and that it might lead to worse things. Others were more tolerant but hoped their children would find pleasure in other ways. Only a small proportion of the families actively indulged but there appeared to be a growing interest on the part of the young people. During the period of observation dances were being given by three different "crowds." A typical evening with each of these groups is briefly described below.

The most active "crowd" consisted of married couples from a small number of large owning families at the upper end of the community that met every three or four weeks. One evening in the middle of February fourteen couples, including a few visitors from the county seat, assembled at one of the homes for the usual square dances. The three musicians, who also came from the county seat, brought a violin, a mandolin, and a guitar. Acting as master of ceremonies was the popular son of a large owner who knew all of the musicians thereabouts and attended all of the dances. From twenty to thirty minutes was required for each set danced. Every two or three sets a short intermission gave the musicians a "breathing spell." At the midnight rest all present were invited to the dining room where large piles of sandwiches and cake and cups of hot coffee were available for refreshment. This having been accomplished 75 cents per couple was collected and distributed to the players who thereupon found strength to start the music again.

Quite a variety of square dances was used including "Ladies Bow", "Caging the Pretty Dove", "Ocean Wave", "Ladies Walk Across", "Ladies Whirl", and "Lady around the Ladies and Gents also"; the latter set was enjoyed so much that it was repeated twice. Two round dances supplied additional variety. Some of the men, a close observer would realize, had had the foresight to fortify themselves against the exertions of the evening with moderate amounts of artificial encouragement. While their parents danced, several little children in an adjoining room amused themselves with marbles and paper dolls until they fell asleep before the fire. Soon thereafter they were moved to nearby beds where they slept soundly until their elders "gave out all tired but happy", at two in the morning.

The other two dancing "crowds" were less well defined; they met at an earlier hour and less regularly. They were composed mostly of young unmarried people. One of these groups called itself "The Young Peoples' Dancing Crowd." Their parents were landowners chiefly from the lower end of the community. One cold March night ten of these couples, including one or two from a nearby town, were invited to the home of the largest owner in the vicinity to participate in the celebration of his birthday. Each young man "chipped in" 40 cents for the four musicians who played a violin, a banjo, and a guitar and the piano which belonged to the house. Nearly all of the dancing which lasted until 11:30 was "round with cut-ins" which the young people preferred. This was varied, however, with two square sets which were arranged as a special honor to the head of the household who had enjoyed them so much when he was young. A plentiful supply of cake, pickled peaches, and cider was available to strengthen the dancers as they needed it.

Young people from tenant homes, chiefly in the center of the community, comprised the third dancing "crowd." Twenty-two of them, more young men than women, gathered shortly after supper one evening in April at the home of a sharecropper. A violin and two guitars furnished the music for which each young man paid what he could. The dancing was about half round and half square. Several sets of the latter were different from those mentioned above including the "Grapevine Twist", "Partners Walk the Floor", "Gents Whirl", "Right Hand Across", "Ladies Walk Across", and "Thread Big Eye Needle." Sorghum popcorn balls were served about ten o'clock and the party adjourned before twelve.

The square dances which were so substantially represented in the programs above described, it is worth while to note, demanded concerted action according to definite patterns under the direction of a leader on the part of a considerable number of couples. They were less individualistic perhaps but more organized than round dancing and required the development of more elaborate skills on the part of the participants. In this sense the square dances may be thought of as representing a cultural behavior that is comparatively difficult to master. And it is interesting to observe that those of the community who did dance were quite equal to these demands.

No account of social gatherings in a rural community would be complete without reference to visiting and "loafing" at the stores. As occasion offered all classes, both sexes, and young and old alike, "went to the store." The longest visits were made by the men. When their business was done the women usually left while the children "just stopped by" after school. Many interesting things happened in these busy centers of social activity besides the buying and selling of goods. Not a little of the spice and variety of life in the country was to be found there. In an election year, such as was the year in which the study was made, politics went hand in hand with trade, the former being taken little if any less seriously than the latter. Our observations were made during a week of fair weather in the month of April. From the accounts of these visits, which are presented below, the reader can learn much about how the people spent their time. The first two narratives are concerned with the largest of the stores; the third, with one of the smaller.

"April 3rd I visited Prude's store from 2:00 to 3:45 in the afternoon. Many people, who had been helped by the R. F. C. and the C. W. A., were there to receive a distribution of government garden seed.

"Five men were making arrangements with the proprietor "to run them" for the year, mortgaging their crops as security. After haggling considerably over the price an old man bought six pounds of peas at 6 cents. Two little negro boys came in for coal oil.

"An oil-truck man delivered some gas and began to campaign for Mr. Keene who wanted to represent the District in Washington. Several men took positions in favor of the opposing candidate because they said Mr. Keene had never helped the laboring classes.

"Mr. K. came in to check up on his Roscoe (slot) machine. He took out $27.50 half of which he gave to the proprietor. The machine pays off in 2's, 4's, 8's, and 16's and the jack pot. You drop in a nickle, turn the crank and sometimes it pays off as high as $8.00.

"The men discussed the criminal case which was then before the grand jury. An old man tried to persuade two friends to help him get a license in the adjoining county for his thirteen-year-old daughter to marry a seventeen-year-old boy—which the officials of this county had refused to grant. The old man thought it was 'just a matter of pull.'

"Four men were playing dominoes in the rear of the store and several were watching a game of pool between two of the champions of the neighborhood."

The general store not only supplied most of the material goods which families needed or were able to buy. This picture, taken on a Sunday morning when the store was closed, suggests its role in forming public opinion.

"On April 6, from 1:30 to 3:30 P.M., I visited Prude's store. Soon four negro women came. One after pricing many articles exchanged a dozen eggs for 10 cents worth of sugar; the second, a peck of shelled corn for a 5 cent box of salts, a spool of thread, and 8 cents worth of rice. A negro man came for three plow bolts for Mr. C. A young white woman bought some setting eggs, salt, and soda and played the Roscoe machine for a nickle and collected four nickles. Two white men, who came in an old Model T truck, inquired the price of cotton seed. A spool of patching thread was bought by a negro woman who came with her baby. Mrs. R. bought a box of bean seed, a paper of radish seed, two papers of turnips, a box of matches, a block of soda, $2\frac{1}{2}$ yards of cloth, and a thirty-five cent broom. For these she exchanged five dozen eggs and had the rest charged. She then took a bottle of castor oil, quinine, and capsules for a neighbor.

"In the meantime Mr. N. told about his hired hand. When Mr. N. took corn to the mill last Saturday he left the man plowing in the field. When he returned the plow and the mule were there but the man was gone. Mr. D. came in to solicit the proprietor and all present for donations of groceries, clothing or money for Mr. S. whose house had burned to the ground with everything they had while the family was at prayer meeting last night. Some young boys were planning a trip to the annual singing at Mt. Horeb Church.

"Mr. Beasley, candidate for probate judge, appeared, distributed circulars, and discussed his prospects in the election. Mr. E., who came in for garden seed, invited every one present to come to the school house Monday night to hear Mr. J. who wished to represent the District in Congress. Mr. E. also spoke strongly in behalf of one of the candidates for county solicitor.

"At this moment a school truck 'dropped' several pupils, who bought candy, gum, and orange crush drinks."

"April 9th I visited Beasley's store in the afternoon from 4:15 to 5:45. On the outside several men were discussing the gubernatorial candidates. Most of them were for Graves because, they said, he had helped the schools. Sitting on a bench near the door was a real old man surrounded by a number of children for whom he was telling fortunes with face cards. Inside near the stove two men were playing an all-afternoon game of dominoes. Near-by two old negroes were discussing the time to plant corn, beans, and watermelon. Good Friday was the right time, it appeared. One thought it would rain before long because the setting sun was 'drawing water.'

"Two county road workers then drove up and drew the attention of the men in front of the store to their new Caterpillar tractor which burnt crude oil very economically, they said. A patent-medicine salesman, who had just sold a bill of goods and played the Roscoe machine, told the men about the Bankhead cotton bill. They wanted to know if it would help the small farmer. One asked the salesman why the Governor had not appointed a man from the community on the County Board of Revenue to take the place of one who had just died.

"A man who bought seed corn said it was time to plant when the whippoor-will started calling. One of the neighbors reported that Mr. F., who had been very dangerously hurt in an automobile accident, was still alive in the hospital at the county seat."

UPLAND BEND IN THE DAILY NEWS

One can learn much about the people of a community by reading what the newspapers say about them. The News which was published daily at the county seat regularly retained a reporter "to cover" the activities of our community where the paper was widely read. A local high-school senior, who was the son of a landowner, served in this capacity while the survey was in progress. Events of unusual importance were reported as special articles. The ordinary run of local news was presented from time to time in a special column under the heading "Upland Bend Items." Indeed, most of the events which have been described in some detail above were duly recorded in this column soon after their occurrence.

During a period of about ten months, from March to February, nine special articles relating to the community and totaling 100 column inches appeared in The News. Three articles pertained to the school. The longest with twelve inches described the dedication of a $9,000 addition to the buildings. An address by the Congressman of the District was the principal feature though short talks were made by members of the Board of Education and other county officials. Local participants in the program included the president of the local board and three of the teachers. A lecture on the value of forest products to the farmer, which was delivered in the school house by the State Forester under the auspices of the P.-T. A., was the subject of a short article. A third account dealt with the Senior Play.

Four articles using sixty-six column inches with cuts were concerned with the death of one of the community's most prominent men. This distinguished citizen was a large landowner with a numerous and influential family connection. For many years, as a member of the County Board of Revenue, he had controlled the road work in the southern part of the county. On the day of the funeral the court house was closed and the list of honorary pallbearers read like a Who's Who in county politics and business.

An interview with the manager of the team in a large Canadian city, which belonged to the International Baseball League, was the subject of a long article in the sports section. The manager was the son of a large Upland Bend landowner. The occasion of the interview was a visit to this home by a well-known Yankee baseball star. The last of the special articles, which described the social honors accorded the daughter of one of the large owners on a visit to the city, appeared in the society section.

The "Upland Bend Items" column appeared in The News sixteen times during a six months period from December to May. The total amount of space used in that time was 231 inches. As spring approached, the column appeared with greater frequency. For the purposes of this discussion the "Items" which were recorded there have been grouped in two classifications: (1) Institutional Events and (2) Social Events.

In the period above mentioned 100 institutional events were recorded. The school figured most prominently with fifty-three "Items." Twelve of these were concerned with adult activities such as meetings of the P.-T. A., attendance of teachers at the state education association, gatherings of various groups at the school, purchases of new equipment, and official recognitions accorded the school. Most of the events, on the other hand, were concerned with the activities of the children such as meetings, contests, and banquets of the Future Homemakers and Future Farmers Clubs and of the Girl Scouts and plays, health lectures, and basketball games.

Events connected with the churches were next in frequency. Fifteen of these were activities for adults such as decoration, memorial or regular services, conferences, all-day singings, and meetings of the Ladies Aid Society. Three reports dealt with the Young Peoples League and an Easter egg hunt. The churches, it appeared, were much less active than the school, especially in promoting activities for the young people.

Events of economic interest came next with sixteen notices. These were meetings chiefly of the Home Demonstration Club and of the Farm Bureau, which took place at the school. One notice informed the community that a music teacher had secured pupils for instruction in piano. The remaining fourteen institutional events were of a miscellaneous nature such as parties, dinners, weddings, and the activities of the Red Birds, an amateur basketball team which was made up of former graduates of the high school.

Social events, which for the most part were records of the doings of individuals, appeared in the "Upland Bend Items" column with much greater frequency than events of an institutional nature. During the observation period of six months, 184 events, which were classified as social, were reported. Notices of visiting constituted the great majority of these. The remaining few were business trips, extensions of sympathy to bereaved families, and a bridal shower. Most of the visitors, whom the families received as guests and whose place of residence was given, were from around in the county (72 per cent) or from nearby towns in adjoining counties (19 per cent). The others (9 per cent) came from outside of the state.

It is worth while to know what people in the community did the visiting. The social events that were reported in the two months, March and May, were subjected to analysis with this question in view. The grown men and women, it appeared, visited almost twice as much as the boys and girls. Men, strange to say, were mentioned as often as women. Do men in the country have more social prestige than men in the city? Did they do more interesting things? Or was it simply that the "Items" reported all kinds of activities including those of men as well as women? Boys were mentioned, however, only half as often as girls.

It was the landowners' families, especially those of the large owners, that made the news. Once mentioned, these names appeared again and again. Unrelated tenant names appeared only once, when they appeared at all. This, indeed, was true of the overwhelming majority of the entire population in the period under observation. One hundred per cent of the negro, 96 per cent of the unrelated tenant, and 86 per cent even of the landowning families were not mentioned once.

Why were so many of the people given no recognition of this kind? Did they never go anywhere? Did no one come to see them? Had they no part in showers, dances, or dinners? Were there no parts for their children in the school play? Had their boys raised no big hogs? Were birth, marriage, death, a tour of jury service, and a broken leg all they ever did of interest to the community? Or were they simply a small part of the great masses of the American people who toil long at unromantic tasks and do their duty as best they can without ever breaking into the newspapers?

THE CHILDREN'S WEEK

The preceding sections of this chapter have been concerned primarily with the doings of the grown people. The remaining sections will deal with the activities of the children. What the children did in school was treated in the chapter immediately preceding. Here we are concerned with a more general view of their behavior—especially with that greater part of their time when they were not in school. The work and play of boys and girls are topics of fascinating interest in themselves. To those who wish to understand the life of a community, however, more is involved than this, for, what the children do indicates what the community will do a few decades later.

With the cooperation of the school it was possible to learn what the pupils, who were enrolled in the six upper grades, did with every hour of their time during the second week of April. On an ordinary school day the average fifteen to seventeen year old boy whose case will serve as a basis of comparison spent 1.9 hours dressing, washing, and eating, 8.0 hours at or on the way to school, 3.3 hours doing the chores, 1.2 hours in reading and study, 1.0 hours at play, and 8.6 hours in sleep. The girls' day was about the same as the boys' except that a little more time was spent in personal care and in recreation and a little less doing the chores. Longer periods of sleep and study and less of work

Brooms made of broomsedge gathered from the river bottom lands were common in Upland Bend. This picture of a high-school youngster on a Saturday morning represents the first stage in the process.

characterized the routine of the younger pupils (ages twelve to fourteen). Just the reverse was true of the older boys and girls (ages eighteen to twenty-one). Of the facts above set forth, the most striking perhaps is the comparatively extended duration of the working day. The time devoted to school was made exceptionally long by the necessity of riding a considerable distance on the bus. But this was not all for, when the youngster reached home, he found waiting for him a considerable amount of work about the house or farm. The result was that the children's working day was about as long as that of their parents.

On Saturday the situation was somewhat easier. An extra hour went to bathing and dressing and there were twice as many chores to do, but about five hours were saved for play and books were forgotten. On Sunday the inevitable chores took less than an hour of the boy's time but there was about as much house-work for the girl on Sunday as on other days. Neither boys nor girls studied but they read quite a bit more. Two hours were spent attending religious services. There was even more rest and recreation than on Saturday and an hour earlier to bed was the rule on Sunday.

The chores, which made up so conspicuous a part of the usual youngster's week, included a great number of activities. Some things were reported as done by boys and girls alike, but, in general, division of labor was the rule. Plowing, harrowing, cutting stalks, spreading fertilizer, planting corn, repairing fences, cleaning ditches, burning brush, cutting trees, splitting wood, sharpening tools, spreading rock, dragging logs, and hauling and driving out in the fields were reserved for the boys. In the barnyard they caught, fed, and harnessed the mules, "got up" and fed the cows, carried garbage to the hogs and bones to the dog; they repaired the barn, castrated pigs, threshed peas, shelled corn or washed and repaired the car or truck. In the garden they broke ground, dug up grass, hoed, and set out cabbage, onions, and potatoes. Nor did the house escape their attention, for here they brought in wood and water, swept and scrubbed floors, helped with breakfast, washed dishes, cleared the table, fixed school lunches, cleaned fish, made cream, washed curtains or cut the hair of younger children.

Nursing in Upland Bend was usually in the hands of the older children. This eleven-year-old girl has responsibility for her five-year-old brother and baby sister while mother did the house work, the garden, and often worked in the field. The back yard in which they were playing also served as the washing place, the wood yard, and for many other purposes.

No less varied and useful was the work done by the girls. They toiled in the gardens, it was found, like their brothers; but they cultivated flowers about as often as vegetables. In the barnyard the girls fed the chickens, gathered eggs, chopped and stacked wood, swept up trash or fixed the reservoir. The milk was one of their major concerns; they tied up the cows, chased away the calves, milked, churned or made cream. In the house there was bed making and cleaning to do, cutting, sewing, and fitting clothes, washing and ironing, bathing and dressing the younger children, and putting the baby to sleep. Sometimes they worked in the store or ran errands but the kitchen with its three meals a day claimed the girls' time more frequently than any other place. Neither the girls nor the boys worked away from home for pay. The economic classification of their parents, it appeared, made little difference with the chores from which there was no escape for anyone.

Numerous interesting activities were available for the enjoyment of the hours of leisure. Boys and girls alike found pleasure in sitting around and talking or playing games with members of the family. They liked "dating" and going to parties and singings. The boys were fond of playing ball, marbles, wrestling, and working puzzles. The girls played ball, too. Sometimes they flew kites and ran races, but more often they played jacks, cards or checkers, and skipped the rope. Visiting and walking aound with others they did a great deal. They also enjoyed taking pictures and hunting for flowers in the woods. Playing the Victrola or the piano and practicing songs at church were favorite pastimes of the girls. To the boys the river was a great attraction. Several of them had boats tied up to the trees. On its banks they killed snakes, dug bait or seined for minnows. Many happy hours were spent watching their poles or running the trot lines.

When they were alone, as children in the country often are, they entertained themselves with books, magazines, or newspapers. Now and then they wrote letters, listened to the radio and played the organ. The girls climbed trees or gathered flowers occasionally while their brothers slipped off by themselves to hunt, set rabbit traps or go riding on the mule. If there was nothing else to do they just "loafed", "sat around", "watched the rain", or "did nothing."

A slightly greater variety of recreational activities engaged the energies of the children of the owning classes. More equipment that was usable for such purposes, it will be recalled, was found in their homes. About half the things the children did were done socially, i.e., with other children. More different kinds of activities attracted the junior boys and girls than the seniors, but juniors and seniors alike engaged in a less varied round of pleasures than children in urban areas where, generally speaking, more elaborate recreational facilities have been provided. A significant illustration of this point was the cinema. The nearest entertainment of this character was miles away. Only rarely—when they "went to town" did the children of this community see the movies.

To complete the picture of the children's week a few pages from the daily records of individuals will help. The first four cases

are boys; the remaining five are girls. Half of the cases describe
school days; the others, Saturdays and Sundays. Different ages
are represented. Cases A, B, D, F, G, and H were sons and
daughters of owners; Cases C and E came from furnishing tenant
homes. The sharecropping families were very lightly represented
in the population of the high school, in the upper grades especially.

Case A

An 18 Year Old Boy's Typical Thursday

5:30- 7:00 A.M. Got up, dressed, ate breakfast, milked two
cows.

7:00- 4:00 P.M. On the bus or at school.

4:00- 6:30 Repaired pasture fence, fed mules and hogs,
milked.

6:30- 7:00 Ate supper.

7:00- 8:00 Read a book and went to sleep.

Before school, after school, and on Saturdays the high-school students
"help about the place." This young thirteen-year-old could "plow as
good as any man."

Case B

A 15 Year Old Boy's Long But Varied School Day

5:00- 7:30 A.M. Got up, dressed, had breakfast, fed the horse, studied a half hour, and dressed for school.

7:30- 3:00 P.M. In school or on the way.

3:00- 7:00 Plowed, harrowed. Took a half-hour to find a rabbit hole.

7:00- 8:00 Ate supper and read the paper.

8:00- 9:00 Took a nap.

9:00-10:30 Visited fish trap in the river and came home to bed.

Case C

A 15 Year Old Boy's Busy Saturday

5:30- 6:30 A.M. Heard dad call, dressed, had food.

6:30-12:00 Went to the field and harrowed plowed ground. Fed mule.

12:00- 1:30 P.M. Dinner. Read a magazine.

1:30- 7:00 Plowed in the field.

7:00- 9:30 Took supper, read until sleepy, and went to bed.

Case D

A 14 Year Old Boy's Sunday

5:00- 8:30 A.M. Got up, dressed, ate breakfast, and fed the mules.

8:30-10:30 Played around alone.

10:30- 1:30 Sunday School. Visited with other boys on way home.

1:30- 2:30 P.M. Dinner

2:30- 5:00 Played marbles with the boys.

5:00- 5:30 Supper

5:30- 7:00 Did "night work," talked with father, and went to bed.

Case E

A Typical 14 Year Old Girl's Tuesday

5:30- 8:30 A.M. Got up, dressed, fixed and ate breakfast, washed dishes, and dressed for school.

8:30- 3:00 P.M. In school.

3:00- 5:30   Visited at sister's home. Played jacks and ball.
5:30- 6:30   Bathed and ate supper.
6:30- 7:00   Sat around with family and cousins.
7:00- 9:30   Studied (an unusually long time).
9:30-   Sleep.

Case F

A 20 Year Old Girl's Socially Active Friday

6:00- 7:30 A.M.   Dressed, ate, helped clean house, and dressed
                  for school.
7:30- 3:00 P.M.   At school or on the way.
3:00- 4:30   Visited a neighbor and went riding.
4:30- 6:00   Made ice cream and decorated for the party.
6:00- 7:30   Ate supper, bathed, and dressed for the party.
7:30-11:30   At the party.

Case G

A 13 Year Old Girl's Hard-Working Saturday

5:30- 7:00 A.M.   Dressed, helped cook, and ate breakfast.
7:00-10:00   Washed and cleaned bedrooms, and ironed.
10:00- 1:30 P.M. Cooked lunch, ate, and washed dishes.
1:30- 3:00   Heated water and bathed, dressed, and took
                  care of baby sister.
3:00- 6:30   Sewed and started supper.
6:30- 8:30   Read, talked with mother, and rested.
8:30- 9:30   Ate supper and washed dishes.
9:30-10:30   Bathed and got ready for bed.

Case H

A 16 Year Old Girl's Sunday of Recreation

5:30- 8:00 A.M.   Dressed, cooked and ate breakfast, washed
                  dishes, and cleaned house.
8:00-11:00   Read a book.
11:00-12:30 P.M. Helped cook, ate dinner, washed dishes.
12:30- 2:30   Sat around and talked.
2:30- 3:00   Studied
3:00- 5:30   Went visiting. Picked flowers.
5:30- 7:30   Cooked supper, ate, and washed dishes.
7:30- 8:30   Read and went to bed.

READING INTERESTS OF SCHOOL CHILDREN

The part played by books, magazines, and newspapers in the lives of the grown people of the community has been discussed in a previous section of this chapter. A more favorable opportunity to get books of a suitable nature was available to the children than to their parents owing to the facilities afforded by the school. In its high-school and vocational libraries together—besides government publications and other bulletins or pamphlets and the works of reference which constituted the greater part of its 700 volumes—the school had a hundred books of fiction and nearly twice that number on vocations, history, biography, science, travel, and fine arts. In addition to this, substantial monthly borrowings of fiction mainly were made from the county's circulating library of 10,000 volumes. These books, together with the twelve general and sixteen vocational magazines and two city newspapers, were what interested the children most.

The average number of books claimed to have been "read during the last thirty days" by the junior and senior high-school pupils was 3.7. One in nine had read none but several named as many as seven or eight. The juniors had read a little more than the seniors. There were fewer boys in the school than girls, but the boys averaged one book more than their sisters.

In this connection it is interesting to know that two of the boys, both sons of landowners, possessed several copies of books by Zane Gray and Harold Bell Wright. These they were accustomed to circulate for a fee of 5 cents per book. With the proceeds, thus derived, additional volumes were purchased.

Fiction was what the children liked best. Adult fiction, with such titles as *Keeper of the Bees, Age of Innocence, Lena Rivers, Ivanhoe, Mill on the Floss, Shepherd of Gaudaloupe, Rainbow Trail, Elope If You Must,* and *The White Oak of Jalna* accounted for one in every three of those read. To the older boys and girls especially these themes were very attractive. Juvenile fiction, like *Little Women, Old Fashioned Girl, Son of Tarzan, Joe Ann-Tomboy, Campfire Girls, Robinson Crusoe,* and *Treasure Island,* was no less popular, particularly with the younger children. Most of the remaining titles were those of adventure stories such as *Buffalo Bill, Fighting Caravans, Last of the Plainsmen, Silver Chief, The Cowboys, Two-Gun Men,* and *A Son of Ari-*

zona. These stories were mentioned more frequently by the boys, especially by the younger boys, but the girls liked them also. Books indicating an interest in science such as *The Big Trees, Reptiles of the World,* and *The Beetle* were not reported very often.

As far as books were concerned the children, it is clear, were more active readers than the grown people. The children who have been considered included only those who were old enough to be enrolled in the junior or senior high school. In these grades, moreover, the owning families were represented far more often than the tenants. And, among the adults, it was the owners mostly who read books. Nevertheless the facts seem to indicate that the children of the owners read books decidedly more often than their parents.

With those magazines which they were able to obtain the high-school pupils spent a good deal of time. They liked best of those they had read periodicals of general interest such as *McCalls,* the *American,* and the *Saturday Evening Post.* Next in favor was romantic fiction with such titles as *True Stories* and *Love and Romance.* These publications appealed to the girls mostly. Adventure magazines about the wild west, detectives, and airplanes drew the attention of the boys and a goodly number of the girls were fond of home magazines such as the *Ladies' Home Journal* and the *Woman's Home Companion.* Thus it appears that the high-school pupils read the periodicals that were in the school library, perhaps most of the time, but they found ways to obtain others, of some of which their teachers might not have approved.

THE GENERAL PICTURE

It will be helpful finally to sketch the broad outlines of the picture the details of which have been given above. During most of their waking hours, as we have seen, the people were busily engaged wresting a living from the soil. Each family relied on its own strength and everyone worked. They found time, nevertheless, to take an interest in school and church and to visit often with their neighbors. Letters, magazines, and newspapers attracted quite a number. While some of their elders browsed in religious books many of the children read stories of adventure and fiction. There was leisure for hunting, fishing, dancing, music, and parties. Inexpensive sedentary games and gossiping at the store were very popular. Making quilts, raising barns, and attending political rallies mixed pleasure with profit. On Saturday and Sunday, after the chores were done, lots of time remained for rest and recreation. Thus life was varied and not uninteresting for many. It is impossible, on the other hand, to overlook the lack of privilege which was characteristic of substantial elements of the population, white and negro alike. Limited means and economic stratification, doubtless, had much to do with it. Nevertheless the fact remains that some did more with what they had than others.

Chapter X

WHAT THE PEOPLE THOUGHT

The material and social background of a people is of importance because it influences what they do and think. This point has been made repeatedly throughout the earlier chapters. In the immediately preceding chapter the activities of the people of Upland Bend were our chief concern. Here consideration is to be given to what they thought, their ideas, and opinions on various subjects. A certain amount of both direct and indirect attention has been given to the thoughts of the people in the development of most of the topics. It is the purpose of this chapter to present a more elaborate treatment of what the adults and young people thought about a number of current issues, some of local interest others much broader in scope. The materials of the chapter deal entirely with the views of the white people. Although information on what the negroes thought on certain subjects has been presented elsewhere, on most of the topics treated here the negroes consistently took the position that they "left such matters to the white folks."

The opinions of the adults, which are treated first, came from two sources. In the course of making a number of special investigations the persons interviewed were asked to express their opinions on a series of topics most of which were of direct local concern, either to the individual or to the community. In addition, a number of standard "attitude blanks" dealing with issues of national concern or with well-known institutions were administered to certain adult groups. The information on the opinions of the young people came through the high school. The same attitude blanks which were administered to their elders were given to the high-school students and, in addition, they were asked to write their views on several subjects. Their reactions to these various matters constitute the subject matter of the latter part of the chapter.

OPINIONS OF ADULTS ON MATTERS OF LOCAL CONCERN

Special interviews of a selected group of citizens of the community were made for the purpose of getting expressions from a sampling of the population on a series of questions of some local interest. The group interviewed consisted of 37 persons, 25 men and 12 women. The men were more or less evenly divided between the landowning and tenant classes and consequently may be assumed to represent a fair cross section of opinion. All of the women except two were from the landowning groups. The opinions expressed by them should be considered as representative of the thought of the upper economic groups only, but in general they agreed very closely with the men.

To this group of 37 persons the questions listed below were asked and the answers made were written down.

Do you approve of the state income tax law which was recently passed in Alabama?

Would you favor the exemption of homesteads of less than $2,000 value from *ad valorem* taxes?

What is your opinion on the operation of our schools with federal government CWA funds?

What do you think of the TVA, its activities and prospects?

Would you approve of the consolidation of counties and county government in Alabama?

What things most need to be done to improve Upland Bend Community?

Would it be desirable or practical for the churches of Upland Bend to get together and form one church for all?

What are the chief difficulties parents now have in rearing children?

What is your attitude toward playing cards?

Would you advise a bright young boy to stay in Upland Bend or to leave? (to men only)

Would you prefer to have a daughter of yours marry a man in Upland Bend or a man from a larger town or city? (to women only)

The answers given to the above questions will be summarized first, and then we will examine in more detail the responses to each. A large majority of those interviewed favored the income tax, homestead exemption, Federal financing of schools, the TVA, and the consolidation of counties. A good majority opposed the consolidation of churches and they approved of playing cards, if money was not involved. By far the largest number of them favored having their sons or daughters reside in Upland Bend. Only two definitely felt it best for children to leave the community, but a few others gave conditional answers. The two questions that remained did not lend themselves to this sort of statistical treatment. Suffice it to say here that the people conceived the needs of the community to be in terms of material improvements, buildings, roads, etc., and it was their opinion that the most serious problem involved in rearing children was laxness in discipline.

A state income tax law had been passed the year prior to the survey. The proceeds of this tax were "earmarked" for the retirement of a bond issue, which had in turn been made for the purpose of retiring several million dollars of outstanding warrants that had been issued mainly to the school teachers of the state in lieu of salary. It had required a constitutional amendment to pass the law and the vote on this amendment had been preceded by an elaborate propaganda campaign. The teachers and most friends of education in the state very naturally supported this program. These facts may have accounted for the very definite opinions which the people had on this particular subject, and they may have been responsible for the fact that most of them favored the law. In interpreting their reactions, however, it is well to remember that no one in the community had an income sufficient to require him to pay the tax. This fact was reflected in many of the responses. "It is only fair that the wealthy should pay taxes", or "It's only fair that the rich should pay more. I wish I made enough to have to pay it", was the way they expressed it. Whatever the reasons, three-fourths of those interviewed endorsed the law. A part of the others were "not interested" or knew nothing about it. Only six persons were actually opposed.

Many who supported the income tax could give no very satisfactory reason for this support, replying simply "A pretty good law, I reckon" or "I sorta favored it." Some approved of it because they thought it was to be used for operating the schools. One woman took the position, "Get money for the schools at any cost." A man who had originally voted for the amendment, thus making the tax law possible, reversed his position because he couldn't "see any benefits to our school." The opposition, a very small minority, was rather frank in saying they were opposed to all taxes, "We're taxed to death now." One rugged individualist took the position, "Them that is lucky enough or smart enough to make money ought to be allowed to keep it." One of the large landowners thought a sales tax was to be preferred because the "rich ain't the only ones that gets out of paying taxes." Two men thought they saw a point not observed by others, "the poor will pay it in the long run", and "no matter who pays taxes first it will fall back on the farmer."

The exemption of homesteads of less than $2,000 value from state *ad valorem* taxes was an issue in the election that was in progress at the time of the survey. In spite of this, every sixth person interviewed knew nothing about the subject and consequently had no opinion to express. Those who did were in general favorable, but not to the extent that they endorsed the income tax. Their reasoning was similar to that offered in support of the income tax, "the wealthy should pay the taxes" and "the taxes on poor landowners is too heavy." One man expressed it, "It's only fair; the big corporations and rich ones get exemption through slick lawyers." One farmer recognized the soundness of the principle, but thought the exemption limit was too high: "Anybody who had a $2,000 home could certainly pay a tax. $1,000 limit is plenty high enough." Others raised a question as to the practicality of such a plan in view of the great need for revenue, particularly for the schools. The minority who opposed homestead exemption thought, "too many people get out of taxes anyway"; "it's O. K. if you put a sales tax in its place so all the people who ain't paying will have to"; and "every man should carry his part of the taxes, big owners and little owners too." Doubts concerning the tax exemption characterized the replies of all the large landowners except one. The tenants and small owners favored it and the women were non-commital.

The year previous to the investigation state education funds had been exhausted at the end of approximately three and one-half months of school. After considerable bickering certain Federal funds were diverted to the operation of the schools and the term was completed with the teachers on a relief basis. This method of financing the school was acceptable to the people of Upland

Bend, but in an emergency only. To a few the matter of local pride was involved, "We ought to have saved our money and not let the politicians mop up with it", or "the county is in bad shape when they have to call on the Federal Government." Many, however, were frankly hopeful that "we may never have to pay the money back." No one raised the question of Federal control of education. None expressed any concern over teachers being "on relief", perhaps because they knew it was the first time in several years the teachers could be sure of any pay. Two men saw Federal aid to schools as the least of evils, "If this Government has to spend money that (operating the schools) is better than most of the things they have done with it." Only a few were enthusiastic about Federal aid as a permanent thing. These claimed to see "good already done in this community." A number didn't see how the Government could keep on spending money "without ruining its credit" or "raising taxes". One man was convinced that the only honorable thing was to repay the government, and another did not care about the principles involved but saw no need for supporting a "play school like they got up there".

The use of the TVA as a topic for the expression of opinion may have involved an element of bias. The connection the survey had with the TVA was a tenuous one; but because of this slight contact the idea was prevalent in the community that the interviewers represented the TVA, and politeness or policy may have forbade expression of opposition. All of those interviewed except one person professed a certain amount of enthusiasm or remained silent. The one objected because he did not "see anything being done yet and don't think anything will that helps us." A few were frank to say, "I don't know what it's all about." Others reacted to it in terms of the survey work in the community, thought it was all right, "but I don't see why you have to ask so many questions", or "the main thing is are you going to get us (electric) lights?" Many persons who did know something of the plans of the TVA evaluated it entirely in terms of potential good for Upland Bend; but a few thought it would "benefit the South, the farmers, give them electricity and cheap fertilizer." One man was doubtful of the politicians, another didn't think they would "be sensible about it." One hoped "they'd get them high salaried power fellers", and one expressed contempt for "them who is opposed to the government entering business."

The "county consolidation" issue was not a particularly live one at the time of the visitations, with the result that every fourth person questioned made answers comparable to the man who said, "I am not prepared to answer that, I haven't thought about it." A majority of those who did express an opinion were favorable, thought it would reduce taxes or overhead expenses, perhaps make for economy. One man pointed out that roads were now good enough in the state to make it practical. Three of those interviewed thought it would be fine for some of the smaller counties like . . . . (naming several but not their own), another frankly said, "that's all right for other counties, but not for Chehaw." The opposition came from those who thought that the idea was too radical, that it "would throw too many people too far from the court house", or that "it would work a hardship on smaller county seats."

The question relative to the "Greatest Needs of Upland Bend Community" called forth more voluble responses than did any of the previous ones. All persons except one were very sure there were many things wrong with the community, and in general they seemed rather confident of what the troubles were. In the eyes of the typical citizen the great needs were in terms of immediate material improvements. Needed buildings headed the list: new churches, a new school, a brick school, additional school buildings, an athletic field, a school library, a public library, and a community hall were named. Electricity, telephones, a water system, a sewage system, better roads, all-weather roads, paved roads, were other needs mentioned. The homes, too, needed repairs and paint. Most of the needs listed by those interviewed were items such as the above. But not all were such. In the economic realm, unspecified methods of reducing or relieving debt, and "run out people who don't like to work" were suggested as urgent needs. One person named more scientific farming; another, a woman, offered as the greatest need some source of income other than farming; a sharecropper proposed that the government "buy up a lot of the small farms, put the relief people on these and make 'em work"; while another young tenant thought the government ought to make the big owners divide up their farms and sell small tracts.

The homes, schools, and church came in for a large part of their attention. "Beautify the homes", "keep the yards clean", "put out shrubs", "better sanitary conditions" (meaning more and better privies) were named by single individuals. In addition to the building needs in both school and church, more books in the school library, a longer school term, more of the Christian spirit, and the consolidation of churches were named as great needs. Finally, one farmer demanded cooperation among farmers and another not only wanted cooperation but he wanted "to educate them away from dirty politics."

On the subject of church consolidation, the seventh question asked, the first definite cleavage in the opinions of the people was found. More than one-half of the persons interviewed opposed consolidation. The women and tenants were lined up against the landowners who mainly favored this proposal. However, almost one-half of the persons who expressed a favorable reaction to consolidation of the churches doubted that it would be practical in that particular community, consequently the issue was not a vital one.

Reasons given for consolidation were the cheapness, the difference in the quality of the ministers who would be available, and the desirability of welding the people together. One man though it was just as sensible to consolidate the churches as to have consolidated the schools and another expressed the view that "The churches ain't doing no good now and they might not if you joined 'em up, but it ain't going to hurt to try."

Those opposed were usually clearer as to their reasons. It would cause community dissention; would inconvenience people; "everyone should be allowed to hold to his own principles." One woman pointed out that, "History is against it. We've had two (churches) break off here recently." Another felt that "one church might save a soul where another couldn't. Competition is just as good in religion as it is anywhere else." Yet another woman, a Baptist, thought she might be able to join up with the Methodists but certainly not with the Nazarenes. The majority definitely did not agree with one old farmer, who was reputed not to be a very religious man, who said, "I'd as soon go to one church as another.

They could get together if people would stop to reason things out."

Card playing was a harmless pastime, if not accompanied by gambling, in the minds of a majority of the people. Only two men thought it a definite social good. And for almost one-half of the persons interviewed it was dangerous, "led to evil" or was actually "sinful." Because it was sinful or "leads the mind in the wrong way", at least one-sixth of the homes prohibited card playing. Because "it improves the social pastimes of my children" and "keeps the kids home", two others encouraged it. The women joined the landowners in being more lenient toward card games than were the tenants. The men who were against playing feared that "when boys get good at it they start gambling", while to the women who were opposed it was simply sinful. One mother who permitted card playing in her home, said she was "now liberal on this subject but it's contrary to my old ideas."

The question relative to the difficulties involved in rearing children seemed to touch a sympathetic chord in the parents of Upland Bend. Most were of the opinion that "times have changed so much that it seems like raising good children is awful hard." Only two persons saw, "no more difficulties now than there ever was." Most of the parents seemed to accept the responsibility, to recognize the problem as being theirs. Few, however, agreed with one man who thought the chief difficulty was "ignorance of parents as to what is the best thing for children." Lax discipline, not starting it early enough, not being firm, "being too much influenced by your children", was by far the most commonly named difficulty in rearing good children. Quoting one old man, "I don't know. People don't raise children nowadays. I *do* know that mine minded me as long as they put their feet under my table." Other variations of the same theme: "we don't learn them to love work", "we're not strict enough", "you've got to clamp down on them early and stay clamped." Four persons felt that "we don't work them enough" and three said we "just don't try." Five men recognized a different problem, that of feeding and clothing their children. And to the wife of a large owner the problem was an economic one, but of a slightly different nature. As she worded it, "you can't keep their minds on the level with your pocket-book."

Several parents seemed to feel that the main difficulty lay in the general perverseness of present-day children. "They just won't work", "too much inclined to play", "I can't teach them to study", "they don't want to stay home", were forms in which they expressed it. Others saw the problem in terms of the distracting influences of modern life, the "many temptations to lead them off from the way we were taught." Dances, whiskey, and the automobile were the chief offenders. "The automobile is the worst thing that ever happened to try to raise children with. It has caused many a girl to go astray, will ruin boys and bankrupt old men." Bad company, too, the unwillingness of other parents to discipline their children, and the presence of "too many transient people in the community", were involved. At any rate, to most of them it was a serious matter. One grandfather stated it for the community, "Seems like in the old days children just naturally growed up good but nowadays it's a terrible hard job to raise 'em decent."

The last question, though it was asked in a slightly different form to the men and women, had to do in either case with the future of their children. The answers to this question not only expressed their concern over the children, but they threw considerable light on the attitudes which the people had toward their community and toward the world outside. There seems little doubt but that the relatively heavy drainage of the younger population, which was commented on in an earlier chapter, was in spite of rather than as a result of any encouragement received from the parents. Of those interviewed, all except five were very definite in the opinion that the best future for their sons and daughters lay in Upland Bend rather than elsewhere. Only one person felt that a bright young man "should get a college education and check out of Upland Bend for good." Three others gave conditional answers: "It depends on what he wants to do. The city is all right if he can get the right kind of job"; "There is nothing in Upland Bend for a college man"; and "if he is educated he should try something else." One mother preferred that her daughter, "marry a city man if he could afford a good home." All others hoped that their children would stay in the community. This position they justified in various ways. "Farm raised boys should farm, and this is a good community to live in" or "country girls should stay in the country, for that is what she has been used to", seemed to be the consensus of opinion. Many of them pointed out what they thought were the advantages of country life: "a dependable living", "can live better", "country is the best influence", "independent life." Others saw the disadvantages of city life: "Wild bucks should stay away from towns", "educated work is the worst kind of work", "too many city folk lose their jobs", "It's hard to make enough money in a city to be decent", or "girls from Upland Bend don't do too well in cities." One farsighted father of three sons claimed to find another issue involved. "I would rather my sons stayed where they were born. You can't build a community by sending the best out."

ATTITUDES OF ADULTS TOWARD CERTAIN SOCIAL ISSUES

In the attempt to get further light on the opinions of the people a series of standard "attitude scales" were administered to a number of persons in the community. The attitudes dealt with are suggested by the titles of the various scales used: *Opinions on the New Deal, A Scale for Measuring Attitude toward the Church, Attitude toward the Negro, Attitude toward the Law, Attitude toward War,* and *Patriotism.* These scales were made by psychologists for the purpose of getting more complete information on the attitudes which people are willing to express. Typical of them is the "New Deal Scale" that is reproduced immediately below together with the directions for its use.

Directions: Below are a number of statements expressing various opinions concerning the "New Deal." In the parentheses before each statement put a check mark ($\sqrt{}$) if you agree with the statement, put a cross (x) if you disagree. If you can not decide about a statement you may mark it with a question mark (?).

(95) 1. The New Deal is a big step in the right direction.

(52) 2. Time alone can tell whether the New Deal is good or bad.

(21) 3. Relief projects under the New Deal have been a waste of time and money.

(41) 4. The New Deal is not as successful as was anticipated.

(105) 5. No other period of equal length in history has seen such progress as has taken place during the present administration.

(69) 6. Several features of the New Deal are working successfully.

(10) 7. The New Deal is directly opposed to personal freedom in that it is an autocratic, tyrannical attempt at dictatorship.

(7) 8. The New Deal is forcing our country so far into debt that recovery will be practically impossible.

(93) 9. The New Deal has brought the needed hope to the American people.

(106) 10. The New Deal has done more for the United States than any other movement in its history.

(44) 11. The New Deal sounds good but so far it seems to have had but little effect.

(17) 12. The New Deal has tended to send the country further into the depths of depression by raising prices without a proportional rise in wages.

(1) 13. The New Deal is the worst scheme for our country's welfare that could have been imagined.

(27) 14. The New Deal borders too much on socialism to suit me.

(75) 15. The New Deal is a great common leveler.

(30) 16. There are indications that the New Deal is in some ways checking progress of the nation.

(60) 17. Whether due to the New Deal or not, recovery is in sight.

(39) 18. The New Deal may be the right way to prosperity, but so far there are but few indications of it.

(63) 19. Perhaps there are better ways to relieve our distressed condition but no one seems to have suggested them.

(78) 20. The New Deal has tried to set a fair basis for industrial competition.

Note:—The numbers inside of the parentheses at left above did not appear on the scale. They are given here simply to indicate to the reader the degree of favorableness or unfavorableness represented by a statement. High numbers, like 106, represent very favorable attitudes.

It will be seen that such scales include statements representing all degrees of opinion on the subject, ranging from "strongly opposed" through a "neutral" position to "very favorable." By permitting a person to check as many or as few statements as are agreed with, it is possible to get a rather complete picture of his attitude. But, further, since each statement has a score value depending upon how favorable or unfavorable it is, one can average the score values of the statements which a person checks and use this average figure as representative of the extent to which he favors or opposes the issue in question. Thus one may speak of *how* favorable or unfavorable a person is, compare the degree of favorableness or unfavorableness with that of others, determine the average favorableness or unfavorableness of a group of people on the subject, etc. In other words, one has in a measure at least quantified the attitude.

Most of the responses to these scales were obtained through an administration of the series which was made at a community meeting. A few others came through interviews. The persons filling out the blanks at the meeting were asked not to sign them, because it was felt that in this manner franker responses might be obtained. This meant that for most of the blanks it was impossible to identify the individuals who had filled them out; consequently, it was not possible to study differences among the groups within the community. Quite a number of the people did not attempt to check the blanks. Others filled out only one or two. The responses obtained probably represent a sampling of the more literate portions of the community. In general, about fifty persons filled out each blank used.

Opinions on the New Deal, as expressed through the scale reproduced above, were obtained from a total of fifty-three men and women. The people as a whole were extremely enthusiastic toward the New Deal. Three-fourths of them were of the opinion that "No other period of equal length in history has seen such progress", all except a mere handful believed that it "had brought the needed hope." Very few felt that "Relief projects under the New Deal had been a waste of time", and only one person accepted the statement, "The New Deal is directly opposed to personal freedom in that it is an autocratic, tyrannical attempt at dictatorship." Two felt, "The New Deal borders too much on socialism to suit me", and a few others agreed that "The New Deal is forcing our country so far into debt that recovery will be practically impossible." Only four persons checked statements that gave them an average score which could be classed as "opposed to the New Deal." For one of these the basis of opposition was known. He was a recipient of a Spanish War pension which had been seriously cut as a part of the President's early "economy program." As a result, he said he would be "agin anything

Roosevelt done." Eight others were neutral, the remainder were definitely favorable and more than one-half were classified as "very favorable."

To the extent that the attitude scales measured opinion, the people of the community were strongly favorable in their *Attitude toward the Church*. Only five of some sixty persons who checked the church blank could be classified as neutral, one was "somewhat opposed", all others were favorable and the large body were "very favorable." All but two of the persons who reacted subscribed to this statement, "I think the church is a divine institution, and it commands my highest loyalty and respect." Two-thirds of them, all who were known to be women, agreed that "my church is the primary guiding influence in my life." On the other hand, it seems rather significant that almost one-half of the people accepted these statements, "I believe that the church is losing ground as education advances", and "I am loyal to the church, but I believe its influence is on the decline." Six persons admitted indifference toward the church, but only one was willing to go further and admit a "slight tendency to oppose it." This one man regarded "the church as a monument to human ignorance" and thought "the church is stupid and futile." One-third of all the persons questioned admitted, however, that verbal support was the most important aspect of their own contribution, checking this, "I am sympathetic toward the church, but I am not active in its work."

Toward the Negro the average of the opinions which were checked by the 67 adults who filled out the blank is best described by the statement, "After you have educated the Negro to the level of the white man there will still be an impassable gulf between them." The people tended to have more or less the same opinion on the subject. No one checked this statement, "Inherently, the Negro and the white man are equal;" only 5 per cent thought that "the Negro is capable eventually of equality with the white man, but he should not be recognized until he is better trained;" and but slightly more than 10 per cent felt that "the Negro should be given the same educational advantages as the white man". Approximately one-third of the persons who checked the scale might be classified as strongly prejudiced against the Negro. Almost one-third accepted the statement that "no Negro has the slightest right to resent or even question the illegal killing of one of his race", and more than one-half agreed that "no Negro should hold an office of trust, honor or profit." One-third accepted this, "I place the Negro on the same social basis as I would a mule." The following two statements seemingly best represent the opinion of the community as to the true place of the Negro, at any rate, 80 per cent of the people subscribed to them: "It is possible for the white and Negro races to be brothers in Christ without becoming brothers-in-law" and "The Negro should have the advantage of the social benefits of the white man but be limited to his own race in the practice there-of."

Toward the Law, the people had no such clear-cut opinions as they seemed to have on the subjects just treated. They were in general favorable, most of the forty-one persons who checked the *"Attitude toward Law"* blank agreed that "individual laws may be harmful but the law as a whole is sound." They thought, further, that "we should obey the law even though we criticize it." Only a small minority felt that "law is the enemy of free-dom", no one believed "in the use of force to overthrow the law." On the other hand, only one-half classed the law as "the greatest of our institutions", while two-thirds were sure that "we have too many laws." Four-fifths thought "the law is often the refuge of the scoundrel" and a like number felt that "men are not all equal before the law."

Perhaps the trouble was that very few persons had verbalized an attitude toward law in general. Toward particular laws they had very definite opinions but concerning law as an institution they seemed to have given no serious thought. That was certainly true in the case of one man who refused to react to the statements with the remark, "I don't have no truck with the law and don't know anything about it." Other evidence supporting the same point was found. Many more of the statements on this blank, than from the others, appealed to the persons interviewed. Con-sistently they checked more of the statements concerning the law than they had on other blanks. And there were many inconsis-tencies in their responses. It is difficult to see how a man could subscribe to two such contradictory statements as these: "The law is more than the enactments of Congress, it is a sacred insti-tution" and "Law is the enemy of freedom." Yet, 10 per cent of the persons interviewed did just that. And 10 per cent checked this statement, "Law is the greatest of our institutions", then proceeded to check the next following which read, "The Law is just another name for tyranny." Undoubtedly the opinions of the average person toward the law were not very well crystallized.

Toward war the attitude of the community was conservative. The average person was "mildly pacifistic." No extreme pacifists and no radically militaristic persons were found among thirty-six examined. They agreed that "war brings misery to millions who had no voice in its declaration", that "nations should agree not to intervene with military force in purely commercial or financial disputes", and that "an organization of all nations was imperative to establish peace." Further, they thought, "It is almost impossible to have a large military force without being tempted to use it." But none felt that radical moves toward the elimination of wars were desirable. Almost universally they agreed that "compulsory military training in all countries should be reduced but not eliminated." Most of them felt that "it is our duty to serve in a defensive war" and almost as many believed that "if a man's country enters a war which he does not consider justified, he should nevertheless serve at the front or wherever he is needed." No one thought "it is the moral duty of the individual to refuse to participate in any way in any war, no matter what the cause"; only one person would accept the statement "he who refuses to fight is a true hero." On the other hand, no one thought "war is ennobling and stimulating of our highest and best qualities", only two would agree that "the benefits of war outweigh its attendant evils", and every one refused to check the statement, "There is no progress without war."

War seemed a very real thing to most of them. Evidently their last experiences in war were still fresh enough in the minds of many to cause them to have a rather consistent attitude toward the subject. For less than half of them, however, was it "difficult to imagine any situation in which we should be justified in sanctioning or participating in another war." It seemed clear that to the people of Upland Bend there were worse things than going to war, and to a majority of them "militarism is necessary for the proper defense and protection of a country."

There was little doubt concerning the feelings of the people of Upland Bend toward their country. Individually and collectively they were a patriotic group. The statement which best describes the attitude of the average citizen was, "I don't know much about other countries but I'm satisfied with the United States." In fact, every single one of 37 persons examined checked this statement. In terms of their expressed opinions none would be classified as "unpatriotic", none as "neutral." All were patriotic and most were very much so. Statements such as these were checked freely, by more than 90 per cent: "The United States is closer to being an ideal country than any other nation has ever been" and "I think the American people are the finest in the world." A few people did, however, accept this, "I think the American people are the most conceited people in the world." Most everyone felt, "There is no room in the United States for people who find fault with this country"; no one agreed that "I can't feel patriotic because I see too many flaws in my country." In fact, more than three-fourths of them said, "I'm for my country, right or wrong." Although most of them, 80 per cent, agreed that "the fact that I love my country doesn't make me feel less kindly toward other countries", a like percentage also recognized that the "hatred of the United States by foreign countries is caused mostly by envy of our greatness." A rather large number did exhibit some insight into the factors back of their attitudes. Almost one-half were of the opinion that, "I am fond of this country because I was born here but I would be fond of any other country if I had been born there."

WHAT THE YOUNG PEOPLE THOUGHT

The opinions of the young people in the community were investigated through asking the high-school students to write on a number of topics and through having them check the same attitude scales that were used with the adults. Our first concern will be with the papers which they wrote. The subjects dealt with were as follows:

What I would like to do and where I would like to live when I finish school.

What are the most common sources of disagreement between parents and children?

What are the greatest needs of Upland Bend Community?

What I think of the TVA?

Should electric power lines be publicly owned?

The responses made to the first topic, "What I would like to do and where I would like to live when I finish school", were examined with a view to finding out what occupations the children hoped to enter and whether they hoped to remain in the community or to go into the towns or cities. Their reactions lent themselves to a certain amount of statistical treatment. Perhaps because of a lack of knowledge concerning many vocations, the occupational choices of the young people appeared to be limited. A total of only 13 different vocations were mentioned by 68 students, and four occupations accounted for two-thirds of all choices. These, arranged in order in which they were most often mentioned were: teaching, homemaking, farming, and business In addition each of the following occupations were mentioned by two children: minister, musician, aviator, and baseball player.

Many children supplemented their occupational choice with comments on other things they hoped to do. The most common topic mentioned was travel. Large numbers hoped to travel both in this country and abroad. Eventually, however, most of them expected to return to their home state, many of them to Upland Bend, to live. Several implied that they hoped to leave the community when they expressed a preference for "living on a farm, near a large town." About one-half of those who definitely located a hoped-for future place of residence offered this compromise between town and country, which seemed to them to combine the advantages of the life they knew and of the life they did not know. One-fourth hoped to live in a city or town while the remaining one-fourth hoped to stay in the community. One-third expressed a desire to precede the final choice of an occupation and of a place of residence with a college education. The others saw no hope or had no interest in such training.

Such statistical analysis of the replies seems to destroy something of their life. Perhaps the following treatment dealing directly with their writings more adequately portrays their ideas on the subject.

Many of the boys hoped to own farms. These future farmers qualified their choices and defended them variously. The following young men, two of whom were sharecropper's sons, were very serious about it: "I would like to live on the farm and have about three hundred acres of land under cultivation and about thirty people to tend the soil. I had rather live on the farm than in the city." "I would like to live out west as far as Texas on a big farm because I like to work in the fields and watch plants grow. I like to live in the country better than I do in the city. The ground is level out there and is very suitable for farming." "I like the farm because of its free life and because it is situated in the great open. I admire the man who can own a farm, a nice home, orchard, plenty of animals and work stock. I hope to some day be in this position and to be a master farmer and leader in my community."

These, perhaps just as serious, saw other advantages in country life, advantages which were of more immediate concern to them: "The thing I would like to do in later life is to be a farmer. You can quit work when you get ready. The work is hard sometimes, but you can get through." "I would like to be a farmer when I am grown because I have always done farm work. I like farm work because you can be your own boss and you can quit and go to a ball game, or go to town to the show most any time you want to. You can go fishing or hunting any time." "When I am grown I would like to live in the country because . . . . I like to go fishing and swimming. People don't charge to go in swimming and fishing in the country and most of them do in the city."

One of the men in the community had an older son who had become a "Big League" ball player. This son commonly wintered in Upland Bend where he took advantage of the "open seasons" to catch up on his hunting and fishing. His influence on the vocational choice of the young man, a high-school senior, who wrote the following was rather evident: "In baseball you get plenty of exercise both physically and mentally. You can make an easy living playing ball, that is if you play well enough, which is my weakness. Therefore you would enjoy the pleasure of seeing different sections of the country without any cost of traveling, but would be making a nice living. Then after ball season is over you can enjoy a long vacation during the winter months, which is the season for all kinds of game hunting. So why not be a sport and enjoy life."

The religious life seemed to call three young men. This prospective young minister was rather clear as to what he wanted: "If I had some church in a rural community like Upland Bend I would be happy or at least I think I would. I have always dreamed of helping others, so most of all I want to be where I can do much for those that love me, for those so kind and true, for the Heaven that is above me, and the good that I can do." Another was not so concerned over his vocational choice as he was with the principles that should guide him: "I hope to be a preacher but regardless of what I do in life or where I go I want to be successful. I have set up as my guide these following few lines. To be glad of life because it gives you the chance to live and to work and play and to look up at the stars; to be satisfied with your possessions but not content with yourself until you have made the best of them; to despise nothing in the world except falsehood and meanness, and to fear nothing except cowardness; to be governed by your admiration rather than by disgust, to covet nothing that is your neighbor's except his kindness of heart and gentleness of manners; to think seldom of your enemies, often of your friends, and every day of Christ; and to spend as much time as you can, with body and spirit, in God's out-of-doors." And the third prospective entrant into the religious field might be suspected of ulterior motives: "My greatest desire is to travel. I would like to visit all the foreign countries. I want to learn their customs and manners. I would like to learn their language so I could talk to the foreign people in their language. I think I shall be a missionary in different countries and spread the gospel to those who know nothing of it."

Several of the young people exhibited a certain amount of confusion concerning the nature of the occupational world outside of Upland Bend. One 17 year old boy wanted to go to Switzerland and be a cattle boy and "Yodel and sing and watch and sleep." Another young man who hoped to graduate from high school in the next year or so wrote: "My greatest ambition is to take a business course in Civil Service in some business college. I want to be prepared to do anything, that is be successful in life, and I think that I can do this in Civil Service. I know many things about the subject of civil service because Daddy has at one time took a Civil Service exam and he has told me things and I have studied rules of it and I know the salary that a man of that position gets, that he can have a living, a bank account and show the womens a good time. The good things about is that it is a sure pay, a sure living, and is easy to do, but on the other hand it is confidincy on a person and a person to hold the job has to be a citizen."

Others, on the other hand, were very definite in their choice and in the reasons for them. The following young man, for example, seemed to have had from some source or other a certain amount of vocational guidance; "I would like to spend four years in college and then study Civil engineering. I like this occupation for several reasons. First it is an out-door occupation in general. Second, it contains problems of algebra and geometry which I like to try to master. Third it pays a reasonable income and fourth it is a field fairly open to new competitors." This one, too, seemed to know what he wanted: "When I grow up and finish high school and maybe a course in some business college I am going to be a rural mail carrier. This occupation appeals to me because it is one sort of an outdoor job. I do not want a collar and tie job in some office because that kind of work just doesn't appeal to me."

Most of the girls looked forward to marriage and homemaking. The number expressing a desire to enter other occupations was limited. Several wanted to teach, like this young lady: "But amid all the mishaps and discouragements I still have dreams. A dream of the future which time alone can tell whether it will come true. When I have finished my high school I want to go to college. After that I want to start my career as an English teacher." A few others planned to enter the business world. The three reported below are typical: "I would like to finish high school and then go to college. I want to get a good college degree. I want to be a secretary for some business man. I want to buy a beautiful home about one-half mile from town. I want to work during the winter months and travel all during the summer." "When I finish school I would like to be a seamstress. I would like to be a seamstress and sew for Sears, Roebuck and Company in Memphis, Tennessee. I would like to make dresses for small children." " . . . I would like to be a saleslady in some nice store making my own living. In doing this I would have only myself to look after. I could get the things which would suit my taste and there would be no complaints from the rest of the family. But still there are some bad points about this. As you all know a lady has to be very particular what she does, where she works and whom she associates with. But if the place was a nice place what could there be to worry about?"

Those who wanted to be homemakers were usually very definite as to the kind of home desired: "I would like a large house in the country with all the modern conveniences in and around the house. I want a pretty flower garden with bird baths, benches covered with vines, and fountains all around." Or this, "The home I want is a 'Log Cabin' made in the right way and painted. I want lots of beautiful flowers growing around my home. I want the yard beautified by a good landscaping man. In my home I want pretty furniture. Not the veryest expensivest furniture but furniture that is nice."

One young 14 year old would have nothing of such life as Upland Bend had to offer. The attractions of the outside world were great for her: "I want to finish high school then go to college four years and after I finish college I want to go to school and get the highest degree I can. When I have finished school I want to take flying lessons then I want to fly to all parts of the world and then to the North pole and South pole. If I can not be an aviatress I want to be a basketball player and get to go to many parts of the world playing basketball. If I can not be a basketball player I want to be a tennis player and go to most all parts of the world. When I get ready to marry I want a big ranch to live on and a herd of cattle so I can get on my horse and ride over my ranch."

And a final young lady showed little concern with the realities of life, but took the opportunity to record a dream that reflected her reading or limited movie experiences more than it did the life of Upland Bend: "I would like to own a large plantation in Virginia when I am grown. I would love to have a large Colonial home, (a green trimmed in white) nestling among cottonwood and water oaks. Around the house I would like to have rambling vines growing, especially on the chimney. Then I would want a large lawn, with an evergreen hedge; lower down I would want the servants quarters among the trees. I would love to live in this house, and go to college in day time and at evening come back home, and be met in the hall by the butler to take your wraps. Then go up to my room and find my bath already drawn. After I have bathed and dressed go out and set on the large winding porch, and listen to the negroes singing and playing their banjoes. Then the cook announced supper. The old fashioned kind of supper, where you have hot-country biscuits and homemade jam that only Nora, my colored cook, can make. We dined in a stately dining room with a cozy fireplace, which made the food much better. Later friends dropped in and we sang and danced, then, went to bed. I hardly realized I had been asleep when my maid woke me next morning. I ate breakfast in bed then read my mail, then go up and dressed. As I walked out on the porch, the sun looked brighter than ever, the birds seemed to sing louder, and all around me negroes were singing as they went about their work. I walked to the southside of my house and saw my gardener pulling grass out of the petunia beds. The garden is one of my treasures with its lovely curved walks, lily ponds, birds bath and numerous other things. Then I went out and sat on a bench on the lawn and thought 'What a grand old world after all.' "

The limitations of their environment were rather obviously reflected, either consciously or unconsciously, in the dreams of most of the young people. Perhaps the definitely "aircastle" type of response most clearly makes this point. The last quotation above, for example, contains a total of 19 items that were not found, or were found to a very limited extent, in the homes of Upland Bend. Also evident from the replies was the fact that someone, perhaps the school, had been pointing out the advantages of country life. The very clever solution to this problem which was mentioned earlier was hit upon by many of them. It involved moving to a farm just outside a city, thus having the advantages of both. The lack of knowledge concerning occupations seems to point out a serious problem for the school. On the other hand, the simplicity of their dreams, the general wholesomeness of outlook should not be overlooked. Not a girl wanted to be a movie star, not a boy seemed to have heard of gangsters, none even wanted to be G-men, no one cared to get rich. A large farm represented the wildest dream of the boys, and the girls accepted motherhood. Even those who planned to teach hoped "after about five years to meet the man of my dreams, marry and settle down about one mile outside of a town where I can have a garden and flowers and two nice babies."

All of the young folks in Upland Bend recognized the problem involved in the topic concerning "things over which children and their parents disagree most nowadays." Twenty-eight senior high-school students, who wrote on the subject, listed a total of more than 75 specific points on which they and their parents disagreed. In addition, many of them volunteered the opinion that "old folks" were too conservative, that they were ignorant of modern ways, that they had no education, and that they thought all the young people today were "going to the dogs."

The subjects of disagreement were varied. The most common one reported was the keeping of late hours. The parents, "disagree about how late children should stay out on Sunday nights. The parents say they should be in by nine o'clock, and the children want to stay out until eleven or twelve o'clock," or, "the boys stay out as long as they want to but the girls cannot stay out later than nine o'clock. Why shouldn't the girls stay out late?" One young man even complained, "they expect us to make good in school and won't let us have much time to work on our books at night, but make us go to bed early instead."

The second problem most often causing trouble was that of proper associates. The younger girls, particularly, felt the restraint of their parents here. " . . . Some parents don't want their children to go with boys until they are seventeen or eighteen. It wouldn't matter for a girl to go with boys when they are young. Some girls have to slip and go with a boy they like and when their parents find it out they make a fuss over it. Some parents say something to their children about going with a certain boy or girl and that will make them afraid and they sometimes marry."

Modern dress, party clothes, and the use of cosmetics came in for a share of comment. "Parents don't like the way girls dress these days like making their dresses without sleeves and sunback." "The parents want us to dress like they did when they were children." And, "The girls of today do use more makeup than they normally should, but I think that is their own affair. If some girls didn't use makeup they wouldn't appear neat and attractive."

Taboos by parents on dances, parties, cigarettes, and jazz music rather than "old-timey sacred songs", were other points of disagreement. Finances, interestingly enough, were mentioned as a source of friction by only two persons. "Too little time for play" may or may not have been involved in this statement made by a sharecropper's young daughter, "Most girls think they should not work hard in the fields as they used to but most parents think they should." The family car, "who will drive it, when and where," caused trouble in only one home according to the reports. And one serious youngster complained that "fathers can't agree with their children about the modern ways of farming."

The varied ways in which the children reacted to this disagreement with their parents were also reflected in the responses made to the subject. Many, like this young high-school senior, were very philosophical about the matter: "History teaches us that each rising generation is criticized and contradicted by the generation preceding them. When people reach maturity and have offsprings, that is children, they immediately forget the frivolous small things they believed in their youth. They cease to enjoy the many things they enjoyed in their earlier life and begin to tell each other how the rising generation is going to the dogs. They seem to forget that their parents said the same things about them when they were children. So it is under these circumstances that most parents and children disagree." Another youngster perhaps more colorfully stated the same position, "Old folks are old folks with old time ways, young folks are young folks with young folks ways. The parents never stop to think what pleasure is today was not pleasure a long time ago." Several had a lot of friendly advice to offer parents: "I think parents should take into consideration the things they did in their youth and try not to be unjust to their children. The parent will naturally say 'I got a kick out of it but it was wrong, so I don't want you to do it son.' This parent seems to forget that we have only one life to live and that any person should get the most out of life possible even if they do a few things that is not right. We all do, so why should the parents make home life unpleasant for his children by constantly criticizing or finding fault in their action."

A few, like the following young lady, sweetly defended the parents' position: "Parents are not as strict on their children these days as they should be. Children need strict parents now just as bad as ever. If parents would be more positive and strict with their children, perhaps the children would have more love and respect for them and not be so ready to disagree with them. Often mothers tell their daughters not to go to certain places, or with certain boys, but they often go on, even if they know they shouldn't. In the end they are sorry they didn't obey their mother, for their name has been dragged through the mud and their 'rep' lowered. They are shunned by the nicer boys and girls and feel as if they were outcasts. They think if they had only listened to what their mother said, they would be one of the nicest of girls. So it is always best to obey mother and think that she is always right, for she is."

Others may have accepted the parents' rights in the matter but they, at least, did it unwillingly. As, for example, these: "Some parents do not allow their children to go to parties and dances. Personally I can see no harm in either one. Where I can't see harm mothers and fathers can"; and, "Another thing about which many parents disagree is drinking. I know there is harm in it but I do think when you are off at a party it is alright to take a drink to help you out." Another boy felt that "parents of to-day expect more than children can possible live up to."

The high-school students, as well as the adults, were asked to express themselves concerning the greatest needs of Upland Bend. Their responses, in general, followed very closely those of their elders. Perhaps because of greater familiarity with the school, they appeared to emphasize needs in this field; but other places of community life were not neglected. In the school they pointed out the building needs; repairs to the roof and replacement of broken window panes, lights, water, indoor toilets, shrubs. The scarcity of equipment in the library, in the laboratories, and on the playground was noted by several. But the intangible needs were not overlooked. A longer school term, more cooperation between parents and teachers and between teachers and students, more care for school property on the part of students, and more honesty in school work were matters often mentioned. One high-school senior felt the need for a college in the community. Typical excerpts from their responses are the following: "One of the first and most important things to be done is the planting of shrubbery about the school building and grounds." "Better ventilation, proper drainage, sanitary toilets, better lights, and many other things are needed in our school." "The school house needs repair work done on it. The pains are all out. The building needs painting and put new tops on the building. That would help Upland Bend community more than anything." "Another thing needed is equipment by giving plays and other entertainments. The main thing is to improve the school grounds. We can do this with the cooperation of the men coming and working on them." "This school has plenty of cooperation, but it is in the wrong way. For example a student does something that he should not, his classmates cooperate with him by not telling if they are asked about it, even if they knew he did it."

Material improvements in the community outside of the school were mentioned by several students, but not so often as by the adults. Sanitation, a pure food law, a local health officer, protection for birds, animals, and trees, and more completely equipped stores were items considered important community needs by certain students, although they had been overlooked by the grown people. One young woman believed, "There should be more places of entertainment. There is scarcely any place to go except to occasional parties given by friends or a play at the school." The houses came in for a share of their attention. Sodded lawns, cleaner yards, shrubs, flowers, and a pride in the property were among the needs given. The church, however, drew but scant attention. Individual comments were made on the need for better attendance, more giving, more services, and better care of the church property, "the graveyards should be sodded to become more attractive." One wrote, "People would take more interest in the church if the seats were comfortable. . . . In winter time they sit back and freeze and that causes bad health. If the church had proper heating facilities they wouldn't mind sitting there and hearing the preacher preach an hour."

Larger social problems drew the attention of a small number. Better farming was advocated by one high-school senior, "Improve the soil by planting winter legumes and turn them under at the right time. If crops were planted on all the land cultivated, in two or three years no commercial fertilizer would have to be bought and would be cheaper and the farmers would have more money to buy more library books which they need very much." Another believed, "the people should take more interest in the (State) Agriculture Department from which they could get information on progressive farming." A young lady wrote, "Upland Bend Community could be improved by some great mill or factory being built, the people who are out of jobs could work in their own community and help to build it up more." One of the prospective ministers saw the problem in terms of its moral aspects, "The one most outstanding thing to be improved in this community cannot be done by one man or a small group of men, every citizen must help to improve the morals of the Upland Bend community, to rear better and more worthy citizens. Citizens that can stand up and say, I have never done anything to prevent the growth of Upland Bend community or give it a black eye." A young man may have pointed the direction in which many of them were thinking when he summarized his comments on the needs of the community with the statement, "If all of this is done or by the time it is completed this small Upland Bend community will be a large prosperous town."

The same "Attitude Scales" which were given to the adults were also administered to the high-school students. The most striking fact brought to light through their use here was the great similarity between the attitudes of the students and those of their parents. The average score of the students was practically the same as that of the adults on every scale used. The adults and young people had exactly the same score on attitude toward war and toward the law. The young as compared with the older people were slightly more favorable toward the Negro and toward the New Deal, they were slightly less favorable toward the church, and were slightly less patriotic. In no case were the differences great enough to be considered very significant.

An analysis of the responses to the various statements within each scale supports the same conclusion. Toward the New Deal, toward war, and toward law the students accepted the same statements that the older people did. In the patriotism scale there was only one statement on which they differed seriously from the adults. Perhaps because it seemed to involve travel, in which already the young people have been shown to be interested, they thought more often than their parents did that they would "pre-

fer to be citizens of the world rather than of any one country."
Toward the church they were very favorable but not quite to the
extent that their parents were. That they were more indifferent
is seen when consideration is given to the statements over which
they disagreed with their parents. The three statements on the
blank which the young people checked much more often were:
"I am sympathetic toward the church, but I am not active in its
work"; "I have a casual interest in the church"; and "I know too
little about the church to express an opinion." Three other statements they did not check nearly so often as the adults did: "My
church is the primary guiding influence in my life"; "In the
church I find my best companions and express my best self";
and "I believe that anyone who will work in a modern church will
appreciate its value."

Toward the Negro the children expressed attitudes that varied
slightly from those of their parents. Although the differences
were not great, one or two points seem worthy of comment. To
the statement, "I place the Negro on the same social basis as I
do a mule" many less students than adults would agree. On the
other hand, 50 per cent of the students as compared with but 5
per cent of the adults accepted this one: "The Negro is fully
capable of equality with the white man, but he should not be so
recognized until he is better trained."

The high-school students were also asked to give impromptu
expressions of opinion on the Tennessee Valley Authority, and a
number of them were invited to write "compositions" on "Public
Ownership of Electric Power Lines." The young people were
more confused on the subject of the TVA than were their parents. Almost one-half of them thought the TVA consisted of the
work which the survey was doing in the community. Although
the survey may have been involved in their associating it with the
TVA, certainly members of the staff had not been presumptous
enough to pose as representatives of the TVA! Typical of the
ideas of those who made this confusion is the following: "The
reasons for this Tennessee Valley Authority is to see what the
children of this community really needs. Later on we can see
what the Tennessee Valley Authority has done for us. Lot of
people say that it is just a way to let people have jobs and for
us to have to work more than we generally do. When the Ten-

nessee Valley Authority finds out what we need, maybe they can help us in many ways."

Most of those who did grasp something of the significance of the TVA evaluated it entirely in terms of the possible good to the community. From it they seemed to expect a great deal. Aside from comments on its general goodness, a number mentioned electricity, relief from hard work, greater leisure, telephones, better roads, better homes and schools, and more jobs as being goods that would accrue to the community. Only one boy felt that it was "bad for the government to spend so much money now." The young man who wrote the following seemed to have been attempting to summarize the opinions of the entire group: "The Tennessee Valley Authority is an organization that is trying to help the people in the country. It is to help the people in their hard work at the house. It will save our time and strength. In this day and time people have other things to take their part-time. Not only that it is going to furnish our community with electric lights, telephones and other things that gives us good comfort. It is going to improve our roads for good transportation over Alabama. This will bring great·progress to the State of Alabama. The Tennessee Valley Authority is going to lower the prices of electric devices that are used in the home. So it may be possible for poor people to use."

On the subject of "Public Ownership of Electric Power Lines", because they had more time to prepare it, and probably because they treated it more as a school assignment, the answers were more complete and indicated more grasp of the subject. The following treatment is more or less typical of the position of those who favored public ownership.

"I think the public should own and conduct all the activities and management of electric power lines. It is so large in its operations and cost that it can hardly be carried on by private owners, and give all parties concerned their fair and right consideration. Usually private owners do not consider anything but paying dividends when operating these power lines. Costs are unjust and all parties are not treated equally fair. Under private control the development is not even, just those near the source of power are developed. If the public owned it there would be a general and even development all over the country and all would get benefits not otherwise received. When owned by private concerns the power lines tend to get into politics and many scandals and unjust actions are pulled over the public by the influence of the owner.

"These power lines are becoming so important that the government should take them into their hands. Electricity is now the most used source of power in the world. It is carried over these power lines, lighting systems, railways, factories, signals, automobiles, and almost all public activities are operated by electricity. If the government had control it would reduce prices of things made by electricity, reduce the cost of currents, power would be more evenly distributed. In cases of emergency the government could use electricity to the best advantages and in general the public would be more satisfied for they know their wants and needs better than any one else."

Several recognized the dangers involved in government ownership. "If they are conducted as many other governmental enterprises they will not be managed efficient as private ownerships and will cost the public in the long run more than previously under existing conditions." Only one person, however, was definitely opposed. Perhaps because he stood alone, he appeared to be slightly on the defensive. His paper: "If electricity became a political ball we might not get the service that should be rendered for the price paid. Too, the lines might not get the proper attention where they branched off from the more important lines. Probably since the lines are private owned they receive more attention, because of competition than they would if there was no competition. This is only personal opinion and I am not a well read person on the subject. Any way electricity is one of the most important and mysterious things the world has ever known."

In spite of a certain degree of isolation the people of Upland Bend had developed many of the viewpoints which are commonly accepted among our people. Their loyalty to the country was unquestioned, their own community, too, was a good place in which to live. They accepted the church as a divine institution, felt that there are too many laws, that the children had changed from those of yesterday, and that the Roosevelt Administration was the greatest in history. Rapid social change in the church, in the government, or in other institutions, they did not consider desirable. Progress was to be measured largely in terms of material improvements. And so on through a wide range of beliefs that are typically American. Toward the Negro, perhaps toward the TVA, their opinions would probably be better classified as Southern. Only in their attitude toward playing cards was there a suggestion of historical lag.

To some their opinions may represent a too limited social outlook. The restricted nature of their background, however, would hardly lead one to expect anything else. To others their patterns of thought may appear too typical of conventional America. The nature of the environment in Upland Bend might have led some to expect a greater deviation from the mode. But after all the background of Upland Bend is the background of America. Though for some people this background may be more mediated, one must recognize that in no realm is social change slower than it is in the ideational.

On social issues the children in large measure reflected the attitudes of their parents. In general the school either built attitudes that paralleled those of the adults or it did not build them. On personal matters there was some divergence of opinion. A certain restlessness noted among the young people may indicate more rapid change for the near future or it may merely be a manifestation of the age old tendency of youth to rebel, however futilely, against the restraints of its elders.

An equable acceptance of their fortune seemed to characterize most of the people. The naivete of the children accented this acceptance, but it characterized the adults, too, for many of whom it took on a form approaching complacency. Bitterness toward the social order, toward life, if it was present was not in evidence. Any unrest which may have existed was in most cases kept well below the surface.

CHAPTER XI

LEADERSHIP OF THE COMMUNITY

A leader is "one who occupies a chief or prominent place, especially one who is fitted by force of ideas, character or genius or by strength of will or by administrative ability to arouse, incite, and direct men in conduct and achievement." The chief function of leadership in a community is to organize the masses and focus their efforts on getting things done that make for a better and happier life. No aspect of a people's situation is of greater interest to the student of social life than the leadership that is available to guide them in this eternal struggle with their own natures and with the environment that surrounds them. In several of the previous chapters, most notably in those on religious and civic affairs, incidental attention has been given to the leaders who managed the institutions of Upland Bend. In the present chapter it is our purpose to probe more deeply into the background, capacities, training, ideals, and achievements of these influential persons. The significance of the services which they have rendered to the community will be assayed. Attention will be given to the leaders who were in charge at the time of the survey and to those who were in training for the future. On account of differences in the nature of their work it has been deemed advisable to treat separately the men, women, and negro leaders, and the young leaders who were then in school. In connection with each of these groups an attempt will be made to point out any significant indications as to the course of events in the future that the facts make apparent.

IDENTIFICATION OF ADULT LEADERS

The problem of identifying the men and women who influenced substantially the round of life in Upland Bend developed elements of complexity. It was difficult, if not impossible to draw a sharp line of demarcation between leadership and mere prominence. Some leaders, moreover, stood out as of greater weight than their colleagues but the latter also made contributions that were indispensable. It was decided, for these reasons, to include in the leadership groups those who were less influential as well as the very few who were outstanding. The method of selecting the adult leaders that was finally adopted consisted in asking the persons who were interviewed in the survey of families to name the five leading men and the five leading women of the community. In the case of the negroes the request was for the names of negro leaders but some of the negroes had difficulty in understanding what was meant by "leaders" and some persisted in their inclination to give the names of white persons.

Approximately 195 men and women took part in the voting. Nearly 800 votes were cast for 103 white men, nearly 700 for 97 white women, and 50 votes were cast for 18 negro men. The thirteen white men who received the greatest number of votes (from 15 to 121) were taken to represent the white male leadership. The twelve white women who ranked highest (from 15 to 77 votes) were selected to represent their sex. The negro votes were so widely scattered, except in the case of one man, that it seemed best to treat only this outstanding individual as a leader. Practically every family in Upland Bend participated in the voting. Other sources of information, furthermore, indicated that the lists as finally selected included all of the leaders who were outstanding and probably most of those who were at all important.

THE MEN LEADERS

Because of the preponderating weight of their prestige in the affairs of Upland Bend consideration will be given first to the white men leaders. These thirteen men, with but one exception, were landowners. Among them were nine of the community's eleven large landowners. The only leader who was not an owner was a retired farmer and merchant who maintained the teacherage and acted as justice of the peace. The leader's group included a retired Baptist preacher and a young farmer who also preached. Three were local school trustees, one was a member of the County Board of Education, two were veterinarians, another was the most substantial merchant of the community, and several held official positions in the church. All were or had been farmers. All had been born in Chehaw County and had lived practically all their lives in Upland Bend. They were well along in middle life, averaging fifty-one years of age, but they had married later (at 23 years of age) than the average of their fellow citizens. Seven was the usual number of years of schooling. The fathers and mothers of nine had been born in Chehaw County and the fathers of all but one had been landowners.

The leaders were among the wealthiest men of the community. The average one owned 266 acres of land, had 4 tenants, owed $246.00, had $2615.00 wealth outside of land, enjoyed an income of $1256.00, paid taxes of $58.38, carried $1153.00 life insurance and $311.00 fire insurance. In addition to favorable economic background there were influences early in life that moved them in the direction of leadership. In most cases the encouragement centered in the inspiring personality of a father, mother or older brother. Sometimes the stimulation came from a minister, a successful farmer or from "The Lord." The inspiring personality was described as a strong man of affairs, a school builder, a good father, a real Christian, a great hunter or simply as one who was unusually honest, upright, sincere, progressive or helpful. The older man encouraged the younger in these desirable qualities and to lead others to the Christian life, to participate in church work, to be a good business man, to help his fellowman or to be worthy of his community.

Inspiration from older people is indispensable to the development of leadership in younger people but actual participation in organized group activity also plays an important part. Several of the men leaders were able to recall significant experiences of this nature during the school years. Most of them had been reared in church or Sunday School. As a young man one had served as superintendent of the latter. Four had been members or leaders of a baseball team. Debating clubs had attracted three; fraternal orders, two; and the Future Farmers of America, one. When the leaders were boys opportunity along these lines in school and Sunday School was none too plentiful in Upland Bend. The value to youth of actual experience in group activities had not been widely recognized. Only in comparatively recent years were young people's societies and organized Sunday-School classes provided in the churches and student organizations in the school. The lack of adequate early training may account for the reluctance of the local leaders to preside over public functions when visitors from the county seat were present. On such occasions as political rallies and school celebrations, as has been shown elsewhere, they were accustomed to turn the meeting over to one of the visitors.

Most of the men leaders' experience in the management of organizations came after they were old enough to be entrusted with responsibility in adult institutions. They had to pick up what training they could on the run, so to speak. By the time they were grown all of them had joined the church and all but one had become members of fraternal orders. Nine were members of adult organizations connected with the school, eight had affiliated with farmers' societies, and two reported that they had been members of the Ku Klux Klan.

Two of the leaders failed to report official positions in these organizations. The average number of offices they had held was 2.8 but the range was from 0 to 7. The most widely experienced man had been president of the Farmers' Union, Director of the Farm Bureau, local school trustee, member of the County Board of Education, and the holder of several positions in the Masons and Odd Fellows. Another active man had done most of his work in the church. He had served as pastor, moderator of the county Baptist Association, Sunday-School superintendent and teacher, clerk of the B. Y. P. U., and chaplain of the Masons. A more typical record was that of one who had been president of the United Farmers, a deacon in the church, and secretary of a nearby Masonic lodge. A similarly typical record was that of another who had been director of the Farm Loan Bureau, incorporator of a crop loan association, and local school trustee. In addition to services of this nature two men had talked for Liberty Loans during the World War, one had served as a private soldier in the National Guard when he lived in Shallow-Ford, and another had served in the Army in some capacity during the Spanish-American War.

The men leaders were not great readers of books. Only four of the thirteen had looked into a manual of parliamentary law. During the last two months two had read from the *Bible* and one had read parts of Harold Bell Wright's *God and the Groceryman*. But at that they read more than the average householder. In their homes there were eleven books, on the average, three magazines, and two daily or weekly newspapers. In magazine and newspaper reading they placed more emphasis on articles about farming, politics, the market, prominent people, and foreign news than did the ordinary citizen. Their reports concerning the great men of whom they had read were interesting. In youth five had been attracted by stories of American pioneers like Captain John Smith and Daniel Boone or of heroes of the West such as Buffalo Bill and Wild Bill Hickock or of Civil War leaders like Robert E. Lee and Stonewall Jackson. Two had been interested in the Biblical characters, David and Jesus.

In later years two of the leaders had paid attention to notable religious evangelists like Charles Spurgeon and George Stewart. More were interested in presidents like Washington who was "brave and loyal to the people", Lincoln who was "an honest farming man", Theodore Roosevelt who had "strong ability to manage others", William McKinley who was a "consecrated Christian", and Woodrow Wilson who was "fairminded and managed the War so well." Franklin D. Roosevelt was mentioned more frequently than any other president. "Trying to help the farmers and laborers" and "a broad vision" were what they admired in him. One man mentioned Senator Norris as the "builder of Muscle Shoals" and another, William Jennings Bryan as "a good Christian." Four prominent Alabama statesmen were recognized. Senator John H. Bankhead "rose from farm boy to Senator", and he was "for the farmer." Governor W. W. Brandon "once drove the mules on a dinky street-car line." Congressman_____was a "friendly personality and a skillful lawyer." And Richmond P. Hobson was a "brave naval officer" and a "powerful fighter for prohibition." The leaders also knew the names and something of the deeds of men who were prominent in agricultural affairs such as Tait Butler, Clarence Poe, R. J. Redding, J. F. Duggan, and Henry Wallace. Some of these things they read in books but most of what they knew of prominent men came from magazines and newspapers. Three of the leaders, however, had no recollections whatever of reading along these lines.

The interest in heroes, which the leaders reported, developed along traditional lines. When they were boys they liked best men who led romantic, adventurous lives including two characters in the Bible. In later life interest shifted to individuals who occupied conspicuous positions in current affairs or in history. The mention of names that were prominent in religious, agricultural, and governmental circles reflects preoccupation with vocational motives and with politics. With the significance of the contributions of their heroes to the public welfare the leaders were concerned to some extent. But they were impressed most of all with the possession of sterling qualities of personal integrity and with the ability of men of humble origin to rise in the world. These virtues and the unusual opportunity of the common man in this country must have been greatly emphasized in the teachings of home, church, and school in Upland Bend. With broader problems of an economic and political nature, it has been shown elsewhere, these institutions had concerned themselves but little. The devotion of the leaders to great men who were "for the farmer" suggests the existence of feelings of inferiority concerning their situation as farmers. The leaders occupied positions of superiority in Upland Bend, but they came in contact frequently with the more prosperous business men, ministers, and politicians of the county seat. Inevitable comparisons of their lot with that of the "big men" of the city may have been at the bottom of their appreciation of statesmen who were "for the farmer."

It is interesting to observe the points in respect to which the views of the thirteen men leaders differed from those of the average citizen. The New Deal was approved by the leaders without exception. They were more favorably disposed toward the law, the church, and the Negro than some of their followers. The state income tax, reform of county government, the Tennessee Valley Authority, and the consolidation of churches were supported by the leaders in greater numbers. Of playing cards the leaders were decidedly more tolerant than the ordinary man. One of the leaders whose father had been a Populist was the only man in Upland Bend that drank whiskey openly. In naming him as a leader quite a number of people qualified their votes by saying "he ain't no Christian." Concerning the social problems above mentioned the views of the leaders were different probably because they read more and got about more than the ordinary citizen. One of the latter indeed in response to questions on these problems described his situation quite aptly when he replied "I'd need three months to think over this passle of questions. All I know is plowing and hoeing." And another answered "City fellows talk about such things as this and a country man ain't got no business hanging around town."

The leaders told how they went about working with the people to get something done. First they called together a number of their colleagues, discussed the project with them, and formed a committee to carry it on. If the undertaking was a large one they called a general meeting. They then put their own names on the petition or subscription list and canvassed from house to house explaining the proposition in detail and asking for votes or for contributions of money or labor as the case demanded. If a building was to be erected they sometimes asked contributions from friends in town. When the time came to haul stones or drive nails they often pitched in and lent their own hands to the work if this appeared to be needed. When something important had been accomplished they usually called for a meeting of the entire community to celebrate the occasion and "build good will." In such instances they often invited visitors from the county seat to celebrate with them.

Very substantial additions and improvement of the institutional life of Upland Bend had resulted from the exertions of the leaders in the last decade or so. The greater part of their energies in recent years had been devoted to the betterment of educational facilities. The two old school districts had been consolidated and with funds raised in the community two new buildings had been erected on sixteen acres of ground donated by one of the leaders. Old roads had been improved and new ones built for the school busses and for easier travel in general. A vocational agriculture department had been added to the high school to help the farmers improve their soil and grow better crops. Supplementary funds had been raised to assist the library, provide laboratory equipment for the science department, add to the facilities of instruction in home economics, extend the school term, and beautify the grounds.

The churches likewise profited from the exertions of the leaders. They had directed the erection of all of the buildings that were put up in recent years. They helped weaker congregations like that of the Nazarenes to which they did not belong. The leaders were responsible for repairs, for raising pastors' salaries, and for equipment. They also cooperated with the county agricultural agent in the organization of activities for the promotion of better farming.

While the leaders exerted themselves on behalf of the community they were not insensible of the benefits that accrued to them and to their families as a result of their labors. Improved schools, they thought, would enable their children to become better farmers or obtain better positions in life. The farmers would be enabled to pay a part of their debts, the leading merchant thought, if the children were better educated. Good schools induced his children to study harder and to try to be more civic minded, another said. Superior educational advantages, one remarked, would attract a better class of tenants and farm hands to the community. His work for the school, the veterinarian felt, had put him in the way of a greater demand for professional services. There was a satisfaction in setting a good example for the children, in holding a position of authority, and in knowing that something had been done for the upbuilding of the community. Better churches, they said, meant higher moral standards and higher levels of citizenship generally. But, more frequently than anything else, they mentioned their enjoyment of the respect, honor, friendship, and love of their neighbors.

The leaders had thought a good deal about "what is most needed to improve Upland Bend." The minds of several were still concerned chiefly with the school. Much already had been done for this institution, they knew, but many desirable things such as a water system and more adequate compensation for the professional personnel were yet lacking. Better attitudes and more equipment were needed by the churches two of the leaders thought. But, whatever else they mentioned, all of them held that something needed to be done to improve economic conditions in Upland Bend. In emphasizing the need of better material conditions the leaders saw eye to eye with the ministers and with other elements of the population whose views were set forth in previous chapters. With this emphasis the reader of this volume can scarcely fail to agree. The fact that the leaders were wealthy as compared with other men had not blinded them to the nature of their own needs or of those of the community. The other men who were asked about the needs of Upland Bend had fewer ideas to express on the subject but they, too, placed the great emphasis on improvement of economic conditions. The solutions they suggested, however, were strikingly different from those indicated above. Something ought to be done, they said, to get people out of debt, to make the small farmers get to work, or "to run out people who do not like to work." One advocated dividing and selling the larger holdings of land. With the last idea, it is scarcely necessary to add, few of the leaders could have been very sympathetic.

The discussion of the topics immediately preceding suggests that the attitude of the leaders toward the church was not the same as that toward the school. In mentioning their outstanding achievements they emphasized what they had done for the school. As regards the benefits that accrued to them as leaders they dwelt most on those that came from the school. When they thought about what remained to be done they stressed further additions to the school, next to improved economic conditions. In all three cases the school appeared to have a stronger hold on their minds. In the chapter on the churches the point was made—that the major leaders apparently had turned the church over to the lesser leaders and to the women. Not many years had passed since the reorganization of the community around the new consolidated school and the feeling of triumphant achievement on this score was still fresh in their minds. For the churches nothing of comparable significance had been undertaken in recent times. These circumstances may have led to a disproportionate appreciation of the school that would prove to be temporary. They may be indicative, on the other hand, of an increasing confidence in secular education and a declining interest in the type of religious activity with which these men were familiar. If the church is to continue to fulfill adequately its noble historic mission of cultivating the highest ideals of life something of a stirring nature will need to be done, apparently, to restore the enthusiasm of the leaders of the community for the church. A gradual plan of consolidation, if this were the wise thing to do, might capture their imagination —as it did in the case of the school. The ministers of Upland

Bend, divided by sectarian lines and serving part time as they did, were not in a very good position, however, to develop and sustain in the minds of the lay leaders stimulating visions of this nature.

The leaders were alike in some ways but in others they were quite different. Several were well along in years, had practically retired from active participation, and were remembered for what they had done. Others were in their prime. Only two were in the thirties. Some of the leaders were much better "mixers" than others. Some were especially good at raising money; others were noted for great personal integrity. Several had the reputation of helping people in trouble. Professional activity, the ownership of a popular store, and willingness to give land for good causes had helped to bring some to public attention. All were or had been energetic and willing to work but it is doubtful if any would have won wide respect if he had not been an unusually successful farmer.

Further understanding of the qualities that tended to raise men to positions of influence in Upland Bend was gained by comparing the leaders with an equivalent number of unselected citizens who had received few votes in the leadership poll. The names of both leaders and non-leaders were arranged alphabetically and a number of competent judges were asked to rate them on eleven traits of personality. In respect to two traits only were the leaders and non-leaders rated the same namely, ability to estimate one's self correctly and selfishness. The leaders, it appeared, did not need to understand themselves better than other men and, while they worked for the community, they did not need to neglect their own interests. It would seem, indeed, that to be a leader one had to be able to look out for his own requirements unusually well and, at the same time, retain a reserve of strength that he was able to use in the service of others. The leaders were also judged to be more dominating, more sympathetic with people, more conservative, and of more excellent character than other men. The most marked differences, however, were in ambition, energy, and persistence and in an understanding of people that was informed by intelligence. In these respects the leaders were adjudged decidedly superior to ordinary men. The traits of personality in which the leaders excelled had a good deal to do with their rise to leadership but these same traits lead to success in private as well as in public affairs.

A few individuals in any group of leaders, ordinarily, stand head and shoulders above the rest. These few men possess superior prestige. They see what needs to be done and by persuasion or force of personality they win the cooperation of lesser leaders. To the superior leaders everybody in the community looks for guidance. Following them, in time, becomes a habit. In Upland Bend two men and two alone exercised this predominating influence. One of the two died while the survey was in progress. For this reason his name was not included in the group of thirteen leaders whose work was discussed above. But his fondness for foxhunting and the newspaper accounts of his death were described in the chapter on how the people spent their time. His place in the life of the community until he passed away, however, was such that attention must be given to his influence here. The death of this man left the community practically in charge of the other superior leader who survived him.

Both of the two men belonged to large family connections. The oldest son of one had married the oldest daughter of the other. The numerous families to which they were related by blood or by marriage supported them loyally. Being a Baptist in one case and a Methodist in the other, they were members of the two predominating religious groups. The families of both had lived in Upland Bend for several generations. Both inherited land and money and both were conspicuously successful farmers. Their homes were the best in the community. Each had a capable grown son who was able to look after the farm and manage the tenants. Each was thus free to visit frequently at the county seat where he knew many leading business men and all of the prominent politicians. With the latter especially both had influence. When a question affecting Upland Bend was raised in county political circles these men were consulted. All candidates for county offices sought their approval. When an Upland Bend man had trouble at the court house he asked one of these men to help him out. This they did to the best of their ability as they were proud of the community and well aware of the manifold responsibilities that leadership entailed.

Both men held important official positions in the government of the county. The one who was a member of the Board of Revenue controlled all of the road work in the southern part of the county. Where roads were to be built, which were to be improved, and who would do the work were questions which he largely decided. The other man was a member of the Board of Education. In this capacity he secured money for the local school, determined who worked on the buildings, and had an important voice in the selection of bus drivers and teachers. Each man supported the other. It was as if they had reached a working agreement to the effect that one would supervise the roads; the other, the school; and that each would back the other in everything he did. Thus there was peace and cooperation where there might have been strife and division and the community got what was coming to it. Any proposition that had the approval of these two men was likely to go in Upland Bend. Nothing could succeed that they opposed. The passing of one was a serious blow to the influence of the community in official circles and some loss in income from political sources was to be expected, at least for a time. No younger man who was capable of taking his place had come in sight. Yet such a man might appear at any time. If he failed to cooperate with the surviving leader there would be division. If an outsider he would be less interested in Upland Bend. But the surviving leader was patient, shrewd, and farsighted. He knew the ropes and whatever was in the power of one man he would not fail to do. If this man should lose his grip, however, Upland Bend would not be represented officially at the county seat, a central figure to unify the community would be lacking, and marked deterioration might ensue.

THE WOMEN LEADERS

The twelve women leaders of Upland Bend were all married and all but one were members of landowning families. Ten of the twelve women were wives, daughters or daughters-in-law of men leaders. One of the exceptions was herself a teacher and the wife of a teacher in the local school who was also a landowner. The other exception was a landowning widow, a fine old Christian lady who was most useful in caring for the sick and whom everyone in the community loved. One of the women leaders ran a small store which supplemented the income her husband derived from the farm, another kept the teacherage, and two had been teachers before they were married. Prominence of husband or father contributed much, doubtless, to a woman's rise to leadership but it was far from being the only determining factor. The wives of seven of the most prominent men, not to mention daughters, were not included in the list of women leaders. Evidently the possession of qualities of leadership in her own right was required to raise a woman to a place of influence.

Their mothers, fathers, and teachers, the women leaders, said, were the persons who had inspired them in youth to undertake civic responsibility. The encouraging older person possessed admirable personal qualities such as devotion to duty, a sweet, lovable, sincere, religious character, lived an upright Christian life, was interested in the community or she was a wise and kind teacher. The older person encouraged the younger woman to emulate this respected behavior, to work for the church or to become a teacher. When the women leaders were girls their mothers had not been drawn into the movement for better schools. The example set by the older women was that of working for the church. It was not until later years, when they were grown and married, that the energies of the women leaders were directed to the improvement of educational facilities.

In school days the women leaders took about the same advantage of the limited opportunities to gain social experience in student organizations as did the men. But they made much greater use of the facilities of the Sunday School in which several had played the organ, led the singing, acted as secretary or taught classes. In adult years they continued with the Sunday School and extended their efforts to include the Ladies Aid and the young people's scoieties. These organizations together with a flourishing Home Demonstration Club and a very active Parent-Teacher Association were practically under the control of the women leaders. With fraternal, political, and farming organizations they had nothing to do. Thus their experience was less varied than that of their husbands.

The women leaders, according to the observations of the interviewers, were decidedly superior to the average woman of Upland Bend in housekeeping ability and in the readiness with which they responded to questions. But differences in interest, ability, and experience were marked. Most of them labored in a number of organizations but some concentrated on the church or the school, on home improvement work or on the leadership activities of their husbands. Some of the older women tended to be more sure of themselves in the church whereas several of the younger had risen through work for the school. Those who had been teachers were the best educated and the broadest minded. They had married landowners, but like the others, they tended to leave public questions to their husbands.

Most of the women leaders were well aware of their prominence in the community and of the responsibilities that prominence entailed but others were modest, retiring persons who simply liked people and were willing to help whenever they were asked. The latter had held few offices but worked readily on committee assignments. One of these had taught Sunday School nearly thirty years and another was the most welcome visitor of the sick in the community. Being useful in small ways such as furnishing chickens for suppers, lending her truck for the transportation of coffins, giving wood to poor tenants, keeping the children or cooking meals for sick women, singing at public gatherings, and giving good advice were an important part of being prominent. The women leaders were very practical persons working mainly, as they did, for immediately attainable objectives and with things and for persons who were directly before their eyes. Some, on the other hand, stood out in the matter of holding office. One of the most active ladies tended to be the chief officer of the organizations to which she belonged. For a period of several years, in each instance, she had been president of the Ladies Aid, the Home Demonstration Club, and the P.-T. A. She was described as a determined "go-getter" who knew how to explain her projects and how to win the cooperation of the men. She had been a teacher. Another was interested in minor offices such as secretary, treasurer, and group leader of the same organizations. Thus there were many things for the women leaders to do and each worked according to the capacities which she possessed. In the eyes of the community, however, the women leaders were thought of chiefly as good, faithful, and willing Christian women.

The women leaders tended to be more like average women than the men leaders were like other men according to the opinion of several competent judges who rated them on eleven traits of personality. In respect to ability to estimate one's own importance correctly, possession of dominating attitudes, selfishness, and general intelligence the women leaders were marked about the same as an ordinary group of unselected women. As regards sympathy, conservatism of outlook, and excellence of character they were given definitely higher ratings. The highest differences to the advantage of the women leaders, however, were in energy, perseverance, and understanding of people. As far as these ratings may be used for a basis of judgment—and they were statistically consistent—devotion to accepted standards of conduct, social tact, and persistent work for home, school or church were the qualities that most distinguished a leader in feminine circles from other women.

Some acquaintance with books on parliamentary law was claimed by two of the ladies who had been teachers. Most of them had read one or more books, chiefly fiction, during the past two months but they were not interested in great leaders of state or nation or other notable personalities as much as their husbands were. When they mentioned such names, however, they did not fail to include prominent women such as Mrs. Franklin D. Roosevelt, Mrs. Alice Roosevelt Longworth, Dorothy Canfield, Joan of Arc, and Florence Nightingale. One was attracted by the Biblical story of Ruth. Two mentioned distinguished women of Alabama, Helen Keller who "triumphed over natural infirmities" and Mrs. James Fitts Hill whose services on behalf of the State P.-T. A. commanded general admiration. The attitudes of the women leaders were more favorable than those of other groups toward the church and toward the Negro and they were overwhelmingly in favor of the use of Federal funds for schools. The women proceeded with public activities in much the same way as the men except that they gave a good deal of time to raising comparatively small sums of money by means of parties, suppers, quiltings, encouraging the saving of eggs laid on Sunday, and collecting donations of food and clothing.

The women leaders were proud of the work they had done for the school. They had helped to beautify the grounds, equip the

playfield, enlarge the library, and keep the schools open. They
were no less pleased with what they had been able to do for the
church. They had raised money for song-books, Sunday-School
leaflets, and pastors' salaries, presented the pastors with gifts of
food and quilts, repaired chairs and carpets, beautified the church
and cemetery grounds, and improved the programs of the Sunday
School. Much had been accomplished for better homes. Demon-
strations of good canning, cooking, sewing, and interior decoration
had been arranged. Magazines and new books on home economics
and how to raise better poultry had been provided for the Home
Demonstration Club library. All of these things, the women felt,
had been helpful to them in about the same ways as the men had
named. But the women were especially grateful for the more
attractive homes that had been provided for their children. As
for what needed to be done in the future the women leaders
thought about the same as their husbands, but they also wanted
to continue to add to the effectiveness of their homes and to do
something for better health and sanitary conditions.

As between the men and women leaders of Upland Bend the
principle of division of labor operated in obvious ways. The most
widely known and the most powerful leaders were the two men
whose great weight in the counsels of the community has been described. It was the men who traveled to the county seat and discovered what was going on and what new enterprises needed to be
developed locally. They initiated the major undertakings such
as the consolidation of school districts, erection of buildings, and
the improvement of roads. They organized movements, raised
the larger sums of money, and supervised construction activities.
When an institution had been established the men filled most of
the higher administrative positions. In all of these developments
the women leaders were interested. They gave freely of their
time, energy, and encouragement and they were especially helpful
in preparing the dinners and suppers which are an indispensable
feature of large scale community enterprises.

When the major objectives of the institution were established
and its building erected the interest of the men tended to subside
to some extent and the services of the women were in greater
demand. It was the women who were in closer touch with the daily
lives of the children, the young people, the teachers, the pastors,

and with men and women in general who were the beneficiaries of the institution. Their keen insights and quick sympathies made them determined to see that the work of the institution was such as to meet the needs of those who were intended to profit from it. So they thought about additions and improvements, formed auxiliary organizations, and raised the small sums of money that were necessary. By these means new departments were developed, additional professional workers were secured, desirable equipment was provided, and all were encouraged to work more effectively. In these several ways and according to their special talents the men and women leaders labored together for the upbuilding of the community.

The Negro Leader

The one outstanding leader of the negroes was a man far advanced in years but still active and in complete possession of his faculties. At his initiative and under his direction buildings had been erected for the Mount Gilead Negro Church, for the local school, and for several other negro schools in adjoining communities. As set forth in the chapter on the churches this man controlled the activities of the Mount Gilead Church to which he belonged. He owned free of debt 161 acres of land which he had bought with his own savings. As a farmer he was capable but conservative terracing his land properly, owning two mules and three cows, but making no use of winter covering crops. Two barns, a corn crib, a smoke house, a pig shed, a small orchard, a garden, a tenant house, and his own home constituted the improvements. He made about $150.00 cash a year, paid $17.00 in taxes, and carried burial insurance. Thus he was the most prosperous of the negroes. When he was a small boy he had been brought as a slave to a community adjoining Upland Bend by a planter from Virginia. His mother had always told him, he said, that his father was a white man. Evidently he had been carefully instructed in farming. When he was freed two successful white farmers took an interest in him, showed him how to buy and pay for his farm, and encouraged him to take the lead in developing institutions for his people. Having had no formal schooling he took neither magazine nor newspaper and the only books in his home were the *Bible* and a copy of the *Ladies Birthday Almanac*. He had married late in life. Two children were born but only one survived, a son who worked for a packing house in Chicago.

There was no doubt in this man's mind concerning his leadership among the negroes. When he decided that something needed to be done he explained it to the others and told each what he had to do. On public questions he was little informed and hesitated to express the opinions he might have held, preferring to agree with any suggestions that were advanced by the members of the staff who interviewed him. Like the other negroes he did not vote. Such problems as taxes, the TVA, and the reorganization of county government were affairs which he left to the white man. He was free to say, however, that "I likes the President we got better than any one I ever heard of." His real interests were confined to personal business and to the progress of the church and school. Improvement of their school was what the negroes needed most, he thought, and the evidence available on this subject indicated that he could not be far wrong in this opinion. He did not look to the future of the negroes in the community with very great assurance. The children, he thought, were being reared with too little respect for their elders. And he was troubled with the foreboding that when he died there would be no one to look after the church and the school as he had done.

Leaders in Training

Having studied the leadership that served the community at the time of the survey consideration will now be given to the young people who may be available for this purpose in later years. The leaders of the future were the boys and girls of school age who were making themselves useful in the management of organizations specifically designed for the training of young people. In the course of ten to fifteen years these youngsters will begin to make themselves felt in the counsels of the community. Who they were and what they were doing to prepare themselves for the responsibilities of leadership are the questions with which we are most concerned.

The organizations which were available for the training of the youngsters included some that were connected with the church and others that were connected with the school. The nature of both types of organizations and the activities that took place under their auspices have been described in detail in the chapters on the church and on the school respectively. When the facilities that were available in both institutions are considered together it is apparent that the young leaders were being offered an equipment for leadership which was far superior to that provided for the leaders who governed the affairs of the community when the survey was made.

Discovering the identity of the young leaders was a task of no great difficulty. It was necessary simply to locate those boys and girls who were enrolled in the senior high school and who had participated most extensively in the activities of the organizations that were open to them. The measure of participation was the number of points earned in the last four years. For each year's holding of a presidency two points were counted, one point was assigned to each minor office, and one for each year of membership. In the assignment of points both school and out-of-school organizations were considered. When computations were completed the fifteen pupils who ranked highest were taken as the leaders. Nine of the fifteen were boys and six were girls. Seven were enrolled in the 12th grade; five in the 11th; and three in the tenth. Together they constituted one-third of those in active attendance. The extent to which the pupils thus selected stood out from the others may be shown by contrasting them with the sixteen boys and girls who ranked in the lowest one-third in respect to points of participation and who may be described as non-leaders. The average number of points earned by the latter was six whereas the leaders averaged twenty-three points or almost four times as many. Thus the pupils who have been designated as leaders undoubtedly included those who ran the juvenile organizations to which they belonged both in and outside of school.

The points earned by the fifteen leaders were derived in greater part from memberships (58 per cent) than from office-holding. In this respect the leaders differed radically from the non-leaders. In the case of the latter 90 per cent of the points earned were derived from memberships. Thus the greater distinction between leaders and non-leaders was in extent of office holding but volume of experience, as determined by the average number of memberships was also greater for the leaders (13 points) than for the non-leaders (5 points). A majority (57 per cent) of the leaders' points were earned in out-of-school organizations. Just the reverse (28 per cent in out-of-school organizations) was true of the non-leaders. Thus the leaders were much more active in the Sunday School and in the young people's societies than the non-leaders but they were also more than twice as active in the school organizations. The superiority of the leaders in average number of points earned in the previous three years (6 as compared with 1 point) was decidedly more marked than their superiority in respect to number of points earned in the present year (4.5 as compared with 3.0 points). The advantage of the leaders, therefore, consisted largely in having started to gain social experience at an earlier time of life.

The nature of the social experience of the leading pupils may be revealed by brief descriptions of the four-year records of a few individuals. The most outstanding record was that of a young man twenty-one years of age who was a member of the graduating class and the son of a large landowner. This young man had been president of his Sunday-School class and president of the Free Will Baptist League during each of the past four years. In the school he had been chairman of the program committee of the student council one year and of the Future Farmers two years. For two years he had been president of a glee club and a member of a dramatic club both of which had passed out of existence when the teacher who sponsored them left the school. This young man was planning to become a minister.

A second young man who ranked fourth in participation points was twenty-one years of age, a member of the graduating class, and the son of a furnishing tenant. For four years he had belonged to the Sunday-School and to the League. Of the latter he had been vice-president two years. For three years he had been patrol leader of a Boy-Scout troop that disbanded when the scoutmaster resigned. He was a member of the student council. For four years he had been president or secretary of the Future Farmers. During the last half-year he had served as janitor of the school. In the future he intended to become a farmer.

The leader who ranked second was a girl sixteen years of age who was in the 11th grade. She had attended Sunday School and the B. Y. P. U. for the last four years and for two years had been president of the latter. A member of the Girl-Scout troop three years she was now senior patrol leader. In the school she was a member of the student council, the home-economics club, and the history club. Of the latter she had been vice-president two years. She had also served as president of a debating club one year and of the 4-H Club two years and as secretary of the girls' athletic association one year.

With these active careers those of the non-leaders made but poor comparison. In the main the non-leaders were merely members of the few organizations to which they belonged. Some were affiliated only with church or only with school organizations. In the case of the latter they tended to report only those societies, such as the class organizations, to which everyone belonged. Many of these pupils were underprivileged in the matter of social experience. Even in the highly selected population of the senior high school not all pupils need or can be expected to be outstanding leaders. All, however, should obtain a volume and variety of social experience that is sufficient to prepare them for active participation in one capacity or another in the civic life of the community. In the cases of a number of the pupils in the high school at Upland Bend the evidence shows that this function was not being very adequately served.

Before going into the question as to who the young leaders were it will be necessary to take account of the fact that not all were residents of Upland Bend. The consolidated senior high school received a majority (54 per cent) of its pupils from communities adjoining Upland Bend. Two-thirds of the leaders of the school, however, were Upland Bend's boys and girls which shows that the youngsters with whom we are most concerned were fully capable of taking care of themselves in a competitive situation. There were no facts to indicate, on the other hand, that the leaders who were not residents of Upland Bend differed in any essential way from those who were. For this reason the two groups will be treated as one.

Most of the young leaders were members of landowning or related families, mainly large owners, but this was true of the entire enrollment of the senior high school. Thus there was no greater representation of owning families in the leadership group than in the school at large. The unrelated tenant families that did send their children to the senior high school were probably the most able and ambitious of their group. Such families might well be expected to produce a reasonable number of unusually promising youngsters. If these young people continue as tenant farmers when they are grown it is possible that the tenant groups will be represented in the leadership of the community in the future which was not the case when the survey was made. On the other hand, it is possible that able and ambitious youngsters of this sort will become landowners themselves thus leaving the tenant groups again without direct representation. In either event the large preponderant representation of owning families in the group of young leaders indicates that most of the leaders of the future will be landowners as they have been in the past.

There were more boys than girls in the leadership group, the boys' average rank in participation points was slightly higher, and their experience tended to be more varied. The finding of so many girls in the group of leaders, however, indicates that women will continue to occupy a prominent place in the counsels of the community. The leaders made slightly higher scores on a test of general intelligence than the non-leaders. Even a small margin of superiority in this trait would allow the leaders to take more time from their lessons for outside activities in which social experience was to be gained. Superior scores on two tests of socio-economic status (Sims and Burdick) showed that the leaders came from homes that were better equipped and of higher cultural background. The children of such homes are more likely to be stimulated to higher ambitions than those that come from a less favorable environment. The leaders had also read more books in the last thirty days than other youngsters. These facts indicate that those who are likely to be leaders in the future have greater natural ability and have enjoyed greater advantages than others of the same age.

Would the young leaders who were being developed in the school and in the churches of Upland Bend remain in the community to enrich and build up its life? Or would they finally give themselves and their talents to other communities than the one that had nurtured them? What the future will bring forth can be predicted with considerable assurance on the basis of what has happened in the past. Of those who graduated from the Upland Bend High School in the last ten years 54 per cent of the boys and 38 per cent of the girls (44 per cent in all) had left the community. Of those who had gone to college 90 per cent failed to return. Only one, a woman, of those who had graduated from college ever came back to live. Thus it was the boys especially and the ablest of the boys and girls in general who tended to leave. Most of those who went away did not go far but they were lost to Upland Bend as far as leadership was concerned.

The life of Upland Bend possibly did not provide sufficient opportunity for many individuals of superior ability. Had the ablest leaders remained they might have been dangerously thwarted in the effort to exercise their talents by the limitations of Upland Bend. Barren and bitter lives might have been the outcome: lives that to the persons first concerned were not worth the living: lives that contributed little to the community that failed to give them a chance. To the extent that these conditions obtained individuals of superior ability had no choice but to seek their fortunes elsewhere. And it may have been better so for all concerned. Reflections on this issue, however, must not be allowed to blind our eyes to the other side of the significance of the drainage that has been revealed. The tendency was for only those young leaders to remain who had less ability and less training. Thus in the future, as may have been the case in the past, the fate of the community did not seem to lie in the hands of the best talent that it had produced. And this, indeed, may well be one of the great tragedies of the American countryside.

THE BROAD LINES OF DEVELOPMENT

Certain broad lines of development emerge from the details that have been presented above when we attempt to look at the situation as a whole. As the people of Upland Bend, like men everywhere, strove to obtain the good things of life for themselves and their children, leaders rose from the mass to direct and unify its energies. These guiding spirits were superior in many ways including especially unusual success in the conduct of their private affairs. A few leaders stood high above the others but the latter also were needed and contributed yeoman's service. The men leaders got movements under way, designed the main features, and held the most conspicuous posts of administration. But the women helped all along and, when an institution was set up, they fostered and nurtured it in order that the human needs which it was intended to satisfy might be better served. A wise old negro led his people to set up institutions that worked for the enrichment of their lives. The leaders of all groups had shown courage and vitality and the community was moving forward on several fronts, especially in the direction of providing physical facilities that were superior to those they had enjoyed in the past.

What good would come to Upland Bend from the improved material equipment which they sought to provide? Most prominent in the leaders' eyes was the vision of a nobler personal life. They wanted their children to be more prosperous, to have more attractive homes, to avoid temptations, to be sober and honest, and to live like Christians. These were the traditional individual virtues which have long been taught in church and school and which, indeed, are indispensable in any social group where wholesome development is wanted. They desired their children to become better citizens also. Ideas as to what this meant were a little vague but the leaders did not doubt that better churches and schools would achieve it, whatever it was.

The leaders were not vividly aware of the conflict of interests that was beginning to register more deeply on the minds of the American people after the disasters and disillusionment that followed in the wake of the great depression of 1929. In Upland Bend problems connected with a better distribution of wealth and income lay all about. In these matters the leaders were among the most fortunate people in the community though none had more than enough to guarantee his own security. It was scarcely to be expected that people so situated would initiate the consideration of these questions as local issues. The masses of the people lacked more but they were not well informed as to the nature of the difficulties that beset them. They, too, accepted striving for personal development as the chief goal of human endeavor. As a result pressure from the less fortunate groups was not soon expected to induce the leaders to think seriously of a better distribution of the materials of privilege.

Promising young people who were capable of assuming the burdens of leadership in due time were growing up in the school. As regards practical experience in the management of institutions they were obtaining a far more adequate training than was given their parents. In other ways, too, their intellectual development was being fostered more effectively. In regard to problems of a civic and economic nature, however, our study of the school has shown that their courses of instruction were but little better adapted to an understanding of the social environment in which they lived than those that were offered to previous generations. The indications were, moreover, that a considerable number of the ablest young leaders would leave for greener pastures elsewhere. Their going would deprive the community of much of the talent that was most capable of coping with difficult problems. Those who remained, however, might be expected to do the best they could for themselves and the community as the older leaders had done before them.

But whoever the leaders may be it did not appear reasonable to believe that the community was capable of making the adjustments that were needed through its own efforts alone. Fortunately for the people of Upland Bend the problems that shadowed their lives were equally provocative in other communities throughout the land. Of these sources of social irritation leaders of thought and action in state and nation alike are well aware. Trained professional workers in many fields are laboring devotedly with expert skill to find solutions. Under their auspices plans for improvement are available already and better plans are in the making. To learn about and seize upon help from the outside that is waiting to be used is one of the chief functions of the leadership of a small community. This the present leaders realized on several occasions in the past when they moved forward for farm and home and for church and school. Thus the greater community helped the smaller and both made progress for neither can live without the other.